INTRODUCTION TO
CHRISTIAN
THEOLOGY

Bradley C. Hanson

FORTRESS PRESS / MINNEAPOLIS

For Julie, Carter, and Kim,
my beloved daughter and sons,
and for Michelle, my dear daughter-in-law.
Their faith in God and participation in
the church's worship life
are a great joy to me.

Cover and text design: David Lott
Author photo: Chip Peterson

Library of Congress Cataloging-in-Publication Data

Hanson, Bradley.
    Introduction to Christian Theology / Bradley C. Hanson.
        p.   cm.
    Includes bibliographical references and index.
    ISBN 0-8006-2984-1 (alk. paper)
    1. Theology, Doctrinal.   I. Title.
BT75.2.H365   1997   96-52886
230—dc21   CIP

Manufactured in the U.S.A.   AF 1-2984

01   00   99   98   2   3   4   5   6   7   8   9   10

Contents

Preface

One of the most important questions to ask about a book is, What audience does the book address? Most introductions to theology are written for seminary students who are assumed to have some knowledge of the Bible and the history of Christian theology. This book is especially for those college and seminary students who do not have much background in the study of Christian theology, and thus may not know biblical figures such as Sarah and Paul, when a theologian such as Augustine lived, or what technical terms such as hermeneutics and eschatology mean. If you are a student who already understands these references, all the better; you will find more than enough to think about here. The point is that the intended audience of this book is neither the professor nor the advanced theological student, but the beginning student of Christian systematic theology. This does not mean the text is simplistic or unchallenging, but the book does not assume a student comes to it with a considerable fund of knowledge in Christian beliefs and history. Consideration of this audience has also meant that the book does not begin with an extensive prolegomena or foreword on theological method and context.

My primary concern in this book is to engage the student's interest in the great issues of Christian theology. I have not written it in order to convince you that my personal views are the best. I shall certainly express my own position on a number of issues and let you know when I am doing so, but the student does not have to agree with me. What matters most is becoming personally involved in thinking through the fundamental issues of Christian theology. The book is designed to acquaint students with some of the important options in dealing with an issue and then to nudge them toward formulating a personal stance on it. The student need not be a Christian believer to do this, for most of the questions are relevant to universal human concerns that deeply touch everyone. When a student wrestles with the underlying issues, then study of Christian theology becomes not only interesting but exciting.

Like every other theological book, this one reflects the author's interests and convictions. I shall briefly identify five commitments that shape my approach to theology. If you are a beginning student in theology, these comments will make more sense after you have read several chapters; it would be helpful to return to these remarks later. Those who are experienced in theology will find that these five commitments express my perspective on Christian theology. First, I am convinced of the importance of *biblical narrative* for Christian theology. That is, when we are involved in describing the basic beliefs of Christians we must keep close to the primary way these beliefs are expressed and passed on—in stories. This means being familiar with the Christian foundational stories in the Bible. Obviously we cannot retell all the biblical stories, but after reading this book students should be acquainted with a select number of important biblical stories, even if they had not previously heard them. Biblical narrative is the soil in which Christian theological reflection should grow.[1]

Second, I am persistent in seeking to show that Christian faith is *reasonable*. Not that I think it is possible to prove or disprove the faith. But I believe it is important to show that Christian faith is reasonable by establishing links with beliefs and theories in other fields of knowledge. Not all theologians who stress the biblical narrative do this.

Third, my own views and ways of formulating issues reflect my rather considerable agreement with *liberation and feminist* theologies. This agreement, however, is tempered by my more basic commitment to the biblical narrative for Christian theology. When I think a major thrust of biblical narrative is compromised in the thought of a liberation or feminist theologian, I will criticize that position. Nevertheless, I fundamentally support the central concerns of liberation and feminist theology.

Fourth, I have strong *ecumenical* interests; that is, I am deeply concerned about better understanding and closer relations among the various Christian traditions. I have my own roots in the Lutheran tradition, but where there are differences of belief and practice between Catholic and Protestant, for example, I will discuss them in a fair, balanced manner. Most variations in theology do not follow denominational lines, but when they do, I feel it is important to understand the differences and see whether greater agreement is possible.

---

1. Gary L. Comstock, "Two Types of Narrative Theology," *Journal of the American Academy of Religion* 55 (Winter 1987): 687–703.

In addition, I share an even wider ecumenical interest in dialogue and mutually respectful relations with adherents of religions other than Christianity.

Fifth, I think Christian theology is intimately connected with Christian *spirituality*. One understands the symbols and ideas of theology only if one has some grasp of what it means to live the faith. This estimate of spirituality influences somewhat the choice of topics; for instance, this book treats prayer and devotional practices, subjects that are often left out of such introductions to theology. Attention to spirituality will also surface in our discussion of whether belief in God is reasonable.

Finally, I wish to thank various people for their help in the writing process. The students in my Essential Christian Teachings class over the years have stimulated my reflection many times by their sharp inquiries, challenges, and proposals informed by study in a host of different majors. Recent students have also improved the clarity and flow of thought in this book by evaluating in detail all the chapters. Among my colleagues at Luther College, Will Bunge read the first two chapters and made helpful suggestions about the role of narrative. Richard Ylvisaker made very insightful comments on chapters 3, 5, and 11. Marcia Bunge, now at Gustavus Adolphus College, recommended certain improvements in chapter 4, and John Sieber checked my use of biblical materials in chapters 6 and 12. H. George Anderson, former President of Luther College and now Presiding Bishop of the Evangelical Lutheran Church in America, read the majority of the total manuscript. The fluid hand of my good friend Richard Simon Hanson has helped to conceive a couple illustrations. The entire department discussed chapter 11 and assisted me on specific points in the whole book. I especially want to thank Lawrence Cunningham, Chair of the Department of Theology at the University of Notre Dame, for his useful feedback on chapter 8 (The Church) and all but the last section of chapter 10 (Sacraments and Devotional Practices). The entire project has also been sustained by the love and support of my wonderful wife, Marion. And again Judy Boese deserves high praise for her capable and careful help. To all these people I say thank you.

1

Faith and Theology

Life is a journey, a movement from a starting point (birth) to an end point (death). Theology can be an extremely interesting area of study, because it deals with fundamental questions about the journey of life. What is the purpose of this journey? Is there a God who has established a purpose for it? Is death really the end of us or is there another destination? How is one's individual life journey linked to the larger trek of the human family? To the development of nature? We all give personal answers to these questions, if not explicitly, then implicitly by how we live our lives. Our answers flow from our faith. Faith is not the same thing as theology, although the two are closely related.

Faith is a complex word; like "love" it has many meanings that vary with the context in which it is used. For our purposes, though, three aspects of faith are especially significant. The first aspect is *belief*. Of course, we have a great many beliefs. We believe that Jupiter is a planet in our solar system. When we admire the beauty of a tree, we believe that the tree is really there, that we're not being deceived by our senses. So belief involves holding something to be true. The beliefs pertinent to faith are those that together make up our interpretation of the journey of life. For instance, a peach-robed devotee of the Hare Krishna sect believes that we humans are properly disembodied souls that have become attached to the pleasures of physical things, but our true destiny is to exist in a bodiless heaven praising God Krishna. A convinced secularist might believe that human life has arisen as a result of a fortunate turn of events and, like all other forms of life, will eventually die out; meanwhile people should contribute to the survival of the species by being productive. Each vision gives a certain understanding of life's journey.

The belief aspect of faith is commonly communicated in story. Since a story narrates events of conflict involving one or more characters and ending in some sort of resolution, it is well suited to expressing an interpretation of life's journey. Story is the chief means of articulating the Christian faith, for this faith is integrally linked with the history of Israel, Jesus, and the church; history has temporal movement that requires narration.

A second important aspect of faith is *commitment*. It's probably true that we have numerous commitments—to family members, friends, school, and nation, but our highest commitment belongs to faith, the allegiance that takes precedence over every other. We give our ultimate loyalty to what we care about most of all, our top priority. For example, if a person is devoted primarily to career success, family and friends will receive less attention than career. The person may have a family and friends, but if a serious conflict arises between them and career, career will win out.

Belief alone is not enough. Faith is more than claiming certain things to be true, it involves faithfulness, commitment, giving oneself. For several decades polls have shown that well over 90% of Americans indicate a belief in God, but experience suggests that a far lower percentage actually give their primary loyalty to God.

On the other hand, commitment is not given except in a context of supporting beliefs. During World War II there were some members of Hitler's youth organization who showed extraordinary fidelity to Hitler by reporting remarks their parents had made criticizing him. Such devotion would not have been given, however, if the Hitler youth had come to believe that the Führer was insane. Likewise, highest loyalty is given to God only in the context of beliefs which support that loyalty (for instance, God is perfectly good).

A third vital aspect of faith is *trust*. Again, we all trust in a great many things. When we drive a car, we trust the steering wheel will turn the vehicle in the desired direction. When we eat at a restaurant, we ordinarily trust the food will not make us sick. The trust that belongs to faith is our most fundamental trust. On what do we rely for our ultimate security and meaning? This may be difficult to identify, since we often take trust for granted. But in a situation where our very existence or meaning is threatened, we quickly become aware of whether our ultimate trust is well placed. While living a very dangerous existence as an itinerant Christian missionary the apostle Paul expressed profound trust in God, "For I am convinced that neither death, nor life, nor angels, nor rulers, nor things present, nor things to come, nor powers, nor height, nor depth, nor anything else in all creation, will be able to separate us from the love of God in Christ Jesus our Lord" (Romans 8:38-39).

When faith is understood as involving belief, commitment, and trust, it becomes clear that not only religious people have faith. The devout followers of Hitler also had a faith. Within the framework of beliefs about the superiority of Germanic culture and people provided by Hitler's National Socialist ideology, they gave their primary loyalty to the Third Reich and trusted that the Reich would deliver on its promises. A faith may not be so sweeping in its claims. In the play *Death of a Salesman*, Willie Loman's faith is in becoming wealthy through being a well-liked salesman.

People sometimes think faith is a marginal matter in life, but that is only true if the so-called faith is merely an external label that has little relation to their life. People's actual faith shapes their whole lives. For instance, if I truly care most about always being first, then that primary commitment influences how I allocate my time (especially to what will advance me over others), what sort of friendships I have (always with inferiors), how I spend my money (even my "contributions" benefit me), and how I play games in my spare time (winning is the main goal). Along with highest loyalty to personal preeminence, I place fundamental trust in myself. This affects my relations with others, for I rely upon others only if they do not threaten my position and I distrust any rival. My faith in winning involves beliefs that shape my interpretation of the world. I view the journey of life as a big race and regard other people as either supporters or opponents in the competition. With this perspective I see my work as a series of contests to be won, not as opportunities for service, and I evaluate individuals and social groups according to their prestige. Thus my real faith powerfully influences the sort of person I become on life's journey.

Faith gives unity to a person's life. A person who lacks faith has no overall understanding of the pathway and flits from one thing to another without any consistent direction, like a college student who changes majors every two weeks. Just as students discover direction in their studies only when they form some idea of what they want to do in life, so human beings set a consistent course for the journey of life when they come to a steady faith. A person's life gains some degree of unity through having a highest commitment that prioritizes all the other commitments.

Of course, a person's faith develops over time. In recent research James Fowler distinguishes seven stages in faith development beginning with the basic sense of trust (or mistrust) that an infant has in its caregivers. Fowler shows that when we undergo major changes in our life situation, our faith usually changes as well. For instance, when late teenagers leave home for college or a job, they often enter different social circumstances. Leaving the familiar beliefs and values of family and high school peers, they are plunged into a setting with greater diversity in beliefs and values. The process of sorting out what they themselves believe, which probably had started already in their early teens, is now carried further. It is common to examine carefully the faith one has known in the past as well as the other faiths one now encounters. The question is not so much *whether* one will have faith, for few of us can travel aimlessly for long; the real question is, *In what* is one's faith to be placed? Young adulthood is frequently a time for serious reflection on faith. This is what theology does.

What Is Theology?

Theology is personally involved reflection on a religious faith. Let's break this definition down into its parts. First, "theology is reflection on a religious faith." There is a distinction between faith and theology, although the two are very often closely related. One can see the difference by comparing the act of devoutly praying the Lord's Prayer and reflecting on what is meant in the prayer. To genuinely pray by addressing God as "Our Father" is a direct expression of faith in God. To ask what is meant by speaking to God as our father is to take a step back from full involvement in the prayer. Theology is taking a step back from a religious faith, examining it, asking questions about it.

Second, theology is reflection on *a* religious faith, a specific faith. It is not thinking about generic faith or about religion in general. Theology is Christian theology or Islamic theology or Jewish theology.

Third, "theology is personally involved reflection" on a religious faith. It is possible to avoid personally involved reflection by carrying out an arm's-length examination of a religious faith. This happens when a religious faith is treated as a curiosity piece or a mere body of data, an object to observe, but not as something to take seriously to inform one's own understanding of life's journey. For example, if we learn a bit about ancient Greek religion, we may find the various deities and practices interesting, but probably we do not regard Greek "mythology" as having much to teach us about life and reality. We keep ancient Greek religion at arm's length. In contrast, personally involved reflection takes a religous faith seriously as a potential source of wisdom for understanding the world and for traveling life's pathway. This requires neither mindless acceptance of that faith nor consent to it. Critical questions may be asked, but they are pursued within the context of a personal quest for wisdom.

In this book the religious faith examined is the Christian faith. For those who claim this as their own religious faith, theology is an effort to understand their faith more fully. Traditionally this has been called "faith seeking understanding." For those whose stance of faith is more uncertain, this undertaking in theology represents more of a search *for* a faith. For others who hold a different faith, studying Christian theology can be both a way of understanding Christians and of enriching knowledge and practice of their own faith. I know many Christian students who have been brought to a deeper understanding of the Christian faith as well as an appreciation for their Jewish neighbors through taking a colleague's course on Judaism, but this only happens when the Jewish faith is regarded as a possible source of wisdom, not just as dead mythology.

However you identify yourself, the key thing to remember is that Christian theology can be an exciting activity in which you can be involved. Theology is not just a body of information, nor something done only by professional theologians. Theology wrestles with questions basic to human existence. If you make those questions your own by asking them with passion and if you look at the Christian answers as wisdom that might inform your own understanding of life's journey, then theology comes alive as your own thoughtful consideration of fundamental issues.

The Sources of Christian Theology

If it is granted that theology is reflection on a religious faith, then what sources do we draw upon for Christian theology? As we ruminate, on what do we chew? At this point we will focus on four sources: Christian tradition, Bible, experience, and culture. In the following section, we will discuss the fifth and most basic source—revelation.

Christian tradition generally refers to Christian teachings and practices outside of the Bible that are handed down from generation to generation. That sounds terribly abstract, but in reality tradition is concrete. The Christian faith is a living tradition, not a dead mythology, because it is carried by Christian communities and persons who embody the faith. It is impossible to name all the Christian churches here, but most of the major church families are represented in the chart on p. 6 (Figure 1). This arrangement of churches is not accidental. In general, the churches closest together on the chart have most in common; those furthest apart have least in common.

Those who have been part of a Christian family or been involved with a church already have come into contact with some elements of Christian tradition. Someone from a practicing Christian family will have learned patterns of prayer and church attendance and observed how religion informed the lives of adults in the family. Usually the family religious tradition is linked with a larger current in the broad stream of Christianity; for example, the family ties with the Methodist or Catholic Church. The devotional and worship patterns one learns as a child are commonly drawn from that larger church tradition. In Western societies even those who do not come from a Christian family have been exposed to Christian tradition as it has had an impact on the broader culture. The impact is most noticeable in how our calendar has Christmas and Easter as major holidays and Sunday as a day off from work for most people.

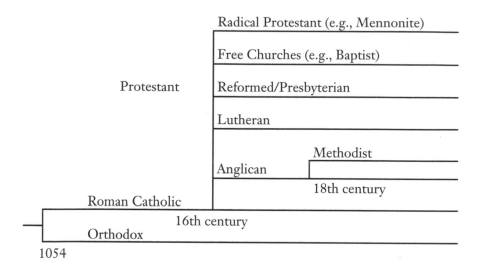

Figure 1
The Major Christian Church Families

Disciplined theological study enables us to become more self-conscious about the Christian tradition. In addition to any knowledge of Christianity already gained from family, neighbors, or from a particular congregation or parish, we can examine some of the great theologians, creeds, and denominational strands within the broad Christian tradition. In the process misimpressions are sometimes corrected and our understanding of this living tradition is deepened.

The Bible—Old Testament and New Testament—is a crucial source in Christian theology. The image of the Bible being read by an isolated individual is seldom true to life. Nearly all Christians have their first direct exposure to the Bible through hearing biblical stories used in a group—their family, a parish, or youth group. Private reading and study of Scripture ordinarily comes later, and then is also generally combined with use of Scripture in some Christian group. Sound Christian theological reflection must pay close attention to the Bible.

As I said earlier, the Christian faith is communicated mainly through story and centrally the story of Israel and of Jesus. The biblical writings are the most significant sources for the history of ancient Israel and the life of Jesus. We can say without exaggeration that the Christian faith has been created anew in each generation through the biblical story as it has been retold in families and churches down through the centuries.

A closely related function of Scripture in theological thinking is to provide a *norm* for what is genuinely Christian. These foundational documents of the Christian story have been taken as the standard or canon by which to evaluate later interpretations of the Christian faith. This may sound simple, but actually the situation is far more complex. Several questions have been debated.

First, how is the Bible actually to function as the norm of Christian faith and practice? In practice the entire Bible—a collection of at least sixty-six books written by different authors over many centuries—is not treated as equally authoritative. That is, most Christian interpretations of Scripture regard something within the Bible itself as the central clue to the meaning of the whole. Some scholars call this the canon within the canon, the standard within the standard. While there are very substantial agreements among Christians, significant disagreements stem largely from differences over the canon within the canon. It is a sign of growth when we become more aware of what interpretive key is operating in our own theological thinking.

Second, what is the relation between Scripture and the traditions of the church? Protestants say Scripture is clearly the higher authority, for all church traditions must be evaluated according to their consistency with Scripture. Roman Catholics and Orthodox Christians see Scripture and church tradition as complementary sources for Christian faith and practice; a tradition cannot contradict Scripture, yet they emphasize that the traditions of the church help interpret the meaning of Scripture. Many theologians today would say that the difference in positions is not nearly as clear-cut as it was once thought to be, yet a difference in emphasis remains. In our personal reflection, the Christian traditions significant to us will very likely color our own understanding of the Bible; one major task of Christian theology lies in testing how well our preconceptions agree with Scripture.

A third question about Scripture that continues to receive plenty of attention is how the authority of the Bible is to be understood. Although there is a range of views on this subject, a brief comparison of two positions opens up the issues. On the one hand, the *fundamentalist* view emphasizes that the Bible is inerrant (without error) at least in its original manuscripts. Any apparent discrepancies in the Bible can be explained. On the other hand, what we might call the *neo-orthodox* view stresses that the Bible *becomes* God's communication or revelation when God uses its foundational testimonies to speak to people today. Historically relative human perspectives and even some errors are seen in the text, but God makes use of such limited means to speak an authoritative message to persons in every period. Our own sympathies on this matter may not be immediately clear to us, but they are likely to become evident later when we discuss an issue on which these positions divide—miracles. In any case, what counts most in Christian theology is not which *theory* of biblical authority one holds, but whether Scripture actually is used as a normative source for one's thinking about Christian faith.

Experience is the third source for theological reflection, and is an inescapable factor in all our thought. Consider, on the one hand, what the word *Jesus* is likely to mean to a person whose main exposure to it was in a family where "Jesus" was only used in curses. On the other hand, what about someone nurtured in a Christian family that used it frequently in prayer and always with reverence? When these two people come to think about the Christian understanding of Jesus, they probably approach it from very different perspectives. We do not come to Christian theological reflection as blank slates; we come marked by our past experience. Family experiences are especially influential, since they come during very formative years of our lives. Out attitudes toward God, Jesus, church, and Scripture are powerfully influenced by the behavior and attitudes of our family. We are not simply products of our past experiences, but they certainly influence how we look at the Christian faith.

While our past affects our attitudes, so can new experiences. Many a person has had an eye-opening experience. Peace Corps volunteers are commonly changed for life by their service abroad; even those who visit another culture for a few weeks tend to see the world differently. Not all new experiences are welcomed, yet however they come they can bring fresh insight that enables us to reinterpret the past.

A fourth source for Christian theological thinking is *culture*. Culture is an unavoidable source, because everyone who carries on theological reflection does so as one shaped by a certain culture. I often am not aware of how my sharing in the American version of Western culture affects my thinking, but I quickly recognize differences in perspective when I engage in dialogue with an African or Latin American theologian. Culture influences our theological considerations in at least two respects: what issues we think are important and what we regard as evidence in determining truth.

Several years ago when I was visiting Zimbabwe, I had an interesting conversation with an African who asked me whether it is permissible for Christians to show respect to spirits of their ancestors. I sputtered something, but frankly I had never even entertained the question. The reason is that in Western culture we generally assume that the dead are further off; heaven and hell seem far away. Traditional African cultures, on the other hand, often believe that spirits of the dead are nearby and deserve special attention. Our culture affects the questions we raise.

Until recently Western societies were dominated by modern culture fundamentally shaped by the Enlightenment (c. 1650–1800). Impressed by the extraordinary scientific achievements of Galileo, Newton, and others, Enlightenment leaders were confident that science was the fully reliable means to discover truth and that the advancement of scientific knowledge would result in the progress of humankind. They were suspicious of traditions and especially Christianity; to be enlightened meant for each individual to affirm only what he or she could justify before the supposedly neutral bar of reason. This outlook put Christian faith on the defensive. The main questions all boiled down to whether Christian faith could be reconciled with the natural (and later the social) sciences. The names of Darwin and Freud call to mind some of the questions. The undisputed means for attaining truth was the scientific method; religious belief seemed weaker even to believers. Since most of us still operate much of the time on Enlightenment assumptions, our theological reflection will have to address many of the questions raised by modern culture.

Many astute observers, however, are saying that Western societies have been undergoing a slow change toward what many call postmodern culture. Triggered partly by the natural sciences and wars of the twentieth century, postmodern culture is marked by a loss of confidence in science to discover more than a limited realm of truth. Indeed, there is a deep skepticism whether we humans are able to discern the nature of reality at all. Not only is there loss of confidence in progress through science, there is no sense of any overarching direction. Set adrift from any transcendent meaning and any objective values, individuals look upon their own goals and values as personal preferences, like tastes in hairstyles. Relativism reigns.

It is difficult to become conscious of how culture influences us, since we take it for granted much like the air we breathe each moment. If we looked closely we would likely find elements of premodern, modern, and postmodern culture within ourselves. In theological reflection it is vital to understand our own culture and how it may be changing. If we unthinkingly adopt our culture's way of putting questions and deciding what is true, we simply accommodate Christianity to the prevailing attitudes of our culture. That yields a monologue in which we are prisoners of our own time; we may perhaps be hip or cool, but we are prisoners nonetheless. Sound theological thought involves a dialogue between the present and the Christian past, between contemporary experience and culture on the one hand, and Scripture and the Christian tradition on the other hand. The conversation should move in both directions, for contemporary experience and culture raise questions to the Christian heritage, but that heritage also challenges the current scene. So theological reflection is an ongoing conversation involving these four sources of Christian theology. The technical term for this process is *hermeneutics*, which simply means interpretation. The important point to remember is that in theology the hermeneutical task involves a complex conversation in which both the past and present are interpreted.

Revelation

An even more basic source for Christian theology than experience, culture, Bible, and tradition is *revelation*. To reveal means to uncover, unveil, and hence to disclose and make known. What Christians claim is that they have received a revelation of God given by God. In other words, generally Christians do not think that they discovered God through their own ingenuity; rather, they believe God has come to them and revealed something of God's character and goals for the world. For instance, the early Christian missionary Paul speaks of "the revelation of the mystery that was kept secret for long ages but is now disclosed" (Romans 16:25-26). The mystery that has been disclosed in the life, death, and resurrection of Jesus Christ is God's will for the world and the heart of God's own character. Christians do not believe they know everything about God and God's intentions for the world, but they do claim that in the biblical events and literature God has revealed the basic meaning of life and reality. This is a lofty assertion indeed. In examining this assertion we want to do three things in this section: first, clarify further the meaning of the Christian assertion of revelation, so that we understand what is being claimed; second, ask how revelation happens; and third, ask how the Christian claim of revelation can be evaluated.

1. *The meaning of revelation.* A good place to begin to understand the notion of revelation is to pay attention to some Christian accounts of a revelatory experience. We shall look at two accounts. The first is given in the New Testament in the book of Acts that tells about the very earliest days of the Christian church. A pious young Jewish man named Saul was actively opposing the new Christian movement that had arisen within Judaism; in fact, he was traveling from Jerusalem to Damascus to continue his opposition.

> Now as he was going along and approaching Damascus, suddenly a light from heaven flashed around him. He fell to the ground and heard a voice saying to him, "Saul, Saul, why do you persecute me?" He asked, "Who are you, Lord?" The reply came, "I am Jesus, whom you are persecuting. But get up and enter the city, and you will be told what you are to do." The men who were traveling with him stood speechless because they heard the voice but saw no one. Saul got up from the ground, and though his eyes were open, he could see nothing; so they led him by the hand and brought him into Damascus. (Acts 9:3-8)

Another account of a revelatory experience is given in 1545 by Martin Luther as he reflected on events from twenty-five to thirty years earlier. Luther's call for reform in the European Christian church of his time had sparked the Protestant Reformation and shattered the unity of Western Christendom. At the heart of his appeal for reform was the doctrine of justification by faith. A year before his death, Luther recalled the time when he came to this insight of justification by faith. As a professor of Bible at the University of Wittenberg Luther regularly gave lectures on various books of the Bible, and at one point was struggling to understand Romans 1:17 where Paul says, "For in it the righteousness of God is revealed. . . ." What troubled him was the word *righteousness*, because he had been instructed to interpret it as God being a judge who punishes sinners.

> At last, by the mercy of God, meditating day and night, I gave heed to the context of the words, namely, "In it the righteousness of God is revealed, as it is written, 'He who through faith is righteous shall live.'" There I began to understand that the righteousness of God is that by which the righteous lives by a gift of God, namely by faith. And this is the meaning: the righteousness of God is revealed by the gospel, namely, the passive righteousness with which merciful God justifies us by faith, as it is written, "He who through faith is righteous shall live." Here I felt that I was altogether born again and had entered paradise itself through open gates.[1]

When we consider these two accounts of an experience of revelation, several common features appear. First and most fundamental is the fact that each experience involves a new understanding of God and God's purposes for the world. Saul, who later changed his name to Paul, now believes that Jesus is central to God's purposes, and Luther comes to understand God as merciful rather than as a demanding judge. So revelation is not advance information on who is going to win the World Series or Superbowl, but a disclosure of God's character and will. Second, both Paul and Luther believe that the revelation has been given to them by God. This is obvious in Paul's case, for he believes the Jesus whom God raised from the dead suddenly and very dramatically appeared to him on the road to Damascus. For his part, Luther had no unusual visionary experience such as Saul's, yet Luther says his insight came "at last, by the mercy of God." Thus the revelation is experienced as a gift. Third, the revelation brings a new outlook on life. Saul now supports the Christian message that he had previously attacked, and becomes the leading missionary spreading the new faith. Luther feels altogether reborn after seeing that God freely forgives sins, and his new understanding fueled his call for reform in the church. Fourth, the revelation has a public side, yet is not necessarily seen by everyone. Acts 9 tells us that Saul/Paul's traveling companions on the road to Damascus also heard the voice, but we are never told whether they too believed it was the risen Jesus speaking. In Luther's case the revelation came through a biblical passage which many people had read and which he himself had often read before, yet it was on that one occasion that the light dawned for Luther.

Many theologians have distinguished between general and special revelation, and with some modifications it is a helpful distinction. *General revelation*

---

1. "Preface to Complete Edition of Luther's Latin Writings," in *Martin Luther: Selections From His Writings*, John Dillenberger, ed. (Garden City, N.Y.: Doubleday, 1961), 11.

means a revelation that is generally available. The clearest example is the order and beauty of nature that suggest the hand of a creator. A person may sense this when appreciating the beauty of a lovely day or gazing up at the stars at night. The Bible considers this a disclosure of God that is readily accessible to everyone in every culture and era. "The heavens are telling the glory of God; and the firmament proclaims his handiwork" (Psalm 19:1). Paul agrees, "Ever since the creation of the world his eternal power and divine nature, invisible though they are, have been understood and seen through the things he has made" (Romans 1:20).

Special revelation has traditionally meant the revelation of God given through the events and literature of the Bible with Jesus Christ as the center of that disclosure. So Christianity is based upon special revelation that Christians believe is a fuller understanding of God's will and character than can be ascertained from general revelation. For instance, while God's power and grandeur can be disclosed through nature, one would not conclude from observing nature that God loves the world with a self-sacrificial love. The special revelation of the Bible goes beyond the message of general revelation in nature.

One difficulty with the distinction between general and special revelation, however, is that many Christian theologians have said that religions other than Christianity are based on general revelation.[2] This does not make sense, for to the extent that Hinduism, for instance, is based on revelation from God, it is not readily available to everyone in every time. It is a specific revelation given within a particular cultural context, so it should be considered a special revelation. Thus I will use general revelation to refer to God's disclosure in nature and any other universally available source, while special revelation will refer to whatever particular manifestations of God may lie behind the religions of the world, including Christianity. Since Christian faith is based on the special revelation given in biblical events and literature, I will refer to this as *biblical revelation* or the revelation in Jesus Christ. As we will see later in our discussion of the relations among the religions, this position need not mean that all special revelations are to be seen as equal.

2. *How does revelation happen?* In every revelation there is an objective side and a subjective side. The objective side is what is shown, the subjective is someone seeing what is shown. For instance, imagine that you get an overpowering urge to run about naked. The reason for this need not concern us now, but just think of yourself having the urge to go about without a stitch of clothes on. So on a warm Tuesday night at 4 AM you slip out of your room or house buck naked, and you run across campus or down several streets and return home. But at no point on your outing does anyone see you. Now the

---

2. For a recent example see Daniel L. Migliore, *Faith Seeking Understanding: An Introduction to Christian Theology* (Grand Rapids, Mich.: Wm. B. Eerdmans, 1991), 25.

question is, Have you revealed your naked body or not? Objectively, you have shown all that you had to show; not an inch of your body was covered. But a revelation of your nakedness has not occurred, because the subjective side is lacking—no one saw you. Another possibility is that several people may have seen you running naked, but interpreted it differently. One may have thought you were an escaped mental patient and called the local mental hospital. Another person may have seen you as a sex maniac and run for safety. Still another may have thought you were the victim of a crime and sought help for you. Whether you were seen or not, the point is that in every event of revelation there is both an objective and subjective side.

Involvement of the subjective side means that every revelation includes human experience, for revelation is always an experience of some individual or community perceiving what God discloses. The objective side of God's disclosure can be made through various means: nature, Scripture, and the many ways Christian tradition is expressed in the lives of individuals, families, congregations, and other groups. Divine disclosure can also occur through events in contemporary culture, such as the ecological movement calling attention to God's care for the entire earth. Thus divine revelation is mediated through nature and the other four sources of Christian theology: experience, culture, Bible, and tradition.

The various disclosures of God are not all on the same level of importance, however, for the revelation given to the biblical authors is foundational for Christianity. We can call this *original revelation*. Examples are the revelation of God to Abraham in the call to leave his home, to Moses and others in Israel's exodus from Egypt, and above all the revelation given in the life, death, and resurrection of Jesus to Peter, Mary Magdalene, Paul, and others among the first generation of Christians. These occurrences of revelation are the foundation on which Christianity is based; without them, there would be no Christian faith. These events are original both in the sense that they are at the origin or beginning of the Christian faith and in the sense that they originate or cause this faith to arise.

Continuing revelation is insight into God that in some way builds on and continues the original revelation. As a result of his encounter with the risen Christ, Paul became a Christian missionary and eventually wrote the letter to the Romans expressing his understanding of the faith in Jesus Christ. Almost fifteen hundred years later Martin Luther gained a fresh understanding of God through pondering some of Paul's words in Romans. Luther's revelatory experience derives from Paul's original revelation.

The revelations given to the Israelite community and early Christian community have a privileged position in Christianity, for all later Christian revelatory experiences are based upon the original revelation underlying Scripture. This does not mean that Christians never have any new insights into God's ways, but they believe any fresh revelation will not contradict or fundamentally alter the original revelation given in Jesus Christ. Thus when Reverend Sun Myung Moon, founder of the Unification Church (Moonies), said he had received a revelation that a second messiah was needed to complete the work of Jesus Christ, Christians regarded this as a fundamental break with the Christian faith. Moon's teaching about a second messiah conflicts with the New Testament belief that Jesus is the only messiah. The situation is much more complicated for those Christian feminists who believe the feminist movement is an expression of God's grace today that challenges many sexist elements within the Christian tradition and the Bible itself, yet also believe that the heart of the Bible and Christian tradition addresses feminism with divine revelation.[3] So revelation continues to happen in Christianity, yet any putative revelatory experience today must be tested for its consistency with the original revelation given in Jesus Christ. For Christians, a genuine revelation today continues and builds on the original revelation in Jesus Christ.

The distinction between original and continuing revelation is not absolute. Jesus and his first followers already were recipients of earlier revelation to the Hebrew people, and Martin Luther's insight into Paul's teaching of justification by faith played a major role in starting the Lutheran tradition and other classical Protestant traditions. In fact, John Wesley (1703–1791), founder of the Methodist movement, writes of a conversion experience he had:

> In the evening I went very unwillingly to a society in Aldersgate Street, where one was reading Luther's Preface to the Epistle to the Romans. About a quarter before nine, while he was describing the change which God works in the heart through faith in Christ, I felt my heart strangely warmed. I felt I did trust in Christ, Christ alone for my salvation; and an assurance was given me that He had taken away *my* sins, even *mine*, and saved *me* from the law of sin and of death.[4]

In this case, the connections in a revelatory experience are complex, for John Wesley has a transforming insight while listening to Luther's words on Paul's Epistle to the Romans. Those very same words of Luther were heard by others at that religious gathering, but very likely those words *became* revelation only for John Wesley.

3. *Is the Christian claim to revelation justified?* It is not unusual to find people (some of them in mental hospitals) who say that God has given them a message, such as the world is going to end on a certain day or they are divinely

---

3. See Anne E. Carr, *Transforming Grace: Christian Tradition and Women's Experience* (San Francisco: Harper & Row, 1988), 112–13.
4. "Extracts From John Wesley's Journal," in *John and Charles Wesley*, Frank Whaling, ed. (New York: Paulist, 1981), 107.

appointed to rule the earth. It is perilous to accept every avowal of divine revelation at face value, so we must ask whether the Christian claim to have received revelation of God can be justified. Theologians have addressed this question in a variety of ways, but we shall look at just two broad approaches.

One important method for defending Christian belief in revelation is to appeal first to some experience common to everyone; we can call this the *generalized approach*, for in essence it appeals to general revelation. An intriguing yet clear example of this approach is given by a contemporary American theologian, Schubert Ogden.[5] Ogden begins by pointing to a simple, taken-forgranted fact of our experience: We trust in the meaning and worth of life. If the place where we are currently present began to fill up with smoke, we would immediately seek to escape to safety. When our life is threatened, we instantly respond with an effort to protect it. Hidden beneath this response is the assumption that our life is worthwhile. One might object that in some circumstances a person under threat from a repressive government or assailant may sacrifice their life for a cause or another person. But such heroic actions themselves assume that human existence is meaningful.[6] It is important to see that our trust in the meaning or worth of life undergirds all our moments, however, not just those in which our existence is threatened. Everyday we get up and go about our tasks, we make plans for the future, and strive to make them into reality. Our moment-to-moment existence rests on confidence in the worth of our life. Schubert Ogden's argument asks us to become conscious of this usually implicit trust.

Next, Ogden says the word *God* refers primarily to the objective ground in reality for our fundamental trust in the meaning and worth of life. That is, whatever it is about reality that invites and undergirds our trust in life's meaning is what is meant by "God." Thus when we trust in the worth of life, we are trusting in God, whether we consciously recognize it or not. Belief in God is really inescapable for us. Even the atheist, who explicitly denies that there is a God, really does trust in God as the ground of confidence in life's meaning. What the atheist rejects is merely a certain idea or concept of God.

What does this argument have to do with the Christian claim to having received a revelation of God in Jesus? Ogden says that the various religions and faiths of the world, including the Christian religion, are all particular expressions of the deeper faith in God that everyone has by virtue of trusting in the worth of their life. At the root of this faith in life's worth is what Ogden calls original revelation, for in this root experience the supporting reality of

5. A very important variation of the generalizing approach is the transcendental method of Karl Rahner. See his *Foundations of Christian Faith* (New York: Seabury, 1978), 208–12.

6. Someone committing suicide usually suffers from deep depression in which the body's chemical balance is severely disturbed and thus does not freely choose suicide.

God is apprehended. This original revelation is a general revelation, for it is given to everyone in every time and place. The decisive revelation in Jesus Christ is a special revelation that makes explicit the reality and love of God that all people already apprehend in a rudimentary way. In fact, Ogden holds that the revelation in Jesus Christ does not add any new content to general revelation, for it only makes explicit what a person already implicitly believes. In essence, Ogden's argument is a defense against both the denial of God (*atheism*) and the belief that we do not know whether God exists (*agnosticism*). Of course, the atheist and agnostic deny the Christian claim to revelation in Jesus Christ, because they do not believe there is any revelation of God whatsoever. Ogden argues that even the atheist and agnostic are recipients of original revelation by virtue of trusting in the worth of their life, and so the possibility of a special revelation should not be ruled out.[7]

There are several criticisms that can be made of Schubert Ogden's generalizing approach for evaluating the Christian assertion of divine revelation; we shall consider only two. One criticism is that those who deny the reality of God may ground the meaning of their life merely on the fact that the universe is organized in a rather stable way that usually sustains human life for a reasonable lifespan and provides opportunities for happiness in relationships and work. To call that stable order "God" is misleading, for there is nothing that transcends the physical order of the universe. In other words, Ogden's argument from our confidence in the worth of our life need not entail belief in God. Another criticism of Ogden's argument is that even if one accepts it as a convincing argument for implicit faith in God, it does not give a defense for most Christian beliefs such as that in Jesus Christ God entered deeply into the suffering of the world or that Jesus' resurrection is God's promise for the future of the world. Ogden's view of God is very vague, as it must be in order to include the conceptions of God in various religions as well as those faiths such as Buddhism that recognize a transcendent reality while refusing to call it God. So even if one agrees with Ogden's transcendental argument, it would still leave open the question whether one should believe the Christian claim to have a special revelation in Jesus.

A second major approach to defending the Christian avowal of divine revelation has a different starting point than an experience that is generally available, for it begins with specific Christian beliefs, for instance, that the life, death, and resurrection of Jesus are the key to understanding God and what humans are intended to be. We can call this the *particularized approach*. How can one judge whether these particular beliefs of Christians are truly based on revelation from God? Several tests may be proposed. One is to determine

---

7. Schubert M. Ogden, *The Reality of God and Other Essays* (New York: Harper & Row, 1963), 21–43; (Dallas: Southern Methodist University Press, 1992), 22–44.

whether the reputed revelation is *fruitful for living*. In 1978 James Jones, leader of the People's Temple, said he was the reincarnation of Jesus Christ, and directed the mass suicide of his nine-hundred-member colony in Guyana. In Texas in 1993 David Koresh led his Branch Davidian followers in a bloody shootout and long-term siege with law officers. These faiths produced wretched fruit. On the positive side, a faith that yields good character, high purpose, and noble resilience in the face of loss has good reasons for being considered solidly grounded. An assignment that I often give to students is to write a brief faith autobiography. These autobiographies clearly show that students who have experienced an effective faith in the lives of their family or friends are very strongly inclined to accept that faith as well, whereas those who have received mixed or negative messages about faith from their family are very likely to express confusion about their faith. All of the students are employing the fruitfulness test.[8]

Another test is to see whether the avowed revelation is *consistent with major theories* in various realms of knowledge. This can be a very sophisticated intellectual enterprise, but it is also something most persons do on some level. Thus it is common for people reflecting on Christian faith to explore how it fits with other ideas such as scientific theories about the beginnings of the universe and the evolution of life, sociological theories about religion, psychological theories about personal development, and philosophical theories about human nature. We all tend to seek cognitive coherence. However, an error quite often made in this endeavor is to forget that every view reflects the limitations of its own place and time in history, so a person may assume that a philosophical or scientific theory is a fully adequate account of the truth. Then a philosophical or scientific theory, rather than the Christian message, becomes the primary ground for Christian faith. Yet if one remembers that all our perspectives are partial apprehensions of reality, the quest for coherence of revelation with major theories is sound. What Christian faith seeks in this endeavor is secondary corroboration, not primary grounding. Here Christian faith seeks to show it is not only fruitful for living but also fruitful for understanding. Coherence is a mark of truth, for ultimately truth is one.[9]

This particularized approach of evaluating the Christian claim to revelation of God is also subject to criticism. The main critique is that the approach

---

8. The contemporary American theologian Francis Schüssler Fiorenza calls this test a retroductive warrant, and gives examples of its use by philosophers of science as well as by theologians John Henry Newman, Sallie McFague, and Karl Rahner. "Systematic Theology: Task and Methods," in *Systematic Theology: Roman Catholic Perspectives*, Vol. 1, Francis Schüssler Fiorenza and John P. Galvin, eds. (Minneapolis: Fortress Press, 1991), 77–80.

9. Francis Schüssler Fiorenza calls these related theories background theories, a term in the philosophy of science to refer to implied theories that impact upon a hypothesis under consideration. He cites the use of background theories by the theologians Augustine, Karl Rahner, and Bernard Lonergan. Ibid., 74–77.

is ineffective in meeting the objections of those who are skeptical of the Christian faith. These critics contend that testing specifically Christian beliefs by their fruitfulness in living is to appeal to a standard of truth peculiar to the community of Christian believers rather than to a standard readily open to everyone. That is, an outsider cannot adequately assess the fruit that Christian faith produces in its adherents without becoming quite familiar with some Christians. Skeptics of Christian faith are therefore left untouched by this theological method, for it asks them, in effect, to become involved with the Christian community of which they are skeptical.

While I can see merit in both the approaches, I think the particularized way of dealing with the question is more in keeping with our actual situation as human beings unavoidably rooted in time and space. It would indeed be easier if we were able to stand outside time and survey the whole sweep of world history from the very beginning of the universe; then we might ascertain the degree of truth and falsity in every avowed revelation. But we are immersed in a given cultural context and can see only a part of the total picture. So in fact all people chart their course in life by a more or less particular faith—by affirming a set of beliefs of what life is finally about, by committing themselves to certain ultimate values, and by trusting that reality will confirm their particular faith. There is no safe, unchallenged path open to us. Even Schubert Ogden's supposedly universal experience of trusting in God shows the influence of Christian beliefs and modern Western culture. While I think God is indeed present to everyone, how that presence is interpreted varies. Calling ultimate reality "God" in itself is an interpretation. Solid ground cannot be found through rational argument alone; it can only be discovered by testing a particular faith for its fruitfulness in living. Aside from those obviously bad examples of faith, such as James Jones and David Koresh, this testing requires a substantial degree of self-investment.[10]

The sort of argument that Schubert Ogden presents still has secondary value as a background theory that employs a particular philosophical analysis to point to the *likelihood* of God's presence undergirding human life. Ogden's argument may be helpful for the skeptic as well as the Christian believer who is searching for coherence, because it suggests that there may be an ultimate reality that bears some resemblance to what Christians talk about as God. There is no substitute for the test of fruitfulness for living, however. Since faith is a matter of fundamental direction in life, it cannot be decided merely on the theoretical level. The crucial test is to see how a faith actually does shape people's lives.

---

10. Mark I. Wallace, "Can God Be Named Without Being Known? The Problem of Revelation in Thiemann, Ogden, and Ricoeur," *Journal of the American Academy of Religion* 59, no. 2 (Summer 1991): 294–95; Martin L. Cook, *The Open Circle: Confessional Method in Theology* (Minneapolis: Fortress Press, 1991), 61–62.

2
God

How we think about God powerfully influences *what* we think about God. Because members of the International Society for Krishna Consciousness take their ideas about God from their founder Swami Prabhupada, they understand God as a personal being named Krishna who summons people to detach themselves from the material world by repeatedly chanting "Hare Krishna" and abstaining from sex. Because those who belong to the esoteric group Eckankar look to the living Eck Master for their conception of God, like him they view God as the destination of a long human quest for spiritual advancement through a many-leveled universe. *How* we think about God, that is, what sources we use, powerfully influences *what* we think about God.

The sources we use to think about God might not be explicitly religious. A student once said in class, "I think God is an idea, the human idea of what we would like the world to be." As discussion continued, it became clear the student drew this suggestion from a psychologist. Another student of mine once wrote, "I believe there is a God for everyone and the way people choose to interpret this God is a personal choice." This student is saying either that there are many gods and we can take our pick or that if there is one God, that God will honor whatever view we hold. In either case, these ideas have their source in the highly relativistic culture of postmodern Western society, for they imply that God is whatever a person wants God to be. How we think about God influences what we think about God.

Since God is ultimate reality, our ideas drawn from finite things always fail to fully grasp God's infinite reality. Indeed, it would be hopeless for us to ever know anything at all about God if there were no revelation from God. But as we saw at the end of our previous chapter, it is a basic New Testament and Christian conviction that the heart of God's character and purpose for the world has been revealed in the life, death, and resurrection of Jesus. Christians do not foolishly claim to comprehend, that is, fully understand God, but they have commonly held that Jesus is the key to discerning the character of God. This means that for Christian reflection on God, attention must be focused on the biblical story of Jesus understood within the context of the story of Israel.

This chapter carefully considers a Christian conception of God that should help to clarify both one's own notion of God and the sources one uses in forming that notion. Of course, the two-thousand-year-old tradition of Christianity, with some sources still much older, includes diverse views of God, yet to one degree or another all of them take the biblical story seriously as a source for understanding the identity of God.

The primary way in which Scripture speaks of God is to tell stories. Some of these stories, like Jesus' parables, are not necessarily about historical events, but other stories, like Israel's exodus from Egypt and Jesus' death and resurrection have roots in history. Indeed, in the biblical books God is identified primarily by stories in which God is an unseen actor. Thus, while we will use some metaphors and abstract terms for God, we must be careful always to draw their meaning from the biblical stories.

This way of identifying God is similar to procedures we use to identify human persons. If someone were to ask me who Abraham Lincoln was, I might reply that he was President of the United States from 1861 to 1865. That bit of information from Lincoln's life story surely distinguishes him from everyone else, yet it does not tell us much about what sort of person he was. So I might describe him as the Great Emancipator or use character traits such as eloquent, courageous, moral, and religious. Yet the metaphor Great Emancipator and the general character traits do not convey the specific character of Abraham Lincoln. We come to know him better through a good account of his life story, which tells the specific challenges he faced and the particular decisions he made. A faithful biography of Abraham Lincoln would reveal his character and give concrete meaning to the metaphor Great Emancipator and to the abstract terms eloquent, courageous, moral, and religious.

While the biblical story is lengthy, Christians also have developed shorthand ways of referring to God. *We shall consider three shorthand ways of referring to the God made known in the biblical story: major metaphors for God, attributes of God, and the doctrine of the Trinity.* These do not speak of three different gods, but they are three perspectives on the one God made known in the biblical story.

Metaphors: Heavenly Father/Eternal Mother

Scripture uses a multitude of metaphors for God; among them are rock, shepherd, fortress, king, judge, and eagle. Perhaps the best-known metaphor that Christians use for God is Heavenly Father. This metaphor has solid roots in the biblical story, because Jesus addressed God as *abba*, the Aramaic word for dad or father. The Lord's Prayer, which Jesus taught to his disciples, begins with "Our Father in heaven." So to speak of God as Heavenly Father immediately connects one's conception of God with Jesus' life story and his understanding of God.

The Father metaphor has two main aspects. One aspect is that God is compassionate and merciful toward his children. The classic expression of this comes in Jesus' story of the prodigal son. In this story or parable, a prosperous land-owning father has two sons. The younger son is unhappy at home, so he asks to receive his inheritance and he goes far away into a foreign land. There the son wastes his entire inheritance, so that he ends up feeding hogs and would be glad to eat what the pigs ate. Finally, he decides he would be better off as a mere servant in his father's household, so he returns home. The parable says, "But while he was still far off, his father saw him and was filled with compassion; he ran and put his arms around him and kissed him." The father pays no heed to the son's speech about being treated as a servant, for the father immediately calls for the dress befitting a son and orders a feast to celebrate the son's return (Luke 15:11-24). Clearly the father in Jesus' story is a symbol for God. As the father is compassionate toward his son, so God is compassionate and merciful toward his wayward human children.

The other aspect to the Father metaphor for God is that God is someone to whom humans are responsible, even as children are responsible to their father. In the New Testament's Gospel of John, Jesus says that God has sent him on a mission and that he is called to obey the Father. In addition, God as Father is the source of one's existence. Thus the Father metaphor also indicates a relationship of dependence upon God for both one's existence and meaning in life.

Of course, to address God as Father does not mean that God is literally a father, that is, one who has begotten children through sexual intercourse with a woman. To add the qualifier, "heavenly," suggests that God is Father in some higher sense, as the ultimate source of one's existence and as the perfectly caring One. Every human father has limitations and faults, but the Heavenly Father does not die and is consistently compassionate. Thus for a great many Christians who use this metaphor, Heavenly Father suggests One with whom they have an intimate, caring relationship and to whom they are responsible.

Some people cannot resonate positively to the Father image, however. Some persons whose human father has been hateful and abusive find it uncomfortable to call God Father. Furthermore, feminists argue that the image of God as Father has often functioned to support a male-dominated society. God has often been understood as a distant, authoritarian Father who controlled all events in the world. Consequently, some feminist theologians completely reject the Father metaphor for God.[1] Others, such as Sallie McFague, say that Father can be properly used of God when the metaphor is understood to mean a nurturing rather than authoritarian father. Nonetheless, McFague argues that the Father metaphor has been overused, so it is time to propose other metaphors for God.[2]

One of the metaphors McFague and other feminists propose is the metaphor of Mother. This proposal has met with some criticism from those who argue that various fertility religions have traditionally referred to a mother deity, and that one way biblical religion sought to distinguish itself from these surrounding fertility religions was to avoid using the Mother metaphor for God. There is some truth in this argument. Indeed, today the Mother image is frequently employed in Goddess religion, which shuns the biblical story and draws its inspiration chiefly from processes in nature. The Mother metaphor has not been traditionally used in the biblical tradition. Nevertheless, the fact that the Bible uses such a wide variety of metaphors for God should free us up to adopt new metaphors. Furthermore, while God is not spoken of directly as Mother in the Bible, some feminine and maternal images are used of God. God is compared to a woman giving birth in the Old Testament book of Isaiah (42:14) and to a woman searching for a coin in the New Testament Gospel of Luke (15:8-10). A word derives its meaning from the context in which it is used. The key for Christian use of Mother for God is that the metaphor be placed solidly within the biblical story, so that the meaning of God as Mother is taken from that story rather than from some nature religion.

To be sure, God is no more literally mother than literally father. It is therefore appropriate to add some qualifier such as "eternal" to the Mother metaphor. As Eternal Mother, God is not subject to the restrictions and flaws of human mothers. In fact, Mother can communicate the same two meanings we saw in Father, namely, that God is compassionate and the One on whom we are utterly dependent for existence and meaning.

It is true that for this or that individual the metaphor of Father or Mother will not communicate these meanings, so for some people one or the other

---

1. Mary Daly, "After the Death of God the Father," in *Womanspirit Rising*, Carol Christ and Judith Plaskow, eds. (San Francisco: Harper & Row, 1979), 53–62.

2. Sallie McFague, *Models of God: Theology for an Ecological, Nuclear Age* (Philadelphia: Fortress Press, 1987), 181–83.

metaphor will simply not work. The church's usage, though, should be broad enough to include both masculine and feminine metaphors for God. If some individuals and groups find either the Father or Mother metaphor offensive, then it is legitimate for them to avoid the troubling metaphor. But it would be a mistake for the church as a whole to shun either metaphor.

Attributes of God

A second shorthand way that the Bible and Christians have for speaking of God is to identify certain attributes or traits of God. Doing this adds specificity to one's conception of God, so that sketching out the major attributes of God fills out the picture of God given by major metaphors. However, again we must be careful to draw our understanding of God's attributes from the biblical story rather than from some philosophy or ideology. The Bible often tells stories in which traits of God may be discerned. The central story in the Old Testament is the exodus, when Moses led the people of Israel out of their bondage in Egypt. We shall look only at a portion of this long story—God's call of Moses.

> Moses was keeping the flock of his father-in-law Jethro, the priest of Midian; he led his flock beyond the wilderness, and came to Horeb, the mountain of God. There the angel of the LORD appeared to him in a flame of fire out of a bush; and he looked, and the bush was blazing, yet it was not consumed. Then Moses said, "I must turn aside and look at this great sight, and see why the bush is not burned up." When the LORD saw that he had turned aside to see, God called to him out of the bush, "Moses, Moses!" And he said, "Here I am." Then he said, "Come no closer! Remove the sandals from your feet, for the place on which you are standing is holy ground." And he said, "I am the God of your father, the God of Abraham, the God of Isaac, and the God of Jacob." And Moses hid his face, for he was afraid to look at God.
> Then the LORD said, "I have observed the misery of my people who are in Egypt; I have heard their cry on account of their taskmasters. Indeed, I know their sufferings, and I have come down to deliver them from the Egyptians, and to bring them up out of that land to a good and broad land, a land flowing with milk and honey, to the country of the Canaanites, the Hittites, the Amorites, the Perizzites, the Hivites, and the Jebusites. The cry of the Israelites has now come to me; I have also seen how the Egyptians oppress them. So come, I will send you to Pharaoh to bring my people, the Israelites out of Egypt." (Exodus 3:1-10)

The most prominent quality of God in this brief story as well as throughout the exodus account is God's compassionate love for Israel. "I have observed the misery of my people who are in Egypt; I have heard their cry on account of their taskmasters. Indeed, I know their sufferings, and I have come down to deliver them from the Egyptians. . . ." God cares about the plight of the suffering Israelites, and this loving God takes action to deliver them.

The other divine characteristic that stands out in the call of Moses is the mystery of God. The divine mystery is suggested by several events in the story. Moses encounters a bush that is on fire, but is not burning up. This is puzzling, for when we burn wood or paper, they turn to ashes. So the burning bush itself eludes understanding. Then Moses hears a voice speaking to him out of the burning bush. This disembodied voice instructs him to come no closer and to remove his sandals, for he is treading on holy ground. Finally Moses hides his face in awe and fear as the voice identifies itself as the God of his ancestors. All of these elements in the story strongly suggest the mystery of God.

Exodus 3 interprets the call of Moses and Israel's release from Egypt within the framework of a larger narrative in which God is the principal actor. This everlasting God has created the world, and has called Israel into a special relationship and responsibility that is called a *covenant*. Later, when Israel is persistently unfaithful to this special relationship, the nation is penalized by conquest and exile. Yet God again generously rescues Israel and calls the people to revive their faith.

Exodus 3 and the larger biblical story convey a richly textured message of who God is. We cannot retell all those stories, but from them we can identify the most significant biblical characteristics of God. The two divine attributes that perhaps best help us grasp something of God's character are mystery and love.

God Is Mystery

In general, a mystery is something that is beyond our understanding, inexplicable. Very often *mystery* designates something we do not *yet* understand, such as a mystery story that will be solved at the end of the book or a puzzle in nature that scientists are working to answer. In the Christian tradition, however, there is a strong abiding sense that God will always exceed our comprehension. We can distinguish three major meanings that Scripture and the Christian tradition give to God's mysteriousness.

1. One important element in God's mysteriousness is the unsurpassable greatness or *majesty* of God. There are many awesome signs of this majesty or grandeur. The opening words of the Bible point to the divine greatness: "In the beginning when God created the heavens and the earth." While all things in the universe have their ultimate source in God, the story assigns no origin to God; God is not derived from something else. God's power to exist is unique, for God exists from God's own self; this is called God's *aseity*. Another sign of the divine majesty is that God is *eternal*. Whereas all things in the

universe and the universe as a whole have a beginning and will have an end, God has neither beginning nor end: "From everlasting to everlasting you are God" (Psalm 90:2). As eternal, God's relation to the passage of time is also different than ours, for while we often face the future with anxiety or fear, God looks to the future with the assurance of being able to cope with anything that may arise.

The divine majesty is also evident in that God is *almighty*. In the call of Moses, the burning bush that does not burn up is suggestive of the almighty power of God. Yet while God can do extraordinary things, it is a mistake to identify the almighty God as a sort of overgrown Superman who goes about performing all sorts of dazzling feats of strength. To have power means to be able to bring something about, to accomplish it. For God to be almighty means that God is able to accomplish whatever God sets out to do. Thus, when the last book in the Bible proclaims, "Hallelujah! For the Lord our God the Almighty reigns" (Revelation 19:6), what is being celebrated is the fulfillment of God's long-intended victory over evil.

Yet another element of God's majesty is *holiness*. This too is evident in the call of Moses when the voice tells him to remove his sandals, for he is standing on holy ground. To speak of God's holiness is to refer to the otherness of God, the difference of God's ways from human ways.[3] This divine otherness is manifest surely in judgment on human sin, but also, surprisingly, in God's saving people from their waywardness. This latter meaning is expressed in these prophetic words from God, "How can I give you up, Ephraim? How can I hand you over, O Israel? . . . I will not execute my fierce anger; I will not again destroy Ephraim; for I am God and no mortal, the Holy One in your midst, and I will not come in wrath" (Hosea 11:8-9).

God is certainly majestic, for God exists by God's own power and is eternal, almighty, and holy. With these qualities God meets us as the mysterious reality that always exceeds our understanding.

2. God is mystery also in that God's ways of relating to humanity and the world are *surprising*. The actual word *mystery* is most often used in the New Testament by Paul. In a letter to the Christian congregation he founded in the Greek city of Corinth, Paul says, "When I came to you, brothers and sisters, I did not come proclaiming the mystery of God to you in lofty words or wisdom" (1 Corinthians 2:1). Notice that "the mystery of God" is not concealed but is openly proclaimed by Paul. Furthermore, the particular mystery he proclaims is that God has acted supremely in Jesus Christ who was cruci-

---

3. S.v. "Holy," in *The New International Dictionary of New Testament Theology*, Vol. 2, ed. Colin Brown (Grand Rapids, Mich. : Zondervan, 1975–1978), 223–38; s.v. "Saint," in *A Theological Word Book of the Bible*, ed. Alan Richardson (New York: Macmillan, 1960), 214–16; Karl Barth, *Church Dogmatics* II/1, eds. G. W. Bromiley and T. F. Torrance, trans. T. H. L. Parker et al. (Edinburgh: T & T Clark, 1957), 360.

fied. Paul goes on to say that the message about the cross is regarded as foolishness by those who were considered wise. So God is mysterious partly because *God behaves in ways that run contrary to people's usual expectations.* It is difficult for those of us who have grown up in a culture strongly influenced by Christianity to appreciate the extraordinary, even shocking character of the claim that God is centrally revealed in a man whose life ended in rejection and brutal criminal execution. This aspect of the Christian message does not surprise us today. Yet in another way Jesus' crucifixion frequently comes as a surprise to contemporary Christians. They may share in the cross of Jesus when they suffer, but when suffering comes, they often ask, "Why me?" It goes against their expectations.

Another side to the surprising mystery for Paul was *the inclusiveness of God's work of salvation.* Paul teaches that Gentiles were included along with Jews; this went against the opinions of many in his day. Paul himself seems to have had difficulty living up to his own additional insight that the Christian community has no divisions between male and female (Galatians 3:28), for he also says the husband is head of his wife and women shall not speak publicly in church (1 Corinthians 11:3; 14:33-36).

Thus, in a Christian understanding, God is mystery partly because God upsets the usual ways of thinking and acting, so even Paul was inconsistent about some implications of that mystery. However, this surprising quality of God's behavior is not aimless, not just random flakiness. In retrospect one can see a pattern of aiming toward a more Christlike life in individuals and communities. This surprising, often disturbing character contributes to the mystery of God.

3. God is mystery also, for even in being revealed God remains *hidden.* One aspect of this is that *God is not an object under our control.* An object is observable to everyone whose senses are physically functional no matter what their attitude is toward the object. Thus, the White House is available to the eyes of all who tour through it, whether their attitude toward the building is respectful or scornful. God is not such an object. This is suggested in the call of Moses story when God spoke to Moses as a disembodied voice coming from the burning bush; Moses looked at the bush, but could not see God.

According to Mark, who wrote one of four New Testament interpretations of Jesus' life called *Gospels,* Jesus' parables were a reflection of the fact that God is not an object observable by any bystander. *Parable* is a term applied to a variety of figurative sayings of Jesus. Jesus' parables are like those words that have a special meaning within a family. One such word in my own family had its origin when one of my children was in diapers. Once when either my wife or I (I can't remember who) encountered an especially messy and smelly diaper, our reaction was to say, "Ach." Ever since in our family "ach" has meant a messy diaper. I doubt that anyone else in the world understands the expression this way, so the only way an outsider could understand our special meaning was to become a close friend of our family. In other words, understanding of the term came through a special relationship. Jesus' parables also can be understood only by those who enter into the special relationship of being his disciple. Of course, others grasp something of what he says, but only the ones who follow Jesus are able to see some part of the deeper, hidden meaning.[4] This is true not only of Jesus' parables but of the God to whom so many of them refer. God is present in each moment, yet God is hidden from those who are closed to the Spirit of God (1 Corinthians 2:6-16).

Another aspect of hiddenness is that *God is also in many respects hidden to the believer.* Although Moses was specifically commissioned by God to lead Israel out of Egypt to the promised land, Moses was often in the dark about what God was doing. The Old Testament figure Job, who lost his family and property, struggled to understand God's ways. And Mark's Gospel shows Jesus on the night before his death trying to ascertain God's will for him (Mark 14:32-39). Indeed, Jesus' dying words, "My God, my God, why have you forsaken me?" (Mark 15:34), seem to express considerable puzzlement about what has happened. It is a common experience of the faithful that they do not understand what God's will is in some trying experience. They suffer or see others suffer, and cannot grasp how that suffering fits with what they believe about God. Some people respond to this experience of darkness by giving up their faith in God. Those who continue to believe in God frequently go through a process of rethinking and modifying their conception of God. They also commonly grow in humility before the mysteriousness of God. This humility brings with it the ability to live with paradoxes and unanswered questions, even to be at rest amidst them. Christian humility in the face of God's mystery enables the believer to wait in darkness for God. Waiting for God perhaps sounds as though one has given up hope, but that is far from the case. Waiting for God is possible only for those who trust and hope in God. In fact, one of the paradoxes of Christian experience is that as faith in God grows, the sense of God's mystery also grows. So faith does not dispel the mystery of God. God remains hidden from our probing questions. Yet our comfort with and confidence in the hidden One may increase.

To summarize, for Christians God is mystery, a reality that remains beyond human comprehension, yet this divine mystery is not complete darkness; some contours are visible, for God is majestic, surprising, and hidden even while being revealed. Many other religions and philosophies speak of an ultimate reality whose greatness eludes our understanding, yet for the Christian the shape of the divine mystery becomes centrally apparent in the bibli-

---

4. Eduard Schweizer, *The Good News According to Mark.* trans. Donald H. Madvig (Atlanta: John Knox, 1970), 85, 86.

cal story of Israel and of Jesus. Thus, God's majestic holiness is also a readiness to help the wayward, God's surprises include divine suffering for others, and God's hiddenness is revealed to the humble.

God Is Love

Love is a very prominent theme in our culture. Whereas many cultures in history have built marriages on social utility, our marriages are supposed to be grounded on love. While families in most cultures have been governed by the authority of the father, our ideal family is ruled by mutual love. Our popular songs sing about romantic love, our most wholesome television shows portray devoted love between family members. We long to receive love, and we often strive to be loving. Yet love is elusive both in relationships and to the understanding. It cannot be taught or packaged in human relations programs, and it escapes our attempts to fully define its nature. We know something about love, enough to yearn for it and sing about it, but not enough to say precisely what it is.

In our cultural context to say that God is love is simultaneously to appeal to our deepest longings and to invite all sorts of confusion about the nature of God's love. To avoid undue confusion, we must be attentive to the meaning of God's love suggested in the biblical story. Only when we have a clearer understanding of the divine love can we appreciate how profoundly that love meets human longings. We can distinguish four aspects of God's love.

1. God's love is a *compassionate, self-giving* love. Compassion is evident in the story of the call of Moses. "I have observed the misery of my people who are in Egypt; I have heard their cry on account of their taskmasters. Indeed, I know their sufferings" (Exodus 3:7). God has tender sympathy for those who suffer and especially for those whose suffering arises from being marginal in society. God's compassion expresses itself through God's own involvement in bringing deliverance; God gives of God's own self. God says to Moses, "I have come down to deliver them from the Egyptians, and to bring them up out of that land to a good and broad land" (Exodus 3:8). Throughout the extended story of the exodus, God is very much involved acting through Moses, accompanying the Israelites on their journey as a pillar of cloud by day and a pillar of fire at night, and giving them the law at Mount Sinai.

The self-giving character of God's love is most memorably articulated in the New Testament in this summary of the Christian story in the Gospel of John: "For God so loved the world that he gave his only Son, so that everyone who believes in him may not perish but may have eternal life" (John 3:16). Above all John emphasizes that God's love is a love that gives of itself. In human relationships self-giving is also a feature of genuine love. A loving parent devotes time and concern to the child, and years later the loving son or daughter may give time and personal attention to the elderly parent. In a romantic relationship if one partner takes without also giving, then a vital ingredient of love is missing. In human relationships the greatest self-giving involves real sacrifice in which something one values highly is given up for the sake of the other. In dangerous situations a person may even give up their life for another. Clearly the story of Jesus' life and death is the chief clue to the meaning of God's love, for the giving of God's own Son shows the depth of God's self-giving. God suffers for the sake of humans.

Many feminists have been cautious about the Christian emphasis on self-giving love, because patriarchal cultures have encouraged women to continually deny themselves for the good of their family. In this way the Christian teaching tends to legitimize the subordination of women and the restriction of their development as capable persons. There is some truth in this argument, for the message of self-denial and self-sacrifice can stultify someone who lacks a solid personal identity. Then self-sacrifice is not done out of free choice, but out of social inertia. However, genuine self-sacrifice flows as a free act from a strong personal identity. Surely Jesus was just such a strong person who had well-developed convictions. So self-giving love is not necessarily harmful to human adulthood, but when freely done is a sign of a very mature person.

2. God's love *aims at mutuality*, it aims at an appropriate response from the one that is loved. God's loving us is not an end in itself but seeks to evoke our response of love. The purpose of God's call of Moses and the exodus is that Israel may live in their own land as a people responsible to God and as a blessing to all nations. Israel is called to fulfill a very important role.

The human response God seeks is also emphasized in John 3:16: "For God so loved the world that he gave his only Son, *so that* everyone who believes in him may not perish but may have eternal life." For John eternal life is not just something that comes after death, but is a quality of existence possible now; and the essence of eternal life is to respond to God's gift with faith and love.

Sometimes in human relationships one person has a love that smothers the other; occasionally a parent loves a child in this way. In some respects the parent's love can be self-sacrificing, yet the parent lives their life in and through the child so that the child is never invited to emerge as a distinct person. Here self-giving and domination are a destructive combination for both persons. God's self-giving love does not aim at control but at a free response of love. The goal is mutuality even while very great differences exist between the eternal God and a mortal human being.

A few feminist theologians have tried to avoid any hierarchical connection with God by entirely avoiding parental language and using images of equality such as sister or brother in reference to God.[5] Their concern is to emphasize that God calls both women and men to responsibility and maturity. To speak of God as a loving parent, they argue, can foster the attitude that we are permanent children without adult responsibilities. While I agree with the basic

---

5. Cited by Letty M. Russell, *The Future of Partnership* (Philadelphia: Westminster, 1979), 62.

intent of fostering mature responsibility in all persons, I think the method is flawed. To suggest that mortal, limited creatures are equal with God just does not make sense. We are forever dependent upon God for our existence and fulfillment. What we need to ask is whether every unequal, hierarchical relationship is bad. The common assumption in feminist thought is that hierarchy is always harmful. But consider the parent-child relationship when the child is not yet an adult. The child as infant is totally dependent upon the parent or other adult caregiver to feed and nurture it. It would also be foolish and harmful for a parent to treat an eight-year-old child as an equal in making judgments about permissible activities and bedtime. Although it is true that most hierarchical relationships are harmful because they involve domination of one party over the other, inequality in power is not necessarily bad. The key to a healthy relationship is whether each party is able to contribute according to her or his ability. Mutuality rather than equality is the goal. Thus it is important to say that God's love aims at mutuality.

3. God's love is *faithful and forgiving*. God's faithfulness to Israel is apparent in the call of Moses, for God has not forgotten Israel. The Old Testament prophet Hosea gives a dramatic image of the forgiving as well as the faithful character of God's love. Hosea portrays the nation of Israel, the Northern Kingdom, as God's wife, a wife who has become a whore by turning to other gods. Hosea announces God's judgment and punishment upon the people of Israel for their unfaithfulness, yet he also proclaims God's mercy: "I will now allure her, and bring her into the wilderness, and speak tenderly to her" (Hosea 2:14). In the background is the idea of God's covenant or agreement with the nation of Israel. A marriage is also a covenant between two parties. The point is that although Israel has not been faithful to its covenant bond with God, God will be faithful to Israel. Such fidelity involves forgiveness of Israel's betrayal. As Hosea puts it, this is "steadfast love and mercy" (Hosea 2:19).

4. God's love is *strong*. Its strength lies partly in its *purposefulness*, God's insistence upon seeking what is best for humans and the world. A family that has a member addicted to alcohol or another drug has to show tough love by refusing to go along with the person's destructive behavior. This is hard to do in a culture that places a high value on independence of the individual, for tough love involves confrontation and saying no. It is common in our culture to view God as superpermissive, to think that God blesses whatever we choose to do. We saw an example of this in the student's statement, "There is a God for everyone and the way people choose to interpret this God is a personal choice." We find no such weak-loving God in the biblical story. After delivering the people of Israel from their bondage in Egypt, God expects Israel to be faithful to God and gives them the Ten Commandments as standards for their behavior (Exodus 20). When King David arranged the death of Bathsheba's husband so that David could take her as his wife, the prophet

Nathan came with words of God's judgment on David (2 Samuel 12). In the New Testament when a pious rich man asked Jesus what he should do to gain eternal life, Jesus told him to sell all and follow him (Luke 18:22). God's love is not a doormat but a tough love that makes a claim upon people.

God's love is also strong in *its ability to reach its goals in spite of opposition.* The strength of God's love is more like Mother Teresa than Russia's Empress Catherine the Great. Its strength lies more in perseverance and high purpose than in overpowering force, yet it is a love that will finally overcome resistance and achieve its purposes.

God is both mystery and love. Both affirmations are needed if one is to have a sense of God as envisioned by the Christian faith. Mystery suggests the *transcendence* of God. To transcend means literally to go beyond, and surely God is beyond anything else. So one cannot talk truly of God without doing justice to God's greatness or transcendence. Yet for Christians this is not just any mystery, for God is the One who also loves. Love expresses the *immanence of God*. Immanence (not *eminence*) refers to God's nearness, the divine presence within the creation. Again, for Christians, this is not just any immanence, but is a divine presence with a self-giving, strong, and faithful love that aims at mutuality with the creature.

A balance of transcendence and immanence is required for a sound understanding of God. If we speak only of transcendence, of God being almighty, eternal, holy, omnipresent, we tend to portray a distant, unapproachable deity, or a controlling tyrant, and a biblical notion of divine mystery is abandoned. On the other hand, if we speak only of God's love, compassion, and mercy, we end up thinking God is a pushover who just goes along with whatever we want. Another concept of love is substituted for a biblical concept. In either case, a Christian understanding of God is lost. When we pay attention to the biblical story, we discern a pattern of mystery and a pattern of love. Thus a genuinely Christian vision of God includes both mystery and love, both transcendence and immanence.

The Doctrine of the Trinity

Another pattern that Christians have seen in God's dealings with the Christian community is the pattern of the Trinity, most commonly expressed as Father, Son, and Holy Spirit. So the doctrine of the Trinity is a third shorthand way that Christians have spoken of God. The doctrine of the Trinity is not basically a logical puzzle about God being one and yet three. The formal doctrine of the Trinity was forged in the fourth century during a dispute over the significance of Jesus Christ, and today as well the doctrine is intimately linked with the centrality of Christ for Christian faith. In order to appreciate this link, we will look briefly at the history of the doctrine of the Trinity in the early church.

The New Testament does not contain the explicit doctrine of the Trinity in which Jesus Christ and the Holy Spirit are recognized as fully divine, but it does make affirmations that point in the direction of the doctrine. To begin, a threefold formula is used twice for God. Jesus' followers are instructed to make disciples, "baptizing them in the name of the Father and of the Son and of the Holy Spirit" (Matthew 28:19). And Paul ends one of his letters with a trinitarian benediction, "The grace of the Lord Jesus Christ, the love of God, and the communion of the Holy Spirit be with all of you" (2 Corinthians 13:13). Furthermore, in several instances the New Testament speaks about God with a two-part formula. For example, Paul says, "Yet for us there is one God, the Father, from whom are all things and for whom we exist, and one Lord, Jesus Christ, through whom are all things and through whom we exist" (1 Corinthians 8:6; cf. 1 Timothy 2:5). In addition, the New Testament makes some very exalted claims for Jesus Christ. In the passage just quoted, Paul speaks of "Jesus Christ, through whom are all things," meaning that everything in the universe somehow receives its existence through Jesus Christ. In another letter it is said of Jesus Christ, "For in him all the fullness of God was pleased to dwell" (Colossians 1:19). John's Gospel makes the loftiest claims using the symbol of the Word: "In the beginning was the Word, and the Word was with God, and the Word was God. He was in the beginning with God. All things came into being through him, and without him not one thing came into being. . . . And the Word became flesh and lived among us" (John 1:1-3, 14). Thus, while the New Testament does not explicitly teach the doctrine of the Trinity, it provides the foundations for that doctrine.

For some years after the New Testament writings were completed, the church did not probe deeply into the relationship of Jesus Christ and the Holy Spirit to God. One early suggested way of conceiving the relationships was called *modalism*, which held that Father, Son, and Spirit designate only passing expressions or modes of God, not permanent distinctions within God. One modalist by the name of Sabellius seems to have taught that after creating the world God expressed himself as Son in the activity of redemption and then after withdrawing that expression came forward as Spirit. In other words, modalism proposed that God is like an actor who plays one role and then another, but the roles are temporary and come one after the other. Against this Tertullian (d.c. 220) held that Father, Son, and Spirit are permanent distinctions or persons who have the same being, but Tertullian did not explore the meaning of this in great depth.[6]

Christian thinking about God entered a new phase in 318 when a radical idea was put forward by *Arius*, a priest in Alexandria, Egypt. His basic premise was that God is utterly transcendent and cannot have direct involve-

6. J. N. D. Kelly, *Early Christian Doctrines*, second edition (New York: Harper & Bros., 1960), 110–23.

ment with the world; this is the Father. However, God created the Son or Word and then the Holy Spirit. It was the Son who went about the work of creating and redeeming the world. This means that for Arius the Son of God or Word and the Holy Spirit are creatures "made" by God; the highest of all creatures, to be sure, yet clearly creatures. As a creature, the Son is not eternal but has a beginning; thus the Arian slogan, "There was when He was not." As scriptural support for his view, Arius appealed to the words of Proverbs 8:22 about Wisdom, which Arius and many other theologians identified with the Son of God: "The LORD created me [Wisdom] at the beginning of his work, the first of his acts of long ago." Arius's radical proposal prodded other theologians to reflect more carefully on the relationship of the Word or Son with the Father, and a heated controversy quickly erupted and lasted through most of the fourth century.

An initial authoritative answer to the Arian position was given at the Council of Nicea (325), the first ecumenical or worldwide council of Christian bishops that took place in Nicea, a city in what today is Turkey. Roman Emperor Constantine, who probably converted to Christianity partly to use its growing influence to bolster the wavering strength of the Roman Empire, called the council to settle the doctrinal dispute. The council approved the Creed of Nicea:

> We believe in one God, the Father almighty, maker of all things, visible and invisible;
> And in one Lord Jesus Christ, the Son of God, begotten from the Father, only-begotten, that is, from the substance of the Father, God from God, light from light, true God from true God, begotten not made, of one being [*homoousios*] with the Father, through Whom all things came into being, things in heaven and things on earth, Who because of us humans and because of our salvation came down and became incarnate, becoming human, suffered and rose again on the third day, ascended to the heavens, and will come to judge the living and the dead;
> And in the Holy Spirit.
> But as for those who say, There was when He was not, and, Before being born He was not, and that He came into existence out of nothing, or who assert that the Son of God is from a different hypostasis or being [*ousia*], or is created, or is subject to alteration or change—these the Catholic Church anathematizes.[7]

Note that while the creed proper is organized into three paragraphs devoted to Father, Son, and Holy Spirit, the size of the paragraphs reveals that the controversy is over the status of Jesus Christ. In fact, the bishops have hardly thought about the Holy Spirit, for they merely affirm belief in the Spirit without any explanation. Note also that the creed and the anathemas (condemnations) are intended to clearly exclude the Arian view of Jesus Christ.

---

7. Ibid., 232 (I have substituted "being" for "substance" as the translation of *ousia*, and "human" for "man." Parenthetical additions are also mine).

The creed does this with the key phrases "begotten not made" and "of one being [*homoousios*] with the Father"; neither of these could be said about a creature. Athanasius, one of the great Nicene supporters, distinguished between creatures that are "made," and the Son of God, who has the *eternal* relationship of being "begotten" by the Father. And whereas all creatures come from God, no creature was of "one being with the Father." The anathemas complete the exclusion of Arius's teaching by explicitly rejecting Arian slogans such as "There was when He was not."

In fact, the Council of Nicea did not settle the theological controversy even though Arius had rather few supporters; more time was needed to clarify some unanswered questions about the unity and distinctions within God. After several decades the contributions of three Cappadocian theologians led to general agreement to speak about God's unity as one in substance or being (Greek: *ousia*) and to speak about the distinctions as three hypostases. These two technical terms from Greek philosophy—*ousia* and *hypostasis*—had been used interchangeably in the anathemas of 325 but were now distinguished in meaning. These Greek terms were translated into Latin as *natura* and *persona*; hence the classic doctrine of the Trinity is commonly expressed as *God is one nature in three persons.* This theological agreement, fed in part by further reflection on the Holy Spirit, led to an amplified version of the Nicene creed being approved by the second ecumenical Council of Constantinople in 381. While this creed is accurately designated as the Niceno-Constantinopolitan Creed, in Christian worship it is commonly referred to simply as the Nicene Creed.[8]

> We believe in one God the Father almighty, maker of heaven and earth, of all things visible and invisible;
>
> And in one Lord Jesus Christ, the only-begotten Son of God, begotten from the Father before all ages, light from light, true God from true God, begotten not made, of one being with the Father, through Whom all things came into existence, Who because of us humans and because of our salvation came down from heaven, and was incarnate from the Holy Spirit and the Virgin Mary and became human, and was crucified for us under Pontius Pilate, and suffered and was buried, and rose again on the third day according to the Scriptures and ascended to heaven, and sits on the right hand of the Father, and will come again with glory to judge living and dead, of Whose kingdom there will be no end;
>
> And in the Holy Spirit, the Lord and life-giver, Who proceeds from the Father, Who with the Father and the Son is together worshipped and together glorified, Who spoke through the prophets; in one holy Catholic and apostolic Church. We confess one baptism to the remission of sins; we look forward to the resurrection of the dead and the life of the world to come. Amen.[9]

8. Ibid., 226–69 (again I have substituted "being" for "substance" and "human" for "man"). See also Jaroslav Pelikan, *The Christian Tradition: A History of the Development of Doctrine*, Vol. 1, *The Emergence of the Catholic Tradition (100–600)* (Chicago: University of Chicago Press, 1971), 172–225.

9. J. N. D. Kelly, *Early Christian Creeds*, second edition (London: Longmans, 1960), 297, 298.

While details of the Trinitarian Controversy are of interest mostly to experts, of wider significance are the two main reasons *why* the vast majority of bishops opposed the Arian view of Jesus Christ. One reason for rejecting Arius's ideas is that they conflicted with ancient Christian practices of worship and prayer. From the early days of their movement, Christians had been baptizing people "in the name of the Father and of the Son and of the Holy Spirit" just as it says in Matthew 28:19. It had also been a very early practice to worship Jesus. These long-standing liturgical practices were powerful arguments for Christian belief in the deity of Jesus Christ, for to worship a creature or to baptize in the name of a creature would be idolatry, treating a creature as though it were God. Since early Christian worship practices implied the divinity of Jesus Christ, making the belief explicit is a genuine development rather than a mistake. The Arian view of Jesus Christ implied that the Christian church had been wrong on a fundamental point of its belief from early on.

Another reason why the bishops rejected the Arian proposal was that it undercut the Christian idea of salvation through Jesus Christ. According to Arius, God does not have immediate contact with the world, but acts through second-class intermediaries—the creaturely Son and Holy Spirit. God remains in the distance, untouched by the human predicament and the death of Jesus Christ. Basic to the Nicene outlook, however, is the belief that God is intimately involved in Christ's work of salvation. As we saw before in John 3:16, "God so loved the world that he gave his only Son." The supporters of Nicea held that unless God personally comes to the rescue of humans, we are still trapped in sin and death.

What then is the significance of the doctrine of the Trinity for a contemporary understanding of God? Three meanings stand out. First, since Jesus Christ and the Holy Spirit are fully divine, contemporary Christians may affirm that God is directly involved in their salvation through Jesus Christ and the Holy Spirit. The implications of this can be spelled out only when we discuss the work of Jesus Christ and the Holy Spirit, but now we can simply point out that a perennial human tendency is to place the weight of our liberation or salvation on our own shoulders. Conceptions of the nature and mechanism for liberation vary, yet the common underlying conviction is that the decisive role in liberation is played by humans. For some the central human problem is ignorance, and advancements in science and education are the answer. For others the main difficulty lies in oppressive social structures such as racism, sexism, or classism, and liberation will come chiefly through social reform or revolution. Such outlooks often interpret Jesus Christ as a great moral/religious leader among a number of religious leaders in world history. Jesus is an example to follow in carrying forward the human responsibility for salvation. In the process of this interpretation, God recedes into the background much as for Arius God was removed from the struggles of the world. The Bible contradicts this trend of thought by emphasizing God's deep, primary involvement in the work of liberation or salvation. The Nicene Creed goes against that trend also by teaching that the Father, Word, and Holy Spirit are *one* God. In other words, Nicea teaches that the God who gives existence for all things is the same One who in Jesus Christ shares the human predicament and overcomes it in struggle, death, and resurrection and the same One who in the Holy Spirit renews individuals and communities. God is not off at some safe distance leaving the dirty work to others, but God is fully engaged in that work of healing things.

A second important meaning of the doctrine of the Trinity is that it underscores the relatedness of God; that is, God's character is to be social or in relation rather than in isolation. To get at this issue I once asked a class what they thought God did before creating the world. One person proposed, "God just sat around." She thought that sounded boring. Another offered that God was busy making plans for the world. However, both suggestions assume that without a world with which to interact God is inactive and lonely. Both suggestions also fit with Arius's ideas, for in the thinking of Arius God exists in transcendent isolation from any other reality.

In contrast, the doctrine of the Trinity affirms that there are relations within God's own being, for there are the relations between Father and Word, Father and Spirit, and Word and Spirit. It is extremely difficult to describe the nature of these relations, so difficult, in fact, that some theologians say these relations exist only as God appears to us humans. That is, when God goes out of God's own self to create a world and give revelations to humans, God takes on the distinctions of Father, Son, and Holy Spirit. This is to limit the distinctions to what is called the *economic Trinity*, the Trinity as it is revealed outwardly to humans. On the other hand, there are theologians (and I count myself among them) who argue that the distinctions between Father, Son, and Holy Spirit are eternal distinctions, so God's innermost nature is to be in relation. This is to maintain that there is also an *immanent Trinity*, a Trinity within God's own being. Admittedly, we don't understand much about the character of these eternal relations when we say that the Father "begets" the Son who is "begotten," or when we say that the Spirit "proceeds" from the Father (and the Son). God cannot be captured by our words, and here we stammer even more than usual. Yet one very important idea behind affirmation of the immanent Trinity is that relatedness belongs to God's own eternal nature.

We must use analogies to speak of God; that is, we say God is like this, while also acknowledging that God is also unlike this. Analogies that suggest relatedness are those from the human experience of community, such as the experience of the lover and beloved. However, the modern meaning of "person" is different than the ancient philosophical concept of hypostasis or persona. To us, person means a distinct center of consciousness. But if we use such a notion to speak about a community of three persons in God, we end up with the idea of God as a committee of three separate individuals. It helps considerably if we come to understand persons not as separate, autonomous individuals, but as intrinsically relational. Nevertheless, it is difficult for us to entirely leave behind the concept of a person as a distinct center of consciousness, so social analogies for the triune God need to be balanced by psychological analogies based on the individual human person. One common psychological analogy has been to speak of one subject or mind that includes memory, understanding, and will. These are three distinct mental functions, yet they are aspects of one mind. Multiple analogies are necessary as we struggle to express relatedness within the one God.

A third meaning of the doctrine of the Trinity is that it affirms life and movement within God's eternal being. Sometimes God is viewed like a placid pool of clear water. There is absolutely no movement in the pool, not even a ripple, and every part of it is composed of the very same clear water. There are no distinctions, and there is no motion. The pool of water is in some sense perfectly one, but it is a lifeless unity. To think of God in this way is also to think of a lifeless God. The doctrine of the Trinity says there are distinctions, life, and activity within God's eternal being. This movement is suggested by the metaphor of Word, for the image is that the divine Source expresses a Word. A word is an articulate, rational expression, not just a grunt. So the act of uttering the Word is an act of God going out of herself in a rational expression. The Spirit is the divine activity of unifying, bringing together. So God's inner being may be seen as an eternal activity of Source going forth in the Word and Spirit bringing them into unity or the Father sending the Son and the Spirit unifying them. Such images can be merely suggestive, but the point is that they suggest life and movement eternally within God, a two-step dance that is expressed in ever-new ways. This is especially important when we think about God as creator of the universe.

We will say more about the doctrine of the Trinity when we discuss the doctrine of creation and the teaching about the Holy Spirit, but for now it is sufficient to see that these three meanings of the doctrine support each other. God lives and acts eternally in the relatedness of God's being, so God reaches out to create the world and to heal its complex broken relationships.

Feminist Criticism of Trinitarian Doctrine

Feminists are centrally concerned about the liberation of women and men from sexism, that is, discrimination and oppression based upon sex. Feminist scholars say that down through history the oppression of women has taken a variety of institutional forms in which males have dominated, and they commonly call this institutionalized male domination *patriarchy*, literally "rule by the father." They argue that wherever it occurs—in ancient Israel, medieval China, or contemporary America—patriarchy pervades the institutions, practices, and laws of the society as well as the dominant ideas and images of the society. For instance, in the United States today males have the dominant positions in nearly all institutions—government, business, health care, and education. While the subordinate positions of secretary, nurse, and elementary school teacher are typically filled by women, the leadership positions of president, senator, CEO, physician, and school superintendent are usually occupied by men. This domination of American institutions by males is supported and justified by ideas and images that portray men as strong, aggressive leaders, while women are often pictured as dependent, passive persons who follow their men.

Feminists argue further that a patriarchal society is hierarchical in nature, that is, certain individuals and groups have power over others below them on a social scale. The feudal society of medieval Europe was clearly hierarchical in structure, for at the very top of the civil order was the Holy Roman Emperor, then came kings and princes followed in descending order by dukes, barons, knights, craftsmen, and peasants. Women were represented on the various levels of the social hierarchy, so that a princess had a far higher standard of living than a peasant woman, yet women were subordinate to men on their own level. In any case, a patriarchal institution is hierarchical in nature, and males occupy the relatively more privileged positions in the hierarchy.

One might ask what all this has to do with theology and the doctrine of the Trinity. The connection is that feminists generally say both the Israelite society of the Old Testament and the Christian church have been patriarchal. For instance, Christian churches have typically had a hierarchical organization dominated by men. The Roman Catholic Church is still led by an all-male clergy that is itself arranged in levels of pope, bishops, and priests. Some Protestant churches have ordained women, mostly in the last thirty years, but it is uncommon for women to hold top positions of leadership either in congregations or in the larger church body.

A number of feminists have also charged that the doctrine of the Trinity is a teaching that has supported male domination; criticism has focused especially on the language of God as Father. They say that when God is spoken of consistently in male imagery as Father, King, Lord, Shepherd and is referred to always as he, then it is almost unavoidable that people will think of God as masculine. Of course, nearly everyone denies that God is literally a male; nonetheless, exclusively male language produces a masculine conception of

God. This is fortified by referring to the second person of the Trinity by another male image—Son of God. What this does, say the critics, is give subtle religious justification for male domination throughout a patriarchal society. When a masculine God rules over the world and the church, it seems appropriate that men should rule in the family, church, government, and other social institutions.

Feminists differ widely in their views on the doctrine of the Trinity; for simplicity we can distinguish three positions. Radical feminists such as Mary Daly think Christianity is so thoroughly corrupted by patriarchy that women should completely abandon Christianity, including its trinitarian doctrine, and create a female-affirming religion using elements from some religions that include a Goddess.

Another position is taken by liberal feminists who continue to identify with the Christian faith, yet believe major changes are needed to make Christianity a force for liberation rather than oppression. One of the most fully developed of such interpretations is given by Sallie McFague in her book *Models of God: Theology for an Ecological, Nuclear Age*. McFague argues that a longtime emphasis on God as a transcendent, controlling Father has promoted many social ills, for the image of an independent, dominating God has justified male domination of women, human control over nature, and a readiness to destroy the earth through nuclear war. She wants to stress God's close relationship with the world. She does not speak of God revealing something of God's character, however; rather, our ideas about God are mostly fictions, constructions of our own imaginations. These theological constructions are to be evaluated by Christians according to their social usefulness and their faithfulness to the core of the Christian tradition. In our time, says McFague, what is needed is a theology that teaches mutuality between men and women and between people and nature. She proposes three metaphors that accent God's immanence: Mother, Lover, and Friend. These three names are proposed as an effort to unseat not only the traditional language for the Trinity (Father, Son, and Holy Spirit) but also the heart of doctrine of the Trinity. As we noted above, the doctrine of the Trinity was formally stated in the fourth century to claim that God was truly and most fully revealed in Jesus. McFague rejects this view of Jesus, for she believes Jesus is one of a number of great religious teachers. She does not reject the father image for God if it is interpreted in a nurturant direction, but this fatherliness refers only to God's relation with the creation, not to an eternal relation between Father and Son in God. In short, Sallie McFague believes major modifications should be made in the Christian tradition if it is to be relevant to the needs of our time, and in the process the doctrine of the Trinity should be drastically reinterpreted.[10]

10. McFague, *Models of God*, 181–83.

A third, moderate feminist position sees fundamental Christian affirmations being made in a proper trinitarian understanding of God as Father, Son, and Holy Spirit. Catherine Mowry LaCugna agrees with critics that sometimes the doctrine of the Trinity has been understood in a patriarchal manner, yet she claims that a faithful rendering of the doctrine embodies a revealed truth about God that is genuinely liberating for women. This truth is that God's own nature is relatedness; that is, within God's eternal being there are the relations between Father, Son, and Holy Spirit. LaCugna argues that when feminists totally reject the doctrine of the Trinity, they end up seeing God as distant, like Arius did long ago. In defense of the doctrine of the Trinity she says, "The total identification of God with Jesus the Son, even unto death on a cross, makes it impossible to think of God as the distant, omnipotent monarch who rules the world just as any patriarch rules over his family and possessions."[11] Since the trinitarian God of relatedness fosters inclusivity in human community, the doctrine of the Trinity has liberating power for women. However, LaCugna argues that Christians need not express the truth of the Trinity only in the language of Father, Son, and Holy Spirit. She suggests other analogies to express God's self-relatedness: Mother-Daughter, Father-Daughter, Mother-Son, Lover-Beloved, and Friend-Friend.

I basically agree with LaCugna's position. As I indicated in the previous section, God's inner relatedness is one of the essential insights of the doctrine of the Trinity. Primarily this is a truth about God's nature, but as LaCugna says, it is also an encouragement to have more positive relationships in human life. For centuries domination of one person over another, one group over another, and humans over nature has often been justified as part of the fabric of reality; "power over" rather than "connection with" has been emphasized. An additional development in much of modern Western culture has been the exaltation of the individual's independence, so that the accent has fallen on separation rather than relationship. The isolated God of Arius fits in with such worldviews. But when God's own nature is to be in loving relationship, then there is the highest permission and summons to live in upbuilding relationships. Relatedness is an absolutely fundamental feature of reality. To recognize our complex connections with God, other humans, and nature is to go with the grain of things rather than against the grain.

I also think Catherine Mowry LaCugna is correct when she says that many critics of the doctrine of the Trinity end up with a vision of a remote God. This is even true of Sallie McFague, contrary to initial appearances and perhaps her own intentions. To be sure, McFague seeks to emphasize God's inti-

---

11. Catherine Mowry LaCugna, "The Baptismal Formula, Feminist Objections, and Trinitarian Theology," *Journal of Ecumenical Studies* 26, no. 2 (Spring 1989): 243. See also her chapter on the Trinity in *Freeing Theology*, Catherine Mowry LaCugna, ed. (San Francisco: HarperSanFrancisco, 1993), 83–114.

mate, caring relationship with nature and people, and she proposes some useful and evocative metaphors for God. Yet all of that is set against the background of a barely knowable God. While she rightly protests against too close an identification of God with certain metaphors of male power, I fear she errs in omitting any notion of revelation from God. She so underscores the fictional nature of theology as imaginative constructions that God seems ultimately hidden in clouds.

Furthermore, I go along with LaCugna's suggestion that in addition to the traditional language of Father, Son, and Holy Spirit, Christians can use other analogies to speak of God's inner relations. Surely Father, Son, and Holy Spirit should continue in common use, partly because Jesus addressed God as *abba* (the Aramaic familiar word for Father) and Scripture often refers to Jesus as Son and to God's presence as the Holy Spirit. But the deeper reason for continuing to use Father, Son, and Holy Spirit is that these terms help to anchor the Christian understanding of God in the events of the biblical history. The divine Father of whom Christians speak is the One whom Jesus called Father; thus the One who called and guided Israel through its long history and the One who sent Jesus on a special mission and raised him from the dead. And the divine Spirit of whom Christians speak is the Spirit who leads people into friendship with this Father and with the crucified and risen Son. The key is that our understanding of God is given centrally through the stories of these particular communities—Israel and the early church—and through this particular man, Jesus. Merely using the names of Father, Son, and Holy Spirit is no guarantee of preserving the linkage with this particular history, for other religious groups competing with Christianity (for instance, ancient Gnosticism and its modern descendants) often incorporate those names into their own theological framework and give them very different meanings. However, to reject altogether these names, which play such prominent roles in the biblical story, is to run a serious risk of severing the link with this particular history.

On the other hand, to use only male metaphors for God does give the impression that God is male and does tend to support male domination in church and society. Thus it is generally beneficial for Christians to refer to God with a variety of terms, as long as the whole context of use has a clear linkage with the biblical story. In addition to calling God Father, it is appropriate to speak of God as Mother and like a woman in some respects. Scripture itself uses considerable diversity in its language for God. For instance, in the Old Testament God is addressed not only by the proper name *YAHWEH*, but is also called God (*Elohim* in Hebrew), the Most High, the Almighty (Psalm 91), your Redeemer, and the Holy One of Israel (Isaiah 43:14). In the New Testament, while the names Father, Son, and Holy Spirit appear frequently, they occur only once all together in a trinitarian formula (Matthew 28:19). Other names for Jesus Christ besides Son are the Word, Wisdom, the

Lord, and Lamb of God, and another name for the Holy Spirit is the Advocate. Although it is true that Scripture never addresses God as Mother, we have already noted that God is compared to a woman giving birth (Isaiah 42:14) and to a woman searching for a coin (Luke 15:8-10). Thus Scripture itself suggests that we should use female as well as male imagery for God. We are currently in a fluid, experimental stage in our language about God, and no alternative trinitarian formula has yet won wide acceptance. With an understanding of the doctrine of the Trinity close to that of LaCugna, Elizabeth Johnson suggests Spirit-Sophia, Jesus Christ, and Holy Wisdom.[12] The formula of Creator, Redeemer, and Sustainer clearly is not adequate, for these terms refer only to God's relations with the creation, not to an inner divine life. In the future we should be open to using female and male imagery for God, provided it occurs in context with the biblical story. While it is possible to avoid all gendered words in speaking of God, the result is a rather depersonalized view of God. Throughout the rest of this book I will use both male and female metaphors for God, and I will refer to God alternately with the personal pronouns she and he.

To conclude this discussion of the Trinity, I agree with many feminist theologians that Christian interpretations of God have relied too much on male images, yet I believe the doctrine of the Trinity expresses some central Christian affirmations. While the names of Father, Son, and Holy Spirit should be supplemented with other appropriate names, all Christian talk about God should be closely connected with the story about God's dealings with Israel and Jesus.

Looking back over this entire chapter, we may recall the importance of not assuming everyone has the same idea of God, for when we look closely we find that conceptions of God vary considerably. *How* we think of God influences *what* we think of God. The basic source for a Christian understanding of God is the biblical story. We identified three shorthand ways in which Christians speak of the God known in the biblical story: the metaphors of Heavenly Father and Eternal Mother, the divine attributes of mystery and love, and the doctrine of the Trinity. Although there have been feminist criticisms of the doctrine of the Trinity, the doctrine makes three major affirmations: that God is directly and fully involved in the work of salvation through Jesus and the Holy Spirit, that God's own nature is relatedness, and that there is movement and life in God. Saying that God is Heavenly Father and Eternal Mother, is mysterious love, and is triune surely does not exhaust what Christians believe about God, but it lays a solid foundation for further affirmations about God in our discussions in the chapters that follow.

---

12. Elizabeth A. Johnson, *She Who Is: The Mystery of God in Feminist Theological Discourse* (New York: Crossroad, 1992), 213–14.

3

Is Belief in God Reasonable?

lthough belief in God is fundamental for Christian faith, the question often arises whether or not the belief is reasonable. There are several sources of this question. A major reason for doubting Christian beliefs about God has arisen chiefly in the last hundred years with increased awareness of the plurality of religions. When there is such a diversity of beliefs about God or ultimate reality, how can Christians claim theirs to be true? This issue will be examined in chapter 11 on Christianity and other religions. Another source for questioning belief in God, indeed the very existence of God, is the experience of evil. Already in the Old Testament we find sufferers doubting the existence of a just God. In our own century the systematic killing of fifteen million civilians by Nazis has caused many to wonder whether a good and powerful God exists. We shall consider this problem of evil in chapter 5 in connection with the doctrine of providence. The third main source of questions about belief in God is the subject of this chapter—challenges from a modern scientific worldview that are reflected in philosophy and the humanities as well as the natural and social sciences.

Someone taking a college biology course is very likely to encounter ideas of the evolution of life that have no role for God. Many students in psychology classes will meet Sigmund Freud's view that belief in God is wishful thinking by insecure human beings who create the image of a caring heavenly father to still their anxieties in a threatening world. In a sociology class one might be confronted with Emile Durkheim's proposal that religious beliefs about a deity are more a reflection of society than knowledge of a transcendent reality. When an author or professor touches on belief in God, sometimes one gets the impression that the belief is considered naive, outmoded, and mistaken. This leaves a person wondering whether belief in God is reasonable.

How do we go about answering the questions regarding belief in God raised by the modern scientific worldview? It is not easy, since a religious perspective and a scientific perspective are such different ways of approaching these issues. The difference is evident in how medical science and religion approach the death of a family member. On the one hand, medical science as science is interested mostly in the cause of death. Researchers will seek to determine what specific illness or trauma brought about the end of life. Perhaps an autopsy will be performed on the body. This connection of medical science with the dead person's family may be enacted in a ritual in which a physician explains the pathologist's report to the family in language suitably simplified for those unacquainted with the technical terminology. On the other hand, a Christian perspective on the death of a family member focuses attention primarily on the meaning of human life. This is enacted in the funeral ritual in which the living and dead are viewed within the great context of God's love and purpose for the world as expressed in verbal and nonverbal symbols such as cross, resurrection, and heaven. Whereas the scientific researcher dwells on causes, the minister or priest emphasizes ultimate meaning and purpose. To use Aristotle's distinction, science looks only for efficient causes, religion focuses on final causes. Indeed, what often makes it very difficult to compare a scientific worldview with a Christian worldview is that the scientific worldview in principle excludes questions of goal or purpose. Science need not deny the legitimacy of such considerations, but science itself omits goals from its own explanations.

The point is relevant to the issue of belief in God, for a person's worldview will powerfully affect whether belief in God is considered rational. In the Western world belief in God has been widely questioned only since the cultural movement of the Enlightenment, which urged people to be free from the shackles of tradition and authority by using their own power of reason to judge matters. The key question has been, What do we mean by "reason"? Often reason has been equated with the causal explanations given by the natural and social sciences. The natural sciences explain events by identifying their natural, physical causes, such as the cause of a person's death or the atmospheric conditions that produce a thunderstorm. The social sciences explain events by detailing their psychological, social, or economic causes. When these naturalistic explanations are regarded as exhaustive, as telling us all that is significant, then religious interpretations of events appear superfluous or wrong. Indeed, religion itself is often explained by the social sciences purely in terms of psychological, social, or economic factors; anything "supernatural" is simply discounted. Such naturalistic approaches make belief in God seem unreasonable, a throwback to a more primitive age.

The issues involved can be clarified by creating a scenario that considers the different situations of three college students. Three psychology majors— Peter Pan, Jill the Firm Believer, and Jack the Freudian Skeptic—have become friends, yet they have conflicting views on belief in God. We shall discuss first the situation of Peter Pan.

The Shaken Faith of Peter Pan

Peter Pan was raised in a Christian family and had accepted belief in God, but he has not had much experience involving God. A few times in his life Peter has sensed that God was present and listening to his prayers, but no such experience has occurred for some time. Now the Freudian understanding of religion really has him wondering, for it illuminates some of what he has observed about himself and other religious people. So Peter Pan's belief in God has been seriously shaken. While he is drawn to Christian belief in God, the Freudian interpretation of religion seems to make sense. He feels suspended between the two belief systems. The question is, What should Peter Pan do to resolve his uncertainty? My answer is that Peter might simultaneously do two things—one of them primary and essential, the other secondary and optional.

We shall begin with the secondary procedure, which is that Peter might look at the relevant arguments. This means he would thoroughly examine both the Freudian interpretation of religion and arguments for belief in God. This examination *might* solidify his skepticism of belief in God. On the other hand, more thorough study of the Freudian view and criticisms of it *might* reveal flaws so serious that he would be justified in rejecting it. Peter *might* also be helped by examining the arguments for the existence of God, for they might support plausibility of the belief and undermine the naturalistic assumptions of the Freudian view. It is to these arguments that we now turn.

There are a number of arguments for the existence of God, each of which has generated a sizable literature. We shall briefly consider only three: the argument from contingency, the ontological argument, and the argument from design.[1]

Our first argument is the *argument from contingency*, which received its classic formulation from Thomas Aquinas (d. 1274). Of course, one can only begin to understand the argument when one knows the meaning of contin-

---

1. A clear discussion of these arguments is given in John Hick, *Philosophy of Religion* (Englewood Cliffs, N.J.: Prentice-Hall, 1963), 15–26. For fuller discussion see John Hick, ed., *The Existence of God* (New York: Macmillan, 1964), and Diogenes Allen, *Christian Belief in a Postmodern World* (Louisville: Westminster/John Knox, 1989).

gency. Contingent things might never exist. I am a contingent being, for if my mother or father had died before I was conceived, I would not be here. So a contingent being is dependent upon something else for its existence; a contingent being has received its existence. The argument from contingency calls our attention to the fact that all the persons and things we know in this world are contingent. If I ask why I exist, I can look first to my parents, who gave me existence. But then I see that they received existence from their parents, and on and on. It is the same when I inquire about dogs or trees, rocks or galaxies. Everything is dependent upon something else for its existence. Everything in the world is contingent. But if everything in the universe is contingent, why then does the universe exist? If everything in the universe is dependent upon something else for its existence, then why does anything exist? The only adequate explanation, says the argument, is that the universe of dependent beings has received its existence from a necessary being, that is, from a being that is not contingent but exists by its own power. This necessary being is God.

There have been criticisms of the argument from contingency, especially from the philosophers David Hume (d. 1776) and Immanuel Kant (d. 1804). While their charges of logical flaws probably can be answered, the argument's chief shortcoming is that it is unlikely to convince the full skeptic. Implicitly the argument sets up an either/or: either there is a necessary being (God) or the universe is without explanation. The argument is persuasive only to those who rule out the second option. But the thorough skeptic says that the universe is without explanation, it just is. Thus the argument depends upon what is called the principle of sufficient reason, which is that whatever exists has a reason or cause for its existence. While a doubter such as Peter Pan might accept the principle and find an unexplained universe abhorrent, the full skeptic sees the universe as a brute fact and finds the argument unpersuasive.

Perhaps the most intriguing argument for God's existence is the *ontological argument*, formulated initially by Anselm (d. 1109). Anselm begins the argument with a concept or idea of God: God is "a being than which nothing greater can be conceived." When he says "greater," Anselm means better or more perfect, not larger in size. His idea of God agrees with the biblical notion that it is appropriate to worship only that which is the highest; God cannot be second best. It is also important to understand what is meant by a concept or idea. This can be illustrated by thinking of an architect's idea of a building. This idea exists in the mind of the architect and may be expressed in a set of plans. But the idea of the building is distinct from the actual building.

Now Anselm says that the atheist uses this same idea of God, namely, "a being than which nothing greater can be conceived," for the atheist and the believer understand each other when they talk about God. The difference between them is that the atheist says that God is merely an idea, that God exists only as a concept in a person's mind and does not exist in reality. How-ever, Anselm argues that the atheist is involved in a contradiction when saying that God does not exist. The contradiction is this: When the atheist says, "That than which nothing greater can be conceived exists only in the mind," even the atheist can conceive of something greater, namely, that "that than which nothing greater can be conceived" exists in reality also. Thus Anselm concludes that there is no doubt that God exists not only as an idea in the mind but also exists in reality.

The ontological argument sparked criticism. A contemporary monk named Gaunilon claimed that Anselm's argument would lead to absurd results if applied generally. Gaunilon said Anselm's argument implies that if one forms the concept of the most perfect island, then that island must exist. The German philosopher Immanuel Kant followed in Gaunilon's footsteps when he said that Anselm makes the logical error of treating existence as a predicate or characteristic. For example, the concept of a particular house is enlarged if I add the characteristic of insulation to the house plan. But if I say that the house now exists, I do not add anything to the concept of the house. To say that the house exists moves beyond the realm of concepts altogether and asserts that there is such a building in reality. Thus existence cannot be regarded as a characteristic included in the concept of God. To say that God exists is to step outside the realm of concepts and asserts that there is such a being in reality. Kant's criticism has been accepted by most philsophers and theologians.

A recent philosopher, however, claims that a second formulation of the ontological argument is valid. Anselm's reply to Gaunilon relied upon his sec-ond formulation of the argument, one that stresses the difference between creaturely beings that may or may not exist and God's necessary existence. In short, Anselm answered that his argument applies only to the unique being of God. In this formulation Anselm begins with the idea of God as that which exists necessarily, an idea which the atheist also employs when thinking of God. Neither religious believer nor atheist thinks of God as receiving exis-tence from something else. Now it is rational to think of contingent beings as not existing, for contingent beings by definition might never have existed. But it is inconsistent, says Anselm, to think of that which exists necessarily as not existing. Thus, the statement, "God necessarily exists," entails "God exists."

The third argument is the *argument from design* or the *teleological* argument (from the Greek *telos*, goal). This is a very old argument, for one form of it was stated already by the ancient Greek philosopher Plato (d. 348/7 B.C.), and Aquinas included it among his five arguments for God's existence. A classic statement of the argument from design was made by the British philosophical theologian William Paley (d. 1805). Suppose, says Paley, that in walking in the countryside you come upon a (non-electronic) watch. You open up the back of the watch and observe the intricate gears, main spring, and jewels all moving in such a way as to mark the passage of time on the watch face. Now if you were asked how the watch came to be, you would surely infer that the watch must have a maker. So also with the natural world, says Paley, if we observe carefully, we also see signs of design in great variety and number. For example, the human eye is like a very small camera that adjusts quickly to various light conditions, is sensitive to colors, and operates continuously for hours. Paley's point is that the order of parts in the eye is so well suited to producing vision that it is reasonable to infer that the eye is the handiwork of a designer. So when we see that the intricacies of nature are suited again and again to a particular purpose, we must infer that they have been made by God.

There have also been criticisms of the argument from design. Among David Hume's objections was his counterproposal of accounting for the order of nature simply by chance. He suggested that the universe is composed of a number of particles in random motion. Given enough time these particles may come together in a stable order, which may be the universe we know. However, this explanation of order through sheer chance was generally less persuasive to people than divine design. Charles Darwin (d. 1882) offered a much more convincing explanation for the order in living things—evolution. What Darwin supplied was a principle within nature itself which explains the particular order or organization that organisms have. There is no need to say that the order has been designed by God. The difference between Paley and Darwin can be illustrated in the following way. Paley might say that the existence of the ozone layer in the upper atmosphere to filter out rays harmful to life is an indication that the ozone layer was placed there by God for the purpose of protecting life on earth. The Darwinian would say that given the prior existence of the ozone layer, only those forms of life developed that could exist in this level of radiation.

Recently, discussion of the argument from design has moved into a new phase. Whereas evolution accounts for the development of living things by a process of chance mutations and natural selection over long periods of time, many scientists have noted that the previously existing physical constants of the universe are such that they make the development of life possible. Scientists generally think that our universe was born in the Big Bang, that it began as a very small mass of extremely dense matter that exploded and has been expanding ever since. The physical constants of our cosmic order arose in the initial seconds of the Big Bang. Many physicists and astronomers are struck by the fact that this particular cosmic order makes life possible and that even very slight alterations in these constants would rule out life. For example, if the universe were not expanding, it would be too hot to support life. If the rate of expansion were just a little faster or slower, the universe would already have collapsed back into dense matter or the stars could not have formed. If the force of attraction between protons in the early mass of hydrogen atoms had been just a little stronger, all the hydrogen would have turned into helium and no stars or life would have formed. Also, if the electric charge of the electron were slightly different, no chemical reactions would have been possible. Now it is still possible to explain the universe by randomness, for it is conceivable that there was a series of big bangs and universes until ours happened to arise with the necessary features for life. But it seems much simpler to think that the physical make-up of our universe has been intended. The philosopher Holmes Rolston III concludes, "Christians caught up in the debate over creation in biology may not have noticed how congenial physics and theology have become. The physical world is—shades of Bishop Paley!—looking like a fine-tuned watch again, and this time many quantitative calculations support the argument. The forms that matter and energy take seem strangely suited to their destiny."[2]

Peter Pan's examination of the arguments for God's existence might have several outcomes. He might think the Freudian case is stronger. Or he might still be uncertain. Let's say, though, that after considering the argument from design Peter concludes that the universe very likely has its source in a divine being. What does this accomplish for him? It certainly makes unpersuasive the Freudian idea that belief in God is merely a human wish for security and meaning; thus the objection to belief in God that was troubling him is overcome. Nevertheless, the argument from design has not established Christian faith in God, because the argument yields only a higher rational being as the source of the order of the universe; Christians go on to speak of a God who loves people and cares for the world. There is some overlap in the two notions of God, but they are surely not identical. In addition, belief in God held on the basis of a very likely argument seems to be a pale, intellectualized faith that lacks the deep commitment of Christian faith. Arguments for God's existence *may* overcome certain objections to belief in God and thereby clear away an obstacle to Christian faith in God, but in themselves they are not adequate grounds for Christian belief in God.

The Ground of Christian Faith

Christian belief in God has its primary ground in the Christian story as that story forms one's understanding of the world and shapes experiences that confirm Christian faith as fruitful for living.[3] This is such a pregnant sentence

---

2. Holmes Rolston III, "Shaken Atheism: A Look at the Fine-Tuned Universe," *The Christian Century* (December 3, 1986), 1095.

3. Alvin Plantinga, "Reason and Belief in God," in *Faith and Rationality: Reason and Belief in God*, Alvin Plantinga and Nicholas Wolterstorff, eds. (Notre Dame: University of Notre Dame Press, 1983), 85. Plantinga rightly says that a high proportion of beliefs are accepted at least partly by way of training or testimony. For instance, nearly all of our beliefs about geography are

that you should read it again before we begin to unpack its meaning. Implied in this statement is the distinction between training or exposure to the Christian story and Christian experiences. The relationship between training in the Christian story and Christian experience that confirms some aspect of the story must be clarified. Certainly, experience can affect a person's perspective. For instance, sometimes the experience of travel abroad leads persons to see their own nation in a new light. But the reverse is also true, namely, that people's perspective influences their experience. When two people have different outlooks, what one sees the other may ignore or minimize. An example may clarify the point.

Goldilocks is a college sophomore who has recently decided she wants to major in art, but her father, a hard-nosed business man, is opposed. He wants her to major in a field that will likely lead to a good-paying job. "What can you do with an art major?" he asks. "Very few art teachers or advertising artists are well paid. Go into management or law where the money is good." Goldilocks is not the least bit interested in business or law. Art is her passion, and she doesn't worry about being poorly paid; to her it is more important to do what she loves. Several times Goldilocks and her father try to discuss this, but they end up arguing; neither one is able to appreciate the other's concern. Their lack of understanding stems chiefly from their divergent perspectives. What matters to Goldilocks are the creativity and beauty she finds in art; these are largely ignored by her father. On the other hand, she discounts his concern for earning a good living. It is as though Goldilocks looks at her future with blue-colored lenses, while her father looks at it through green lenses. Each filters out different aspects of the scene and highlights others.

Outlook or perspective actually influences *what* one sees or hears, *what* one experiences. Two people hear the same music on a car radio; one hears "some classical music," the other hears "the second movement of Beethoven's Eighth Symphony." At a high school reunion, two men watch a few minutes of a professional basketball game on television. One of them sees "a nifty basket," the other man, a basketball coach, sees "he came off a pick and drove for the basket; as the defense rotated, he shifted the ball to his left hand, and split the defenders." Two women in an art museum in Amsterdam come to a van Gogh painting entitled "The White Orchard." One sees "a pretty picture; it reminds me of my uncle's orchard." The other woman, an art professor, sees

---

taught us by books, maps, or oral instruction from authorities. Such training is *prima facie* or initially adequate justification for holding our geographical beliefs, unless there are reasons to doubt a particular authority. Similarly a person learns Christian beliefs about God from the testimony of other Christians expressed in the New Testament, church practices, and in their daily lives. Being raised in a Christian family is *prima facie* justification for a person to hold Christian beliefs, unless challenges are raised to this teaching.

a picture "done within the first few months of his arrival in Arles." Then, after detailed thoughts about the painting's composition, she concludes, "Yes, I agree with van Gogh that this is superior to 'The Pink Orchard.'" In each of these three cases, the two persons have different experiences. The point is that the perspective or mental resources a person brings to an experience powerfully shape the nature of that experience.

Furthermore, in order to have access to certain experiences, one must ordinarily be trained in the appropriate perspective. If the woman seeing only "a pretty picture" in the van Gogh painting wants to have a richer experience of it, she must receive more training in art. Similarly, if a person is to experience God speaking to them, as Christians often do, then one must receive some instruction in the Christian perspective. Training in the Christian perspective on life make it possible for some people to experience a passage in the Bible *as* God speaking to them. Such experiences confirm their belief in God. If another person approached the Bible with the firm conviction that there is no God, that person is highly unlikely to hear God speaking through the scriptural words.

What this means for Peter Pan's situation of being suspended between Christian and Freudian perspectives is that *Peter needs more than arguments for God's existence to reaffirm Christian belief in God. He also requires further training in the Christian story.* Peter has already had a childhood training, but now further instruction is required. This continued education is partly a matter of gaining fuller information. Far too many people are trying to answer adult religious questions with a middle school Christian education or less.

Yet the necessary further education is more than acquiring information. I might become knowledgeable in the traditional religious practices of the Lakota Indians of North America, yet never have Lakota experiences. Let's say that I smoke a sacred pipe with some Lakota men. With some knowledge of Lakota beliefs and practices, I would be able to recognize that this is a practice for interacting with the realm of spirits. But I would not experience the pipe smoking *as* an interaction with multiple spirits. For me it would be an experience of observing other men who believe they are encountering spirits. While I may understand some elements of the Lakota worldview, I see that worldview only from the outside. If I were ever to truly share some of the Lakota's experiences, in some measure I would have to live within their worldview. This has happened to some non-Indians who have come to know an American Indian culture well; they come to see the world in part through Indian eyes. For this to happen, non-Indians must relinquish their distant, observer relation with the Native American worldview and get inside it.

How does one get inside a religious outlook, so that one can possibly begin to experience life from its perspective? It is not merely a mental exercise—reading books and thinking about certain ideas; one must also engage in doing certain religious practices. This is not strange; consider parallels. Imagine that you are the one who sees only "a pretty picture" when looking at a van Gogh painting, but you feel attracted to it; you sense that visual art might just enrich your life. How does one go about discovering whether art will indeed bring enrichment? Reading words about art and artists will provide some information, but one must also look carefully at pieces of art. To go further, one must also try one's own hand at drawing or painting and receiving firsthand instruction from an artist. Learning to appreciate art involves looking carefully at what artists have created and perhaps doing art oneself. To experience much of what it is possible to see in an artwork requires training. A similar thing is true with learning to appreciate the music of Mozart. Reading a book about him or visiting one of his residences might pique one's curiosity, but one must actually listen to Mozart's music. In order to go into much depth, one must also have some facility in playing or singing his music. To experience the beauty and mastery of Mozart's music requires training.

In like manner, to see what it is possible for a Christian to see requires more than gathering information about Christianity. One must engage in such practices as consorting with a community of Christians, participating in their worship, praying in ways this community prays, and taking part in their acts of mercy. It's true that some people participate in these activities without ever experiencing God's presence or voice, just as taking a drawing class or receiving music lessons does not always awaken deeper appreciation of art or music. The activities do not automatically produce the confirming experience. Yet the confirming experience comes only through participation in such practices. As the philosopher William P. Alston says, "God is not available for *voyeurs*. Awareness of God and understanding of His nature and His will for us, is not a purely cognitive achievement; it requires the involvement of the whole person; it takes a practical commitment and a practice of the life of the spirit, as well as the exercise of cognitive faculties. . . . God is always present. . . . But only to those who have responded to His call, have made a stable commitment to Him, have put Him at the center of their lives, and have opened up themselves to His influence."[4]

In short, in order for Peter Pan to deal with his uncertainty raised by the Freudian challenge to belief in God, he can do two things. One is to examine the relevant arguments such as the arguments for God's existence and arguments for and against Freud's interpretation. This may help overcome the Freudian objection to belief in God, which has been troubling him. The other primary and essential thing is to go further into the Christian outlook both by increasing his knowledge of Christianity and by continuing or even deepening his involvement in Christian religious practices such as prayer and

4. William P. Alston, "Christian Experience and Christian Belief," in *Faith and Rationality*, 13.

worship. It is especially difficult to continue praying and worshiping once serious doubts are raised, for the tendency is to reduce or even withdraw from such Christian practices. But to give up prayer and worship is to abandon some of the basic means by which God may communicate with people. To abandon prayer is like a person refusing to communicate with a friend from whom she has become alienated; it only increases the alienation by destroying the bridge by which reconciliation might come.

In this double strategy reason and faith perform different roles to meet the challenge. On the one hand, Peter's reason seeks for a rebuttal to the Freudian objection. On the other hand, his less than full-hearted faith, like that of the psalmists of old (Ps. 79:5; 89:46), is called upon to trust the promises of God's presence while seeking fresh confirming experiences of God.

Jill the Firm Believer

The other two friends of the trio of psychology majors are in different situations than Peter Pan. Jill is a convinced Christian who prays daily, quite often reads the Bible, and usually attends church. Jack calls himself an atheist. For the past year or so he has been much taken with Sigmund Freud's entirely naturalistic interpretation of religion and, following Freud, he thinks that belief in God has its roots in a deep human wish to be special, to be key players in a grand cosmic drama. The belief in a loving and righteous God is simply a powerful human wish to have a good, all-powerful father give us meaning and care in a threatening universe. Jack and Jill have friendly but sometimes heated discussions about religion. "How can you believe that stuff about a loving and righteous God?" says Jack. "Can't you wake up and see that it's just one of our dreams? Christianity doesn't come from God; it's just a human creation." Jill steadfastly replies that her trust in God is not shaken. She knows there is a God and that this God loves her. Sometimes God speaks to her through a passage of Scripture, a hymn, a sermon, or nature. Quite often when she prays, she has a sense of God's presence. So Jill is firm in her faith in God. Yet while her faith is unshaken by Jack's skeptical arguments, she feels inadequate and even a little stupid since she is unable to counter Jack's ideas. She wonders whether she is being naive, less than the intelligent adult she wants to be.

Jill's situation is different than Peter Pan's, for Peter's faith in God was shaken. Yet Jill's situation raises another question, Should Jill give *other reasons* to support her faith in God, reasons such as arguments for God's existence? Is Jill cognitively justified in her belief in God or does she have to refute Jack's skeptical argument before she can legitimately reaffirm her belief in God? I will argue that she is justified in affirming her belief in God even though she may not refute Jack's argument against it. Jill's calm reply to Jack can be justified on the philosophical grounds that for her, belief in God is a properly basic belief. This argument involves three steps.

1. *First we must clarify what is meant by foundationalism and a "properly basic belief." Foundationalism* is a philosophical account of human knowing (epistemology) which distinguishes between basic beliefs and nonbasic beliefs. A basic belief is foundational for one's system of beliefs. In this respect, a basic belief is like a premise of some logical arguments. The classic syllogism is an example of a logical argument.

> All humans are mortal. (Major premise)
> Socrates is human. (Minor premise)
> Therefore Socrates is mortal. (Conclusion)

A basic belief is like a premise that is held to be true without previous argument. Nonbasic beliefs are those that we arrive at as conclusions; or, to state the same thing differently, nonbasic beliefs are the result of inferences.

2. *Critics of classical foundationalism argue that it has been too restrictive in what it accepts as properly basic beliefs.* Classical foundationalism accepted only two or three conditions for *properly* basic beliefs, that is, beliefs that deserve to be basic.

a. A condition agreed to by all foundationalists is that statement of the belief is self-evident. A self-evident statement is seen to be true as soon as one comes to understand it. For instance, very simple truths in arithmetic ($2 + 2 = 4$) are self-evident.

b. Ancient and medieval foundationalists said statements that are "evident to the senses" also express properly basic beliefs. "I see a tree" and "I am wearing shoes" are examples.

c. Some modern philosophers have preferred a more cautious claim than "evident to the senses"; instead they have spoken of statements that are "incorrigible" or immune from error as properly basic. An example is: "I seem to see a tree." Even though one might be feverish and mistaken about seeing a tree, it is undeniable that one *seems* to see a tree.

Foundationalists have usually said that belief in God is not a properly basic belief, for it does not fall under any of these categories; hence, belief in God must be inferred from other beliefs. So if Jill were to follow the foundationalist view, she would be rationally obligated to provide other reasons for belief in God than her own faith experiences.

Various theologians and philosophers have sought the reasons or evidence for concluding that God exists by providing arguments for the existence of God. This endeavor is customarily called *natural theology*, the name Thomas Aquinas gave to his arguments for the existence of God. Thomas divided his theology into two very unequal parts—natural theology, in which reason alone works to discover truth about God, and *revealed theology*, in which faith accepts truths revealed by God through the Bible and Christian tradition. Thomas Aquinas was convinced that his five arguments for God's existence were compelling, and for centuries many other philosophers and theologians agreed that one or another argument for God's existence was solid rational evidence for belief in God. But, as we noted previously, after criticisms of the arguments by the philosophers David Hume and Immanuel Kant, doubts about their persuasiveness increased. In the twentieth century most theologians and philosophers have not regarded any of the arguments as compelling. The result has been that *if* one accepted the classical foundationalist interpretation of human knowing, belief in God has appeared to be unsupported by reason and perhaps even in conflict with reason. Some theologians and many Christian believers were not troubled by this, because they held that faith is superior to reason and needs no support from reason. This position is called *fideism* (from the Latin *fides*, faith).

In the last twenty years or so, however, many philosophers and theologians have come to reject some features of the classical foundationalist account of human knowing. One of the leading philosophical critics is Alvin Plantinga, who agrees with the distinction between basic and nonbasic beliefs, but says classical foundationalism's three criteria for a basic belief are too restrictive. Plantinga offers a more inclusive account of human knowing in which it is possible for belief in God to be a properly basic belief.[5] He begins by pointing out that the restrictive criteria of classical foundationalism do not account for some very common basic beliefs. For instance, I believe I ate dinner yesterday. This and many other memory beliefs are basic beliefs for me, since I do not arrive at them by argument or inference from something else. Yet the belief does not meet any of the three classical criteria, for it is not self-evident, evident to the senses, or immune from error (incorrigible). The *ground* of my belief is my experience of remembering having had dinner yesterday. I do not go through some complicated reasoning process of first remembering lunch, then thinking my memory on such matters has been reliable, and finally inferring that this memory is sufficient evidence for believing I had lunch. No, in the very act of remembering lunch, I believe I ate lunch yesterday. Plantinga argues that my experience of remembering justifies my belief as properly basic in most circumstances. It is appropriate to immediately trust our memory, unless we have good reason to doubt it, such as when we are taking a drug that often causes delusions or when past experience has shown that our memory is frequently faulty.

5. Plantinga, "Reason and Belief in God," in *Faith and Rationality*, 59–63. See also Joseph Runzo, "World-Views and the Epistemic Foundations of Theism," *Religious Studies* 25 (March 1989): 31–51.

3. *For firm believers like Jill, belief in God is a properly basic belief, for she has adequate grounds for her belief.* The grounds of her belief in God are complex. As a child she had *prima facie* or initially adequate grounds for belief in God by virtue of her Christian family upbringing, but as she has matured her belief has been confirmed by her sense of God speaking to her through Scripture, her sense of God's presence, and her appreciation of how the faith informs the lives of certain family members. Some of what Jill has been taught about God has been confirmed in her own experience. This in turn gives her good reason to trust the Bible and the Christian tradition for further instruction. Jill often experiences the world *as* God's world and herself *as* God's daughter. This rich interplay of Christian tradition and Jill's experience is the ground for her belief in God as a properly basic belief. If she were a mental patient subject to delusions, then she should not trust these experiences. But as a mentally sound person she is justified in trusting them. However, Jill does not go through some complex reasoning process to arrive at her belief in God. For Jill, belief in God is a properly basic belief, not an inference from other reasons.

Jack implicitly wants Jill to adopt his atheistic Freudian perspective and to try to defend belief in God from within it. Jill quite rightly refuses to do that. She continues to reflect on life from the framework of Christian beliefs and practices of worship and prayer. Jill grew up in the church and was taught these beliefs and practices, but over time they have become her own. Not only has she seen Christian faith in God shape the lives of her parents and sustain them through trying times, Jill herself has often experienced God speak to her through Scripture and be present with her in the everyday events of life. What she has been taught has been at least partly confirmed in her own experience. To expect Jill to abandon her religious perspective and adopt some other framework, is to ask her to do what we do not expect physicists, sociologists, or historians to do, namely, to give up the framework of beliefs and ideas with which they encounter the world.

Of course, Jack might object that Jill's religious perspective is simply mistaken. The comic strip "Peanuts" portrays Linus having experiences with the Great Pumpkin, so Linus sees the world from a Great Pumpkin perspective. Yet no one but Linus believes there really is a Great Pumpkin. Sincerity of belief is not enough. Followers of James Jones sincerely believed in him, but they were wrong. Some followers of the People's Temple were deceived by James Jones, who conducted healing services in which he supposedly extracted tumors from people's bodies, although the tumors were really chicken livers. Those who believed in Jones experienced these events as divine healings. Yet sincerity of belief is not sufficient. There must be some other way to distinguish among beliefs.

As I pointed out in connection with the discussion of revelation in chapter 1, I think there are two tests for distinguishing among beliefs. Primary is the *test of fruitfulness for living*. Fruitfulness for living involves seeing whether a belief system enables people to deal constructively with the diverse situations of life, and whether it produces high character. Whereas there is no enduring community of Great Pumpkin followers or James Jones followers, Jill has seen the positive fruit of Christian faith in God in her own life and the lives of her family. So Jill's firm affirmation of faith in God is intelligent behavior, for she is reasserting a belief and worldview that has demonstrated its fruitfulness for living.

What remains for Jill to do is to take up the challenge of a secondary test for evaluating beliefs, the *test of fruitfulness for understanding*. Again, as I said in relation to revelation, this is the endeavor to make connections between Christian faith in God and significant ideas and theories from other fields of study. In this case, it involves the effort to establish coherence between Christian faith and some aspects of psychology. Jill does not need to suspend her faith in God until she has accomplished this task, however, for the task may take years and never be completed. Similarly, you are not obligated to formulate a theoretical response to the skeptic's challenge to your belief that there is a book in front of your eyes right now before you can continue reading it. A skeptic might charge that the book and other objects in the room with you now are simply projections of the mind. It might be interesting to attempt a rebuttal to the skeptic's challenge, but even if you were to try, most likely while you were doing so, you would assume the existence of books, tables, chairs, computers, and such. Your belief in the existence of the book and other perceptual objects around you simply wells up within you. The point is that very likely you would not genuinely doubt the existence of perceptual objects, so there is no obligation to suspend belief in them until you can satisfactorily answer the skeptic's charge. In like fashion, Jill does not doubt the existence of God when Jack raises his objection. For Jill, belief in God is what some philosophers call a properly basic belief.

Jack the Skeptic

Both Jill and Peter Pan, in varying degrees, live within the Christian worldview. But what about Jack, the Freudian skeptic, who stands outside the Christian worldview? He has challenged the beliefs of Jill and Peter. How might they challenge him?

First, Jack's confidence in the adequacy of a godless worldview might be shaken by careful consideration of some arguments for the existence of God.

The argument from design is especially strong when one thinks how a number of very slight alterations in the physics of the universe would make the development of life impossible.

Second, Jack does not realize how much our experience is influenced by the perspective and concepts we bring to it. In his discussions with Jill, Jack may feel that she does not play fair, for her belief in God is grounded partly on special experiences of God speaking to her and simply being present, experiences that Jack does not share. He may want her to debate the question of God's existence on the basis of experiences readily open to everyone. Like many people, he has assumed that the truth of any claim can be tested by experience common to all times and places. This idea of universal experience is fostered by the practice of scientific testing of hypotheses, which should yield identical results whether the researcher is in France or India, the seventeenth or twentieth centuries. What is overlooked is the fact that these researchers must be looking at the data with common assumptions. It makes a huge difference whether the researcher is a modern chemist or an alchemist and whether a modern chemist uses Newton's or Einstein's paradigm of the physical world.

Jack should also be challenged on his assumption that the naturalistic perspective of modern science rules out a religious understanding of reality. Just as a scientific study of the sounds of a Beethoven piano sonata will not tell us all that music theory might enable us to hear and appreciate in those sounds, so the scientific approach to reality might miss some dimensions that religion makes accessible. Such arguments may convince Jack that the Christian perspective is worth serious consideration, that it may also be an avenue to truth.

There are limits to what can be accomplished with arguments, however. Jack will not be able to see what the Christian sees unless he "tries on" a Christian perspective, that is, tries to see things from a Christian outlook. To be sure, one can try it on only if one believes that there *may* be something *true* in this perspective. Yet one is unlikely to try it on unless one also senses that there is something *good* in it. Why? Because Christianity is a practical guide for the journey of life, not an hypothesis for laboratory research. As we saw before, a major test for assessing a claim to revelation is its fruitfulness for living. Above all, Christianity presents a vision of human life healed from its alienation from God, self, others, and nature. Thus, to try on a Christian perspective is to involve oneself in a personal quest for wholeness. Arguments alone can never move a person to engage in this undertaking. Indeed, here Freud's point that religion has its impetus in human needs for meaning and wholeness could be put to use in Jack's own quest.

In this chapter we have reflected on the question whether belief in God is reasonable. We approached the question from three different angles, because our personal context in life affects the meaning this question has for us. First, we looked at the situation of a person such as Peter Pan whose belief in God is shaken by an objection. I suggested that such a person follow the dual strategy of examining the relevant arguments and strengthening his understanding of Christian faith through study and religious practice. Second, we considered the situation of a convinced Christian such as Jill for whom belief in God is a basic belief confirmed by her own experiences of God. I argued that it is reasonable for her to continue believing in God even though she does not refute a skeptical objection, just as it is reasonable for her to believe in the existence of perceptual objects without countering skeptical challenges to it. Third, we gave attention to the position of the skeptic like Jack for whom belief in God seems unreasonable. It is often difficult to know how deep a person's skepticism runs. It is not uncommon that those who claim to be atheists or agnostics are not as firm in their view as it might appear. A study revealed that nearly 20 percent of Americans who identify themselves as atheists or agnostics pray daily.[6] If the skeptic is open to reflecting anew on the question of God, then arguments for the existence of God should be pondered since the arguments attempt to meet skeptics on their own ground. To the skeptic, however, Christian talk about God may sound like music to a tone-deaf person, unless, through contact with Christians and their practices, the skeptic comes to sense that there is something highly valuable in the belief.

6. "Talking to God," *Newsweek* (January 6, 1992), 39.

4

Creation

The universe inspires wonder. When we gaze at the stars on a clear night, we may wonder about the ultimate origin of the universe and ourselves. What is the source of this unbelievably vast universe that exhibits both randomness and order, complexity and simplicity? The Bible addresses the issue of origin by telling stories that recognize God as the ultimate source of the universe and human life. In fact, the Bible begins with two stories of creation. The first portrays God creating the world in seven days with male and female humans appearing simultaneously on the sixth day (Genesis 1:1—2:3). The second creation story recounts God's creation of a human followed by animals and then woman as the suitable companion (Genesis 2:4-25). The biblical belief in creation has been a constant teaching also in the history of Christianity. Thus, our experience of the wonder-inspiring universe, the Bible, and Christian tradition all lead us to reflect on the doctrine of creation.

Our thinking about creation, however, needs to pay attention to the major questions that modern culture has raised about this belief. One such question is how belief in divine creation fits with scientific thinking about the evolution of the universe and of life. Another question is whether the doctrine of creation is compatible with concern about ecology. The ecological issue also prompts a fresh look at a perennial question within the Christian doctrine of creation, namely, What are we human beings? Thus, our reflections in this chapter will be divided into four main parts: first, a brief look at the two biblical creation accounts and some key ideas in the Christian doctrine of creation; second, how creation and science relate; third, creation and ecology; and, finally, what the doctrine of creation says about being human.

Bible and Christian Tradition on Creation

Since the two biblical accounts of creation are too lengthy to quote here, you should read them in the opening two chapters of the Bible. At this juncture we can only call attention to a few points about each. The first account (Genesis 1:1—2:3) is more a hymn than a story with characters, and it portrays God as creating in a very orderly manner. God creates on six days and rests on the seventh day, thereby providing an anchor in God's creative activity for the Jewish religious practice of observing the sabbath. Certain features of the creation are emphasized through frequent repetition. God creates on the six days simply by speaking; for example, "Then God said, 'Let there be light'; and there was light" (Genesis 1:3). This way of representing God's creative activity emphasizes God's sovereignty in creation; God does not struggle with some other limiting power. Another oft-reiterated theme is the declaration, "And God saw that it was good." In this account the last creature to be brought forth is humankind, and they appear simultaneously as male and female.

The second creation account (Genesis 2:4-25) is a story about the first human couple. Here the human being is created first, and plants and animals follow. The distinction in humans between male and female emerges only at the end, however. In this story God is very much a hands-on creator, for God is pictured like a potter forming the initial human from dust of the ground. God also works here more by trial and error than by some orderly plan, for the distinction between human male and female is introduced by God only after the animals failed to provide a suitable helper and partner for the initial human being.

Why does the Bible have two quite different accounts of creation? While it probably seems strange to us today, it is fully consistent with two common practices in ancient Hebrew literature—repetition and balancing. On the one hand, just as the first account's frequent refrain "and God saw that it was good" underscores the essential goodness of the creation, so having two accounts that trace the origin of things to God is a literary device for stressing that fundamental point. Repetition emphasizes.

On the other hand, balancing one version of creation with a quite different version enables Genesis to suggest the complexity and ambiguity we encounter when we try to understand the profound mystery of creation. For instance, we experience the world as having both rational order (Genesis 1) and trial and error (Genesis 2). Again, the distinction of humans into female and male may suggest both a special human community with God (Genesis 1) and a deep bond of humans with one another (Genesis 2). Thus, having two different renderings of creation makes it possible for Genesis to underscore certain convictions through repetition and to express some of the complexities of creation by balancing one perspective on it with another perspective.

Down through the centuries, Christian reflection about creation has continually drawn upon the two accounts in Genesis, while at the same time Christian theologians have confronted other ideas and questions. We can come to a reasonably good understanding of the theological tradition on creation and stir up our own reflection on the matter if we consider three key ideas: creation *ex nihilo*, models of how God creates, and why God creates.

Creation *ex nihilo*

When we speak of a human being creating something, we mean that the person has brought into existence something new. Neither an assembly line worker nor an author of formula romance novels is creative, for they do not produce something new. Human acts of creation suggest both giving existence and newness. God's activity of creating also involves giving existence to what is new but in a far more fundamental way. Shakespeare's writing of *Macbeth* was indeed an act of creative genius, but in the process he made use of materials that he received from others—seventeenth-century English language, literary traditions, London theatre practices, and, generally, Elizabethan culture. Like an imaginative architect, he used existing building materials to bring about something original. Those building materials would have continued to exist even if William Shakespeare had died as a baby and never written *Macbeth*. Christian theologians have generally held that God's act of creating is more radical, for it does not employ building materials that exist independently of God. Divine creation is the act of giving existence to what cannot in any way exist on its own.

Second-century Christian theologians called this creation *ex nihilo*, which means creation out of nothing; it came to be a core Christian teaching even though it does not appear to be taught in either creation story of Genesis. The first creation story says, "In the beginning when God created the heavens and the earth, the earth was a formless void and darkness covered the face of the deep" (Genesis 1:1-2). This suggests that God creates by giving order to chaotic matter. However, the unchallenged sovereignty with which God creates by merely saying, "Let it be," is not far from the idea of creation *ex nihilo*. The second creation story focuses on the creation of humans by fashioning them from existing materials.

As they reflected on the fundamental issue of creation, though, most Christian theologians have affirmed creation *ex nihilo* even though it is not explicitly taught in either Genesis creation account. By creation *ex nihilo* theologians have asserted two things about God and the world. The first is that creatures receive their existence from God, whereas God exists by her own power. So there is an absolutely fundamental difference between God and creatures. Everything in the universe ultimately relies upon God for its existence, and this remains the case in every moment.

A common misunderstanding of the doctrine of creation is to regard God as the first in a series of factors bringing about the universe. An influential eighteenth-century version of this was called *deism*. The deistic God was viewed like a great watchmaker who made a watch, wound it up, and then sits back as the watch runs mostly on its own. Such a deity played a key role back at the very beginning of the universe, but ever since has had little to do. Today people often express a form of deism when they encounter the contemporary Big Bang theory that the universe started from an extremely dense mass of matter that exploded and has been expanding ever since. When people go on to identify God's creativity chiefly with being the source of that initial mass of matter, then they are thinking in deistic fashion. God was the first link in a chain of events back at the very beginning of the universe, but since then the universe has operated on its own. In its various forms deism sees God's creativity as merely getting things started long, long ago. A more personal form of deism thinks God creates each person at the beginning of his or her life, but since then it is as though one runs on a long-lasting battery. We assume the battery will keep us going for many years as long as we are not foolhardy or unlucky.

In contrast to deism, the Christian idea of creation *ex nihilo* sees God as the source of existence for all things in every moment of time. No creaturely thing at any time exists by its own power, whether it be the great Rocky Mountains or an ant. Creatures are always poised over an abyss of nothingness, and each moment of existence is a fresh gift from the Creator. The fundamental difference in being between the Creator and creatures remains.

The basic dissimilarity between God and creatures also rules out *pantheism*, which literally means all is God or God is all. Pantheism is a fuzzy notion, very difficult to define, but its crucial feature is no clear distinction between God and creatures. Whereas all Christian theologians say that God is present *in* creatures, a pantheistic outlook in some way believes that creatures *are* God. In pantheism fern, fish, and frog are forms God has taken. Creation *ex nihilo* denies that creatures are somehow fragments or forms of God. The distinction between God and creatures is preserved.

A second implication of creation *ex nihilo* is that all spheres of the created world are inherently good since they have their ultimate origin in a good God. Of course, this conviction is solidly grounded in the biblical creation accounts. In Genesis 1 on each of the six days of creation God saw that what had been created was good. In the second creation account in Genesis 2, the world is also initially portrayed as good; only later in Genesis 3 does sin enter. Thus, in both the Bible and Christian tradition, any final *dualism* is denied.

In some religious outlooks, the world is divided into inherently good and evil areas. In Gnosticism, an influential religion that has competed with and sometimes mixed with Christianity, the material world and the human body are essentially flawed, for they have their source in a lesser, flawed deity, while the soul has its source in the highest deity. The gnostic key to salvation is a secret knowledge (*gnosis* in Greek) that enables the soul to free itself from attachments to this physical world. Christianity has often been affected by dualisms in which spirit is good and the body evil, reason is positive and emotions are negative. All such dualisms are undercut by the teaching of creation *ex nihilo*, which implies that all areas of the world are inherently good, because they have their common origin in the one, good God.

This is not to deny that there is evil in the world, but creation *ex nihilo* rules out seeing an original chaos or stuff as the ultimate source of evil. The presence of moral and natural evil does not nullify the essential goodness of the world. Human freedom is misused, but that does not mean human freedom as such is evil. Even the biblical figure of Satan or the devil is not understood as essentially bad but as a rebellious angel. Similarly, humans now suffer ill affects from a cold virus in their body, but the cold virus itself is not essentially evil; the evil arises in the relation between human and virus. This is such a complicated issue, though, that we will return to it in the next chapter. For now it will have to suffice to point out this second implication of creation *ex nihilo*: since all creatures receive their fundamental being from the one, good God, they all have some essential goodness and value.

Models of Creation

Since God's creating is different from other instances of creating, no model or analogy we can suggest is fully satisfactory; yet some models are more appropriate than others to the biblical traditions about God. In the Christian tradition four major analogies or models of divine creation have been suggested.

1. *Making* is the language used in the Genesis 2 creation story, which portrays God forming a human figure out of dirt and then giving it life by blowing air into its nostrils. The analogy of making or forming something calls attention to the patterns present in the universe as well as to God's intention of giving those patterns. Thus this model emphasizes that the world has come about through the purposes of God. A shortcoming of making or formation as an analogy for divine creation is that the maker so obviously begins with already existing materials which are a second, independent factor in creation and may place external limits on God's creativity.

2. *Emanation* is a model proposed by ancient Neoplatonic philosophers and sometimes employed by Christian theologians. The best example of emanation is a star giving off light just as the sun radiates light. When creation is understood in this way, it seems to be a necessary divine activity rather than something God decides to do. As long as the star is a star, it gives off light. When its light ceases, the star has died and become what astronomers call a

black dwarf. Most Christian theologians have been critical of emanation as an analogy for divine creation, since it portrays creation as a necessary mechanical process rather than as a free personal action. Yet some theologians defend emanation for emphasizing that creating belongs to God's nature and is not just a capricious act.

3. *Giving birth* or procreation has been a model used by many religions, but it has generally been avoided by Christianity until recently. Sallie McFague has proposed giving birth as the dominant model for creation, because it emphasizes God's kinship and similarity to the world as a mother is close to her offspring. McFague rejects the idea of creation *ex nihilo*, for she believes its stress on the difference between Creator and creature pictures God as a distant ruler over the world, which promotes domination of men over women and humans over nature. Another reason McFague approves of the birthing model is that it implies in some sense God is physical as well as beyond the physical. The virtue she sees in claiming that God is both spiritual and physical is that the dualism of spirit and body is thereby eliminated at its very root.[1]

I agree that the birthing model of creation powerfully expresses God's intimate connection with the world. This is especially so if we think of God's birthing process stretching over billions of years and involving pain for God. The metaphor declares God's enormous personal investment in the creative process and in the world that is being born. Nevertheless, the model also has some flaws. One is that in all instances we know the mother gives birth to an offspring very like herself, generally of the same species. Does the birthing metaphor suggest too close a likeness of Creator and creature? Another flaw is that speaking of God as physical suggests to most people that God has a tangible body we could see and touch. Perhaps speaking of God's "energy" would be more appropriate, for energy has connections with inanimate matter as well as with a variety of life forms, including human persons. In any case, I think McFague's underlying concern for a close divine relationship with the physical world can also be satisfied by appropriate use of the next model of creation.

4. *Artistic expression* likens God's creating to creating a drama, painting, quilt, building, or symphony. This is an analogy with several aspects.

a. Like the model of making, artistic expression suggests giving form to some material, but the work of a great artist has much more originality than ordinary making or fabricating. In this respect great artistic expression is closer to creation *ex nihilo*. There may be some element of the striking originality of artistic expression in the six-day creation story in Genesis 1 where God just speaks a command and the thing appears.

---

1. Sallie McFague, *Models of God: Theology for a Ecological, Nuclear Age* (Philadelphia: Fortress Press, 1987), 109–10.

b. The artist's work is an expression of the artist's own self. In other words, artists put themselves into their work. Indeed, the more of themselves they put into it, the more they value their handiwork. Sallie McFague criticizes the model of artistic expression on the grounds that artists relate to their completed work with a distant, critical eye that evaluates it as good or bad by aesthetic standards. That may be the case with an artist who creates a multitude of works, but it is different with someone who puts many years, perhaps most of his or her life into creating one great, complex work such as a medieval cathedral. Then the artist has an enormous personal stake in the endeavor. God may indeed have other universes unknown to us, but even apart from the revelation of God in the biblical story, it would seem likely that the Creator has invested much in such a huge project as our universe with its ten-to-twenty-billion-year-old evolution, immense size, and amazing complexity. In fact, the Bible gives many testimonies to God's deep concern for this world, not least of which is John 3:16, "For God so loved the world that he gave his only Son." The Greek word for "world" here means the cosmos, not just earth. Rather than standing aloof from the cosmos, God pours himself into it.

c. The artist's expression takes place in a medium other than the self of the artist. An author works with language, a potter with clay, a musician with sound. As George Hendry says, "Art builds a bridge between mind and matter."[2] Considered in this light, it does not seem at all strange that God should go out of herself to create a material universe. Like working with clay enables a potter to express something of herself and even through the process come to a fuller knowledge of herself, so through the incredibly long history of the universe, God expresses herself and finds fulfillment in her grand creative project.

d. The products of artistic expression tend to take on a life and history of their own that gives them a certain independence from the artist. A Ming dynasty vase can take on a significance in the history of art and a value in the marketplace that the artist never foresaw. Characters in a drama acquire new meaning when they are interpreted by directors and actors in a different cultural situation. This discovery of new possibilities is even more likely to occur if the artist produces something that itself requires actualizing new potentialities, such as a play that calls for the actors to ad-lib.

The best analogy to God's creativity that I know is jazz.[3] The heart of jazz is improvisation on a given theme. When a jazz band swings, all members of the band are contributing to the music. While one person takes the lead in improvising, the others are also improvising in response to the lead. So the jazz analogy suggests that while God is the chief improvisor in creating the

---

2. George S. Hendry, *Theology of Nature* (Philadelphia: Westminster, 1980), 156.
3. I owe this suggestion to my colleague and fellow jazz lover Richard Ylvisaker.

world, the creatures are also thoroughly involved in the creative process through their responses to what God and the others are doing.

While each of these four models of creation has some legitimacy and, in combination with another model, can be used to highlight certain things, I think the model of artistic expression is the most appropriate and helpful one.

Why Does God Create?

Although neither biblical account of creation addresses this question and we cannot come up with the definitive answer to it, it is fruitful to consider some of the major options. One answer sometimes given is that God creates the world because God is lonely and seeks company with humans. This view has been criticized both as inadequate for God and as anthropocentric. That is, a God who starts out with such a major deficiency as being lonely seems far too weak to be the ultimate source of the universe. The suggestion is also anthropocentric (human-centered), for it says the purpose for this entire universe lies in the humans who dwell on one of its small planets.

A second proposal is that God creates the universe simply out of an overflowing love. This is a more difficult view to grasp, for it begins with a certain interpretation of the doctrine of the Trinity. It uses the distinction between the immanent or internal Trinity, which refers to the eternal relations among the three persons of the Trinity, and the economic or external Trinity, which concerns God's relation with the world. The basic idea is that eternally God has relationship or community within God's own inner life in the fellowship among Father, Son, and Holy Spirit. This means that God does not "need" to create a world, for God already enjoys relations within God's own eternal life. Thus, God's act of creating is a free act of pure generosity, an act of overflowing love that gives but does not seek anything for itself. God does not need to create, but freely decides to do so out of sheer benevolence.

This suggestion has had many influential supporters such as Karl Barth and contemporary German theologian Jürgen Moltmann, but it has also been criticized. One critique is that the creation of the world in this model seems to be a wholly arbitrary act of God, a mere divine whim. Since, in this view, God would have been just as happy and fulfilled without a world, creation seems not only generous but capricious. Another criticism of this view has been made by some feminist theologians who argue that the idea of a self-sufficient deity giving existence to a completely unneeded world tends to give religious support for hierarchical human relations in which one party dominates over another.

A third proposal also makes use of the doctrine of the Trinity, but focuses on a different pattern in God's trinitarian life. It says the pattern of God's work of salvation in Jesus Christ and the Holy Spirit is also evident in God's work of creating. In Jesus Christ the pattern is that the eternal Word goes out from God into a physical form, in order to bring the physical realm into a higher unity with God. Indeed, the "going out" of God involves a going into the depths even as Jesus Christ experienced the depths of suffering and alienation, in order to move toward a greater well-being and harmony. The Holy Spirit also has the pattern of this double movement of going out and moving toward greater unity, for as the Spirit went out into Jesus in the wilderness, Jesus resisted the tempter and was obedient to God (Matthew 4:1ff.). The Holy Spirit continues to move out into the lives of believers and draws them into the church's unity of praising God and serving others.

This pattern in the work of salvation is also apparent in the divine activity of creating the universe. God goes out of himself and gives existence to a complex physical world other than himself, indeed, a world that includes much negativity and suffering, in order to eventually bring that world to a higher unity and fulfillment.[4] Elizabeth Johnson speaks of a similar trinitarian dynamic, "Unoriginate source, unknowable mother of all, she forever comes forth from hiddenness as her distinct self-expressing Word. The Word is Wisdom in the movement outward from light inaccessible . . . and this eternal divine movement of self-distinction, when posited externally, grounds creation. . . . Simultaneously, Holy Wisdom forever unfurls as distinct self-bestowing spirit . . . in the spiraling movement of liberating love freely and inclusively given."[5] I believe this is the most satisfactory suggestion of why God creates the universe. Here the divine activity of creating is filled with a generous, self-giving love, just as in the second proposal, but there is no hint that God might have been just as happy if she had not created a world. Rather, the immensely complex and long-term activity of creating the universe is seen as a magnificent project fitting for the divine Artist who expresses herself, experiences genuine trials, involves creatures in the creative undertaking, and fulfills herself as well as creatures in accomplishing the project.

I have likened God's activity of creating to an intricate, fluid performance of a basic dance step. Another good artistic analogy for God's creating is jazz. As the jazz musician expresses himself or herself through the medium of musical improvisation and thereby interacts with the other musicians in the band to achieve a fresh harmony and unity, so God goes out of himself into the medium of matter and creaturely spirit to achieve ultimately the richer harmony and unity of the reign of God.

---

4. A clear, perceptive presentation of this view is given by Hendry, *Theology of Nature*, 163–71.

5. Elizabeth A. Johnson, *She Who Is: The Mystery of God in Feminist Theological Discourse* (New York: Crossroad, 1992), 214.

So far in this chapter we have looked at the two biblical accounts of creation, the traditional teaching of creation *ex nihilo*, different proposals on how God creates (models of creation), and why God creates. These ideas lay the foundation for addressing two urgent issues. The first issue is whether belief in creation by God is compatible with science. The second is the relation between the doctrine of creation and ecology.

Creation and Science

In today's culture almost everyone feels some difficulty in putting belief in divine creation together with modern science. Not only beginners in fields of science and theology struggle with this; renowned scholars also strain to bring their understanding of the world through science together with their understanding of reality in Christian faith. Four main ways of dealing with the issue have emerged.

1. *Fundamentalist rejection of science when it contradicts the Bible.* Fundamentalism is a complex religious movement that emerged at the end of the nineteenth century and remains strong today. A significant part of the fundamentalist outlook is seeing a basic opposition between the biblical teaching of creation and the Darwinian idea of evolution. In the early decades of the twentieth century there were fierce battles in many churches over this issue. In recent decades many fundamentalists have advocated what they call *scientific creationism*, that is, they want the biblical account of creation in Genesis to be taught in the public schools as another scientific explanation in competition with the evolutionist account. What this reveals, of course, is that fundamentalists think the two creation stories in Genesis 1–2 are trying to do the same thing as scientific theories such as the Big Bang and evolution; hence the Bible and these scientific ideas contradict each other. Faced with this either/or, fundamentalists side with the Bible and reject some major ideas of modern science.

Some people see no other viable way to go than the fundamentalist path, but it has many difficulties. One major difficulty is that while the two biblical accounts of creation agree that God is the source of things, they speak about the *process* of creation in very different ways. Whereas Genesis 1 speaks of the initial state as a watery chaos, Genesis 2 describes the beginning situation on earth as a desert. While Genesis 1 represents humans as the final act of creation, Genesis 2 places the creation of a human before the plants and animals. Perhaps there are strained ways to reconcile such differences, but the basic question they raise is whether the biblical accounts of creation are intended to be accurate portrayals of the *process* of creation and hence in direct competition with scientific accounts. Fundamentalism is not a live option for someone who seeks some degree of coherence between faith in the Creator and modern science. Fundamentalism forces a choice between them.

2. *Scientific reductionism* in one respect closely resembles fundamentalism, for they both share the assumption that Genesis 1–2 is a form of science. In another respect, though, scientific reductionism is the opposite of fundamentalism, for it regards the scientific account of things rather than the Bible as the only source of truth. But why call it scientific "reductionism"? If this view proceeded merely to endorse science and reject religion, the term would not apply. What in fact often happens, though, is not a simple rejection of religious beliefs, but a reinterpretation that reduces them to some scientific insight.

makes little distinction b/t worldview + worldpicture

For instance, a strong tendency toward scientific reductionism is evident in leading proponents of sociobiology such as E. O. Wilson in *Sociobiology— The New Synthesis* (1975) and Richard Dawkins in *The Selfish Gene* (1976). In the sociobiological scheme social behavior in humans (as well as other life forms), such as a mother's care of her young, is explained as a way in which her genes are most likely to survive. A human mother may sincerely believe she acts out of love for her children, but the sociobiological explanation tends to imply that gene survival is what is "really" going on. Religious beliefs can be interpreted in similar fashion as tools for survival; if a belief works to enhance reproduction of the genes, then it is functional. So religious beliefs are not entirely rejected, but are construed as survival strategies, something that religious believers themselves generally do not realize. This approach could reconcile belief in divine creation with science by reinterpreting God's act of creation as a fairy tale that helps people live with confidence of purpose in a meaningless world and thereby better enables their genes to reproduce.

reduces humanity to natural processes.

Many students of science feel a powerful clash between science and religion, for science is sometimes presented to them as the only path to truth. And they usually sense that reductionistic efforts to reinterpret religious belief end up with empty religious symbols. Like fundamentalism, scientific reductionism pushes a person to choose between science and creation.

3. *Separation of science and religion.* Many people cope with the difficulties of relating religion and modern science by regarding them as different perspectives that can be entirely separated. There are reflective and unreflective forms of this separationist approach. One reflective version has been advanced by Karl Barth and other theologians strongly influenced by him, for Barth emphasized that God is known only through God's self-revelation in the historical events of Israel's history, Jesus' life, and the early church. God cannot be known through observation of nature. Science deals with nature

and the finite causal relationships between natural occurrences, while theology treats God's relationship with the world. Since God is not a finite being, science is in no way concerned with God. God and nature are different levels of reality, so belief in God and science operate on different levels as well. This means that there is no conflict between science and religion as long as each observes its proper limits.

An unreflective form of the separationist approach is exemplified by a biology professor and an active church member I know. Once I asked how he related biology's mechanistic approach to human beings with his own experience and attitudes about human freedom. He replied, "I don't think about it much." I answered, "So you just avoid the issue?" He chuckled and said, "Yes, I guess the most honest way to put it is that I avoid the issue." His way of handling the difficult problem of scientific determinism and human freedom is often followed by religious believers who practice science: they keep the two ways of thinking separate.

The separationist strategy is grounded in the genuine insight that religion and science are two different perspectives on reality. Reality is so complex that it allows, indeed, invites, a variety of perspectives in order to grasp and appreciate its richness. As a great novel encourages viewing it from various points of view and continues to elicit new interpretations through the years, so even more does reality call forth a multiplicity of responses and interpretations: music, visual art, literature, religion, sociology, psychology, physics, biology, and more. It is indeed foolish and arrogant to claim that one of these perspectives has the inside track on truth, and the others must follow it. Reality has many dimensions or levels, so a variety of perspectives is warranted. Thus the separationist strategy is an advance over fundamentalism and scientific reductionism both of which insist that science and religious belief in creation are addressing the same dimension of reality from the same perspective. Nevertheless, separation of religion and science is not satisfactory, because we all yearn for integration of understanding. Granted, we are unlikely to achieve complete unity of knowledge on earth, yet we should at least seek to make connections where we can among diverse areas of understanding. Hence, I think the best approach is to explore possibilities for dialogue between science and religion.

4. *Dialogue between religion and science.* This method recognizes that science and religion are different perspectives often looking at different dimensions of reality, but it also operates with the assumption that reality, while complex, is also one. Thus religion and science should complement one another. There have been some important efforts to bring science and religion into a synthesis that respects the integrity of each. Probably the most influential has been the process philosophy of mathematician-philosopher Alfred North White-

Two diff.
perspectives on
reality that do
overlap.

head (d. 1947), for his religious philosophy has inspired a number of process theologians such as John Cobb. The Jesuit paleontologist Teilhard de Chardin (d. 1965) offered another creative synthesis. However, no proposal to date has won widespread support from both theologians and scientists. What counts, though, is working at the dialogue between science and religion, for it is an essential part of the human quest for understanding.

An excellent example of someone writing today on the creation-science issue is the Oxford biochemist and theologian Arthur Peacocke. The fundamental problem he tackles is how God's purposive activity in creating can be compatible with scientific explanations of natural events in terms of chance and orderly necessity. For instance, in biology the heart of evolutionary thinking is that random genetic changes produce variation, say, in the tongue length of anteaters. If environmental conditions produce a shortage of ants, those anteaters with a longer tongue have a slight edge in obtaining food. Over time this means that more of the longer-tongued anteaters will survive to reproduce. While the genetic change was introduced by chance, the new genetic information is passed on mechanistically from generation to generation by a fixed chemical process. Chance and necessity combine to bring about modifications in anteaters.

The difficulty this scientific explanation poses for religious faith is that there seems to be no room for intentional action by God. To be sure, some religious people look for God in the gaps of scientific explanation; perhaps in the lack of explanation for life first emerging on earth or for the human brain suddenly undergoing a huge increase in size. But this is a defensive maneuver that over time has less and less need for God.

Arthur Peacocke addresses the issue with three main points. First, he *distinguishes two types of causation: bottom-up and top-down causation.* The notion of causality is usually understood as bottom-up, that is, the behavior of the constituent parts of a system account for the behavior of the system as a whole. The activity of atomic particles explains the state of the atom. The statistical behavior of oxygen molecules accounts for the condition of a whole tank of oxygen. Peacocke agrees with several other scientists that there is also top-down causation in which the system as a whole influences the behavior of its constituent parts.

Peacocke cites several examples of top-down causation. A very simple case is when a tank of oxygen is dropped on the ground, and the effect is passed on to the molecules within. Another example is the Benard phenomenon in fluids being heated, like heating a pan of liquid on the stove (see Figure 1, p. 74); the difference in temperature between the liquid at the bottom from that at the top causes upward movement of molecules. At lower temperatures the molecules move randomly in relation to each other. Beyond the critical point of temperature, molecules now move in co-ordinated fashion within hexagon-shaped groups or cells. In fact, the width of the cells is roughly equal to the distance between the upper and lower surfaces of the fluid. Peacocke says this phenomenon illustrates top-down causation, because *the system as a whole* influences the behavior of its constituent molecules, such as the organization into cells whose width varies with the distance between the upper and lower boundaries of the fluid. In other words, beyond the critical point a new regime or order takes over; what was impossible before, now occurs.

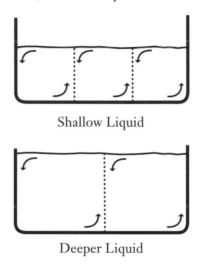

Shallow Liquid

Deeper Liquid

Figure 1
Benard Phenomenon

Yet another example cited by Peacocke is in the evolution of an organism such as the anteater. Evolution is not only influenced by genetic code and environmental conditions, but also by the nature of the organism as a whole at a given time. An anteater with a dramatically larger tongue might seem to have the advantage over its competitors for ants during a food shortage except that the tongue is much too large for its body, so it ends up being far slower than other anteaters. The overall body of the anteater acts as a check on which genetic mutations will be viable, thus constraining natural selection to move in certain directions rather than others. Peacocke suggests that top-down causation is better understood as taking place by a transmission of information rather than a transmission of energy or movement of matter (this pushing that).

Second, Arthur Peacocke proposes that *top-down causation is helpful in understanding how our minds influence our bodies.* None of us doubts that we continually decide to make all sorts of movements with our body, yet we do not know *how* we do it. Science tends to explain human behavior in purely bottom-up, mechanistic fashion. One result of using only the mechanistic account of human action is that it becomes impossible to allow for human freedom. Using the analogy of top-down influence, however, Peacocke says thought influences the body through a transmission of information. This does not require postulating a separate entity called the mind. Rather, when matter becomes highly organized, as it does in the human brain, thought emerges. A new regime comes about that makes possible new events. Thought influences the body in top-down fashion without contradicting the ordinary bottom-up relationships.[6]

Third, Peacocke recommends that *the top-down relation of the human mind to its body is the best analogy for God's relationship with the world.* That is, as our mind over time influences the conscious activities of our body in unified fashion, so God is the unifying influence on the world as a whole. This analogy avoids the difficulties of thinking of God affecting the world like a physical object pushing another object or a power source emitting a jolt of electrical energy. God's influence on the world comes as a flow of information like our mind affects our body.

Fourth, *God's activity of creating the world may then be likened to the human activity of aesthetic creation.* Arthur Peacocke thinks music that involves improvisation is the most apt analogy. He cites the case of Johann Sebastian Bach who, one evening in 1747, was called upon by the Prussian king to improvise spontaneously on a theme provided by the king; Bach responded by developing the theme in a three-part fugue. The next evening Bach chose a theme of his own with richer possibilities and produced a six-part fugue. A great jazz musician also responds to each situation afresh by extemporizing on a given melody, doing it one way and then another way. Peacocke says, "God as Creator we might now see as a composer who, beginning with an arrangement of notes in an apparently simple subject, elaborates and expands it into a fugue by a variety of devices of fragmentation, augmentation and reassociation."[7] The world is like a musical composition, for there is the basic stuff of the universe with its definite properties and lawlike behavior, but this fundamental God-given theme is rich with possibilities for elaboration. One cannot predict what an outstanding composer will do next with a theme, yet in retrospect one can see the logic of what has been done. So also with God's creative activity. The role of chance in exploring the possibilities also rules out prediction of many events in the universe, but looking back over the evolution of the universe one can see an amazing trend toward greater complexity and higher levels of awareness. Randomness and lawful consistencies work together to explore the possibilities in matter. Thus the interplay of law (necessity) and chance, rather than excluding God, is actually part of God's

6. Arthur Peacocke, *Theology for a Scientific Age: Being and Becoming—Natural and Divine,* Theology and the Sciences (1990; Minneapolis: Fortress Press, 1993), 50–61.
7. Ibid., 174.

creative activity. The whole creative undertaking is not just an unfolding of processes working from the bottom up, but is also a top-down activity like the mind giving coherence to conscious bodily movements. Thus Peacocke says we may imagine God using chance and law to unfold "the potentialities of the universe which he himself has given it, nurturing by his redemptive and providential actions those that are to come to fruition in the community of free beings—an Improvisor of unsurpassed ingenuity."[8] I find much that is worthwhile in Peacocke's proposals, although his top-down language is much too suggestive of a domineering, hierarchical relationship. It might be better to speak of whole to part causation. Especially fruitful is the idea that under certain conditions a new regime may come into play. I heartily agree with Peacocke's analogy of musical improvisation except that I conceive this as not the improvisation of a solo performer but as the corporate and mutual improvisation of a jazz band. God makes it possible for creatures to contribute to the creative process.

Creation and Ecology

Ecology concerns the interrelationships of living things with their environment, and there is increasing worry over the damage that we humans are inflicting on our environment. In 1967 ecologist and churchman Lynn White Jr. published an article noting that in Western culture science and technology have combined to produce disastrous affects on nature and charging that this exploitation of nature was based on a common Christian view of nature. White's central argument is that in most of Christianity all of nature has been understood as created *for* humans. In this anthropocentric (human-centered) outlook, nature does not have value apart from its usefulness for human beings. This attitude, says White, leads people to use nature however they please.[9]

White and others have surely identified a crucial ecological issue, namely, how we view nature and our relation to it. Human abuse of the earth through practices such as pollution, extinction of species, and thoughtless exhaustion of resources has been caused in large part by the assumption that we have a right to use nature as we wish. In short, our attitude toward nature has supported behavior that has produced the ecological crisis. The question we must address now is the role of the Christian teaching of creation in all this.

8. Ibid., 175.

9. Lynn White Jr., "The Historical Roots of Our Ecologic Crisis," *Science* 155 (March 10, 1967): 1003–1007.

To begin, a thoughtful, not too hasty response to White is appropriate. On the one hand, a confession of collective guilt by Christians is in order, for Christianity has contributed to the arrogant attitude toward nature. For most Christians in history and today, the faith has centered entirely on people and their relationships with God and one another; nature has generally been regarded as the background or stage for the drama of human history. Most Christians have not viewed their relationship with nature as an important ingredient in their divine calling, but have taken nature for granted as a necessary but minor factor in the unfolding of the human story.

On the other hand, it is a mistake to regard Christianity and its doctrine of creation as the chief culprit for the world's ecological difficulties. Several factors should lead us to doubt that claim. Environmental problems occur all around the globe, including those societies that do not have significant numbers of Christians. Although it might be argued that these societies have unwittingly contracted Christian assumptions toward nature by their adoption of modern Western technology and science, if their own religious assumptions and practice toward nature were so opposed, why have Western technology and science so often been eagerly sought by non-Christian societies? Moreover, history shows examples of humans causing erosion, over-grazing, and desertification in Egypt and elsewhere before the time of Jesus. In addition, it is probably a mistake to compare the ways of small indigenous societies with the practices of technologically advanced societies with large populations.[10] For instance, before the arrival of whites in South Africa, the Bantu-speaking peoples lived very well with a mixed economy of farming that periodically let some plots lie fallow, raising as many cattle as they could acquire on open range, and hunting.[11] Their system worked well as long as good land was plentiful and the human population was limited by disease and occasional famine. Today if the Bantu-speaking peoples of South Africa were to follow their old ways, their much greater population would cause terrific strain on the land, trees, and game of the region. As Lynn White himself recognizes, human beings have always used resources and polluted the environment with their smoke and waste products (broken pottery, arrowheads, and so forth), but their restricted numbers and technology reduced their impact on the environment. These points suggest that the main root of human misuse of the earth goes deeper than the Christian doctrine of creation, to the human heart and what Christian theology calls sin. As we shall see later in greater detail, one important aspect of sin is a prideful, excessive estimate of the needs and worth

10. James A. Nash, *Loving Nature: Ecological Integrity and Christian Responsibility* (Nashville: Abingdon, 1991), 88–90.
11. Leonard Thompson, *A History of South Africa* (New Haven: Yale University Press, 1990), 15–21.

of oneself or one's group in comparison to those of another. Not only does this attitude lead one person to abuse another and one group to oppress another group, but it also prompts humans to dominate nature.

Nonetheless, ideas about the natural world do influence behavior, and formulating Christian teachings in such a way as to enhance respect for nature is consistent with the depth of those teachings. While it is true that the Bible and Christian teachings have often been interpreted in ways that have left nature at the periphery, there are ample precedents within the Bible and Christian history for recognizing a more prominent role for nature. White himself appeals to Francis of Assisi as a model of ecological responsibility in Christian history. The Bible has other examples: a central part of God's promise to Israel was the land; the God who delivered Israel from its bondage in Egypt was understood as Lord of heaven and earth; and an integral part of Jesus' message about the coming Reign of God was a renewal of the entire cosmos.[12] We shall want to be alert to the role of nature in all Christian teachings, but now we must focus on the doctrine of creation.

This is the central question, What is our relationship with nature? Unlike some perspectives that speak to this issue without reference to God, Christian theology should begin ecological reflection with the primary question, What is God's relationship with nature? Our answer to this shapes the understanding of our own relationship to the earth and the cosmos.

The foundation for an ecological theology lies in our view of why God creates. The revelation of the triune God suggests that it is God's very nature to reach out to another and to interact with that other so as to bring about a richer unity. Eternally in God there is the activity of the Source going out in the Word and having communion in the Spirit. This dynamic of God's trinitarian life finds expression also in creating the universe, for God goes out of herself into matter with the aim of arriving at a fuller unity of all creatures with one another and with God. Since it belongs to God's being to go forth into what is other, God's creating a physical universe is consistent with God's character. God is at home with matter, gets deeply involved with it, and finds joy and satisfaction in expressing himself through the manifold possibilities of matter. In human beings the marvelous possibility of self-consciousness has been actualized. So humans play an important role in God's creative undertaking, but we are part of a far larger drama on earth and in the cosmos.

Integral to God's going out of herself to explore the potentialities in matter are diversity and complexity in the world. As Arthur Peacocke suggested with his analogy of God as a composer, a great musician improvises on a

---

12. H. Paul Santmire, *The Travail of Nature: The Ambiguous Ecological Promise of Christian Theology*, Theology and the Sciences (Philadelphia: Fortress Press, 1985; reprint, 1991), 189–202.

theme with bountiful originality. The Psalmist expresses wonder at the pro-fuseness of God's handiwork on earth: "O Lord, how manifold are your works! In wisdom you have made them all; the earth is full of your creatures. Yonder is the sea, great and wide, creeping things are innumerable there, liv-ing things both small and great. There go the ships, and Leviathan that you formed to sport in it" (Psalm 104:24-26). The Leviathan is an expression of God's playfulness, created just for delight.

Since the rich variety of beings in the world have their ultimate origin in God who is good, these beings also are intrinsically good. In Psalm 104 just quoted, there is no suggestion that Leviathan and the innumerable other creatures have been made merely for human use. These beings have their own value simply as creative expressions of a good God. Thus the teaching of creation *ex nihilo* affirms the goodness of this diverse world even apart from any benefits it may give to human beings.

At the same time the abundant diversity of things in the universe and earth are interconnected. Every life form on earth is linked in intricate ways with other life forms and with physical conditions such as water, atmosphere, light, and temperature. Physicists tell us that even minute physical events occurring in one part of the universe have an effect on other parts of the universe bil-lions of miles away. Thus the universe already has an amazing coherence as well as variety. This certainly does not constitute a proof of divine creation, but a universe and earth with such complicated relationships among different things is consistent with belief in a Creator whose eternal life is differentiation in unity. The interrelated world reflects the interrelated life of the triune God.

In addition, the biblical story speaks of a unity of the universe that God will actualize in the future. Already the universe has had an extremely long existence, and life on earth has gone through a lengthy history that has seen many life forms become extinct; yet evolution continues. The story of the universe is not yet finished. When the New Testament writers look to the ultimate future, they look forward to the reign of God. The reign of God is a symbol that suggests a situation in which God will have achieved his purpos-es for the world, a situation in which there will be a perfect harmony of all creatures with God and with one another. Since the reign of God has not yet been fully actualized, God is still in the process of exploring the possibilities of matter and working toward that harmonious unity.

What then should be our relationship with nature? A great deal could be said, but in this context of the doctrine of creation, I will highlight three points.

1. *We should recognize and welcome our many links with nature.* Too often Christians join with forces in our culture emphasizing the distance between people and the rest of nature and minimizing the close ties that exist. Unlike

Aristotle who acknowledged both our similarity and dissimilarity by describing humans as rational animals, we generally feel uncomfortable admitting our similarities to other animals. Like social climbers who try to forget their humble social origins, we often deny our connections with other life forms. We treat them like poor relatives or even total strangers. However, God's full embrace of matter in creation should free us to accept our own bonds with the earth and with other animals.

2. *We should acknowledge that other life forms have value whether or not they are useful to us.* Part of this is to recognize that all living things are expressions of God's goodness and profuse creativity and are therefore valued by God. A consistently Christian view of reality is neither human-centered nor nature-centered, but God-centered. In a theocentric (God-centered) outlook, the appropriate stance is appreciation of how every created thing participates somehow in the value and beauty of created being. Another part of this is that every living thing has a good of its own. This good can be known if we come to understand the life cycle of an organism. The good of a particular beetle is different from the good of a certain bird. Fulfilling its life cycle may take the bird on long-distance migrations, whereas the beetle might spend its lifetime within a small area. Yet each in its own way may grow to maturity and reproduce. The beetle and the bird have intrinsic value or worth, that is, each has value actualizing its own good regardless of whether they are appreciated or useful to humans. To recognize that other life forms have intrinsic value or worth is to suggest that they make a claim upon our respect.[13] This is not necessarily to say that all life forms are of equal value, but it is to say that all living things have some objective value.

3. *We should hope for the final unity of all creatures with God in the promised reign of God.* The universe continues to change and evolve. To be sure, not all is change, for there is also a stable order. Yet there is much in the present system of things that is not good. While we may say that even the HIV virus and the polio virus have an intrinsic value, their effects on the current breed of humans are disastrous. Thus respect for nature should not take the form of venerating the status quo as though it were perfect.

Having briefly considered our view of nature, we must now direct our attention to an understanding of ourselves. Our conception of what it means to be human deeply affects our attitude toward God, one another, and nature.

---

13. Paul W. Taylor, *Respect For Nature: A Theory of Environmental Ethics* (Princeton: Princeton University Press, 1986), 71, 72.

Human Beings as Creatures

What are we humans? Since we are extremely complex beings, a complete answer to this question would have to embrace a variety of perspectives. The perspective of biology would focus on our ties with other life forms in earth's biosphere. Sociology would emphasize the social nature of humans. Psychology would dwell on human mental and emotional processes, anthropology on culture, and the arts and literature on some of the self-reflective, creative productions of humans. All these fields and others help us understand something of what it means to be human. Our question now is, What insight into human being does Christian theology give? Not surprisingly, the distinctive emphasis of theology is to view human beings in relation to God, and in this context of the doctrine of creation the emphasis is that human beings are creatures. Christian theology's understanding of human being as creaturely being can be condensed into four insights.

1. *Humans are absolutely dependent upon God for their existence.* This is implied in both the biblical creation stories and the doctrine of creation *ex nihilo.* Of course, humans have this reliance in common with all other creatures. Nonetheless, it is important to make this point explicitly, for *recognition* of dependence on God for existence itself from moment to moment adds a distinctive tone to the life of an individual or community. To believe that God is Creator is to live with a sense of thanks and praise to God for existence and the many good things of life. Just thinking that the universe had its beginning in God long ago or that one was given a long-lasting battery at birth is not Christian faith in the Creator. Believing in the Creator is to live moment by moment with gratitude to God for one's life and whatever blessings of sustenance, love, friendship, beauty, and pleasure one may receive. Whereas others may take the good things of their existence for granted or feel they have earned them, living with a sense of life as a divine gift fosters a powerful attitude of gratitude to God.

This Christian affirmation conflicts with the perspective of modern and postmodern culture that we human beings are or should be independent and autonomous (self-ruling). Especially among young adults who are working to establish their own identity over against parents, dependence is often viewed with suspicion. In a recent class with about thirty-five students I asked whether they felt any reservations about being dependent; about half raised their hand. When I asked whether they had any doubt about the value of independence, no one expressed concern. In contrast, Christian teaching says that as creatures we are fundamentally dependent upon God for our life. This conflict between the two perspectives should prompt us to ask whether complete autonomy is a dangerous delusion and whether dependence on

God is a very solid basis for confident, self-reliant relationship with other people.

2. *The essential makeup of human beings is good although it is liable to distortion.* This too is an implication of both biblical creation stories and the doctrine of creation *ex nihilo*. Whereas some religions have regarded the body or some other aspect of being human as fundamentally flawed, Christian faith teaches that the basic structures of human being are good. Two polar structures of human existence deserve special attention here.

a. Human beings are *limited and free*. Limitation or finitude runs throughout human existence. We are bound by time and space, and are restricted in knowledge and power. Our finitude is evident as well in the many conditions that are simply given to us, conditions over which we have no choice: the time when we are born, the very fact that we are born, our genetic composition, family of origin, and our childhood economic and social status. If we look only at the chemical, biological, social, and psychological "givens" of life as studied by the natural and social sciences, we appear to be entirely determined.

While we share finitude with all other creatures, we are different from them in that we are also free. Freedom is far from simple, but in part it means that we can reflect on our situation, consider various possibilities, and choose a course of action. We are not simply determined by our past, but can take a new path. Novelty and surprise belong to human life. Yet our freedom is always within limits. Human freedom and limitation are polar realities. Like the two poles of a magnet, they always coexist (you can't have one without the other) and they exist in tension with each other.

b. Humans are *individual and communal* beings. Every human being is unique; each has his or her peculiar life history and point of view. Even twins with the same genetic code have their own sequence of experiences and personality. Much of modern Western culture, and especially American culture, has emphasized individuality. In our politics and law, prominence has been given to the rights and freedoms of the individual. In our psychological theories and films it is commonly expected that persons arrive at their own distinctive identity.

Humans are also communal beings. Our first community is with nature, the environment of elements and compounds, plants and animals within which we exist. We are intricately linked to the rest of the cosmos through common physical forces and chemical processes. We have complex interactions with plants and animals, depending upon many of them for food and affecting them in ways known and unknown. Of course, we humans are also connected with one another in families, peer groups, ethnic groups, nations, and a host of other social groups. No one goes through life entirely alone. We live in a family, whether happily or unhappily. We go to school and do various activities with peers, again happily or unhappily. Even though a person may at times feel alone, our lives mesh with others in home, school, work, community, nation, and world.

The relationship between individuality and human community is complicated. While there are certain groups such as clubs that we as individuals decide to join, in most cases groups influence the individual prior to that person's choice. Apart from our choice, we are powerfully affected by the family of our early years. Our first language is usually taken from our ethnic group, and our speech patterns are shaped by regional custom without our early awareness or consent. Human communities have deep and pervasive influence on the individual. Yet we are not just carbon copies of one another. Siblings may be very different. And as we mature, we sift through the influences from our communities, accepting some influences and rejecting others. But we never start with a clean slate. So the individual and communal are polar elements of human existence; one does not occur without being affected by the other.

This estimate of individuality and community as polar realities of relatively equal weight and value conflicts with the assumption of American culture that individuality is of much higher value than community. Americans generally have ambivalent feelings about community. They long for it, yet they often want to have community on their own terms. Following one's own star is frequently primary, and community seems too restrictive. American Christianity has been powerfully influenced by this individualism, yet within sound Christian teaching there is a fundamentally positive view of community that promotes service to the common good. On the other hand, Christianity has frequently emphasized individual sacrifice in such a way as to legitimate subordination of women; this has aroused criticism from many feminists. This clash of ideas should challenge us to rethink our own understanding of the relationship between individual and community.

Recognition of the polarities of limitation and freedom and individual and community is not peculiar to Christianity, but the doctrine of creation does add that these basic structures of human being are essentially good. A being that is finite and free is vulnerable to misuse of that freedom, but limited freedom as such is good. Likewise, humans are susceptible to exaggerating the importance of the individual or the community, yet being an individual in community as such is good. Human "nature" is not evil but good. Thus the doctrine of creation lays the groundwork for a positive, accepting view of human life.

3. *Humans are created for community with God, one another, and with other creatures.* This vision of humans is initially grounded in the assertion of the

Genesis 1 creation story that human beings are created in the *image of God*, but it is supported and amplified by Christian beliefs about Jesus Christ and by Christian hope for the future. Here we will focus on the symbol of the image of God.

In the creation story of Genesis 1, when God creates humans on the sixth day, it says, "Then God said, 'Let us make humankind in our image, according to our likeness.'. . . So God created humankind in his own image, in the image of God he created them" (Genesis 1:26-27). The meaning of this symbolism is not clearly explained in the Bible, for it was probably so well understood by its original audience that explanation was unneeded. Yet the image of God seems to involve four main things.

First, *human beings are intended for communion with God*. This is certain, although there is considerable debate over details of interpreting Genesis. When Genesis 1 says human beings are created in the image of God, there seems to be a suggestion of similarity or likeness with God; however, it is very difficult to know for sure just what the similarity is. Some traditional suggestions have been that the likeness is in rationality, freedom of the will, and moral responsibility; in the twentieth century many have interpreted the image as self-transcendence. Karl Barth and the German Old Testament scholar Claus Westermann follow an entirely different tack and argue that "image of God" does not refer to any quality within human beings, but rather to the fact that God created humans for relationship with God.[14] When the dust has settled from these scholarly battles over the biblical symbolism, saying humans are created in the image of God seems to convey at least this basic claim: God intends humans to live in special relationship with God. This implies that humans have been given some distinctive qualities that make it possible for them to enter into such a relationship, but it is not necessary to say whether these qualities are specifically rationality, moral responsibility, self-transcendence, or whatever. In fact, a number of such qualities are required for the kind of relationship with God envisioned in the Bible.

Second, *being the image of God means that humans represent God on earth*. Both ancient Egyptian and Assyrian texts speak of their king as the image of God in the sense of acting for God and standing for God. This is consistent with Genesis 1:26, which after saying "Let us make humankind in our image, according to our likeness," immediately adds, "And let them have dominion over the fish of the sea, and over the birds of the air, and over the cattle, and

14. Gordon J. Wenham, *Genesis 1–15*, Word Biblical Commentary (Waco: Word, 1987), 29–32; Claus Westermann, *Genesis 1–11: A Continental Commentary*, trans. John J. Scullion (Minneapolis: Augsburg, 1984; reprint, Fortress Press, 1994), 148–58; Geoffrey Wainwright, *Doxology: The Praise of God in Worship, Doctrine, and Life* (New York: Oxford University Press, 1980), 16–33.

over all the earth, and over every creeping thing that creeps upon the earth." Having dominion is a kingly function. So being made in the image of God means that the relationship with God to which humans are called is one of accountability as God's representative or vice-regent on earth.

The Genesis symbolism of humans created in the image of God appears to have a third meaning as well: that *humans are created to be in relationship with other creatures.* As we already noted, as God's representatives on earth, humans are given dominion over the animals. So being related to God as representative or vice-regent on earth necessarily involves humans in relationships with other life forms.

Fourth, *the image of God is linked with relationship between human beings.* Genesis 1:27 says, "So God created humankind in his image, in the image of God he created them; male and female he created them." Since humans are made in two kinds—male and female—relationship between humans is inescapable. Thus, being created in the image of God has four interconnected meanings: human beings are intended to live in special relationship with God, part of this special relationship is to be responsible to God as the divine representative on earth, and humans are meant to be in relationship with one another and with other creatures.

What kind of relationships are meant? Lynn White and other critics argue Genesis promotes an exploitive relationship with nature by teaching that humans have dominion over the animals. However, a closer reading of Genesis 1 at two points shows that exploitation is precluded. First, earlier in the creation story, the sun is said to rule the day and the moon to rule the night (Genesis 1:16). A metaphorical rather than literal meaning of "ruling" is intended, like speaking of a mountain dominating the landscape. Similarly human dominion over the animals may mean that humans as rational, free beings are the brightest light among earth's life forms. Second, while humans are given dominion over animals (1:28), God allots humans only plants for food (1:29). Prior to the fall into sin, humans are seen as vegetarians. Hence, while humans do have a certain preeminence on earth as the one creature who is self-consciously responsible to God, the character of this dominion excludes exploitation. To be God's representative on earth means to be God's steward, administering things in a manner consistent with God's own way of ruling.[15]

These four conclusions about the meaning of the image of God are supported by other Christian beliefs, especially beliefs about Jesus Christ and about the ultimate future. In the New Testament Jesus Christ is called "the

---

15. Westermann, *Genesis 1–11*, 159–60; Jürgen Moltmann, *God in Creation: A New Theology of Creation and the Spirit of God*, trans. Margaret Kohl (1985; Minneapolis: Fortress Press, 1993), 24. Moltmann also says that the divine commission to "subdue" the earth in Genesis 1:28 refers only to the nourishment or food supply of human beings.

image of God" (2 Corinthians 4:4) and God's goal for others is to be "conformed to the image of his Son" (Romans 8:29). This indicates that Jesus Christ embodies the sort of relationship with God intended for all humans: a relationship of trust and love for God that includes relationships of love for other persons and creatures, especially the vulnerable.

Jesus' proclamation of the coming reign of God and Paul's belief that "the whole creation has been groaning in labor pains until now" (Romans 8:22) also express a hope for a final destiny involving harmony with God, one another, and nature. To believe in God as Creator is also to hope for the fulfillment of God's creative activity. I spoke earlier of God's creative endeavor as a stupendous project stretching over billions of years; this project is not yet finished. There is much in the present order of things to lament. So to believe in the Creator is not only to be thankful for past and present blessings, but also to long for and expect the completion of God's creative undertaking. Creation in the image of God lays the foundation for this hope.

4. *All human beings share equally in a common human nature and in the image of God.* All human beings are created in God's image, so that there is this fundamental equality among all people whether they are otherwise distinguished by sex, race, or ethnic group. In spite of this affirmation of basic equality among people, the Bible has often been used to justify the domination of one group of people over another. Whites have sometimes used passages of Scripture to argue for their superiority over people of color. This has happened in South Africa when whites defended apartheid or white separatism.[16] In America the Ku Klux Klan claims Christian justification for its racism by its symbolic act of burning a cross.

Arguments have also been employed through most of the history of Christianity to legitimate male domination over females. Thomas Aquinas and Martin Luther are two very influential theologians who present variations on the common theme of female inferiority. In his great work of medieval theology, *Summa Theologica*, Thomas Aquinas uses a mixture of philosophical and biblical ideas to teach the superiority of men to women in two ways. One way is that the power of reason is greater in men, so that even if humans had not sinned, it would have been part of the divine order that men rule over women for women's own good. Aquinas uses Aristotelian biology as the other reason for male superiority: the active power of reproduction belongs to the male, the passive power to the female, and the active male power tends to reproduce itself unless some defect intervenes to make a female. Hence, Aquinas says, "As regards the individual nature, woman is

---

16. "The Kairos Document," in Robert McAfee Brown, ed., *Kairos: Three Prophetic Challenges to the Church* (Grand Rapids, Mich.: Wm. B. Eerdmans, 1990), 29–47.

defective and misbegotten." The main reason for women existing at all is that they are appointed by God to share in the work of procreation.[17] As the philosophy of Aristotle declined in influence, Aquinas' reasons for female subordination have lost weight. Biblical arguments for the secondary status of women have been more enduring.

Martin Luther relies on such an argument in his commentary on Genesis. We must remember that Luther and other theologians until the nineteenth century thought of the stories in Genesis 1–3 as historical accounts in which Adam and Eve were the first two human beings who were created good and then fell into sin. Prior to their sin, Luther says, "Eve was not like the woman of today; her state was far better and more excellent, and she was in no respect inferior to Adam, whether you count the qualities of the body or those of the mind."[18]

Yet Luther goes on to say that woman becomes decidedly inferior to man as a result of God's punishment after the fall into sin when God says to the woman, "I will greatly increase your pangs in childbearing; in pain you shall bring forth children, yet your desire shall be for your husband, and he shall rule over you" (Genesis 3:16). Luther comments that if Eve had remained free of sin, she would not have been subjected to her husband's rule and would have been a partner in the human rule over other creatures. But part of her God-given punishment for sin is to be under the rule of men. "The rule remains with the husband, and the wife is compelled to obey him by God's command. He rules the home and the state, wages wars, defends his possessions, tills the soil, builds, plants, etc. The woman, on the other hand, is like a nail driven into the wall. She sits at home. . . ."[19] Thus, according to Luther, the fundamental equality among women and men affirmed in Genesis 1:27 is vitiated by the divine punishment of Genesis 3:16.

Such biblical justification for the subordination of women has been challenged by feminist theologians. Phyllis Trible, an Old Testament scholar, has led the way in reinterpreting Genesis 2–3, so that it supports the liberation of women rather than their subordination. For instance, Trible argues that it is wrong for Luther and others to read the judgments on the sinful Adam and Eve as divine endorsement of male domination. Whereas the serpent and the earth are cursed by God, the woman and man are not. The words in Genesis 3:16 about woman bearing children in pain and being ruled by her husband are not divine commands or prescriptions of what ought to happen, but are

17. Thomas Aquinas, *Summa Theologica*, Part I, Question 92, Article 1 in *Basic Writings of Saint Thomas Aquinas*, Vol. 1, ed. Anton C. Pegis (New York: Random House, 1945), 880.

18. *Luther's Works*, Vol. 1, ed. Jaroslav Pelikan, trans. George V. Schick (St. Louis: Concordia, 1958), 115. However, Luther's views on women are not fully consistent; see his remarks on Genesis 1:27 (ibid., 69).

19. Ibid., 202–3.

descriptions of the corruptions that do in fact occur in human life as a result of sin.[20] Thus creation in the image of God means there is a fundamental equality of all human beings regardless of differences in race, gender, or social position.

We may conclude this chapter by briefly reviewing the rich meanings involved in the doctrine of creation. First, we looked at the two accounts of creation in Genesis 1–2, and saw how Christian theologians developed this understanding with creation *ex nihilo*. Second, we considered the modern problem of how creation and science are related. Third, we examined the meaning of the doctrine of creation for ecology. And fourth, we reflected on the implications of creation for understanding ourselves as human beings. Having thought about these aspects of God's creative activity of giving existence to the world, now we will turn our attention to the divine work of caring for that world—the providence of God.

---

20. Phyllis Trible, "Eve and Adam: Genesis 2–3 Reread," in *Womanspirit Rising*, ed. Carol Christ and Judith Plaskow (New York: Harper & Row, 1979), 80. See also Phyllis Trible, *God and the Rhetoric of Sexuality* (Philadelphia: Fortress Press, 1978), 126–32.

Providence and Evil

C hristian faith not only holds that God is the creator of the universe, but it also affirms that God continues to care for the world. The traditional name for this continuing care of God is *providence*. The term in its root sense from Latin means to foresee (*provideo*), but theologically it has the added meaning of "seeing to it." Christian faith in providence means that God sees to things by seeking to bring creatures to their fulfillment. Thus, while the doctrine of creation speaks of God's activity of giving existence from nothing, the doctrine of providence talks about God's nurturing what already exists.

In this chapter we will look first at how belief in providence is grounded in the biblical story and then at how belief in providence and miracle may be compatible with contemporary science. In the last two sections of the chapter we will reflect on evil, both on the challenge evil presents to belief in divine providence and on the various aspects of moral evil or sin.

The Bible and Providence

Christian belief in providence is based upon the Bible, for all the diverse writings in the Bible assume some form of belief that God nurtures creaturely life. One of the best known biblical expressions of providence is in the story of Joseph. This story, which spans chapters 37–50 in Genesis, is about Joseph, one of the twelve sons of Jacob, patriarch of the fledgling people of Israel. Among Joseph's many gifts is the God-given ability to interpret dreams. Jealous of the favor Jacob shows Joseph, the older brothers get rid of Joseph by selling him to slave traders who take him to Egypt. After spending some years as a slave and in prison, Joseph is called upon to interpret two dreams of the Egyptian Pharaoh or king. Joseph says the dreams mean that Egypt and surrounding countries will have seven years of good crops and then seven years of bad crops; this is a warning from God to prepare for the seven lean years. Pharaoh is so impressed with Joseph that he appoints him to oversee the massive food storage system that Egypt undertakes. When famine strikes the area, Joseph's brothers come to Egypt to purchase grain. Eventually Joseph reveals his identity to them, and his brothers are afraid of retaliation. But Joseph assures them, "God sent me before you to preserve for you a remnant on earth, and to keep alive for you many survivors. So it was not you who sent me here, but God" (Genesis 45:7-8).

We can distinguish three aspects of providence in this story: individual providence, historical providence, and general providence. *Individual providence* is the belief that in and through the events of one's personal life, God is striving to draw one toward fulfillment. The twists and turns of Joseph's life are amazing. From being the preferred son of a wealthy sheep and goat herder, he descended into slavery. Taken forcibly to a foreign land, he first rises to be overseer for a captain in the Egyptian military. But when the captain's wife makes sexual advances and is rebuffed, Joseph is betrayed again and thrown into jail for two years. Ancient Egyptian jails probably were not pleasant places. Then, astonishingly, Joseph is elevated by Pharaoh to the second most important position in one of the most cultured and powerful nations in the ancient world. After many years of separation from his family, Joseph is reunited ultimately with his father and the entire family who end up moving to Egypt. Looking back over his personal journey, Joseph now sees the hand of God at work in his life: "So it was not you who sent me here, but God." This expresses the conviction that in and through the events of Joseph's life and often unknown to himself and other actors in the story, God was able to accomplish a deeper purpose.

Joseph also recognizes historical providence at work in the same series of events. *Historical providence* is the belief that in the larger sweep of history, God is able to realize some divine purpose. Joseph interprets his life and the move of Jacob's family to Egypt within the context of God's promise to Abraham (Jacob's grandfather) that he be the father of a great nation. Part of keeping this divine promise, according to Joseph, is that God provides sustenance for Jacob's family during a long famine. Joseph says, "God sent me before you to preserve for you a remnant on earth, and to keep alive for you many survivors."

A third aspect of providence is also present in the Joseph story: *general providence*, which refers to God's care of nature. From our modern perspective, this means in part that God gives some direction to the evolution of the universe. In part also, general providence involves the basic fact that the sun and the rain fall on just and unjust people as well as on other life forms; without these supportive conditions, there would be no life to guide toward fulfillment. General providence is also present in the Joseph story, for basic to the narrative is the belief that God somehow directs the course of nature, in this case, the weather in the Middle East. Thus, the Joseph story includes personal, historical, and general providence. They are present here and elsewhere not as separate parts, but as three aspects of one total divine reality of guiding things toward fulfillment.

Now we need to focus on a conviction implicit in this idea of God guiding things toward fulfillment, namely, that God has an overall purpose for human life and the universe. That is, if God is nurturing creatures and seeking to bring them to fulfillment, then God must have some vision of what that culmination is. What is the fulfillment toward which God is working? This is a crucial question for understanding the Christian idea of providence, because so much depends on *what* the goal is for God's nurturing activity.

Christian faith draws its understanding of fulfillment from the biblical history of ancient Israel and centrally from the life, death, and resurrection of Jesus Christ. As we suggested in the previous chapter on creation, we can say that the goal of the world is what the Bible calls *the reign of God*. The biblical symbol of the reign or kingdom of God refers to a situation of perfect harmony—humans in harmony with God, humans at peace with one another, and humans in a new unity with all creatures. Jesus' teachings flowed out of his vision of concord among people grounded in their unity with God: "Love your enemies and pray for those who persecute you, so that you may be children of your Father in heaven; for he makes his sun rise on the evil and on the good, and sends rain on the righteous and on the unrighteous" (Matthew 5:44-45). Harmony among humans will come when they are at peace with God. Less prominent in the Bible is the hope for a new unity in nature, yet it is present. In his vision of a new heavens and earth, the Hebrew prophet Isaiah says, "The wolf and the lamb shall feed together, the lion shall eat straw like the ox" (Isaiah 65:25). This recalls the harmony in the first creation story in Genesis where all animals are vegetarians (Genesis 1:30). So for Christians the culmination of world history is the perfect harmony of the reign of God.

Another way of talking about the fulfillment of human beings is to say that they are intended by God to *become like Jesus*. Jesus called others to follow him, that is, to live in company with him and share his mode of existence. In John's Gospel, Jesus uses the image of a grapevine and its branches to express this relationship, "I am the vine, you are the branches. Those who abide in me and I in them bear much fruit, because apart from me you can do nothing" (John 15:5). Jesus explains that when disciples abide in him they love one another. The apostle Paul uses different imagery to express the idea that the believer's destiny is to be conformed to Jesus Christ. Paul speaks of believers sharing in the death and resurrection of Christ, which includes turning from sin and living a new life and eventually being raised from the dead (Romans 6). Thus, in the New Testament outlook, fulfillment for the human individual is to become like Christ.

Whether we speak of the reign of God or becoming Christlike, it is the same vision of fulfillment viewed from different perspectives. The reign of God is a communal perspective, emphasizing the harmony and unity God is working to accomplish with humans and all creatures. But obviously those individual humans who will share in that ultimate fellowship will be Christlike persons who love God and other creatures.

Very briefly summarized, the fundamental conviction of providence is that God is Father or Mother nurturing the individual person, human history, and nature toward a divinely intended fulfillment. Whereas some outlooks on life see the world as devoid of any given purpose, Christian faith in providence says God has been striving to bring about her purpose for the world and can be trusted to accomplish it.

Although belief in providence may appear to be a safe and comforting idea, it is a belief that has always faced very serious challenges. One major challenge is whether our modern scientific understanding of the world rules out any talk about God's purposive activity in the universe, as well as belief in miracles and belief in prayer that asks God to do something in the world. If science precludes belief in providence and miracle, then those beliefs seem outmoded, even stupid. Thus we must consider whether modern science is compatible with belief in providence.

Providence and Science

In reflecting on the compatibility of modern science and providence, the thought of John Polkinghorne is very helpful. Polkinghorne held a distinguished position as professor of mathematical physics at Cambridge University when in 1979 he resigned his professorial chair to study for the Anglican priesthood. After serving briefly as a parish priest, he returned to Cambridge as Dean and Chaplain of Trinity Hall. Polkinghorne's understanding of the universe and God's relationship with it is similar to the views of the biologist-theologian Arthur Peacocke that we encountered in the previous chapter on creation.

John Polkinghorne says that many people have not caught up with the advances in science during the twentieth century. Nineteenth-century physics thought the whole world was like the solar system: things happened in precise, predictable ways just like the movements of the planets and certain comets could be predicted for many years in advance. The universe was seen as a vast, complicated machine. In this worldview it was extremely difficult to find a place for God. While some people thought of God in deistic fashion as the being who created the machine long ago, there was very little sense of God's ongoing providential care. The mechanistic view of the universe seemed to rule out providence, for it seemed that God's nurture could only take the form of an interruption or break in the normal functioning of the machine. Of course, the mechanistic outlook also had no way of conceiving how human freedom could mesh with the deterministic realm of matter. So human freedom and providence were aliens to the material universe described by science. Unfortunately, this older scientific view of the universe is still widely held in the popular mind.

Polkinghorne, however, says more recent physics pictures a universe in which human freedom and God are at home, for now the universe is understood to have not only reliability and orderliness, but also flexibility and openness. Flexibility appears at several levels in the universe. According to quantum theory, at the atomic level the behavior of individual electrons, for example, is random and unpredictable. While a few people have suggested that this indefiniteness at the atomic level allows room for divine and free human action to intersect with matter, John Polkinghorne doubts that this is the point at which divine providence and human freedom affect matter. Although the activity of an individual electron is random, the overall behavior of a large number of electrons is predictable. Life insurance companies operate on a similar principle. While the time of death for an individual person cannot be foretold, the insurance companies can quite reliably forecast the percentage of a large group of people who will die in a given year.

Polkinghorne thinks the likely juncture of God and human freedom with matter lies in the unpredictability of many complex dynamic physical systems. Whereas some physical systems like the solar system show very little change over time, they are the exception rather than the rule. Polkinghorne says, "The typical case, on the contrary, involves such an infinitesimally balanced sensitivity to circumstance . . . that it results in an almost infinitely multiplying variety of possible behaviours. How the system threads its way through this maze of possibilities is not open to prior prediction." Most physical systems are more like billiard balls that continue moving for an extended period of time rather than just the few moments we ordinarily see in a billiard shot. Although one might think one could forecast the exact path each billiard ball would follow through its many collisions with other balls and cushions, that is not the case. Polkinghorne says, "The way the balls emerge from each separate collision depends sensitively upon the precise details of the impact. Small uncertainties in the angle of incidence rapidly accumulate to produce exponentially diverging consequences." In other words, extremely slight variations on how one ball strikes another do not affect the usual shots in billiards, but when a ball goes through a number of collisions each little variation becomes magnified. Furthermore, the paths of the billiard balls become extremely sensitive to even the smallest outside influence such as a person touching the billiard table. "Such delicate systems are never truly isolated or self-contained. Causality cannot be strictly localized within them or within their constituent parts—once again the fragmentatory approach of reductionism is seen to be only part of the story. 'Downward causation,' such as we experience when we will the movement of our arm, becomes a distinct possibility."[1] In short, whereas the older science saw the physical world like a mechanical clock in which all the parts function without variation, the newer physics sees a universe in which there is a great deal of unpredictability and openness to novelty. In the new view, there is room for taking seriously our own experience of participating in that openness through our free actions. Human freedom is not the same as indeterminacy in physical systems, but indeterminacy in the flesh of our body makes it possible for freedom on the mental level to move the arm without violating any physical law.

In a somewhat similar way, suggests Polkinghorne, we may think of God interacting with the universe without having to break a law of nature. God is not bound to the world as we are bound to our bodies, yet the relationship of human mind and body is the best analogy for conceiving God's relationship with the world. Within definite limits, we are able to pursue our purposes in and through our body. In like manner, God may seek to realize his goals in and through the reliability and flexibility of the cosmos. Thus it is possible to believe in the nurturing care of God's providence without conflicting with the newer science.

Concluding that belief in providence is *possible* without discord with science, however, does not mean it is reasonable to actually hold the belief. Belief in providence asserts that there is a direction to events in the world, a pattern that reflects purpose. The question is whether it makes sense to believe there is such a direction or pattern. We shall wait until later to discuss whether it is credible to see a purpose in human affairs, the issue of individual and historical providence. Now we consider whether it is plausible to believe in general providence, that God gives direction to the evolution of the universe and sustains the basic conditions for life. Here the ideas of general providence and continuing creation converge.

One major evidence in support of general providence is the *anthropic principle*, the idea that the laws of physics in the universe are such that they permit the evolution of life. We encountered this idea before when discussing the

---

1. John Polkinghorne, *Science and Providence: God's Interaction with the World* (Boston: Shambhala, 1989), 28, 29.

argument from design in chapter 3 on the reasonableness of belief in God. John Polkinghorne points out one example of the anthropic principle:

> If life were to be able to evolve there had to be some hydrogen left after those famous first three minutes in which the whole universe was an arena of nuclear reactions. Otherwise there could subsequently be no water, essential to life. When nuclear reactions started up again in the interior of stars, circumstances had to be such that some of those stars would explode, scattering into the environment heavier elements, such as carbon and iron, made in their cores and also needed for the evolution of life. These requirements together place a stringent limitation on the ratio of the weak nuclear force to the other forces of nature. That ratio cannot vary very much from the value we observe, if we are to be here to measure it. This is just one of the many anthropic balances necessary in the fundamental laws of physics if creation is to have the "goodness" which is the capacity to evolve life.[2]

The evidence of the anthropic principle does not *compel* every rational person to conclude that God's purpose is expressed in the very structure of the universe, but the rational grounds for belief in general providence are certainly strong.

In addition, as one looks back over the long history of evolution, there is a striking overall movement toward greater complexity and higher levels of awareness. Both the amoeba and toad are unified life forms that respond to environmental stimuli, but the toad's greater complexity also produces a more variegated awareness. Awareness reaches a new level when matter in the human brain becomes so intricately organized that self-conscious thought occurs. Admittedly the direction in evolution does not require one to believe in God's nurturance, for other rational explanations of the process are possible; nevertheless, belief in the general providence of God is surely consistent with the sweep of evolution.

I have argued that the openness of the physical world allows for the nurturing activity of God's providence, but what about those special instances of providence that elicit surprise and wonder—miracles? Is it sensible for a contemporary Christian to believe in miracles?

Miracles

We must begin by defining what we mean by *miracle*, otherwise our thinking will be all muddled. In fact, there is some disagreement over the meaning of the word. One major approach is to focus on miracle as an event so extraordinary, so counter to customary expectations, that it elicits amazement and

---

2. Ibid., 37.

prompts some people to say the event was caused by God. In other words, the event was so unusual that God must have caused it. Thus C. S. Lewis uses the word *miracle* to mean "an interference with Nature by supernatural power."[3] This conception of miracle concentrates on what the Bible calls signs and wonders, such as exceptional healings, turning water into wine, and walking on water. It also tends to conflict with scientific explanations of such occurrences.

Another approach is to focus on miracle as an event with special religious significance. That is, not every rare event is called a miracle. If a horse that oddsmakers rate a 500-to-1 shot ends up winning the Kentucky Derby, we probably should not call it a miracle. A miracle in the theological sense must be an event with special religious meaning to a person or group. John Macquarrie expresses the viewpoint that "What is distinctive about miracle is God's presence and self-manifestation in the event."[4] With this interpretation, miracle merges with the concept of revelation or, even more broadly, with faith's sense of God, for a miracle is any event in which a person or community sees the presence and activity of God. This view emphasizes God's presence and activity in ordinary rather than extraordinary happenings. In fact, Macquarrie takes pains to show that this understanding of miracle does not conflict with scientific and historical explanations of events. For example, he says Israel's crossing of the Red Sea can be accounted for by a low tide and high wind; what made the crossing a miracle was that the Israelites saw their escape from the onrushing Egyptian soldiers as an act of God. In general, Macquarrie reinterprets or plays down the unusual signs and wonders in the Bible, and focuses on miracle as an event with religious meaning.

While I agree with Macquarrie that theologically miracle must include the idea of religious significance or manifestation of God, he goes too far in explaining away extraordinary signs and wonders. It may well be that some of the biblical miracle stories are embellished, but it is difficult to avoid the conclusion that a regular part of Jesus' ministry was to heal people and that many of those healings were exceptional. Furthermore, central to Christian faith is the astounding occurrence of Jesus' resurrection from the dead. Christians cannot ignore extraordinary events.

The most difficult question about miracles, therefore, is how we should understand their relationship with nature and what science calls the laws of nature. As we have noted, one option is to say that God intervenes in the normal processes of nature. Like the above view of C. S. Lewis, Evangelical theologian Norman Geisler says a miracle is "an event that is beyond nature's

---

3. C. S. Lewis, *Miracles: A Preliminary Study* (New York: Macmillan, 1947), 15.
4. John Macquarrie, *Principles of Christian Theology*, 2nd ed. (New York: Scribner's, 1977), 250.

power to produce, that only a supernatural power (God) can do."[5] Geisler explains that this need not require a violation of the laws of nature, but the addition of an extra, supernatural cause produces an unusual effect. God intervenes in some way, if not by breaking a law of nature at least by adding something to what is ordinarily present in nature. For instance, Geisler thinks many of Jesus' healing miracles were cases in which the body's normal healing processes were speeded up. In any case, according to Geisler, one of the marks of a miracle is that it has no natural cause, so it has no natural explanation. A weighty objection to this view of miracle is that it implies the Creator of the universe is such a poor planner that he must from time to time push the "override button" in order to bring about his desired effects.

A second option is represented by Macquarrie, and that is to explain away extraordinary miracles as really reducible to processes in nature that we already understand. Thus the extraordinary event becomes an ordinary event within our present understanding of nature which the religious imagination tends to embellish.

A third view was suggested by Augustine (d. 430), who said a miracle or portent "happens not contrary to nature, but contrary to what we know as nature."[6] The difference from the first view is that God does not override natural processes to accomplish a miracle, but works within the complex structures of nature. We are amazed by the miracle because it goes against our current understanding of nature. Thus, in this view an explanation of the event in terms of natural causes is always possible in principle if not presently in fact. God works in and through the processes of nature. In all three views a miracle is an act of God; the difference lies in how God's miraculous action relates to nature.

John Polkinghorne gives a contemporary rendering of this third outlook by offering some ideas for conceiving how God may bring about extraordinary events without violating or overriding nature. One idea Polkinghorne uses for interpreting miraculous events centers on the concept of a regime in physics. A regime is a set of circumstances under which a substance will behave a certain way. A familiar example is that below its freezing temperature, water is a hard material, above freezing it is a liquid, and above its boiling point it becomes a gas—three remarkably different patterns of behavior for the same chemical compound. Polkinghorne's suggestion is that since our knowledge of nature and its various regimes is limited, miracles are events in which God is acting within the laws of nature, but in a regime

5. Norman L. Geisler, *Miracles and the Modern Mind: A Defense of Biblical Miracles* (Grand Rapids, Mich.: Baker, 1992), 14.

6. Augustine, *The City of God*, Book 21, Chapter 8, trans. Marcus Dods (New York: Modern Library, 1950), 776.

unknown to us. I think this is an excellent proposal for understanding miracles. God neither violates nor overrides the laws of nature, but is able to make use of physical regimes unknown to us. To use a crude illustration, it is as though we only know how to use four forward gears on a machine and God knows how to use reverse, sideways, and additional forward gears. Miracles are still surprising events with religious meaning, but in them God is working within the intricate system of nature she has devised rather than against it or beyond it.

Evil and the God of Love

Probably the most severe challenge to belief in providence is the occurrence of evil and the suffering it produces. A distinction is commonly made between moral evil and natural evil. *Moral evil* is evil that human beings bring about. Murder and slander are individual wrong actions. Unjust patterns of housing and abuse of the environment are also humanly caused. *Natural evil* refers to unwelcome experiences that are not originated by humans. Examples are earthquakes, floods, and viruses that cause suffering. Actually, the line between moral and natural evil is not always clear; the damage from floods is often in part due to humans cutting down forests; cancer sometimes is partly the result of smoking. Yet, on the whole, the distinction between moral and natural evil is important and helpful. Evil's challenge to belief in the providence of God can come to a person as either predominantly a theoretical question or predominantly a practical matter; we shall first consider the mainly theoretical question.

Evil as a Theoretical Problem

One is most likely to encounter the theoretical problem of evil in a philosophy or theology class or in a discussion inspired by such a class. The theoretical problem of evil is often posed this way: If God is perfectly good and omnipotent, why then does evil exist? That is, if God is perfectly good, it appears that God would not want to have evil in the creation and would not want to have her creatures suffer. And if God is omnipotent, then it seems God is able to create a world in which no evil exists. Yet evil does in fact exist. In this formulation of the problem, the fact of evil becomes an objection to rational belief in God, at least belief in a perfectly good, all-powerful deity. Rational defense of belief in God in the face of evil is called *theodicy*, a Greek term that means a justification of God; the issue is how we can understand that a good, almighty God would create and sustain a world in which such evil exists. We shall briefly examine four answers to this question.

1. *Satan as cause of evil.* Although it is not a formal theodicy, the belief that Satan causes evil is often used in an attempt to explain evil. *Satan* is a Hebrew word meaning adversary or wicked opponent, and in the Old Testament is used mostly for a human adversary. In the late Old Testament books of Job and Zechariah, Satan is a heavenly being with access to God's heavenly court who accuses certain humans before God. Only during the time between the Old and New Testaments does Satan appear in Jewish thought as an angel who has become clearly evil and seeks to disrupt the relationship between God and humans. The New Testament assumes this understanding of Satan, who is sometimes called by that name and other times is called the devil. Quite often suffering is traced to the devil or the demons headed by the devil (for instance, Luke 13:16; 1 Peter 5:8-9; Revelation 2:10).

It is very important to be clear about the status of Satan in the New Testament. Satan is not an evil power totally independent of God; if that were the case, there would be an absolute dualism of two equal powers. Rather, God is the ultimate source of every being and this includes the devil. Hence, Satan is understood as an angel who has fallen away from God. Furthermore, the devil continues to exist by God's permission. This is evident when Paul says, "A thorn was given me in the flesh, a messenger of Satan to torment me, to keep me from being too elated" (2 Corinthians 12:7). The passive "was given" indicates that Satan acts by God's permission.

Our question now is to what extent Satan helps us understand how belief in a good and almighty God is compatible with evil. Sometimes moral and natural evil are traced to the devil as their primary cause. This suggests that moral evil has its most basic root in the sin of the angels who fall away from God; then they tempt humans also to sin. In this view the natural evils of disease, earthquake, and death are the work of the devil disrupting God's otherwise perfect creation. In my own view, this interpretation of evil is of only limited value. Its main significant insight is that evil has a power greater than can be attributed to humans alone. But the existence of Satan does not finally help us answer the various questions of why God allows evil and the suffering it brings, for Satan is ultimately under the power of God. We are left wondering why God allows Satan's continued existence and activity.

2. *Process theodicy.* It is possible to resolve the theodicy dilemma either by compromising the goodness of God (an option few take) or by limiting the power of God. The latter course is followed by the seminal process philosopher Alfred North Whitehead (d. 1947) and leading process theologian John B. Cobb Jr. Since Cobb denies the traditional teaching of creation *ex nihilo*, God is not fully responsible for the nature of the world. God influences the world only by persuasion, seeking to lure other beings toward what is best. Cobb is also unable to endorse the Christian hope for God's ultimate defini-

tive victory over evil. So process theology deals with the theodicy issue by drastically limiting the power of God and rejecting traditional Christian teachings about creation and the ultimate future.

3. *The Augustinian theodicy* bears the name of the early Christian theologian Augustine, because the cluster of four ideas making up this theodicy appear in his various reflections on the problem of evil. We will focus on just two of these key ideas.[7] The first idea is commonly called the *free will defense*. This has taken various forms over the centuries, but in Augustine it takes the form of saying all evil derives from the free will of finite beings—angels and humans. As originally created by God, angels and humans were good and there were no natural evils, but first some of the angels and then humans made the fundamental wrong choice of turning away from God. Augustine regarded natural evils such as disease, drought, and damaging storms as fair divine penalties for sin; not necessarily that each instance of disease is punishment for a specific wrong by that individual, but the general presence of natural evil is a penalty for sin. Thus the basic evil is moral evil or sin.

Critics of the free will defense have commonly said the argument does not vindicate God, for an omnipotent God could create free beings in such a way that of their own free will they would always choose the good. In other words, creating free beings who can do wrong is a botched job that could not be done by an omnipotent God. Recent defenders of the free will argument respond that it is not possible to create genuinely free beings who are unable to do wrong. This response rests on a certain understanding of freedom. A robot has the ability to always act according to its computer program and a hypnotized person may always behave as he or she has been instructed, but we do not regard either of them as free. Genuine freedom includes the capacity to think or act otherwise than what one has done, and this opens the door to possible wrong choices. Thus God might have created robots that could only do the good, but she could not create genuinely free finite beings who are unable to do wrong.[8]

A second important idea in Augustine's thinking about evil is the *principle of plenitude*. This is the notion that it is better for God to create as wide a range of beings as possible, rather than just selecting out a few choice ones. Augustine thought in terms of a hierarchy of beings, and considered it best that God created beings on every possible level. This idea links up with the

---

7. The other two ideas are (1) evil as privation of good and (2) the aesthetic theme, that seen as a totality the world is wholly good, for even the evil is made to serve good. Cf. John Hick, *Evil and the God of Love*, rev. ed. (San Francisco: Harper & Row, 1978), 37–89.

8. Brian Hebblethwaite, "The Problem of Evil," in *Keeping the Faith*, ed. Geoffrey Wainwright (Philadelphia: Fortress Press, 1988), 63–64.

free will defense, since even with the inherent risks involved in creating free finite beings, the world is better for having them.

The British philosopher Austin Farrer developed this idea in recent years to argue that a richly complex world inevitably involves conflicts of one system with another. For instance, it is possible to have a bird species that is strictly vegetarian, but a wide diversity of birds unavoidably produces some who feed on other forms of animal life. In other words, in a very complex world, there will inevitably be some mutual interference of systems; this accounts for natural evil.[9]

4. *The Person-making or Irenaean theodicy* is named for the early Christian theologian Irenaeus (d. 202), who suggested a few themes that have been variously expanded by others. Irenaeus suggested that the first humans (Adam and Eve) were created as immature beings who were expected by God to grow to spiritual and moral maturity. While Augustine saw the sin of Adam and Eve as thankless rebellion, Irenaeus thought of it as an understandable mistake due to weakness and immaturity. And whereas Augustine saw the natural evils of this world as divine punishments for sin, Irenaeus saw them as trials necessary for human development to maturity. So overall the Irenaean theodicy says God is justified in creating a world in which evil exists, because the ultimate goal of making at least some fully mature persons renders it all worthwhile.

British philosopher John Hick has developed the person-making type of theodicy in his own way. Taking over some elements of the free will defense, Hick argues that moral evil is the nearly inevitable consequence of creating free finite beings who have not yet reached their full maturity. God is justified in doing this, for virtues formed over a lifetime through personal risks and choices are "intrinsically more valuable" than virtues given to a person ready made. Natural evil is understood as providing the dangers and challenges necessary for free beings to have real choices and thus be able to grow spiritually and morally. That is, people could not learn to be responsible if their actions, wise and unwise alike, always produced positive results. Hick is aware, though, that evil often does not bring about moral development in a person and sometimes occurs on a horrifying scale (for instance, the holocaust under Hitler in which millions of innocent people were systematically exterminated). Thus he says that God will be justified in creating this world only when all persons are eventually brought to moral and spiritual perfection in an afterlife. The limitless good of that future universal salvation justifies the many evils of this world.[10]

---

9. Austin Farrer, *Love Almighty and Ills Unlimited* (London: Collins, 1962), 50.

10. John H. Hick, "An Irenaean Theodicy," in *Encountering Evil: Live Options in Theodicy*, ed. Stephen T. Davis (Atlanta: John Knox, 1981), 39–52.

Neither the Augustinian nor Irenaean theodicies has gone undisputed. Criticisms have been directed at this point or that in both theodicies, but the most fundamental critiques have called into the question their whole approach. One such critique comes from the various liberation theologies who attack the tendency to accept evil and make peace with it. Rather, liberation theologians stress that evil is to be resisted. They try to understand the sources of suffering, especially the social, economic, and political sources, but they emphasize that God struggles against evil and calls people to join in that struggle. Gustavo Gutiérrez, probably the leading Latin American liberation theologian, has consistently said that in a situation of oppression, God is actively on the side of the oppressed.

Another basic criticism has been to point out the limitations of theodicy's theoretical approach as such. The effort to understand how a good and omnipotent God can create a world in which evil exists is an enterprise for the person who observes suffering from the outside. For those who seek philosophical or theological coherence, evil and belief in God are major issues on which to reflect. For them perhaps either the Augustinian or person-making theodicies will be somewhat satisfying. But for a person actually immersed in suffering, such cool and general arguments will either seem irrelevant or downright repugnant. Imagine talking to a survivor of one of Hitler's concentration camps or of a Serbian concentration camp in the civil conflicts following the breakup of Yugoslavia in the 1990s. That survivor may have seen groups of innocent people—women, men, and children—deliberately and systematically killed; he or she may also know that this was not an isolated incident but part of a much larger plan to eliminate certain kinds of unwanted people. How can one attempt to rationalize God's permission of such evil to someone who has gone through it? Dostoevsky's character Ivan in *The Brothers Karamazov* voices classic objection to both the view of the person-making theodicy that the glory of heaven will compensate for all the suffering of world history and the Augustinian idea that suffering comes from sin.

> Listen: if everyone must suffer, in order to buy eternal harmony with their suffering, pray tell me what have children got to do with it? It's quite incomprehensible why they should have to suffer, and why they should buy harmony with their suffering. Why do they get thrown on the pile, to manure someone's future harmony with themselves? I understand solidarity in sin among men; solidarity in retribution I also understand; but what solidarity in sin do little children have?[11]

11. Fyodor Dostoevsky, *The Brothers Karamazov*, trans. Richard Pevear and Larissa Volokhonky (San Francisco: North Point Press, 1990), 244.

In essence, the whole effort to make innocent suffering morally intelligible seems repugnant to Ivan and to many who experience suffering. The whole theoretical approach to the problem of evil is inappropriate, for the chief questions of those who suffer are about what God does to overcome evil and what we can do. What is needed is a practical approach that will help the sufferer cope, and this includes being in solidarity with those who suffer and listening silently to their sobs and protests.

The emphasis on a practical way of addressing suffering is closely allied in theology with a third fundamental critique of the theoretical theodicies, namely, that they talk only about a generalized God, not about the trinitarian God of Christian theology. The theoretical theodicies speak of a God who is perfectly good and omnipotent, but say nothing of Jesus Christ as the Son of God who died on the cross. In this respect, John Hick has misnamed his two types of theodicy, for both Augustine and Irenaeus considered the mystery of evil in the context of a specifically Christian understanding of God.[12]

Evil as a Practical Challenge

This brings us to a practical approach to the problem of evil that is grounded in a clearly Christian conception of God. This approach admits that there is much about this issue that we do not understand, yet Christian faith can make three key affirmations.

1. *God shares the world's suffering.* Central to the Christian message is the news that Jesus Christ died on the cross. We will reflect on this more fully in a later chapter, but at this point we must emphasize that the event of Jesus' crucifixion tells us something extremely significant about *God.* Christians have seen a definitive presence of God in Jesus, and have spoken of him as the Messiah (Christ) and indeed as the Son or Word or Wisdom of God. So the unjust suffering and death of Jesus is not only a terrible experience for that Jewish prophet, it is also the experience of the Word of God. In Jesus Christ the Word of God suffers and dies. What does this tell us about God? It shows that God does not observe world history from a safe distance, untouched by its suffering. Rather, God enters into that suffering. To be sure, it is nonsense to say that God literally died, for in that moment the entire universe dependent upon God would also cease to exist. But the union of the Son of God with Jesus is so close that the eternal Word experiences his death. Furthermore, God's experience of suffering is not limited to the humiliation and cru-

---

12. Kenneth Surin, *Theology and the Problem of Evil* (Oxford: Basil Blackwell, 1986), 11–19; 101–5.

cifixion of Jesus long ago, but it is an ongoing reality for God as he shares in the suffering of all his creatures.

Perhaps an analogy with our own experience will help to clarify this. Everyday in the world enormous suffering occurs. Those instances of suffering that make it into the news are just the tip of the total suffering that happens. Each of us is largely unaffected by nearly all of this suffering. We may feel momentary pity upon hearing of some cases, but ordinarily we quickly resume our normal pattern of life. Generally the only cases of suffering that have a powerful impact on us are those that involve persons to whom we are very close—a beloved family member or intimate friend. When someone close to us is suffering, we also literally suffer. We are very anxious, we sleep poorly, we cannot concentrate on our usual tasks, we cry, and we may actually ache. Because of our deep bond with the sufferer, we truly suffer with them. On the other hand, because we are in various degrees removed from the agony of others about whom we hear, we do not agonize with them; we merely note or observe their grief. One of the things the doctrine of the Trinity tells us is that God does not merely observe the suffering of the world, for God is deeply involved in the lives of creatures. The crucifixion of Jesus reveals the depth of God's involvement in human suffering. As Wisdom of God uniquely present in Jesus and as the Holy Spirit present within all creatures, God experiences suffering firsthand. God knows our suffering from the inside, not as a distant observer.

The awareness that God shares human suffering is very significant, for suffering is complex. For example, a young college student may find out that she has a form of cancer. Understandably she feels great anxiety, and as chemical or radiation treatments are given, she may feel nausea. In addition to these factors, though, there are social factors. Her family is supportive throughout her illness and at the start many friends at college shower her with attention. But since she needs lots of rest, she cannot stay up as late as others and cannot participate in some of her usual activities. She is also reluctant to continually burden her closest friend with her troubles, so she often puts on a bright face that covers up what she is feeling. As the weeks go on, she feels increasingly isolated at school. Furthermore, her sense of worth declines. Being more alone, she does not feel as valued by others. She also loses some of her ability to do things that were important to her; she may have to drop out of athletics and she finds it much more difficult to do as well in her academic work. She misses more classes, in order to get medical treatments, and ends up dropping a class to get her work load to a manageable level. She feels as though she is inadequate. In sum, suffering has many more dimensions than physical pain. In the complex situation of suffering, therefore, it may be a great comfort to be assured that God knows and shares one's suffering to the depths and continues to love one.

2. *While opposing evil, God is able to bring good out of evil*. If we tell a lie and it destroys a prized friendship, we may realize that we have reaped the just fruits of our wrong. But a common initial reaction to experiencing an affliction for which one is not responsible is, Why me? Why us? or Why him? What did I (we or she) do to bring this on? The assumption of such thoughts is that God has specifically sent the suffering. There are ample precedents for this in the Christian tradition, for one can cite biblical stories of evils sent by God either to punish wrongdoers or to test the faith of the righteous. Thus particular evils are intended to serve an educational purpose. The underlying idea is that God directly wills every event to happen, good and bad alike. In this book, however, the understanding of God's providence has been different. Rather than God directly willing each event, I have argued that providence works within the structures of nature, structures that include both regularities (laws) and chance. Thus it may be that the college student with cancer has a family history of cancer, so that certain propensities are passed on by a genetic process involving elements of both randomness and regularity. Or it may be that we can see no pattern in the family, and this illness seems to be a fluke. In either case, contracting cancer is not viewed as directly willed by God. God's providence also works in and through social structures that are built up over time by human societies rather than given by the Creator in nature. The biblical witness makes it clear that God disapproves of unjust social structures and calls on people to change their ways.

Nevertheless, usually in retrospect, Christians may affirm that God is able to bring good out of evil. This does not mean that somehow the eventual good from a situation will outweigh the evil, for what measure could be used to do the weighing? Could any good counterbalance the horrendous evil of killing six million Jews under the Nazis or the evil of deprivation and uncounted deaths produced by apartheid in South Africa? Without calculating relative weight of good and evil and without necessarily assigning some direct divine reason for the affliction, Christian faith says that God is able to bring good out of suffering. There are glimmers of this in the courage and compassion of those who resist natural and moral evil and strive for healing and justice.

"We know that all things work together for good, for those who love God, who are called according to his purpose. For those whom he foreknew he also predestined to be conformed to the image of his Son" (Romans 8:28-29). These words of Paul express a paradoxical confidence in the steadfast love and strength of God, who not only shares human suffering but continues to work toward our good.

3. *God will ultimately triumph over evil*. The Christian message not only speaks about the death of Jesus Christ, it also proclaims his resurrection

from the dead. Jesus' resurrection is more than a happy ending to his personal life story; it is a promise of what lies ahead for the whole world. It means God will ultimately triumph over evil, both natural and moral evil. So while God struggles with us now to bring good out of evil, Christian faith has the confidence that this will not be an endless struggle; God will eventually be the victor.

This belief and hope are very important in helping people cope with their suffering now, for often there is no happy resolution foreseeable in our lifetime. We like to hear accounts of a person or group that encounters misfortune and through perseverance comes back to surmount it. Unfortunately, this is not always the case. Often a person dies without having "grown" from their tragedy. And it is not uncommon for groups to quickly forget about those who have suffered. Evil is terribly powerful and persistent, and no Las Vegas oddsmaker would bet it will soon be conquered. No doubt about it, to think that evil will be ultimately defeated is an act of faith. It is a bold belief that contradicts present experience and the impartial consideration of current evidence. For Christians that faith is grounded in the resurrection of Jesus, but it is no less a faith. Yet by resting on God's promise for victory and renewal in Christ's resurrection, Christians affirm a deeper meaning and the final vindication of good even when it now appears that evil has destroyed meaning and vanquished good.

Undoubtedly, Christian faith's practical approach to evil goes beyond the theoretical approach of generalized theism. Not content with an armchair discussion of the problem of evil by those who can observe suffering from a distance, it offers resources for actually coping with suffering. A person struck by a tragedy often goes through a period of shock in which they are reeling from the blow, unable to comprehend what has happened. Even after absorbing the initial impact, they may be disoriented for a long time. Their world has been upset. When we come to comfort someone in this condition, we often sense that explanations are out of place. Although they often ask questions, they are not ready for answers, even if they were forthcoming. So we are most helpful, when we talk little and are mostly just present. Similarly, the basic message of the Christian faith is that God is present and shares one's suffering. Someone in the depths of suffering may not be able yet to hear this message, much less the further notes that God can bring good out of evil and will eventually bring victory over evil in the resurrection. Nevertheless, embodied in the presence of family, friends, and the believing community, the strength of this total faith may surround and uphold those who suffer. Thus the Christian faith's practical approach is more helpful for those who suffer than the theoretical approach of philosophical theism.

Nevertheless, theoretical issues are not be to dismissed. Not only are we emotional and social beings, we are also reasonable beings who search for understanding. When our understanding of the world and God has been upset by suffering, part of our long-term task is to come to a revised understanding. Questions abound, and fully satisfying answers are impossible to find, yet we can formulate a provisional view. I believe that God opposes evil and will ultimately bring about perfect harmony in the reign of God. But then I am faced with the question, Why is God so slow in establishing that reign? Why let the suffering in history go on and on? Here I find that the person-making theodicy and the Augustinian free will defense have some useful insights. Let me briefly explain.

At the beginning of this chapter I said that the overall purpose of providence is to bring about the reign of God; therefore the sort of person that God aims toward is the Christlike person. God's intent is not necessarily to have a person be good looking, successful, and carefree. What matters to God are the Christlike qualities of trust in God and solicitude for those who hurt. In order to have such persons arise, the world cannot be a paradise, but must have genuine hazards and trials. Such a view could be diabolical if God were seen as a neutral scientist observing laboratory rats undergoing some electric shock experiment. But if we think of God in Christian perspective as one who shares in the suffering as well as the joys of creatures, then a very different picture emerges. Then God's billions-of-years-long enterprise of creating and guiding the world toward fulfillment in harmony and justice involves deep and long-term risks and suffering for God. Indeed, while the suffering of any one creature lasts a relatively short time, God's participation in the suffering of all creatures endures for a very long time. So God willingly pays a high price for creating finite free beings who have the inherent capacity to misuse their freedom.

Perhaps the Augustinian theodicy's idea about the complexity of the world may also be helpful in reflecting on the immense loss of life in the twists and turns of evolution and the presence of dreadful diseases that cause human suffering. But here, too, the idea that it is better to create a world of tremendous complexity is tempered by the Christian insight that God shares in the suffering of the world. So God's extended action of creating and guiding a richly diverse world toward an ultimate harmony is a costly labor of love.

To be sure, to a person in the depths of suffering, such reflections probably seem irrelevant to current needs. But that same person over time may go through a major revision of their conception of God's relation with them and the world, and then the more theoretical approaches to the problem of evil may prove helpful in fashioning a new Christian outlook. However, there will always be much about evil and God that we do not understand. We will never be able to fit all the pieces of the puzzle into a complete and comprehensive picture.

Sin

As we have already noted, the ills of life are not only produced by sickness and natural disasters, but also by moral evil for which humans are responsible. Human beings abuse one another verbally, physically, and sexually. They steal and kill. They lie and break promises. They are unkind to one another. They ignore the sufferings of other people. They are blind to the delicate balance of nature, and treat nature as though it exists purely for human use. While there is much that is praiseworthy and noble in human beings, there is evidently also some flaw or distortion in them. The question is, What is wrong with us humans? Since moral evil is such a prevalent and obvious fact of human experience, every religion and every view of life gives an answer to this question. Marxism says the fundamental cause of moral evil is the unfair distribution of the means of production. A strong strain in Western liberalism says the root is ignorance. Another popular answer is poor communication among people. The Christian answer can be summed up in one word: sin. Sin is a complex pathology, however, so we must distinguish a number of aspects of sin.[13]

1. *Unbelief and idolatry*. As we said in the doctrine of creation, in a Christian understanding human beings are meant to live with faith in God, love for other people, and respect for other creatures. These relationships are the destiny for which God has created humans. Most fundamental is the relationship with God, the ultimate source and final goal of life. If the relationship with God is sound, then the relationships with other people and other creatures will also be sound. Conversely, if the relationship with God goes wrong, then negative repercussions will occur in human relationships with one another and with nature. So in the New Testament, the most common Greek word for sin (*hamartia*) has the basic meaning of missing the mark or goal intended by God. Thus Christian theologians have commonly said the most fundamental disorder is *unbelief* or lack of trust in God.

The inherent situation of human beings as finite and free calls for faith or trust in God. Humans share with all other creatures the condition of finitude or limitation. Our finitude is evident in a restricted lifetime, confinement to being in one place at a time, and limited knowledge and power. We are insecure beings dependent upon our environment to provide the air, water, and

---

13. Insightful discussions of sin are given in the following: Reinhold Niebuhr's classic study *The Nature and Destiny of Man* (New York: Scribner's, 1941), Vol. 1, 178–264; Rosemary Radford Ruether, *Sexism and God-Talk: Toward A Feminist Theology* (Boston: Beacon, 1983), 159–83; Roger Haight, "Sin and Grace," in *Systematic Theology: Roman Catholic Perspectives*, Vol. 2, Francis Schüssler Fiorenza and John P. Galvin, eds. (Minneapolis: Fortress Press, 1991), 85–107.

food that we require to live. We are also insecure social beings who need support and love from other humans in order to thrive. Like other living things on earth we are vulnerable in a host of ways. Yet far more than other forms of life on earth we are aware of our vulnerability, and so become anxious. We can imagine the possibility of shortages in the things we need to live, we can conceive of possible human betrayals, and we know in advance that we are to die. We can also stand above our situation and imagine ways in which we might be safe. We can ask about ways to give our life security and meaning. While we are finite beings, we also have a measure of freedom to transcend our limitations and imagine possibilities for coping with them. So our very situation as humans produces anxiety in us. Anxiety itself is not sin, but it is the precondition for sin.

God's goal for humans is that in the midst of the vulnerability and threats of life we would trust fully in God. Such a complete faith in God would enable us both to face confidently the insecurities of life and to share fairly the resources with other people and creatures. Our anxious questions would find their answer in God. Although this is God's goal for humans, we have not reached it. Instead, the pathology of sin pervades human life. And the most fundamental aspect of sin is lack of trust in God—unbelief. Given this Christian analysis of human beings as finite and free creatures destined for God, we can understand why Augustine and Luther said unbelief is the root sin.

Idolatry is the opposite side of the coin from unbelief. That is, when people do not place their ultimate trust in God, they trust in something else, which must be a creature. This is idolatry, worshiping a creature rather than the creator. This is probably not the sort of idolatry that has one worshiping a statue, but there are many subtle and not so subtle forms of idolatry: Treating oneself, one's family, one's work, or nation as the highest good is idolatry. Making financial prosperity, personal safety, or national security the highest value is idolatry. Regarding personal recognition or preeminence the top goal in life is idolatry. In order to give our lives some degree of unity, we establish priorities. And when God is not the highest priority, then some creaturely reality takes over as our "god." So along with unbelief in God comes idolatry.

Just as a physical ailment often has a number of symptoms that may be present in various degrees and combinations in different cases, so sin is a pathology with some standard signs that can be more or less manifest. While unbelief and idolatry are the core, four other expressions of sin are especially significant: pride, passivity, concupiscence, and blindness.

2. *Pride and passivity.* Since the polarity of finitude and freedom runs through human existence, sin can take the form of exaggerating either human freedom or human finitude. To falsely inflate the scope of human freedom is the sin of *pride*, which is basically what the ancient Greeks called *hubris*. This

is not a healthy pride that takes rightful satisfaction in having done something well, but a damaging pride that has too high an opinion of oneself or one's group. Such unhealthy pride exaggerates human freedom in the sense that one does not admit the actual limits on one's power, knowledge, virtue, or nearness to God. The sin of pride is obvious in an individual who gets a big head over some achievement, and acts as though he or she is doing everyone a favor just by being present with them. But the sin of pride is more subtly present in us all whenever we fail to recognize our mortality and make plans for the future as though our continued existence were certain. Looking back over the last several centuries, we can also see sinful pride in the pretentions of Western nations who colonized other peoples on the assumption that the West was superior. Pride also plays an influential role in the long-held conviction among men that males are better suited than females for positions of leadership in the family and society.

Passivity exaggerates limitations and minimizes the responsibilities that come with freedom. In effect, passivity throws up its hands and says, "I can't do anything about it anyway." The traditional name for this expression of sin is *sloth*, a sort of moral and spiritual laziness that accepts the evil in the status quo. This acceptance of evil in the current situation can occur both among those who have the advantage in that situation and those who are at a disadvantage. Many of us in the United States who enjoy a good standard of living may feel sorry for the homeless who beg on the streets, yet it is a rare person who actually tries to change the condition of the homeless. It is easy to accept inhumane circumstances that do not directly affect us. On the other hand, the homeless may resign themselves to their plight as well. Defeated by life and weighed down by the burdens of simply surviving, they may reconcile themselves to their unhappy situation, rather than strive to change it. Latin American liberation theologians have exposed the ways in which different forms of passivity, both on the part of the powerful elite who control a country's wealth and the masses who suffer terrible poverty, conspire to perpetuate an unjust social situation. The process of consciousness-raising or "conscientization" is the awakening to a fuller understanding of the causes of suffering and taking responsibility to change the situation.[14]

Some feminist theologians have said that whereas the sin of pride describes the experience of men, women are more likely subject to the sin of passivity.[15] There is considerable truth in this, for men have occupied most of the positions of power in society and in various degrees have often believed they were

14. For a fictional yet realistic account of this awakening, see the novel about El Salvador by Manlio Argueta, *One Day of Life* (New York: Random House, 1983), 19–30.

15. Valerie Saiving, "The Human Situation: A Feminine View," in *Womanspirit Rising*, Carol P. Christ and Judith Plaskow, eds. (San Francisco: Harper & Row, 1979), 37.

entirely deserving of their special positions and privileges. For their part, women traditionally have had lower status and been taught that was their proper place. Influential adults have often encouraged women to accept subordinate status, and many have often supported their case with Scripture. Even when a marriage situation is terribly abusive, women are commonly slow to leave it. So passivity is more likely the sin of the downtrodden, while pride is more frequently the sin of the powerful. Nevertheless, people of both sexes and of all social positions are subject to both the sin of pride and the sin of passivity, often in bewildering combinations. For instance, a woman who has resigned herself to an abusive marriage may feel superior to another person of lower economic status. Although sometimes there are purely innocent victims, often no adult in an unjust situation is entirely without fault due to pride and/or passivity.

It is vital to recognize different degrees of responsibility and guilt. The rich and powerful who have dominated the society of El Salvador are surely far more accountable for the sufferings produced by a grossly unequal society than are those among the poor who have resigned themselves to poverty. Likewise men, who have enjoyed the benefits of male privilege in patriarchal society, bear a far greater burden of responsibility and guilt for the evils of sexism than do the women who passively accept unjust treatment.

3. *Concupiscence and blindness.* Concupiscence is not a household word for most people, although it is more likely to be familiar to Roman Catholics. The sin of *concupiscence* is the sin of inordinate desire; desire that is excessive or misdirected. Having desires is part and parcel of being physical creatures. We have desires for food, sex, and comfort. We also have social longings for warm physical touch, friendly conversation, and the acceptance of others. Such desires in themselves are good and essential to human existence in this world. But as unbelief and idolatry distort the priorities of the self, these desires and the self's ability to direct them also become distorted. The desire for food can take on such excessive proportions that it dominates one's life and endangers one's health. The craving for sex can become lust that drives one to promiscuity. The desire for comfort can exceed the search for clothing that protects from the elements and turn into an endless quest for the best of the latest fashions. The longing for acceptance by others can become an insatiable search for acclaim. In fact, a desire may assume an addictive power that takes control of a person's life and leads them to cheat, lie, steal, or even murder to satisfy their craving. In such cases the sin of concupiscence has taken such a socially destructive form that often civil law and the police are used to contain it.

Up to this point we have discussed how the core pathological condition of unbelief and idolatry manifests itself in misdirection of the human *will* in pride and passivity and in the disordering of human *desires* in concupiscence. Now we must consider how sin affects the *understanding* with *blindness*. There is a spectrum of sinful blindness. At one end of the spectrum is what first comes to mind when we think of blindness: not seeing and therefore not understanding, real *ignorance*. The difficulty in talking about pure ignorance or not seeing is that by its very nature, we are unaware of those particular forms that afflict us. For instance, even though God is present in all times and places, human beings are seldom conscious of that presence. In fact, if they are entirely oblivious to the divine presence, they do not even miss it. It should be clear that rather than being a specific act, not seeing or ignorance is a condition, like being color-blind without realizing it. There are forms of ignorance that do not carry blame; the fact that I do not understand high energy physics does not involve some spiritual or moral flaw on my part. But my unawareness of God's continual presence is a result of my lack of trust in God and my idolatrous concern for other things; the ways in which I am oblivious to the workings of racism and sexism in my society is partly the product of my personal share in exalting white males.

At the other end of the spectrum of blindness is pure *deception*. Sometimes we use the word *blind* in this sense in everyday speech; for example, we may say that a candy store is a blind for an illegal numbers racket. Whereas pure ignorance is unaware of what is being overlooked, full-blown deception is a deliberate covering-up of the truth. In other words, deception involves an awareness that something is wrong or at least disapproved of by others. The tools of deception are legion, but language is a staple. Terms such as "separate but equal," "separate development," "final solution," and "ethnic cleansing" are sanitized labels that have been used to justify and mask brutal actions.[16]

Most forms of sinful blindness are somewhere between the extremes of the spectrum and involve some degree of both ignorance and deception. For example, recently a group of nuns from an overwhelmingly white Franciscan community with a strong record of involvement in peace and social justice issues visited a black neighborhood in another city. Toward the end of their visit, one of the nuns confessed to a reporter that she now recognized racist assumptions and attitudes in herself to which she had previously been blind. Her remarks made it clear that her subtle racism was partly the fruit of genuine ignorance of black Americans, but also partly the consequence of passively accepting racist myths prevalent in American society. The nun had been deceived by racist ideas and social patterns in her surroundings, and most likely had unknowingly passed on those racist attitudes to others. On

---

16. Ted Peters, *God—The World's Future* (Minneapolis: Fortress Press, 1992), 161–65; see also René Girard, *The Scapegoat* (Baltimore: The Johns Hopkins University Press, 1986).

the other hand, the racism of the national leader of the Ku Klux Klan is much more conscious and deliberate, but here also deception is at work. The leader deceives others with statistics, arguments, and slogans that appeal to the anxiety of whites who feel socially and economically threatened. But the Ku Klux Klan chief himself is also deceived, for he is convinced that his cause and view is right. Unlike a con artist who knowingly tricks others without himself believing his tale, the Klan leader is persuaded by his own racist ideology.

We must inquire why sinful deception is employed. Deception of others by con artists is understandable, since success in their schemes depends on tricking other people. We can also comprehend deception of voters by unscrupulous politicians, for it enables them to win support that otherwise might not be forthcoming and protects the public image they need to stay in office. But why self-deception? The answer is that we generally want to think of ourselves and our actions as good. Thus we seek to justify ourselves and the groups to which we are committed, and we do that by giving reasons that validate what we do, reasons that we sincerely believe. Self-deception readily creeps in, because in sinful pride we are prone to claim too much insight and power, in passivity to admit too little responsibility, and in concupiscence to avoid facing the excessiveness of our desires. In the effort to justify ourselves, we may rationalize our behavior, project our faults onto others, simply blame "the system," and even treat another person or group as the scapegoat accountable for troubles. An interesting example of self-justification and self-deception is seen in some representatives of the men's movement who portray men as victims of a warlike, patriarchal social system.[17] There is some truth in this, as there often is in a self-justification, yet it overlooks the inequality of responsibility and guilt for sexism. While today's men did not start male privilege but were reared in a patriarchal social system, nevertheless, they have had relatively greater power and reaped unequal benefits from the corrupt system.

4. *Sin in self and society.* When the word *sin* is mentioned, a common tendency is to think first of sin*s*, particular sinful acts such as telling a lie or speaking an unkind word to someone. Such discrete acts are certainly part of the reality of sin, yet sin is also a *condition* of both the self and society that exists prior to particular sinful *acts.*

Becoming a self is essential for human maturity. Selfhood is complex, but some of its key elements are: arriving at one's own set of values, establishing one's own basic goals in life, and affirming certain relationships as central. There is considerable overlap in the notions of selfhood and personal identity. For most people attending college, maturing in their identity or selfhood is the inner task of those college years. A faith is necessary for selfhood, for

17. Sam Keen, *Fire in the Belly: On Being a Man* (New York: Bantam, 1991), 46–58.

becoming a self requires having some vision of life (belief) and setting priorities (commitment). Sin as a condition profoundly affects the self, for sin is really a misdirected faith, faith in some creaturely thing rather than in God. Thus the self is subject to the distortions of sin: pride and passivity, concupiscence and blindness. For instance, one of the important elements in my own identity is being a college professor who is deeply involved both in teaching and writing. I am prone to using this social role as a vehicle for personal glory, however, and to make success in the classroom and publishing the measure of my self-worth. This is the sin of pride, whereby I cling too tightly to certain expressions of the professorial role. Involved also are a disordered desire for social acceptance and a degree of spiritual and moral blindness to what I am doing. At the same time I find myself shrinking from opportunities in which a college professor might assume a deeper level of care for the disadvantaged in our society; a certain passivity allows me to continue in a comfortable way of life. Out of this complex condition of sin come specific sinful acts of commission and omission.

As we noted in the discussion of human beings in the doctrine of creation, Americans tend to think of themselves as self-contained individuals and of society as just a collection of individuals much like a sandpile is merely a collection of separate grains of sand. However, the human relationship between individual and society is much more complex. Indeed, in very significant ways every human individual is social. That is, the patterns and institutions of a society enter into the very selfhood of the individual. In my own case, as I have already indicated, an important factor in my identity is being a college professor, but this is clearly an option only in a society that has colleges and professors. Even more significant components of my selfhood are being a husband to Marion and father to Julie, Carter, and Kim, yet the nature of these family relationships is strongly shaped by the fact that my wife and I are European descendants living in this era of American culture. Our family ties would be quite different if we were Chinese or recent Vietnamese American immigrants. So, in very fundamental ways, who I am is shaped by the society in which I live.

Our societies have their own patterns of behavior and institutions. Among the many characteristics of American society are the predominant use of the American English language, a national political system that has two influential legislative bodies and a powerful independently elected president, and an educational system that produces a relatively high percentage of college and university graduates. The United Kingdom is marked by the chief use of English, a parliamentary political system with an advisory monarchy, and an educational system that yields a lower percentage of university graduates. Although the institutions and patterns of a society do change over time, they tend to be quite durable and resistant to alteration.

Sin affects all the structures and institutions of a society, so that they are in varying degrees unjust. In the United Kingdom different ways of speaking English are linked with social class, so that one's speech is a sign of social status. And in both the United Kingdom and the United States, the affluent have disproportionate influence on political decisions. In the schools, colleges, and universities of both nations, access to high-quality education is more available to whites than blacks and to rich than poor. Throughout these systems, grades are given on a competitive basis, so that a very bright student who barely tries may get a top grade while a less talented student who works to capacity may receive merely a passing grade.

Since the social structures of a society are resistant to change, the injustices in them are also hard to alter. For instance, I think the current grading system is unfair, but I find it difficult to do otherwise. While I would prefer to assess students on how hard they are working in relation to their abilities, I have no easy and reliable way to measure their abilities. Another option is not to give any grades at all, but my college administration expects grades and students wanting to go on to graduate schools need to have grades on their records. In short, it is hard to fundamentally transform the existing system bit by bit from within; it seems that one must create an alternative educational system.

The relationship between individuals and the social patterns and institutions of their society is complicated. On the one hand, individuals inherit the institutions of their society as part of the reality given to them. Some persons receive many advantages from the social system, others are at a disadvantage, and still others get some of both. In any case, these social structures in various ways and degrees *shape* the individuals who grow up in them. For example, a study of Iowa grade school children showed that females have a lower level of self-confidence than males. The difference was also evident among three thousand first-year students at Iowa State University, for the males were more likely than females to rate their intelligence above average. "Male students also rated themselves higher than females in academic ability, emotional health, originality, physical health, popularity and self-confidence in social skills. The female students rated themselves higher than males only in writing ability."[18] It appears that many families, school systems, media, and other institutions send less positive messages to females than to males. It also seems that the situation is improving, but the changes are coming slowly and unevenly. Some females grow up with parents who strongly encourage them to adopt new roles, while others are reared with very traditional sex-role expectations. These social influences begin at birth to influence a child. Indeed, even during pregnancy the mother's economic and social status affect

18. Kellye Carter, "Female Pupils Lack Confidence," *The Des Moines Register*, January 30, 1993.

the health, food, and medical care of the fetus. Individuals are truly shaped by their society.

On the other hand, individuals have a measure of freedom toward their society. Most of the time individuals confirm the patterns of their society with their own individual attitudes and actions. The study of first-year university students just cited suggests that in a sexist society the majority of men and women live out a sexist pattern, some out of conscious choice, others out of inertia. The nun who went through most of her life with unrecognized racist attitudes is an example of how subtly this happens. But as individuals mature they also have the freedom to go against some patterns of their family, school, religion, or nation. Persons can imagine or learn of other possibilities, and resist the ways of their own social group. Nevertheless, even those who come to resist an unjust pattern of their society such as sexism or racism are in many respects shaped by it, because the sting of sexism or racism has also influenced their feelings, thoughts, and actions.

This pervasive, powerful, and preconscious influence of social evil is a large part of what the Christian tradition means by *original sin*. The idea of original sin as initially formulated by Augustine referred both to the first sin of Adam and Eve at the beginning of human history in the Garden of Eden and to the sinful condition in which each person emerges and participates. Genesis 3 tells the story of the sin of Adam and Eve. As the story goes, they were placed in a fruitful garden, the produce of which they were allowed to eat except for the fruit of one tree, called the tree of the knowledge of good and evil. God warned them that if they ate of this tree, they would die. In the garden was also a serpent that was "more crafty than any other wild animal" (Genesis 3:1). The serpent tempts the humans to violate God's command about the forbidden tree.

> But the serpent said to the woman, "You will not die; for God knows that when you eat of it your eyes will be opened, and you will be like God, knowing good and evil." So when the woman saw that the tree was good for food, and that it was a delight to the eyes, and that the tree was to be desired to make one wise, she took of its fruit and ate; and she also gave some to her husband, who was with her, and he ate. (Genesis 3:4-6)

While a literal, historical interpretation of this Garden of Eden story is not plausible, it is doubtful that the story is meant to be an historical account of the first human sin. Nonetheless, the story of the fall into sin is a very perceptive reading of the sinful situation into which every human being is born. Pride, passivity, concupiscence, and deception are all evident. There is even a preexisting evil force in the serpent. The profound truth of original sin is that the roots of moral evil run more deeply than our own individual choices. This is a very disturbing assertion in our culture, for much of modern Western culture tends to see moral evil only in distinct, deliberate acts for which individuals can be held personally responsible. In contrast, the paradoxical Christian teaching of original sin holds on the one hand that humans are born into a situation that is already sinful, and yet on the other hand individuals share responsibility for sin by confirming it in their own lives in a complex variety of ways.

Sometimes the question is asked whether human beings are basically good or basically evil. It is impossible for a sound Christian theology to choose only one of these alternatives over the other; a more nuanced reply is necessary. On the one hand, based on the doctrine of creation, Christian faith affirms a goodness in the fundamental make-up of humans as finite and free, bodily and spiritual beings. These basic structures of human existence are given by God. Christians should also recognize that humans are capable of good and noble deeds, for deep human devotion to family members, friends, or a larger cause often leads to unselfish actions. And even when evil deeds have been done, the attempt to justify the evil to oneself is an indication that a person still has some awareness of the good. So Christian faith can acknowledge signs of goodness in people.

On the other hand, Christian faith also perceives a deep disorder in human life. Because the Christian perspective regards the relationship with God as the most fundamental dimension of life, it evaluates human life by a different standard than just whether people are honest, hard-working, and loyal to their family and friends. In a Christian outlook, a person can be a thoroughly decent human being and yet be alienated in what is primary—their relationship with God. To those for whom God seems secondary or even nonexistent, the Christian interpretation appears strange. Those who are cynical about moral and spiritual progress find Christians too compassionate, too ready to forgive, too hopeful, while those who think humans will soon turn the corner on evil find Christians too sensitive to corrupt motives, too pessimistic about proposed solutions. Since Christian faith traces the roots of social injustice and abuse of nature to humanity's alienated relationship with God, the pathology of sin cannot be healed without God's own action to save human beings and make them whole. Christians believe the focal point of God's saving activity is Jesus Christ, so Jesus Christ is our next topic.

6

The Person of Jesus Christ

Many religions speak of a deity who in some way creates and guides the world. All religions have some analysis of what is wrong with human life. Yet only Christianity gives a central place to Jesus Christ. Of course, we have already seen that Jesus Christ strongly influences a Christian conception of God, creation, and providence, yet now we turn our attention directly on Jesus.

The perennial questions about Jesus are, Who is he and What has he done? Most people in the world would agree that he was a good and wise man. Many see him as a great moral and religious leader whose teachings and example are worthy of emulation. Muslims go further and regard Jesus as a great prophet from God, although less important than Muhammed. Christian interpretations of him have varied over the centuries, but they have commonly gone still further and taken Jesus as the central clue to understanding God and finding human wholeness. In other words, in practice Christians believe Jesus has preeminent significance for knowing God and for reaching human fulfillment.

Frequently theological reflection about Jesus has been divided into two main topics: the person of Jesus Christ, which asks who he is, and the work of Jesus Christ, which asks what he does. Yet the two topics cannot be neatly separated. Assessments of who Jesus is are never purely neutral and objective. They not only say something about Jesus, they also express something about the evaluator's relation to him and the impact Jesus has on that person. Thus one's evaluation of who Jesus is closely intertwines with one's estimate of what he does. Nevertheless, for the sake of convenience and clarity, in this chapter we will focus primarily on the person of Jesus Christ and in the next chapter on his work. The term *Christology*—literally "thinking about Christ"—can be used either in a narrow sense to refer just to reflection on the person of Christ or in a broad sense to include both his person and work; ordinarily the context will make clear which meaning is intended.

To assist us in thinking through the question of who Jesus is, we will consider three major issues: (1) How much continuity is there between the historical Jesus and what the early Christian church said about him? This is commonly called the issue of the historical Jesus and the Christ of faith; (2) What can we make of the New Testament claim that Jesus was raised from the dead? and (3) What is Jesus' relation to God?

The Historical Jesus and the Christ of Faith

Any thoughtful evaluation of who Jesus is must take account of the main sources about him—the writings of the New Testament, for there is very little other first-century evidence about Jesus. Although the letters of Paul are the earliest writings in the New Testament, they do not say much about the life of Jesus. We can get a good sense of the theological issues involved in evaluating a New Testament portrait of Jesus by looking at the Gospel of Mark, which tells a story of his life.

Jesus in the Gospel of Mark

Most biblical scholars think the Gospel of Mark was the earliest of the four accounts of Jesus' life in the New Testament. It was probably written thirty-five to forty years after Jesus' death, during the A.D. 66–70 Jewish revolt against Rome, which ended with the Romans destroying Jerusalem and the Temple. This must have been a very trying time for the fledgling Christian community, for the separation from Judaism had not yet taken place. This was likely a time when followers of Jesus were being accused by some Jews for believing in a Messiah who had failed to do what the Messiah had been expected to do, namely, to deliver Israel from foreign oppression. Christians would also have been suspected of insurrection by Roman authorities, for they followed one who had been executed as a rebel by the Roman governor Pilate. In this difficult situation Mark tried to make clear who Jesus is by relating a narrative of his public ministry. There is good reason to think the author of the Gospel of Mark made use of earlier written sources about Jesus as well as oral traditions. Although we cannot grasp the richness of his view in a brief treatment, three features of Mark's portrayal of Jesus stand out.[1]

---

1. This understanding of Mark's interpretation of Jesus is based mainly upon Marinus de Jonge, *Christology in Context: The Earliest Christian Response to Jesus* (Philadelphia: Westminster, 1988), 53–70.

1. *Jesus is given a unique authority by God to teach, heal, and call others to reorient their lives.* Near the beginning of the story, Jesus goes to a synagogue in Capernaum and teaches the assembly. "They were astounded at his teaching, for he taught them as one having authority, and not as the scribes" (Mark 1:22). In the next chapter when a paralyzed man was brought with great difficulty to Jesus, he told the man his sins were forgiven. Some scribes or interpreters of the Jewish law thought this was blasphemy, for only God could forgive sin. Jesus then healed the paralysis, "So that you may know that the Son of Man has authority on earth to forgive sins" (2:10). Mark uses several titles to express the special status of Jesus: Son of Man, Messiah (Christ in Greek), Son of David, but he prefers Son of God. Later in history Son of God comes to have a fuller range of meaning, but in Mark it means that Jesus stands in a unique relation to God as authoritative representative.

This authoritative representative calls others to reorient their lives. Mark sums up the message of Jesus, the itinerant preacher: "The time is fulfilled and the kingdom of God has come near; repent, and believe in the good news" (1:15). In the Bible the kingdom or reign of God is envisioned as a situation in which there is perfect harmony of life—harmony of humans with God, with one another, and with other creatures. Jesus proclaims that this situation of harmony has come near. The signs of its nearness are evident in Jesus' ministry—the poor, marginal, and outcast are included in his fellowship, the sick and handicapped are healed, and those generally called mentally ill today are made whole (exorcisms). Since this new order is so close, Jesus calls people to repent, that is, to redirect their lives so that the harmony of God's reign will begin to be reflected also in them.

2. *Jesus suffered widespread rejection and finally a brutal death by crucifixion.* There is a double significance to this emphasis in Mark's story. One is that the early Christian community simply had to explain to newcomers why they followed someone who had met such a dismal end. Mark tells his readers that many of the great prophets in Israel's history had met rejection, and most recently the prophet John the Baptist had been beheaded. In view of this history, Jesus' death is not surprising. Mark underscores the fact that Jesus made no attempt to be either a king or a revolutionary, so he is not a failed political leader. The nature of his messiahship and kingship over Israel will become evident only later.

The other significance of Mark's emphasis on Jesus' suffering and death is that it spoke powerfully to the situation of the young Christian community he was addressing. Remember that they were in a period of trial and persecution probably because of the Jewish revolution against the Romans during A.D. 66–70. In dwelling so heavily on the rejection and death of Jesus, Mark is telling his audience that those who follow Jesus should be prepared to meet a similar fate. "He called the crowd with his disciples, and said to them, 'If any want to become my followers, let them deny themselves and take up their cross and follow me'" (8:34).

3. *God vindicated Jesus as Messiah and Son of God by raising him from the dead, and this will be evident to all when he comes again.* The resurrection of Jesus is the pivotal belief of the early Christian community. Without it Jesus would have been just one more religious leader who failed to maintain a following. Belief in his resurrection enabled Jesus' disciples to sustain their claim that he is in unique relationship with God, for the fact that God raised him from the dead shows he is indeed the Messiah and Son of God.

Views of the Historical Jesus

For centuries nearly everyone in Christian-dominated societies accepted the narratives about Jesus in Mark and the other three Gospels of the New Testament as straightforward descriptions of what Jesus said and did. But the Enlightenment with its new tools of historical research and its general skepticism toward religious tradition produced questions also about the historicity of these biblical reports. The person who initiated a heated debate on this matter was the German scholar Hermann Samuel Reimarus, whose provocative ideas were only published a few years after his death as the Wolfenbüttel Fragments (1774–1778). The contrast between Reimarus and the Gospel of Mark opens up some of the key issues that deserve our attention.

Reimarus argued that Jesus' intention was not to found a new religion, but to bring about a political as well as a moral and religious renewal of Israel; this involved a revolt against Roman authority. The kingdom of God that Jesus proclaimed was a temporal kingdom in this world. Jesus' going to the regional seat of temporal power in Jerusalem was part of his revolutionary effort, for he wanted the people to declare him a worldly king. When support was not as strong as he anticipated, Jesus' plan failed and he was executed. His cry from the cross, "My God, my God, why have you forsaken me?" (Mark 15:34) expressed his disillusionment.

Reimarus went on to say that Jesus' disciples were also deeply disappointed, but within a few days of his death, they stole his body from the tomb and changed their view of him from a temporal savior to a spiritual savior who suffered for the sins of all humanity and was raised from the dead. When these followers of Jesus came to write the Gospels, they created events and sayings in Jesus' life that supposedly demonstrated his intention of dying in Jerusalem and his foreknowledge of being raised from the dead. In other words, the disciples made the account of Jesus' life fit their new, fabricated doctrine about him. The result, says Reimarus, is that there is a profound discontinuity between what Jesus was in his own lifetime and what the early

Christian church said about him.[2] In the nineteenth century, this came to be called the difference between the historical Jesus and the Christ of faith. In the opinion of Reimarus, the Christ of faith (what the church says about Jesus) is deeply discontinuous with the historical Jesus.

Since the time when Reimarus raised the question of the relation between Christian faith and history, there has been quite a range of different responses. It will help us sort out our own thinking on the matter if we simplify the options and briefly consider four major responses.[3]

1. *The radical position says that the discontinuity between the Jesus of history and the Christ of Christian faith is so great that Christian faith in Jesus is unwarranted.* This is basically to agree with Reimarus, at least in broad stroke, if not in specifics. One may admire certain moral and religious qualities in Jesus, as Reimarus did, yet believe that Jesus is fundamentally different from the Savior and Son of God that Christian doctrine came to teach. This view is held by a wide range of groups and individuals. In essence, it is found among esoteric or occult groups such as Eckankar, which says the real Jesus is an adept who learned meditation for higher consciousness in Egypt. A similar conception occurs in Maharishi Mahesh Yogi, who has appealed to Jesus as a model practitioner of transcendental meditation, since in an older translation of the New Testament, Jesus spoke of the kingdom of God being "within" people.

2. *The liberal position emphasizes the discontinuity between the Jesus of history and the Christ of church teaching, but makes the religious faith and practice of Jesus the basis for contemporary Christian faith.* This was the tack taken by liberal theologians in the nineteenth and early twentieth centuries.[4] For instance, the great liberal Adolf von Harnack contrasted the simple teachings of Jesus with Paul's doctrine that glorified Jesus as Son of God; Harnack said Christians today should orient their thinking by the three primary teachings of Jesus: the kingdom of God as a moral task, the fatherhood of God, and the commandment of love.

---

2. *Reimarus: Fragments*, ed. Charles H. Talbert, trans. Ralph S. Fraser (Philadelphia: Fortress Press, 1970), 133–53.

3. A fifth option is the conservative position that sees complete continuity between the Jesus of history and the church's teaching about him in the New Testament. This is basically a Fundamentalist view, for it claims that Jesus said and did all that is attributed to him in the four Gospel accounts of his life. The conservative position is included in a sketch of views given by the prominent New Testament scholar Raymond E. Brown; otherwise Brown's sketch is quite similar to my typology. See Brown, *An Introduction to New Testament Christology* (New York: Paulist, 1994), 605.

4. The term *liberal* is often popularly used to refer to any theological position to the left of strict orthodoxy. Here I use the term in a more restricted sense to refer to a particular movement in nineteenth- and early twentieth-century Protestant theology that sought to reconcile Christian faith with modern culture but tended to do that by accommodating the faith to the culture. This liberal approach has its supporters on the contemporary scene as well.

One of the basic criticisms of this outlook was leveled by another liberal, Albert Schweitzer, who said the many biographies of Jesus produced in the nineteenth century by liberal theologians and others were just reflections of their authors' convictions. For instance, Harnack ignored Jesus' expectations about the end of the world, for they conflicted with the assumptions of Harnack's culture. As a result, Jesus' teachings about the kingdom of God were misunderstood by Harnack. Another criticism of the liberal view of Jesus was that it attempted the impossible task of reconstructing the biography of Jesus.

Although the heyday of Protestant liberal theology ended by about 1920, the liberal perspective has had a revival in recent years among some theologians who reject major church traditions about Jesus, yet appeal to some of his teachings and practice. In fact, several recent widely read studies of the life of Jesus take the liberal approach: *Meeting Jesus Again for the First Time* by Marcus Borg (1994), *Jesus: A Revolutionary Biography* by John Dominic Crossan (1994), and *The Five Gospels* (1993) coming from a group called the Jesus Seminar.[5]

3. The *existentialist position* holds another kind of deep discontinuity: *the historical facts about Jesus are largely lost to us; however, that does not matter, for Christian faith arises through encountering his teaching of the reign of God.* This position, taken by the great twentieth-century New Testament scholar Rudolf Bultmann, is more subtle and difficult to understand. In his book *Jesus and the Word*, Bultmann thought very little can be known about Jesus' personality and actions, because the accounts of his activities in the four Gospels are deeply infused with their authors' theological interpretation of Jesus. Bultmann agreed with Wilhelm Wrede, a scholar of the previous generation, that it is impossible to write a biography of Jesus. A biography requires knowing both the chronology of major events in a person's life and something of the person's motives for their words and actions. In the case of Jesus, though, Bultmann argues that we are unable to reconstruct the sequence of most events reported in the New Testament. For instance, all four Gospels tell us that Jesus rebuked some of those who sold animals for sacrifice in the Temple and even drove some of them out of the Temple and upset the tables of money changers. But when did this happen in Jesus' life? Three of the Gospels say that it occurred shortly before Jesus' death, but John's Gospel puts it toward the beginning of Jesus' public ministry. Similarly, John tells about a three-year public ministry of Jesus with a number of visits to

---

5. For a lucid review of the books by Borg and Crossan see Leander Keck, "The Second Coming of the Liberal Jesus?" *The Christian Century* 111, no. 24 (August 24–31, 1994): 784–87. For a highly critical review of *The Five Gospels* see Luke Timothy Johnson, "The Jesus Seminar's Misguided Quest for the Historical Jesus," *The Christian Century* 113, no. 1 (January 3–10, 1996): 16–22.

Jerusalem, whereas the other three Gospels lead us to think Jesus had only a one-year public ministry and during that time went to Jerusalem only at the very end of his life. Difficulties such as these make it impossible to construct a biography of Jesus. This does not mean that we are totally in the dark about Jesus, for Bultmann believed we can know some facts about Jesus' activities: for example, that he did exorcisms, attacked Jewish legalism, had fellowship with outcasts, and showed sympathy for women and children. Nevertheless, Bultmann claimed that knowledge of such information about Jesus is not really vital for Christian faith; what counts is his teaching.

Bultmann's view is that the essence of Christian faith is trusting in God in each moment. He thinks this stance is set forth in Jesus' teaching, and becomes a possible stance in life for each person confronted by the Christian message at any time in history. And that is all Christians need. Whether Jesus actually said this or did that at a certain point in his life is not crucial. What counts is the basic thrust of Jesus' teaching—trusting each moment in God; the Christian message confronts a person with this possibility today as well.[6]

Bultmann's position has been widely criticized. Although nearly all biblical scholars today agree that it is impossible to construct a biography of Jesus, many disagree with Bultmann's idea that it does not matter for Christian faith whether we can know anything substantial about the activities of Jesus. The central critique can be stated this way: if Jesus taught trust in God but in his own life was quite different—say he was the Mafia boss in charge of illegal drugs, gambling, and prostitution in Palestine—then Christian faith is undermined. In other words, Christians need to know more than the teachings of Jesus; they must have reasonable confidence that Jesus acted in ways consistent with that teaching. What sort of person Jesus was matters for Christian faith. While it is not necessary to know whether Jesus said and did everything exactly as it is attributed to him in the New Testament, there must be some degree of confidence that Jesus' character corresponds with his teaching. Although it is impossible to know what Jesus thought and did in every moment, the broad contours of his character do become evident in the Gospels, as even Bultmann himself acknowledged.

4. *The moderate position holds that there is sufficient continuity between the Jesus of history and the church's teaching about him to warrant faith in Jesus as the central revelation of God.* This view is also subtle, but it is the one that I think is most satisfactory. Some explanation is required.

To begin, it is important to distinguish in history between *event* and *interpretation*. Imagine that the president of the United States comes to your com-

6. Rudolf Bultmann, *Jesus and the Word*, trans. L. P. Smith and E. H. Lantero (New York: Scribner's, 1934), 3–15.

munity and gives an address at a public gathering attended by you and many others. Afterwards a number of you who attended write a brief account of the president's visit, and share it with one another. The differences will be interesting and perhaps quite striking. A person who is an avid supporter of the president and the president's political party portrays the talk as perceptive and courageous; just what the nation and the local audience needed. A strong critic of the president views the talk as a mistaken effort to appease a few special interest groups, a clear but horrible example of political cowardice. Presumably these two saw and heard the same presidential address, but they give it very different interpretations. We might think the report of a more politically neutral person would be more accurate. This may be so, but even with the neutral party there is some interpretation going on, for everyone who remembers or tells about the president's speech selects certain things as significant. The selection is made on the basis of some idea of what is worth remembering. Hence, in historical memory and writing, event and interpretation are not neatly separated. In its fullest sense, the speech as an event refers to everything that happened while it was being given. But event in this complete sense can never be recovered in any historical account of any occurrence. For instance, while delivering the speech, the president may have had thoughts that were never uttered and were soon forgotten by the president. Another side of the event is its impact on the audience, but obviously this varies greatly among individuals in the crowd. So an historical event, for all practical purposes, means what is remembered; and remembering always involves some element of interpretation.

Nevertheless, we can make a rough distinction between event and interpretation. Witnesses of the president's speech are very likely to agree on many aspects of the total occurrence: when and where it took place, many of the words that were said, and some characteristics of the audience. These generally agreed-upon aspects of the total event are often what we call *facts*. It is important to see that the facts are only a portion of the original total event; in other words, "what really happened" should not be equated with the facts. What really happened will always include more than what is remembered as well as more than is generally agreed upon.

As these observations suggest, the relation between event and interpretation is complex. In addition to recognizing certain events taking place with the president's speech, everyone who tells about the occurrence also gives their interpretation of those events. Interpretation involves seeing meaning in what has happened. Sometimes people naively think that if enough data is gathered about an event a self-evident, unequivocal meaning will emerge, but that is not the case. Interpretation involves seeing significance in an event as part of a larger pattern of events and meanings. Anyone construing the president's speech within the context of state, national, and international political currents is relating it to a very complex situation whose meaning is never self-evident. So interpretation does not automatically spring from data about the event.

On the other hand, not just any interpretation of an event will do. The interpretation must somehow fit the event. Van Harvey talks about *warrants* as bridges that allow movement from a set of data to a justifiable interpretaion of that data.[7] For instance, someone offers the interpretation of Jesus' death that he was executed by the Romans as a political offender. The initial data for this is that Jesus suffered death by crucifixion. The warrant for the interpretation of his death as a political offender is the further claim that the Romans reserved crucifixion for political offenses. The interpretation is as solidly grounded as the initial data and the warrant. Thus, if new evidence were to establish with reasonable certainty that Jesus died in his bed after a long bout with cancer or that Romans sometimes used crucifixion for nonpolitical offenses, then the interpretation would not be well founded.

The difficulty in understanding a complex historical event is exemplified by the assassination of President John F. Kennedy in Dallas in 1963. It was a very public occurrence. Thousands of people were watching at the scene and on television, including Secret Service agents and police who were all around the area. Very soon after the shooting, volumes of evidence began to be accumulated. Nevertheless, it is still impossible to make all the physical evidence and personal testimony fit together into one totally coherent account of what actually occurred. Of course, no one doubts that John Kennedy was shot to death, but there is considerable disagreement about the details of who did what and how. Intertwined with that is the whole question of the meaning of the assassination. Why was it done? And what was its significance for the United States? On these issues of interpretation there also continues to be variation and even sharp disagreement. The question one must always ask is whether a particular interpretation is warranted, whether the historical evidence and other reasonable assumptions permit this interpretation.

Similarly, we should not be surprised that the four Gospels often vary in their accounts of Jesus' words and activities and in their interpretations of his significance. Each Gospel was composed by a different author writing at a different time and addressing distinct audiences and situations. In fact, perfect uniformity of their accounts would lead us to suspect tampering with the sources to artificially bring them into line with one another. And again, the question is not whether the New Testament testimony about Jesus compels only one interpretation of his life. Rather, we must ask whether the historical evidence about Jesus *permits or authorizes* the Christian interpretation of him

7. Van Austin Harvey, *The Historian and the Believer* (New York: Macmillan, 1966), 51–54.

as the Messiah and central revelation of God, although it does not *require* that interpretation.[8] The moderate position claims that the historical evidence about Jesus does permit the interpretation of him as Messiah.

Assessing the Four Views

With the distinction between event and interpretation as background, we can now proceed to reexamine the four views above on the relation between the historical Jesus and the Christ of faith. The first position was that of Reimarus. In essence, Reimarus made two major claims. One was that the events of Jesus' life were radically different than what Christians generally thought, for he said Jesus intended to bring about a political revolution and died with disappointment at not achieving this goal. The other claim of Reimarus was that the disciples knowingly invented a false interpretation of Jesus' life by stealing his body, announcing his resurrection, and asserting that he had intended his death to be a source of spiritual salvation. Reimarus sought to strike down both the reliability of some key events in Jesus' life and the soundness of the early Christian interpretation of Jesus.

While the fraud theory of Reimarus gets reworked from time to time, as in Hugh Schonfield's *The Passover Plot*, and finds echoes in claims that Jesus was "really" a practitioner of transcendental meditation or an adept in esoteric disciplines, this whole approach is highly doubtful. The chief reason is that nearly all we know about Jesus is drawn from the New Testament and especially the four Gospels. What Reimarus did was to use selected elements of the Gospels to create a radically different rendering of both the events of Jesus' life and their significance. The point is that the New Testament writings are the earliest detailed evidence we have about Jesus. Why should we trust an account of Jesus' life given by the eighteenth-century Reimarus or the twentieth-century Maharishi more than those given by the first-century Gospel writers? It seems wiser to say that if the Gospel writers Matthew, Mark, Luke, and John are basically mistaken about the major events in Jesus' life, then no one knows; since we have no other substantial sources about him, that information is simply lost. Of course, it is still possible to agree or disagree with the Gospel writers as to the significance of Jesus, just as many of their contemporaries did.

The second position, the liberal view, regards some of the events of Jesus' life as a model for Christian practice today, but sets aside those elements in the New Testament and later church tradition that interpret Jesus as divine Word. Sallie McFague is a contemporary representative of this outlook. On the one hand, McFague appeals to what she calls the destabilizing, inclusive,

8. Leander E. Keck, *A Future for the Historical Jesus* (Nashville: Abingdon, 1971), 127.

and antihierarchical teachings and practices of Jesus; these are a paradigm for Christians today. On the other hand, she says of her view, "It is not the traditional and still-popular message that Jesus Christ, fully God and fully man, died for the sins of all humanity and was resurrected to new life, as his followers shall be also."[9]

One major question about the liberal approach is whether in lopping off important elements of the Christian tradition in hope of being relevant to the contemporary world, it ends up having very little to say to the world. Jesus becomes just one more illustration of what can be discerned just as well through other avenues. For instance, while McFague's themes of inclusivity and nonhierarchical relations are very important, they are common themes in feminist and ecological thought generally, whether one believes in Jesus or not.

Bultmann set forth a third position in which he held that the life and character of Jesus are of little concern for Christian faith, since that faith is based on the message of God's kingdom taught by Jesus and the church. In short, the Jesus of history is of minor significance for Christian faith; what matters is the Christian proclamation of God. The existentialist position rests in part on a deep skepticism about the historical accuracy of the very early church's interpretation of Jesus. For instance, Bultmann doubts that Jesus spoke of himself as either Son of Man or Messiah, yet those self-designations are put on his lips at various points in the four Gospels. This discontinuity between event and interpretation is not troubling to Bultmann, however, for he considers the heart of the matter to be the way of life that Jesus taught and exemplified—complete trust in God. This way of life is still available to people today as a possibility for their lives.

In effect, Bultmann nearly severs the Christian interpretation of life from any rootage in historical events of Jesus' life. This has the virtue of making a Christian view of life virtually invulnerable to the changing opinions of historical scholars about Jesus. But it comes at a high cost, for Christian faith tends to become merely an ideal or vision. An ideal or vision is indeed a good thing. But Christian faith has differed from many other views of life in two respects. One is that Christians believe their ideal has actually been lived out by Jesus; this links the Christian ideal to the historical Jesus. The other difference is that most Christians have sought to trust and follow Jesus as the still-living embodiment of the ideal; this relates the Christian ideal to belief in the resurrection of Jesus.

The fourth position we discussed held that there is sufficient continuity between the Jesus of history and the church's message about him to warrant

---

9. Sallie McFague, *Models of God: Theology for an Ecological, Nuclear Age* (Philadelphia: Fortress Press, 1987), 48.

faith in him as the central revelation of God. Remember that the relation between an historical event and a sound interpretation of it is somewhat loose, although not entirely unconnected. That is, on the one hand, not just any interpretation of a particular event is warranted or permitted. On the other hand, the ways in which an event can be connected to other occurrences and patterns is so complex that not just one interpretation of an event is possible; some variation in understanding is allowed. This means that we should not expect the events of Jesus' life to be so obvious in their meaning as to compel all interpreters to arrive at the same understanding. Indeed, it is not surprising to find considerable diversity in the four Gospel accounts of both what Jesus did and said and the meaning of what he did and said.

We will test the moderate position by briefly discussing whether the historical evidence permits Mark's interpretation of Jesus. The first element in Mark's view of Jesus that we identified earlier is this: Jesus is given a unique authority by God to teach, heal, and call others to reorient their lives according to the reign of God. Scholars generally agree that the core of Jesus' message was the coming reign or kingdom of God, that he summoned his hearers to change their priorities in accordance with God's will, and that he healed many people from various ailments. Interpreters differ on how Jesus brought about healings, but most would agree that he was credited with healing power. So the evidence for Jesus' performing some healings is quite compelling. Scholars also vary on whether they think a particular saying attributed to Jesus by a Gospel writer was actually uttered by Jesus or whether it has been altered by the writer. One reason this question arises is that when we examine the Gospels of Mark, Matthew, and Luke, we often find variations of the same basic saying. This leads one to wonder which formulation (if any) was Jesus'.

Surely each Gospel writer has certain themes or emphases that color his portrayal of Jesus. Nevertheless, it seems foolish to conclude from such variations that the fundamental historical veracity of the Gospel writers is in doubt. Perhaps a simple analogy can best make the point. I believe I know my father and mother quite well. To be sure, I do not know everything about them, but through close association over many years, I know a great deal about their character and thinking. Other members of my family and I can tell stories about my father and mother in which their characteristic behaviors and expressions appear, and we all nod in agreement as we acknowledge the authenticity of the stories. When I think about it, though, I am not sure that any member of my family can reproduce the precise words that either one of them spoke or that anyone can describe exactly what either of them did on a certain occasion. Nevertheless, we recognize the fundamental accuracy of the stories, for they truly capture something about my mother and father.

The major point of contention, however, is Mark's evaluation that Jesus did these things through a unique, God-given authority. By its very nature, this claim is open to dispute by others. God is not visible, so "God-given authority" is not established in the same way that we would ascertain whether a police officer has authority to search a private dwelling. In such a case one could see the search warrant with the judge's signature or obtain verbal testimony from the judge that official permission had been given. Under present conditions, at least, one cannot produce indisputable physical evidence that Jesus had God-given authority. Does this mean Mark's interpretation of Jesus must be rejected? Not at all, for the evidence about Jesus certainly *permits* Mark's interpretation. The activities and message of Jesus are consistent with the conception of God in the biblical tradition, so the interpretation is not unreasonable. Yet Mark's estimation of Jesus is also not *required* by the historical data about Jesus' activity and teaching.

The second major element in Mark's portrayal is that Jesus suffered widespread rejection and finally a brutal death by crucifixion. The critical point here is the crucifixion. Although a few have argued that Jesus was taken down from the cross, recovered, and then died a natural death later, there is no solid evidence to support the idea. In addition to the testimony of the four Gospels, the Roman historian Tacitus at the start of the second century said Christ had been sentenced to death by Pilate. Thus it is safe to speak historically of Jesus' crucifixion as a fact, a generally agreed-upon event. However, Reimarus denied that Jesus had died *voluntarily* when he argued that Jesus' demise came when his revolutionary plot failed. On this score, many scholars think that the several New Testament passages in which Jesus is pictured as foretelling his death are probably later constructions of the early church. Nevertheless, it is highly likely that when Jesus went to Jerusalem for the Passover, he realized that he was in serious risk of being killed. After all, a number of other prophets in Israel had been persecuted by authorities, and he had the very recent example of John the Baptist being murdered by Herod. So even though one might not say Jesus knew for certain and in detail about his future death, one can say with confidence that he willingly accepted the high risk of being killed when he decided to go to Jerusalem. Hence it is highly likely that Jesus accepted his death voluntarily. If one goes further to talk about Jesus' death as in some way bringing about salvation, however, then that is an interpretation which the historical evidence allows but does not require.

The third element in Mark's construal of Jesus is that God vindicated Jesus as Messiah and Son of God by raising him from the dead, and this will be evident to all when he comes again. Whether Jesus comes again can only be determined by the future, so that is not an historical question in the usual sense. The vital historical issue here is Mark's assertion that God has raised Jesus from the dead. The question of the resurrection of Jesus is so complicated that we will devote our next section to it.

The Resurrection of Jesus

Belief that Jesus was raised from the dead has been central for Christian faith in most of its forms throughout the centuries. In fact, many scholars think that it was belief in Jesus' resurrection that gave birth to Christianity, for without it Jesus would not be significantly different than John the Baptist and other religious prophets. Our chief questions are twofold: First, are there good reasons to think Jesus' resurrection actually happened? And second, what meaning, if any, does Jesus' resurrection have?[10]

In reflecting on the first of these questions, the resurrection as event, we see that the historian approaches this matter differently than the Christian believer. Whereas the Christian believer is taught to trust what the Bible says, the modern historian is taught to evaluate sources with skepticism and with standards generally applied to other historical sources. Thus another challenge that Christian faith faces in the modern world is whether faith in Jesus Christ can be affirmed in the face of the questions historians ask.

Before we delve into the historical issues, we should clarify what is meant by resurrection. Resurrection does not mean the revival of a corpse, for it involves much more than a dead person's return to his or her former mode of existence. Rather, resurrection is a divine act of radically transforming a person into quite a different mode of existence. Thus asking whether Jesus was raised from the dead is not to be confused with things we might have seen in horror films about the walking dead. Resurrection is thorough change into another way of existing.

Now we must ask, Was Jesus raised from the dead? Did resurrection happen to Jesus? As we begin to reflect on this question, we should note that there are some unusual features about this matter. One oddity is that no one claims to have seen the resurrection itself. We have accounts of various individuals and groups meeting Jesus after he was raised, but no one in the New Testament is said to observe the actual divine act of raising Jesus. This means that the belief in Jesus' resurrection was an inference or an interpretive conclusion that the disciples drew from their experiences after Jesus' death. This situation is what we should expect, for any divine act is not itself visible. For instance, to say that a particular healing is an act of God is also an interpretation of that occurrence. What one sees is a sick person made whole, but one's eyes do not perceive the invisible God doing it. Hence, resurrection is a very strange event, for the divine act of raising Jesus is not visible, although it would have effects in time and space. Two effects are high-

---

10. Clear, helpful discussions of the major issues may be found in the following works: William M. Thompson, *The Jesus Debate: A Survey and Synthesis* (New York: Paulist, 1985), 220–47; Reginald H. Fuller and Pheme Perkins, *Who Is This Christ?* (Philadelphia: Fortress Press, 1983), 28–40; Norman Perrin, *The Resurrection According to Matthew, Mark, and Luke* (Philadelphia: Fortress Press, 1977).

lighted in the New Testament: Jesus' post-crucifixion appearances to various people and his empty tomb. So the question whether Jesus' resurrection happened leads us to examine his appearances and the empty tomb. We shall begin with the appearances, for they are generally credited with being more important.

The best historical evidence we have for Jesus' post-crucifixion *appearances* is from Paul who refers three times in his letters to his own experience of meeting the risen Jesus (Galatians 1:11ff., 1 Corinthians 9:1, and 15:3ff.). His most ample statement is this:

> For I handed on to you as of first importance what I in turn had received: that Christ died for our sins in accordance with the scriptures, and that he was buried, and that he was raised on the third day in accordance with the scriptures, and that he appeared to Cephas, then to the twelve. Then he appeared to more than five hundred brothers and sisters at one time, most of whom are still alive, though some have died. Then he appeared to James, then to all the apostles. Last of all, as to one untimely born, he appeared also to me. (1 Corinthians 15:3-8)

This is a very significant statement historically, because it is the earliest testimony we have (about A.D. 55) and comes from Paul who speaks not only of the experiences of others but also of his own experience of meeting the risen Jesus. Paul's testimony consists mostly of traditions that are considerably older than his letter to the Corinthians, for he says he handed on to the Corinthians what he in turn had received. Although we are unable to date Paul's earlier movements precisely, his own comments in Galatians 1:18ff. tell us that he visited Peter and James the brother of Jesus, both pillars of the founding church in Jerusalem, probably within five years of Jesus' death. So Paul received his traditions about Jesus very close to the original events. Part of what Paul passes on are traditions about Jesus' appearances on different occasions to various individuals and groups. It seems obvious that one of Paul's motives in listing these appearances in detail is to establish the truth of the appearances, for he notes that most of a group of five hundred witnesses are still alive; presumably anyone in Paul's day who doubted could consult those firsthand witnesses.

What was the nature of Paul's experience of having the risen Jesus appear to him? Paul does not describe the experience in physical or psychological terms; that is, he does not relate what he saw and heard or what emotions he felt. But he does say enough to make it clear that he is confident this is not a creation of his own imagination. He believes he met the objective presence of Jesus, for he says Jesus appeared *to* him and in 1 Corinthians 9:1 says, "Have I not *seen* Jesus our Lord?" Paul also clearly distinguishes between this appearance of Jesus and other experiences of revelation that he had in subsequent years; however, he does not tell how he distinguishes them.

One might think we could easily fill out the picture from the New Testament book of Acts, which gives three versions of Paul's encounter with the risen Jesus on the road to Damascus (Acts 9, 22, and 26), but the historian points out that these are secondhand accounts written by Luke. Acts portrays the experience as a vision in which Paul sees a light and hears a voice that identifies itself as Jesus; his traveling companions do not see or hear all that Paul does. This is compatible with the basic idea of resurrection as a radical transformation into a different form of existence. Paul's own cryptic statements about the encounter are also consistent with this, but are not explicit enough to confirm it. So we are left mostly with Paul's firm conviction that Jesus appeared to him, a conviction that transformed Paul from an ardent opponent of the new Christian movement to one of its greatest leaders.

Three Gospels (Matthew, Luke, and John) give narratives of appearances of Jesus, which are far more detailed than what Paul gives. Matthew and Luke are commonly dated around A.D. 80 and John A.D. 90–100. While Acts presents Paul's experience as a vision, the Gospel appearance stories portray the risen Jesus in very physical terms as someone who ate and whom the disciples touched. However, the fact that Jesus is pictured as having the unusual ability to pass through walls and doors again suggests a dramatically different mode of existence. Many historians value these accounts less highly, for the accounts seem to reflect the concern of the Christian community several decades after Paul to defend belief in Jesus' resurrection against denials. Hence, historians tend to think that the Gospel appearance stories tell us something about the challenges the early church was facing in the latter part of the first century, but they are often skeptical of their accuracy as reports of Jesus' appearances.

The second kind of evidence in the New Testament for the resurrection of Jesus is the *empty tomb*. Historians generally value this less than the testimony about Jesus' appearances for two main reasons. One is that Paul in his statement above and elsewhere does not mention the empty tomb among the traditions he has passed on. The Gospel of Mark (about A.D. 70) is the earliest record we have about Jesus' tomb being found without his body, and the event is treated as well in the other three Gospels. The fact that Paul omits mention of the empty tomb does not mean it is a fiction, however. After all, in his letters Paul says virtually nothing about the life and ministry of Jesus on which the Gospels focus, but we do not conclude from that silence that the Gospel accounts of Jesus' activities are all inventions. Indeed, while the details of the several empty tomb accounts vary, the fact that all four versions involve women discovering the tomb to be empty argues for its historicity, since in Jewish society at that time women could not be legal witnesses. The point is that if the early church leaders fabricated stories about the empty tomb, they would not weaken their story by making the first witnesses female.

A weightier reason historians see less significance in these stories than in the appearances is that an empty tomb in itself would not establish that Jesus had been raised from the dead; his body could have been stolen. Why then do the Gospels bother to tell about the empty tomb? Probably because it would have been very difficult for the fledgling Christian movement to proclaim that Jesus had been raised from the dead if his dead body could be produced.

So when we examine from an historical perspective the testimonies about the post-death appearances of Jesus and his empty tomb, we find that a definitive answer about the historicity of Jesus' resurrection cannot be given. What we have are claims that after his death Jesus appeared at different times and places to quite a number of individuals and groups and that two days after his burial his tomb was found empty. The early Christians concluded from these factors that God had raised Jesus from the dead. The question is whether that is a well-founded conclusion.

The fundamental *historical* issue is this: How do we explain the sudden and dramatic transformation of Jesus' disciples from being disappointed and disillusioned by his death to being bold, courageous proclaimers of Jesus' resurrection? Neither the appearances of Jesus nor finding the empty tomb were publicly accessible occurrences; as reported, they involved selected individuals and groups, all of whom became followers of Jesus. But the crucifixion of Jesus and the disciple's proclamation of him as risen are both "facts," publicly accessible events that people of various religious convictions agree took place. The fundamental historical question is how to explain what happened *between* these two publicly accessible events to produce the remarkable change in the disciples.

It is important to remember that not all occurrences in history are publicly accessible. For example, after a final meeting with two advisers, the president of the United States nominates someone for a vacant position on the Supreme Court. The nomination is surely public. But why was this particular candidate chosen over other finalists? What motives and reasons came into play in this decision? That is not publicly available information. Just three persons participated in the final deliberation, and their accounts of the session might well differ, according to their own perspectives and the audience with whom they might later share their recollection. But one major task of a historian writing on this nomination would be to use all the available sources to reconstruct the controlling reasons for the decision. It would not be possible to absolutely prove any one view of why the nomination was made, but a credible account would reconstruct the available evidence in a coherent, plausible manner.[11]

---

11. Francis Schüssler Fiorenza, *Foundational Theology: Jesus and the Church* (New York: Crossroad, 1984), 32.

Similarly, the historical question about Jesus' resurrection should focus on the enormous change in the disciples. What caused this change in them? There are four explanations that roughly correspond to the four views on the historical Jesus and the Christ of faith.

1. Reimarus claimed that the striking alteration in the disciples' ideas and behavior was the fruit of their own creative and dishonest thinking; within a few hours of Jesus' demise, they hatched the greatest fraud of all time by deceitfully claiming Jesus had been raised. Obviously, this interpretation sees no positive meaning in the so-called resurrection of Jesus.

There are three major weaknesses in Reimarus's view and in other fraud theories. One flaw in Reimarus's argument is that it does not make sense psychologically. The evidence we have indicates that nearly all Jesus' disciples deserted him when he was arrested and all, even the most faithful, were deeply disheartened by his death. They were disheartened, precisely because they were not in the least anticipating Jesus' resurrection. So it is doubtful that such disillusioned followers would suddenly invent the story of their leader's resurrection. The unlikeliness of such an action is increased by a second weakness: what the Christians proclaimed was truly a new teaching, namely, that God had raised this one person from the dead as a promise of a future resurrection of all. While belief in a general resurrection of the dead was common in Jewish apocalyptic thought of Jesus' time, we have no previous examples of believing resurrection would happen to one special person in advance of all the others.[12] The third weakness is that several of the earliest disciples of Jesus suffered great hardships and ended their lives as martyrs for the faith, but it is highly unlikely that people would willingly lay down their life for what they knew to be a fraud.

2. Theological liberalism both in its nineteenth-century and contemporary representatives is fundamentally concerned with making the Christian message relevant to the culture of its time.[13] In his famous lectures of 1899–1900 Adolf von Harnack simply harmonizes the early church's belief in Jesus' resurrection with what Harnack regarded as one of the essentials of Christianity—belief in the eternal value of the human soul. Harnack distinguished between the *Easter message*, which speaks of the empty tomb and the appearances of Jesus, and the *Easter faith*, which simply says that God has given Jesus victory over death and will do so for others as well. In this way Harnack

---

12. Wolfhart Pannenberg, *Jesus—God and Man*, trans. L. L. Wilkins and D. A. Priebe (Philadelphia: Westminster, 1968), 96.

13. Adolf von Harnack, *What Is Christianity?* Fortress Texts in Modern Theology, trans. T. B. Saunders, Introduction by Rudolf Bultmann (1957; Philadelphia: Fortress Press, 1986), 160–64.

sought to free Christian faith from uncertainty about the ambiguities and inconsistencies in the biblical accounts of the tomb and the appearances. But what he affirmed was not really resurrection, but eternal life of the soul. Whereas the notion of resurrection sees humans as a body-spirit whole, Harnack thinks only of the soul. And whereas resurrection involves close links between the renewal of bodily human beings and a renewal of the whole cosmos, Harnack's belief in the eternal value of the soul cuts humans off from the material cosmos.

A thoughtful contemporary example of the liberal approach to theology is evident in the work of Sallie McFague. Her reading of the cultural situation in the late twentieth century is vastly different than Harnack's interpretation of the late nineteenth century, yet they share the same broad approach to theology. In theology's ongoing dialogue between the Christian tradition (past) and culture (present), McFague also gives first and primary place to contemporary culture. In a culture that is marked by concerns about ecology, nuclear weapons, and oppression of women and other disadvantaged groups, McFague believes a thorough reinterpretation of the Christian tradition is in order. This includes belief in Jesus' resurrection. She claims that the traditional Christian belief in resurrection teaches people to look for unity with God by escaping this physical world into some supposedly higher realm. McFague suggests, "But what if we were to understand the resurrection and ascension not as the bodily translation of some individuals to another world—a mythology no longer credible to us—but as the promise of God to be permanently present, 'bodily' present to us, in all places and times of our world?"[14] In other words, the resurrection of Jesus does not say anything about *Jesus*, but is only an affirmation about *God*. Jesus is dead, although his way of life remains as a possibility for later generations to follow. So the traditional understanding of the resurrection of Jesus is set aside. "Christ is risen" is reinterpreted as the promise of God's saving presence always in this world.

The greatest difficulty with McFague's understanding of the resurrection of Jesus, in my opinion, is that it is so strained, as though she is trying to squeeze some usable meaning out of something she no longer believes. There does not seem to be any reasonable route from "Christ is risen" to "God is always present in this world." It would seem far better to simply say what is implicit in this position: the disciples were mistaken in their claim that Jesus continues to live by virtue of being raised from the dead. They were sincere rather than deceitful, yet their interpretation can no longer be accepted as true. This is another example of how the liberal approach of accommodating Christian theology to contemporary culture often results in theology not having anything distinctively Christian to say to the culture.

14. McFague, *Models of God*, 60.

3. The existentialist interpretation of Easter is suggested by Rudolf Bultmann and more fully developed by Willi Marxsen. Marxsen says that the miracle of Easter is the birth of faith among the disciples. This same miracle occurs whenever the Christian message is proclaimed and someone comes to faith. So when considering the resurrection at Easter, Marxsen focuses attention on what happened to the *Christian community* rather than on anything that happened to *Jesus*. In brief, resurrection is a subjective event (a change in the thinking of the disciples), whereas the Christian tradition has thought of resurrection first of all as something objective (a change that happened to Jesus).

According to Marxsen, the meaning of the resurrection for today is also subjective; that is, it is a way of expressing the Christian believer's radical trust in God. In each moment of existence a person faces the choice whether to trust in human schemes or to trust in God. The possible way of life that Jesus and the Christian message declare is to live by trusting in God. So also when a person is confronted with death, to live by faith is to trust that one is safe in God. Marxsen says that resurrection is a certain idea or philosophical notion that Christians have shared with Jews and Muslims, but Christians today are not bound to that idea and surely should not place their trust in the notion. Indeed, Marxsen says it is impossible for modern thinking people to share that ancient idea. What Christians today may do is trust utterly in God without trying to conceptualize, with the idea of resurrection or any other theory, how God will overcome death.[15]

Certainly Marxsen is right that the most fundamental stance of the Christian toward death should be to trust completely in God. However, Marxsen and Bultmann are too ready to dismiss resurrection as an idea incompatible with a modern scientific understanding of the world. As we noted, an underlying assumption of Marxsen's existentialist view is that the resurrection of Jesus simply seems impossible. In fact, this is the most common reason why people reject or question belief in Jesus' resurrection; after all, our ordinary experience tells us that the dead do not return to speak with us. Here one's overall view of reality influences one's assessment of what can or cannot happen in history. No doubt, the apocalyptic worldview of the disciples was very influential in shaping their interpretation of what happened, for in their worldview, the God who had created all things could and would raise people from the dead. In the assessment of Jesus' resurrection today, then, our own worldview is very significant. In short, evaluating whether Jesus' resurrection occurred is not merely a matter of deciding about an isolated event

---

15. Willi Marxsen, *The Resurrection of Jesus of Nazareth*, trans. Margaret Kohl (Philadelphia: Fortress Press, 1970), 126–28; 181–88; see Rudolf Bultmann, *Theology of the New Testament*, Vol. I, trans. Kendrick Grobel (New York: Scribner's, 1951), 45–46.

nearly two thousand years ago; one's whole vision of reality and life is involved. Is it conceivable that the God who created the world would also radically transform it?

A large part of Marxsen's concern is to deny that Jesus' resurrection is a publicly accessible event, a fact that Christian believers and non-Christians alike could recognize. He is correct in this, for it is not accidental that all those in the New Testament who testify to Jesus' resurrection were or became his disciples. To recognize his resurrection is to affirm its profound meaning for oneself and the world. The shortcoming of Marxsen's view, I think, is that it limits the significance of Jesus' resurrection to the present life of the individual believer. To believe in Jesus' resurrection boils down to committing oneself to the way of life Jesus practiced in his own thirty years. There seems to be nothing about a hope for an ultimate, radical transformation of the individual and world into a new mode of existence in which God makes justice reign and overcomes death.[16]

Another difficulty with the existentialist view of Marxsen and Bultmann is that it does not give any explanation for the dramatic turnabout and rise of faith in the disciples. What prompted this radical change? Marxsen does not say. The disciples themselves claim that there were objective grounds for their alteration in thinking—Jesus had appeared to them and the tomb was found empty. From these experiences they concluded that Jesus had undergone the radical transformation of resurrection.

4. A fourth, moderate way of interpreting what happened at Easter is the claim that Jesus was alive again and appeared to various people; this objective reality was the occasion for the rise of faith among the disciples. Jesus was made alive again through the divine act of resurrection, and resurrection is radical transformation into a different mode of existence from what is standard in the current universe. Thus, in the happy phrase of Catholic theologian Hans Küng, Jesus' resurrection is not an historical event, nevertheless it is a real event.[17] That is, resurrection does not happen according to the standard rules of nature and history in this universe, yet it is a real happening, not just illusory or purely mental. Again, this is not just an assertion about an isolated event, but is part of a total vision of all reality as being recreated and set right by its creator. In the context of this view of God and reality, the resurrection of Jesus is coherent and reasonable. Thus, assessment of whether Jesus was raised from the dead is not merely a narrow, historical judgment like deciding whether George Washington made a certain trip to Philadel-

---

16. Ibid., 138–48.
17. Hans Küng, *Eternal Life?* trans. Edward Quinn (Garden City, N.Y.: Doubleday, 1984), 105.

phia. Weighing the historicity of Jesus' resurrection is very closely connected with one's own contemporary experience and understanding of God. For those in the early church and for many Christians today, the presence of God continues to bear the stamp of Jesus. Jesus is not dead and gone. He is not merely known through his teachings like Jeremiah or Socrates. For hosts of Christians today Jesus is a living presence, not as a ghost, but as the abiding human shape of God's presence. Thus the primary ground of belief in Jesus' resurrection for contemporary Christians is not the historical testimony of the original disciples but the Christian's experience of Jesus as a living presence. Nevertheless, belief in Jesus' resurrection is a plausible historical interpretation of what the first disciples experienced in the appearances of Jesus and the empty tomb.

The explanation offered by Paul and the other disciples makes sense: Jesus was raised from the dead and appeared to various people. This explanation cannot be proved beyond a doubt; other interpretations are still possible. Yet, given the available evidence from the Gospels and contemporary Christian experience of the living presence of Jesus, the resurrection of Jesus is a plausible historical explanation of what happened between the disappointment of his death and the intrepid public preaching of his disciples.

In our fourth, moderate view the resurrection of Jesus has enormous significance for the individual, the total community of life, and for the whole physical world. In this view, Jesus' resurrection is his real translation into a wholly new mode of existence by God. What is the meaning of this extraordinary event? A fuller discussion of this must await our consideration of the last things in the final chapter, but at this point I will call attention to two meanings of Jesus' resurrection.

1. *Jesus has been vindicated by God.* While Jesus' horrible death seems to indicate that he is a failure and not a special envoy of God, his resurrection shows that God approves of Jesus. Only God can raise from the dead, so when God raises this one person Jesus, it means that he is truly a unique representative of God. It is no wonder then that Mark and other New Testament authors refer to Jesus with exalted titles such as Messiah (Christ) and Son of God.

2. *What has happened to Jesus is God's promise of what lies ahead for all the world.* We are accustomed to hearing and making verbal promises, but an action can also function as a promise. It is standard practice in buying a house to put down some earnest money as part of the promise to purchase. So it is understandable that Paul speaks of the risen Jesus as the "first fruits of those who have died" (1 Corinthians 15:20). Because Jesus has been raised, others may look forward to being made alive after death and participating in the fulfilled reign of God in which death and injustice are overcome.

Jesus' Relation with God

Perhaps the most crucial theological question in reflecting on Jesus is to ask about his relation with God. There is a sense in which each creature has a unique relation with God as a particular creature in a particular place and time, so every creature shares this sort of uniqueness. However, most of the Christian tradition has claimed that Jesus is unique in the much stronger sense that God has acted decisively in Jesus; in this respect, Jesus' relation with God has usually been viewed by Christians as utterly singular and unparalleled. Nevertheless, Christian opinion past and present has included various degrees of diversity. It will help us think through the issue of Jesus' relation with God for ourselves if we divide our considerations into three parts: first, we will look at some New Testament views on the topic; second, we will examine the classical christological creeds; and third, we will ponder the modern debate about Jesus that continues today.

Three New Testament Views of Jesus

Since the New Testament comprises writings by a number of authors addressing different audiences, we find within it considerable diversity of outlook on Jesus; at the same time, there is substantial unity in their testimony to him. New Testament writers use a wide variety of expressions and titles for interpreting the significance of Jesus: Messiah (Christ), Lord, Son of God, Savior, Son of Man, Word, and more. We can catch the flavor of the diversity and unity in their witness by noting what three New Testament authors mean by calling Jesus the Son of God.

In the *Gospel of Mark*, Son of God is the central designation for Jesus. The opening words of the Gospel are, "The beginning of the good news of Jesus Christ, the Son of God" (Mark 1:1). When Jesus is baptized by John the Baptist, Mark says Jesus has a vision in which a voice from heaven says, "You are my Son, the Beloved; with you I am well pleased" (1:11). This term must be understood against its background in the Old Testament, in which three meanings of Son of God stand out. One was that the Israelite king was called God's Son as a way of expressing the close bond between the two, both in the sense that God appoints this person and that the person is loyal to God (Psalm 2:6-7). When hope arose in Israel for the Messiah as an ideal king like David, it was natural to speak of the Messiah also as the Son of God. Mark believes that Jesus is the Messiah, but he takes pains to point out that Jesus' kingship is not the usual political role. Completely contrary to customary messianic expectations, Jesus suffers and dies.

A second major meaning of Son of God in Jewish tradition was to designate a righteous man who is a perfectly obedient servant of God. Psalm 22 is one of several psalms in which a righteous person is wrongfully harassed, cries out to God, and is finally vindicated. Mark tells us that shortly before dying Jesus quoted the opening words of this psalm, "My God, my God, why have you forsaken me?" (15:34). A Roman officer gathers up both these first and second strands of meaning in his declaration as Jesus breathes his last: "Truly this man was God's Son!" (15:39).

The third meaning of Son of God is given more indirect expression by Mark: the Son of God is a special envoy sent by God. This is suggested by a parable in which the owner of a vineyard leases it to tenants who later refuse to pay their rent and beat up several slaves the owner sends to collect the rent; when the owner finally sends his son, the wicked tenants kill the son (12:1-12). At the end of his Gospel, Mark's brief testimony to Jesus' resurrection shows that he has been approved as God's special envoy.[18]

Did Jesus think of himself as Son of God? New Testament scholars differ on this question, but there are two strong indications in Mark's Gospel that Jesus did think of himself as Son in the senses we have identified. One indication is that Jesus' practice of addressing God as Abba, Father (Mark 14:36), implies that he thinks of himself as a son. Another indication is that Jesus' parable of the wicked tenants, just cited in the previous paragraph, suggests that the owner of the vineyard has a son.

We should notice both what Mark does and does not say about Jesus by calling him Son of God. On the one hand, Mark clearly affirms that Jesus has a very special relation with God, for God has chosen him to proclaim the reign of God in word and deed. Moreover, in raising Jesus from the dead, God has clearly set him aside from all other humans. On the other hand, Mark does not explicitly reflect on Jesus' relation to God prior to his lifetime; the question simply is not raised.

This brings us to our second New Testament view of Jesus—the view held by *Paul*. Although the letters of Paul are commonly dated around A.D. 50–55 and the Gospel of Mark around A.D. 70, Paul probes the mystery of Jesus' relation to God more deeply than does that later Gospel writer. Paul agrees with Mark that the resurrection declares or makes clear that Jesus is God's special representative (Romans 1:3-4), but Paul adds reflections on the status of this Son of God after his resurrection as well as before his life on earth.

While the Gospel of Mark indicates that the disciples will meet the risen Jesus again in the near future, the Gospel up to its original ending at 16:8 gives no other thoughts about the Risen One. Paul sets forth a fuller vision of the future: Christ will return, others will be raised from the dead and conformed to him, Christ will overcome all evil powers—the last of which is

18. This interpretation of Son of God in Mark and those that follow on Paul and John are drawn mostly from Marinus de Jonge, *Christology in Context*, 59–63, 114–15, 144–47, 167–69.

death—and "then the Son himself will also be subjected to the one who put all things in subjection under him, so that God may be all in all" (1 Corinthians 15:28; cf. Romans 8:29). In this vision Jesus Christ the Son of God is the pattern of true humanity and reigns over all creation, yet is himself subordinate to God.

Paul also makes some suggestive remarks about the Son of God *before* Jesus was born on earth. When he speaks of God "sending his own Son in the likeness of sinful flesh," the implication is that the Son has a previous existence without the likeness of sinful flesh (Romans 8:3, cf. Galatians 4:4). A similar thing is implied also in these words from Paul: "Let the same mind be in you that was in Christ Jesus, who, though he was in the form of God, did not regard equality with God as something to be exploited, but emptied himself, taking the form of a slave, being born in human likeness" (Philippians 2:5-7). Here Paul hints at a preceding divine existence of Christ Jesus. And since scholars generally agree that in this Philippians passage Paul is quoting an existing Christian hymn of praise familiar to his audience, the idea of a prior existence of Jesus Christ the Son of God probably goes back to the very first years after Jesus' death and resurrection.

Again, it is important not to read too much into Paul's suggestive statements. While Paul certainly sees Jesus Christ the Son of God ultimately having authority over all things in the creation, the Son is clearly subordinate to God. And while Paul implies some sort of existence of the Son prior to being on earth, he does not offer any ideas on how the Son is related to God.[19]

Our third New Testament view of Jesus is given in the *Gospel of John* which scholars commonly date A.D. 90–100. All three themes we identified in Mark's understanding of Son of God are present in John. John gives memorable expression to the idea that God sends the Son, "For God so loved the world that he gave his only Son" (John 3:16). John also emphasizes that the Son is obedient and subordinate to the Father (10:37). The theme that John develops the most, however, is the close relation that the Son of God has with the Father. John underscores the intimate relation between Son and Father: "The Father and I are one" (10:30). In connection with this stress on their unity, John goes further than Paul in reflecting on the relation between God and the Son of God prior to Jesus' earthly existence. In a prayer John has Jesus speaking of "my glory, which you have given me because you loved me before the foundation of the world" (17:24). And John begins the Gospel with these lofty words that use the metaphor of Word, "In the beginning was the Word, and the Word was with God, and the Word was God. He was in the

---

19. A more developed understanding of the Son appears in Colossians 1:15-20, but the authorship of this letter is debated. Many think it was not written by Paul himself, but by someone strongly influenced by Paul.

beginning with God. All things came into being through him, and without him not one thing came into being" (1:1-3). Here John says that the Word, like Wisdom in the Old Testament book of Proverbs, is the mediator through whom creation of the world takes place. But John proceeds to say that the Word *was* God. John goes on to link this Word with Jesus and the metaphor of Son, "And the Word became flesh and lived among us, and we have seen his glory, the glory as of a father's only son, full of grace and truth" (1:14). This exalted estimation of Jesus is reaffirmed very near the end of the Gospel when the doubting disciple Thomas meets the risen Jesus and confesses, "My Lord and my God" (2:28).

Thus there is both unity and diversity in the views of Jesus' relation to God held by Mark, Paul, and John. They all agree that Jesus is a special emissary of God as evidenced above all by his resurrection. They differ in the extent to which they reflect on the relation between this Son of God and God prior to and subsequent to Jesus' life on earth. While the very early Christian hymn quoted by Paul in Philippians 2:7 suggests some sort of divine status prior to life on earth and Mark hints at a previous existence of the Son who is sent, by the end of the first century John explicitly affirms that "the Word was God." Yet the three are of one mind that the Son of God is in some sense subordinate to God.

While these three New Testament authors in various degrees reflect on Jesus' relation with God, they leave two big questions unanswered. First, since the Son of God has an ambiguous status as divine yet subordinate to God, can we say more precisely what the relation is between the Son of God and God? Second, what is the relation between the preexistent Son or Word and the Jesus who lived about thirty years in Palestine? These were the two questions that dominated Christian theological discussion during the fourth and fifth centuries, and it is to that discussion we turn next.

The Classical Christological Creeds

Reflection on Jesus' relation to God during the fourth and fifth centuries went through two main stages.[20] In chapter 2 on the doctrine of God, we already considered the first stage, which resulted in formal approval of the Nicene Creed and the doctrine of the Trinity at church councils in 325 and 381. These deliberations really focused on the relation of the preexistent Son of God to God. Arius had ignited the debate with his proposal that the preex-

---

20. Excellent treatments of the third- and fourth-century trinitarian and christological debates are given by these two outstanding scholars of early Christianity: J. N. D. Kelly, *Early Christian Doctrines*, Second Edition (New York: Harper, 1960); and Jaroslav Pelikan, *The Christian Tradition*, Vol. 1, *The Emergence of the Catholic Tradition* (100–600), (Chicago: University of Chicago Press, 1971).

istent Son of God is the highest creature that mediates between God and other creatures; in effect, Arius said the Son of God is a sort of demigod. The final overwhelming response to this proposal was to affirm the Nicene teaching that the Son of God is of one being (*homoousios*) with the Father. Thus Nicea sided with the affirmation of the Gospel of John that "the Word was God," but expressed this in the language of Greek philosophy. While John, Paul, and Mark expressed their faith in the suggestive, fluid language of metaphor and story, the Nicene Creed also uses abstract concepts such as *ousia* and *hypostasis*, being and individuation. The great trinitarian theologians of the fourth century affirmed that Father, Son, and Holy Spirit are one in being, yet also acknowledged that the Father is the fountainhead from whom the Son is "begotten" and the Spirit "proceeds."[21]

Agreement on the doctrine of the Trinity and its teaching of the full divinity of Jesus Christ quickly brought another issue to center stage: What is the relation between the divine Son of God and the human in Jesus? Thus began the second great stage of classical thinking on Jesus' relation with God. Two schools of thought dominated most of the discussion. The line of thinking associated with Alexandria in Egypt emphasized a very close union of the divine and human in Jesus Christ. Their favorite Scripture verse was John 1:14, "And the Word became flesh." They stressed that it is really the eternal Word or Son of God who was born to Mary, taught about God's kingdom, died on the cross, and was raised. Their primary concern was religious, not speculative, for they were convinced that only *God* can bring about salvation. Hence, they accent the presence of the divine Son in Jesus. The danger of this position was that it could so accentuate the divinity of Jesus Christ that his full humanity with all its capacities and limitations gets covered up. This danger has been called *docetism* (Greek *dokein* means "to seem") after an earlier trend among some groups of Christians to say that Jesus only seemed to have a human body and only seemed to suffer.

The second great school of christological thought was associated with the city of Antioch in Syria. The main emphasis of the Antioch theologians was on the genuine human development of Jesus, so they underscored the distinction between the humanity and divinity in Jesus Christ. The primary motivation of the Antioch theologians was also religious rather than speculative. Their religious concern was that we humans can only be helped by a Savior who, through his own genuine moral development, brings into existence a new sinless person. So they underline the distinction between the divinity and humanity in Jesus, in order to make room, so to speak, for the humanity to develop. The danger of this position was that it could portray Jesus Christ as two beings in close cooperation, like a very good man being adopted by God.

21. Kelly, *Early Christian Doctrines*, 265.

Supporters of these two schools of christological thinking argued back and forth for several decades until a third, compromise view was promoted by Pope Leo I. Whereas the Alexandrian and Antiochene theologians were steeped in the Greek culture of the eastern Mediterranean, Leo represented the dominant christological outlook in the Latin culture of the western Mediterranean. Leo's compromise took as its central biblical text Philippians 2:6-11, which speaks of Jesus Christ having equality with God, emptying himself and taking human form, and then being exalted as Lord over all things. At the Council of Chalcedon in 451 some key expressions from a document by Leo were put together with phrases from several other writings to produce a formula that the council approved. This is the Definition of Chalcedon:

> In agreement, therefore, with the holy fathers, we all unanimously teach that we should confess that our Lord Jesus Christ is one and the same Son, the same perfect in Godhead and the same perfect in [humanity], truly God and truly [human], the same of a rational soul and body, consubstantial [*homoousion*] with the Father in Godhead, and the same consubstantial [*homoousion*] with us in [humanity], like us in all things except sin; begotten from the Father before the ages as regards His Godhead, and in the last days, the same, because of us and because of our salvation begotten from the Virgin Mary, the Mother of God [*Theotokos*], as regards His [humanity]; one and the same Christ, Son, Lord, only begotten, made known in two natures [*physis*] without confusion, without change, without division, without separation, the difference of the natures being by no means removed because of the union, but the property of each nature being preserved and coalescing in one *prosopon* (person) and one *hypostasis*—not parted or divided into two *prosopa*, but one and the same Son, only-begotten, divine Word, the Lord Jesus Christ, as the prophets of old and Jesus Christ Himself have taught us about Him and the creed of our fathers has handed down.[22]

The Chalcedonian Definition endorsed the main concern of each of the two competing theologies. It affirms the Antioch concern that the divine and human in Jesus Christ remain distinct, "without confusion, without change." The Definition also approves the Alexandrian interest in the unity of Jesus Christ, "without division, without separation" and "coalescing in one *prosopon* (person) and one *hypostasis*." It was a compromise that affirmed the essential common ground, and did not attempt to settle some of the most probing questions with which the Eastern theologians had wrestled. Like the Nicene Creed the Chalcedonian Definition used Greek philosophical language to express the convictions of the church fathers; in this case, the central concepts were nature (*physis*), and two concepts of individuation, *prosopon* and *hypostasis*. The Chalcedonian Definition was accepted by most Christian theologians

---

22. Ibid., 339–40. I have changed manhood to humanity and man to human.

and churches until the eighteenth-century Enlightenment questioned it as well as the Nicene Creed.

The Modern Debate on Christology

Criticism of Chalcedon and, to a lesser extent, Nicea, have abounded since the Enlightenment. The fundamental issue has been Jesus' relation with God, but one's view on this issue generally is related to one's position on our two earlier issues—how the Jesus of history is connected with the Christ of faith and how one understands the resurrection of Jesus. In other words, one's view of Jesus tends to form a fairly coherent whole in which all three major issues of this chapter play a part. Thus focusing on Jesus' relation with God will help us bring together our overall reflections on who Jesus is. To help clarify our thinking about Jesus' relation with God we will again examine our four broad theological positions.

1. *Reimarus* says that Jesus was related to God as a prophet, but he is not worthy of being uniquely esteemed. In general on this view, Jesus is credited with being a prophetic figure who had some wise teachings about God, yet he is only one of a great number of inspirational persons. In particular, Reimarus gives some honor to Jesus, but he also thought Jesus mistakenly believed himself to be the Messiah who would bring political liberation to Israel. With such an outlook, Reimarus did not seek to follow Jesus. Our other three broad positions are all held by those who seek to stand within the Christian faith.

2. *Liberal theologians* generally see the life and death of Jesus as the central model for Christians, but regard Jesus as one of a number of people in history especially close to God. Such a view is often called a *low Christology*, because it does not follow the classical Christian practice of setting Jesus apart from all others. There are various forms of low Christology, but a major contemporary theologian who gives clear articulation to such an assessment of Jesus is Sallie McFague.

> Jesus' response as beloved to God as lover was so open and thorough that his life and death were revelatory of God's great love for the world. His illumination of that love as inclusive of the last and the least, as embracing and valuing the outcast, is paradigmatic of God the lover but is not unique. This means that Jesus is not ontologically different from other paradigmatic figures either in our tradition or in other religious traditions who manifest in word and deed the love of God for the world. He is special to us as our foundational figure: he is our historical choice as the premier paradigm of God's love.[23]

23. McFague, *Models of God*, 136.

Sallie McFague does not merely think the ancient terminology of Nicea and Chalcedon no longer communicates well; she rejects the very substance of those classical Christian credal statements. In addition, she rejects belief in the preexistence of Jesus Christ, which is clearly held by several New Testament authors, and discards belief in the post-existence (after his lifetime on earth) of the risen Jesus, which is shared by all major New Testament writers. Hence, McFague's low Christology is a major departure from these foundational sources in the Christian tradition. On the other hand, McFague avoids some of the conflict that the classical Christian tradition has with contemporary Western culture. Above all, her stance toward the religions of the world fits with the relativism so strong in our culture.

Whether one judges McFague's rendering of the Christian tradition to be good or bad depends on one's fundamental understanding of the Christian faith. What I will do is offer an evaluation coming from my own understanding. My essential reservation about McFague's view of Jesus is that it does not do justice to this element so basic to the Christian story: "For God so loved the world that he gave his only Son, so that everyone who believes in him may not perish but may have eternal life" (John 3:16). The story tells of God taking the initiative in the work of salvation. Taking the initiative was not new for God, since the Old Testament pictures God in this way as well. But the core of the Christian story is that God's urgent love found its utmost expression in giving the "only Son." The story of this giving of God's own self even to the depths of suffering and death is what has won the hearts of millions and given life to the church over the centuries. But McFague cuts out this heart of the Christian story, for there is no "only Son" and the divine initiative of giving is strongly dampened. She retains other elements of the Jesus story—his compassion for the needy, his reaching out to the excluded. But the central element of the story is removed from her theology.

Another major element in the Christian story that McFague cuts out is the resurrection of Jesus. This affects her eschatology, her hope for the future of human beings and the world. Since she reinterprets resurrection as God's promise to be always present in *this* world, her hope for the future is limited to healing the fractures that exist in this world. There does not appear to be any hope for a life beyond death. Again, this is major surgery on the Christian message.

When we compare McFague's Christology with the New Testament, we can say that her low Christology only affirms part of what the New Testament means by calling Jesus the Son of God. An Israelite who was obedient to God might be designated Son of God; such a person would serve both as a representative of God and as a model human being. In this sense, there were a number of persons called Son of God.

3. An *existentialist Christology* confesses that Jesus is God's Word *for me*, but refuses to make objective statements about Jesus. As the foremost existentialist theologian of the twentieth century, Rudolf Bultmann was always concerned to articulate the meaning of Jesus *for the Christian believer*. That is, a religious or theological statement about Jesus is always an expression of faith, and hence says something about the committed relationship between Jesus and the believer. So to confess that Jesus is the Word of God is to say that Jesus is a revelation of God *for me*. Others can only truly confess Jesus to be the Word of God when they too have that faith relationship with him. It is a mistake, said Bultmann, to regard such a statement as an objective truth that Christian and non-Christian should agree upon. Bultmann recognized that there are objective truths, such as the fact that the earth is a part of the solar system, but such truths are not of any special significance for a person's faith. So it was that Bultmann did not show much interest in the Jesus discoverable by objective historical research. So also when it came to the resurrection of Jesus, Willi Marxsen and Bultmann focused on the rise of faith in the disciples rather than on anything that one might find objectively about Jesus.

An existentialist Christology tends to be critical of the Creed of Nicea and the Chalcedonian definition, because they make such extensive use of philosophical language that appears to be objective. Yet it is difficult to classify an existentialist Christology as low or high, since it refuses to make the sort of objective statements about Jesus that both low and high Christologies commonly make.

Existentialist Christology is important for at least two reasons. One is that Rudolf Bultmann has had enormous influence on theology and especially on New Testament scholars, and it is difficult to understand what many of these scholars say about Jesus without a grasp of their underlying approach. The other, more substantial reason for the importance of existentialist Christology is its reminder that our thinking about Jesus always reflects the character of our own relationship with him.

Nevertheless, I do not think that an existentialist Christology by itself is satisfactory, for persons of faith should continually seek to connect their faith with how we generally apprehend reality. In the comic strip "Peanuts," Linus has an existential relationship with the Great Pumpkin, but he understandably has no success in bringing others to share his faith in something so unconnected to the publicly accepted view of reality.

4. A *high Christology* views Jesus as the one in whom God is decisively present; Jesus is the unique Son of God, the highest Wisdom, and ultimate Word of God. There are diverse forms of theology with a high estimate of Jesus; I

will use just two types as examples: a Latin American liberation theology and my own form of narrative theology.[24]

Jon Sobrino, the Jesuit theologian from El Salvador, gives a good illustration of a liberation Christology. In the typical way of Latin American liberation theology, he begins with the historical Jesus in the sense that he dwells on the concrete life of Jesus, but this is done in a way that sets Sobrino off from the Christology of Protestant liberals such as Harnack. The distinctive emphasis is on Jesus' special concern for the poor and marginal, a concern that brought him into conflict with the powers of his society and eventually caused his death. Unlike McFague, Sobrino affirms the resurrection as an event that happened to Jesus, for God raised Jesus from the dead and confirmed the truth of his life.

Sobrino agrees with existentialist Christology that Jesus is known as the Christ only in the relationship of faith in him. One factor that distinguishes liberation theology from existentialism is the liberationist's emphasis on coming to know and believe in Jesus through involvement with the poor and oppressed. The parable in which Christ is present in those who hunger and thirst (Matthew 25:31-46) is central.

Sobrino takes a high view of Jesus' relation with God.

> Any theology must hold that Jesus is God. Liberation christology emphasizes that we only know what God is from a point of departure in Jesus. This, I maintain, is the kernel of our Christian faith, which is at once the Good News and a scandal.

This is a scandal, says Sobrino, for it seems foolish to humans who think they already know what it means to be a human being and to be God. What Jesus does is to redefine both true humanity and true divinity.

> But it is especially a scandal, and remains so even for believers, when [in the life of Jesus] the true human being is revealed as poor, at the service of others, crushed, and crucified, and therefore and thereby exalted, when the true God is revealed as partial to the poor and oppressed, as liberator through love and as the one who hands over a Son. . . . The unification of scandal and good news is a scandal for natural reason. But it is the substance of Christian faith.[25]

In my own understanding of Jesus' relation with God, I also have a high Christology. I think the essential thing for Christology and indeed for all of

---

24. Most of the great theologians of the middle decades of the twentieth century had a high Christology: Karl Barth and Paul Tillich among Protestants, Karl Rahner and Teilhard de Chardin among Roman Catholics. Among contemporary theologians with a high Christology are the major Latin American liberation theologians, feminist theologian Anne Carr, eschatological theologians Jürgen Moltmann and Wolfhart Pannenberg, and narrative theologian Stephen Sykes.

25. Jon Sobrino, *Jesus in Latin America* (Maryknoll, N.Y.: Orbis, 1987), 9.

Christian theology is the main point made by Sobrino in the previous paragraph: the life, death, and resurrection of Jesus are the key to understanding
who God is and what we humans are intended to be. It is not that God is
understood only from Jesus, for God is present and active throughout the
creation and in many religious traditions. But for a Christian all the various
conceptions of God or ultimate reality are not on the same level. Neither is
God seen as the common denominator of all the religious and philosophical
ideas of ultimate reality, which could only be an extremely vague shadow.
While not thinking to grasp all of God's reality, the Christian message does
claim to truly apprehend the contours of God's being as mysterious love. The
central way in which this mysterious love is known is the biblical story, above
all, the story of Jesus' life, death, and resurrection.

The theologians who fashioned the creed of Nicea and the Chalcedonian
definition deserve both praise and criticism for the way in which they witness
to God's love in the biblical story. Nicea does well to make clear that God,
rather than a creature, is the author of the new life given through faith in
Jesus. Chalcedon deserves respect for affirming that both the divine and
human are fully present in Jesus Christ. But it is widely recognized that
underlying both Nicea and Chalcedon are some assumptions that are incompatible with the biblical story about God. The main assumptions are that
God cannot change (immutability) and cannot suffer (impassibility). Now it is
true that in the biblical outlook God cannot fundamentally change in character; thus God's faithfulness and steadfast love can be counted upon. But such
faithfulness includes the ability to respond flexibly to new circumstances, and
is quite different than the Greek philosophical notion that whatever changes
in any way is inferior to what is completely unchanging. McFague and many
other theologians are absolutely correct that a vision of God as immutable
results in a deity that is uninvolved with the world. It follows from the same
Greek assumption that God cannot suffer, for suffering entails change, weakness, and vulnerability. Now it is clear that the idea that God cannot change
and suffer is incompatible with the biblical story and especially with the story
of Jesus, for what gives the story of Jesus such power is the conviction that
"God so loved the world that he gave his only Son." That divine loving and
giving which lead to the cross involve the deepest compassion, anguish, and
self-sacrifice.

When Nicea's doctrine of the Trinity is freed from the constraints of
Greek philosophy, however, it is found to be fully consistent with the biblical
story. As I said in chapter 5 in connection with the question of why God creates the world, we can discern a pattern in God's activity: a going out into
what is other, in order to bring about a higher unity and well-being of that
other with God. In the doctrine of creation we were interested chiefly in
God's going out into the physical universe, in order to eventually draw that
evolving universe into a more complex unity. Here, when we are focusing on

Jesus' relation with God, we highlight God's going out into the depths of alienation in human life, in order to bring about reconciliation of humans with God, one another, and with nature. In both cases, though, it is the same trinitarian pattern of the ultimate source going out of itself in order to produce a richer unity. The doctrine of the Trinity—so understood—is eminently supportive and expressive of the story of God giving her only Son.[26]

Two further important issues about a high Christology must still be addressed. One is whether a high view of Jesus Christ is compatible with a feminist consciousness. The main difficulty here is that the classical symbolism of a high Christology is predominantly male. This is obvious when it is said that God the Father sends his Son. Feminist scholars also point out that in John's Gospel and the later theological tradition the image of the Word (masculine in Greek) crowds out the image of God's Wisdom (feminine). So the question is whether the heavily male symbolism of a traditional high Christology functions to reinforce a sexist view of God and Jesus and to strengthen a patriarchal ordering of the church. That is the judgment of one of the most influential feminist theologians, Rosemary Radford Ruether, who rejects a high Christology and emphasizes how Father, Son, and Word have been used to support patriarchy.[27] On the other hand, I think feminism and a high Christology are not irreconcilable. The respected feminist theologian Anne Carr admits that for this or that person, the language of Son of God may be so heavily laden with negative connotations as to be ineffective. Yet Carr argues that the terminology is generally usable as long as Son of God is set within the context of Jesus' life story, for then it is clear that this Son of God serves rather than dominates.[28] Of course, this is precisely how the terms *Son* and *Word* function in the New Testament and how they ought to be used today. An additional sound way to make a high Christology compatible with feminist concerns is to speak of Jesus as the Wisdom of God as well as the Word and Son. This has precedents in Scripture and Christian tradition, but it needs to be emphasized more today.[29]

The second issue that needs to be clarified is the status of this Wisdom or Son prior to the conception and birth of Jesus. Some of the biblical authors and a number of later theologians hold to some sort of preexistence of Jesus

---

26. For a similar interpretation of the Trinity and incarnation that gives credit to the philosopher G. W. F. Hegel for discerning this pattern, see Carl E. Braaten, "The Person of Jesus Christ," in *Christian Dogmatics*, Vol. 1, ed. Carl E. Braaten and Robert W. Jenson (Philadelphia: Fortress Press, 1984), 540–42.

27. Rosemary Radford Ruether, *Sexism and God-Talk: Toward a Feminist Theology* (Boston: Beacon, 1983), 116–38.

28. Anne E. Carr, *Transforming Grace: Christian Tradition and Women's Experience* (San Francisco: Harper & Row, 1988), 177.

29. A fine example of interpreting Jesus as the Wisdom of God is given by Elizabeth A. Johnson, "Redeeming the Name of Christ," in *Freeing Theology*, Catherine Mowry LaCugna, ed. (San Francisco: HarperSanFrancisco, 1993), 120–31.

Christ. For instance, many but not all interpreters see Christ's preexistence in this passage from Paul, "Let the same mind be in you that was in Christ Jesus, who, though he was in the form of God, did not regard equality with God as something to be exploited, but emptied himself" (Philippians 2:5-7). We must ask, In what sense may Jesus Christ be said to exist prior to his beginning in Mary? The Gospel of John says, "In the beginning was the Word, and the Word was with God, and the Word was God" (1:1). This leads us to think of the divine Word or Wisdom existing from all eternity. But I do not think it makes any sense to think of the human person Jesus literally and physically existing from the very beginning of the world. That would nullify his genuine humanity, for he was that human being who lived his particular life in first-century Palestine; that sequence of life events is rooted in a specific time and space. To think of him literally preexisting conjures up weird images of a cloaked Jesus floating about in empty space as the newborn universe expands. We can take a clue from a New Testament sermon by Peter, which speaks of Jesus as a man handed over to death "according to the definite plan and foreknowledge of God" (Acts 2:23). This suggests that Jesus preexists as part of the intention or purpose of God.

An implication of this view is that the incarnation of the Word in Jesus is not a divine afterthought, not an alternate plan conceived by God after sin enters a perfect world. Instead, the incarnation in Jesus is part of God's intention for the universe from the very beginning. A further implication is that this allows us to see the incarnation in Jesus as integral with the total divine act of "going out in order to bring about a greater unity." The divine activities of creation, providence, and redemption are all incarnational in the sense that God is always going out into the other for the purpose of producing a richer unity. Thus the incredibly long and complex history of the universe and the evolution of life can be integrated with God's going out into humanity.[30] And an understanding of the immanent trinity suggests that all of this divine activity in and with the world has its ground in the inner life of God who is Source who goes out of (expresses) herself in the Wisdom/Son and lives in the unity of the Spirit.

Admittedly, some of these ideas are suggestive and speculative, not the inner heart of Christian faith. Yet these ideas are prompted by the simple story of God so loving the world that he gave his only Son. And it is that very story which calls for a high view of Jesus' relation with God. A high Christology agrees with the prologue to the Gospel of John that God is uniquely present in Jesus, for the fully divine Word and Wisdom is present in the human person.

There has never been just one view of Jesus. Not only have there been those who, for diverse reasons, do not believe in Jesus, but also within the

30. A similar understanding of Christ's preexistence is given by John Macquarrie, *Jesus Christ in Modern Thought* (Philadelphia: Trinity Press International, 1990), 388–92.

Christian community there have always been a variety of interpretations of him. We see considerable diversity already in the New Testament, for there is a range of meanings when New Testament authors call Jesus Son of God. But this does not imply that every interpretation is equal in its power to grasp and communicate the reality of Jesus. For example, I think an existentialist Christology is basically limited to certain intellectual circles, for only certain intellectuals can understand both what is being said and what is not being said in the existentialist approach. What have broader appeal are various forms of low and high Christology. A low Christology apprehends some dimensions of Jesus Christ and part of what New Testament authors mean by calling him Son or Wisdom of God. Since this may express what some persons can in good conscience affirm about Jesus at this point in their life, such a confession should be respected in the Christian community. Nevertheless, a low christological outlook that may be legitimate for this or that individual or small group may not be healthy if it were to become the dominant view in the larger Christian community.

What I have in mind may be illustrated by the Unitarian Universalist Association, which traces its roots back to the sixteenth-century reformation when Unitarians rejected the doctrine of the Trinity and, of course, the divinity of Jesus Christ. For most of their history, these Unitarians with a low estimate of Jesus generally considered themselves Christians, but by 1966 only 43 percent of its members regarded themselves as Christians and by 1976 this dropped to merely 26 percent. Now the most astonishing fact reported about the Unitarian Universalist Association was that in 1979 nine out of ten of its members had not grown up in the Association but "converted" from other bodies, mostly liberal Protestant churches. This would have testified to an amazing vitality of the association, except for the fact that the overall body was declining in membership. So, as a sympathetic interpreter put it, "It is clear that UUA churches are in some sense 'revolving doors.'"[31] Of course, many Christian denominations have suffered loss of membership since the mid-1960s, yet this striking development within Unitarianism suggests that when a low Christology becomes the prevailing opinion within a church, the body gradually loses its Christian identity and perhaps even its capacity to hold members.

My point here is that some form of high Christology is crucial to the long-term vitality of the Christian church, for without a high estimate of Jesus, Christianity tends to merge with the surrounding culture. While the diversity in the New Testament suggests that the Christian community can exist with considerable variety of interpretations of Jesus, forms of high Christology play a crucial role in maintaining a strong Christian faith.

31. Robert B. Tapp, "The Unitarian Universalists: Style and Substance," *The Christian Century* 96 (March 14, 1979): 274.

7

Christ's Work of Reconciliation

Now we turn our attention directly to the work of Jesus Christ. This work is often described as *redemption*, coming from the act of redeeming or setting a slave free. Christ's overall work is also described as *reconciliation*, reuniting those who have been alienated. A term with a similar meaning in English is *atonement*, from at-one-ment. Although all of these terms are broadly interchangeable, I have chosen reconciliation as the main term since it is more immediately understood today.

In the previous chapter, while considering who Jesus is, we already were involved in questions about his work. We could not even begin to say who Jesus is without having some understanding of what he said and did while on earth, so probing matters about the historical Jesus touched on what he achieved. Reflecting on the resurrection of Jesus plunged us further into the issue, for whether one believes Jesus was raised from the dead has enormous impact on what one thinks Jesus has accomplished. And what one thinks about Jesus' relation with God, whether one has a low or high Christology, greatly affects what one thinks Jesus has done and will do. Thus the person and work of Jesus are closely related. Nevertheless, we must probe further into the work of Jesus, for it is one thing to say that in his lifetime Jesus identified with the poor, it is another thing to say what that does for other people. Similarly, even if one believes Jesus was raised from the dead, one must go on to ask what that means for other creatures.

Christians have always employed a variety of metaphors to express what they believe Jesus Christ has accomplished in reconciling the world. Whereas the church formulated standards of orthodox teaching regarding the person of Jesus Christ in the Nicene Creed and Chalcedonian Definition, the church has never settled on one orthodox teaching about the work of Christ. It appears that Christian belief about Christ's work is so rich that multiple images are required to articulate various aspects of it. This was the case already in the New Testament, and it has remained so until today. Nonetheless, certain metaphors have had great durability, so we will organize our reflections on the work of Jesus Christ by considering four chief metaphors: sacrifice, victory, doing justice, and revealing love. We shall take up each image in turn by tracing its use in the New Testament and in some portion of later church tradition and then interpreting its significance for today.

Sacrifice

Because making sacrifices was a common religious custom among the Hebrew- as well as the Greek- and Latin-speaking peoples of the Ancient Near East, it was natural for early Christians to draw upon the practices and language of sacrifice to express what Jesus had done. Some grasp of two types of Hebrew sacrifices is helpful for understanding what New Testament writers say about Jesus' sacrifice.[1] One type was a sacrifice for unintentional sin; this sort of sacrifice offered by individuals was variously called a *sin offering* or *guilt offering* or *whole burnt offering*. Ordinarily this involved the killing of an animal. A special sacrifice for the sins of the nation was made once a year on the Day of Atonement when the blood of a bull was offered for the sins of the priests and the blood of a goat for the sins of the people.

The basic idea for these sacrifices for sin seems to have been that sin was a stain on the fabric of Israel's life and a sacrifice would remove that stain. But there is no consistent answer in the Old Testament as to why a sacrifice should be able to remove that stain. Occasionally it is said that blood of an animal makes atonement since life is in the blood (Leviticus 17:11), but this explanation is not consistently repeated in the Old Testament and, in any case, the poor could substitute an offering of flour for the blood of an animal. In the Old Testament there is no idea of God being bought off or divine anger being appeased by a sin sacrifice. So the sacrifices are not to be ways in which humans strike a bargain with God. Rather, the entire sacrificial system itself seems to be a provision of God's mercy; that is, God generously provides the sacrifices as a way for the Hebrews to be reconciled with God. The sin sacrifices are effective not because they "pay" God something, but simply because God graciously accepts them.

---

1. S.v. "sacrifice," in *The New International Dictionary of New Testament Theology*, Vol. 3, Colin Brown, ed. (Grand Rapids, Mich.: Zondervan, 1975–1978), 415–38; Paul S. Fiddes, *Past Event and Present Salvation* (Louisville: Westminster/John Knox, 1989), 63–75.

A second major type of sacrifice in the Old Testament was the *gift offering*. The New Revised Standard Version of the Bible translates this as the sacrifice of well-being. The fact that this was not an atonement for sin is also indicated by communal eating of portions of the offering of an animal or grain. Like modern-day worshipers who make an offering of money to God, the offering of well-being was a gift to God in response to God's giving. The offering was an expression of gratitude and commitment to God.

Properly understood, the sacrifices did not work automatically, for the outward rituals were to be accompanied with the appropriate inner attitudes: a sin offering with repentance and devotion to God, a gift offering with genuine gratitude and commitment to God. In fact, the motives for any given sacrifice were probably not sharply distinguished, for the worshiper usually came with more than one motive.

New Testament authors use elements of both the sin offering and the gift offering when they use sacrificial language in connection with Jesus. The sin offering is the background for Paul when he speaks of "Christ Jesus, whom God put forward as a sacrifice of atonement by his blood, effective through faith" (Romans 3:24-25). The words "a sacrifice of atonement" are a translation of the Greek term referring to the lid on the ark of the covenant, a wooden container for the two stone tablets of the Ten Commandments, located in the holiest room of the Temple. On the annual Day of Atonement, the high priest was to sprinkle sacrificial blood on this lid to cover the unrepented sins of the nation. There is little doubt that Paul is thinking of Jesus' death as a sacrifice for sin. This kind of sacrificial imagery is also involved when John the Baptist says of Jesus, "Here is the Lamb of God who takes away the sin of the world" (John 1:29).

However, speaking of Jesus' work as a sin offering like the various sacrifices of animals and grain in the Hebrew Temple lost much of its effectiveness after the sacrifices ceased with the destruction of the Temple in A.D. 70. For example, the most involved use of sacrificial imagery in the New Testament occurs in the Epistle to the Hebrews, which probably was written to a group of Hebrew Christians who were very familiar with the sacrificial practices of the Temple. But for later generations of Christians the Epistle to the Hebrews has been comprehensible only if they studied about Hebrew sacrifices. And today in Western societies, animal sacrifices are unknown except as bizarre rites performed by people in Satanic cults. In fact, if most of us in Western societies were to witness an animal sacrifice, we would likely not only be puzzled but repulsed and perhaps stirred into action for animal rights. So it is not surprising that for centuries, Christians have generally reinterpreted Jesus' work as a sacrifice for sin in some other way than as the fulfillment of the sin offerings made in the Hebrew Temple. In the sixteenth century John Calvin interpreted Jesus' sacrifice as taking the punishment sinful humans deserve. And in the twentieth century many have simply focused on the second major type of biblical sacrifice, the gift offering. In what follows, I shall use the main lines of a proposal by contemporary Oxford University theologian Paul Fiddes that is based on the gift offering.[2]

New Testament writers also understand Jesus' work as a gift offering, although the gift is not an animal or grain, but Jesus' own self. This giving of self to God was the essence of any offering in the Old Testament and surely the heart of the gift offering. The psalmist says, "Burnt offering and sin offering you have not required. Then I said, 'Here I am; in the scroll of the book it is written of me. I delight to do your will, O my God; your law is within my heart'" (Psalm 40:6-8; cf. Psalm 50:13-15; 24:3-6). The Epistle to the Hebrews quotes these words from Psalm 40 and applies them to Jesus, whose sacrifice is to delight in doing God's will (Hebrews 10:5-9). Paul's advice to Christians that they present their bodies "as a living sacrifice, holy and acceptable to God" is based upon Jesus' self-giving (Romans 12:1). Paul's counsel, "Look not to your own interests, but to the interests of others" is grounded in "Christ Jesus, who, though he was in the form of God, did not regard equality with God as something to be exploited, but emptied himself, taking the form of a slave, being born in human likeness. And being found in human form, he humbled himself and became obedient to the point of death—even death on a cross" (Philippians 2:5-8).

The self-giving in Jesus Christ occurs on at least three levels. One is Jesus' compassionate care for the needy in his society—the poor, the ill and handicapped, the outcast; he gives himself to them by identifying with them and healing their ailments. A second level is the sacrifice of the preexistent Son of God who becomes incarnate in Jesus. This is what Paul highlights in Philippians 2:5-8 when he calls attention to Christ Jesus emptying himself and being found in human form. A third level of sacrifice is God the Father's giving of the Son: "For God so loved the world that he gave his only Son" (John 3:16; cf. Romans 8:32).

Clearly this notion of Jesus' life and death as self-giving connects with contemporary thinking about sacrifice. Sports commentators describe an unselfish basketball player as someone who sacrifices for the team. Many parents know what it means to sacrifice personally and financially for their child. And in situations of danger, sometimes people make the supreme sacrifice of giving their life to save someone else. So while the practice of offering an animal for sin may be foreign to us, a sacrifice of self-offering is understandable.

Jesus' sacrifice of his life has often been understood in a pious vacuum, however, as though he died a sweet death surrounded by angels and beautiful

2. Fiddes, *Past Event and Present Salvation*, 75–82.

organ music. Latin American liberation theologians have been in the front ranks of those who have emphasized that the death of Jesus arose out of the particular life he lived. His identification with the poor and powerless of Israel brought him into conflict with the political, economic, and religious leaders of his time who killed him in the most cruel way known to them. We will give this more detailed discussion later under the metaphor of satisfying justice. Here it is sufficient to note that talk about Jesus' sacrifice should include attention to what we recognized above as the first level of his self-giving, his compassionate care for the needy in his society that resulted in his violent death at the hands of public authorities. Without this rootage in the historical circumstances of his life and death, Jesus' sacrifice of self-giving readily loses its specific character and therefore its power to both challenge and transform others; his death is turned into a transaction with God that might just as well have occurred in a church or palace as in a place of public execution.

On the other hand, key elements of a New Testament understanding of Jesus' sacrifice are also lost unless the second and third levels of self-giving are included in one's interpretation of Jesus—the altruism of the preexistent Son of God and the astounding generosity of God in giving the Son. Obviously, these levels of sacrifice are sustained only by a high Christology, which in some sense affirms the deity of Jesus Christ.

In every conception of the atonement there is a correlation between how the human predicament is understood and how Christ's work is interpreted. So to speak of Jesus Christ as the redeemer of the world is to imply that the world is caught in a situation of slavery. To think of Jesus as the reconciler suggests that the world suffers from alienation. What then is the human predicament implied in construing Christ's work as making a sacrifice? Behind the sin offering is the notion that human life has been polluted or stained by sin, and the sacrifice cleanses or removes the blot. I have said that the cessation of Temple sacrifices of animals and grains as atonement for sin has drained this metaphor of much of its significance for Western people today. Now we can add that the sense of sin as a dirtying of the self and the community has also been greatly diminished. Such a perception exists in some people involved in a serious crime, such as rape victims who may repeatedly shower in an effort to overcome their feeling of being dirty, but it is no longer a widespread, powerful reaction to personal or corporate wrongdoing. Nevertheless, another set of images undergirds the sacrifice of the gift offering. Here the human predicament is closure of the self and social institutions, so that God and others are excluded and mistreated. Christ's work of giving himself is then seen as creating new bonds of commitment, caring, and community.

This shift in the understanding of Christ's sacrifice from mainly a sin offering to a gift offering also means a shift from a more objective understanding of his sacrifice to a more subjective understanding. The use of these terms, objective and subjective, in the context of Christ's work needs some explanation. Two meanings are most important. One is that *objective* refers to what lies outside us, whereas *subjective* refers to what happens within us as a part of our own experience. A strongly objective conception of Jesus' offering for the sins of humankind would stress that Jesus made that sacrifice long ago and the sin offering was real whether someone today acknowledges it or not. Of course, the hope is that people will indeed recognize the validity of Jesus' sacrifice for sin, but the subjective factor consists mainly in recognition or knowledge. So in such a view the overwhelming emphasis falls on what Christ accomplished long ago outside us. A second meaning of objective and subjective is that God's activity is objective while the human response is subjective. In this sense, a strongly subjective version of Christ's gift offering would place the chief emphasis on what human beings do in response to his sacrifice. In such an outlook Jesus is viewed as setting a good example of unselfishness. This is a significant achievement, but the responsibility now falls mainly on others to live up to his example. Thus it would seem that if we combine both meanings an objective conception of Jesus' work would stress what God has done outside of us, whereas a subjective rendering would accent what we ourselves experience and do.

In actuality, though, the two meanings of objective and subjective are not so neatly separated off from each other when linked with the work of Jesus Christ. It is possible to hold that God is the primary mover in bringing about a human response of faith in God and love for neighbor. This is surely true of Paul and John, both of whom think of the Holy Spirit as the fundamental power that enables persons to open themselves more fully to God and to other creatures. In other words, God acts inside people today as well as outside them. To be sure, this idea of God acting within people to enable them to respond in certain ways runs counter to ordinary human patterns of thought in modern culture, yet it is an extremely important idea to note.

Since sin offerings of animals and grain in the Jewish Temple ended long ago, Christians generally have a diminished sense of Jesus' objective work as the once and for all time sufficient sacrifice for sin. The sacrificial language that continues to communicate is Jesus' sacrifice of self-giving. Yet this does not mean Christians must lapse into the wholly subjective view of Jesus as a mere model of a self-giving life, and the responsibility to follow that model is now entirely up to them. As Paul Fiddes has proposed, it is possible to focus on Jesus' sacrifice of self-giving and see it both as an objective event in the past and as an objective and subjective reality in the Christian's present experience. The self-giving of Jesus becomes a reality in the present experience of Christians not by their striving to imitate a distant example like young basketball players trying to imitate Michael Jordan; rather, it happens as the risen Jesus is present in their lives and enables them to give themselves. Paul expresses it this way: "I have been crucified with Christ; and it is no longer I who live, but it is Christ who lives in me. And the life I now live in the flesh I live by faith in the Son of God, who loved me and gave himself for me" (Galatians 2:19-20). Notice Paul's emphases on Christ's self-giving and on Christ now living *within* him. Here Jesus' sacrifice is both something he did some years previously outside the city gates of Jerusalem and a present work of living in Paul and enabling Paul to give himself in faith to Jesus.

Victory

A second common metaphor for interpreting the work of Jesus Christ is to speak of his victory over evil powers. This metaphor has roots in the New Testament, is prominent in certain strands of the church's theological tradition, and is widely used today.

Although many New Testament books explicitly or implicitly portray Jesus as victor, military imagery is most prominent in the Book of Revelation where the Lord of Lords is envisioned doing battle with the forces of evil and defeating them (Revelation 19:11-21 cf. 17:14). More appropriate to the nonviolent Jesus, he is usually depicted as winning a moral and spiritual battle. So the way that Jesus dealt with temptations is seen as his triumph over the devil (Luke 4:1-13). When Jesus healed a woman crippled for eighteen years, the Gospel of Luke views him in conflict both with Satan and certain religious leaders who object to his "working" on the sabbath. Jesus says, "Ought not this woman, a daughter of Abraham whom Satan bound for eighteen long years, be set free from this bondage on the sabbath day?" (Luke 13:16). Jesus is not an obvious victor, however, for he suffers an early, violent death; indeed, his movement is judged to be so weak that the authorities do not even bother to arrest anyone else but him. And his vindication comes only in his resurrection, which is far from being a publicly observable event. So the actuality and nature of Jesus' victory is disputable.

The interpretation of Jesus' work as a victory over evil powers received its classic expression from a number of the early church theologians, mostly of the second to fifth centuries, commonly referred to as the early church fathers. Attention was called to this outlook by Gustav Aulén in his book *Christus Victor*. In this view, the predicament is that the creation is held in bondage to superior evil powers; the early church fathers identified these powers as sin, death, and the devil, while Paul and later Martin Luther also included the law. Sin was understood as a virulent plague against which people had no defense, so the human position was like being infected with HIV and having no cure. Death also dominated over all living things, just as it does still today. Sin and death were closely allied in the thinking of the church fathers, for as alienation from God, the Source of life, sin is itself a form of death. The devil was felt to be a real, evil personal power that continually seeks to gain more control over mismatched humans. The devil was thought of as the master of sin and death. The law was essentially good, but through the perversion of legalism it became evil. In sum, the predicament is that humans, and indeed the whole creation, are under the control of these evil powers, and are utterly unable to free themselves.

The work of Jesus Christ is then understood as conquering the evil powers and setting the world free. Jesus did this by living a sinless life and overcoming death through his resurrection. He defeated the devil by resisting all his temptations, and some of the church fathers also portray Jesus as winning by tricking the devil. For instance, Gregory of Nyssa (d. 395) says that the deity of Jesus Christ is so hidden under his humanity that the devil seizes him and kills him like a big fish swallowing a little fish, but the devil himself is caught when he takes God's bait. And later Luther could speak in similar terms about the law condemning Jesus, but itself being overcome by his love and mercy.

In recent years one prominent way of reviving the victory metaphor has been liberation theology's practice of speaking of Jesus Christ as liberator. Basic to the liberationist view has been a reinterpretation of the evil powers that hold human life in bondage. This reinterpretation has not been just a mental exercise of intellectuals in an ivory tower, but has been rooted in the experience of bondage and of liberation. For example, Brazilian theologian Leonardo Boff points out that liberationist theological reflection takes place in a situation of oppression, liberation, and resistance to liberation. The oppression is political, economic, and cultural as one group dominates over another group. Boff sees this within nations as the wealthy, powerful, and generally white members of a society control the society's major institutions to their own advantage, while the poor, disproportionately people of color, suffer from insecurity, malnutrition, and lack of medical care. In addition to this real-life experience of oppression, liberation theology flows out of the experience of movements striving for liberation from oppression by working for such basic things as better sanitation, jobs, and health care. In Latin America many of these liberation movements are inspired by faith in Jesus Christ. However, liberation theology also arises from the experience of resistance to change on the part of the powerful. In Latin America this resistance frequently has been violent, for police, military, and vigilante-like death squads imprison and kill those in the liberation movements. So liberation theology's thinking about Jesus takes place in the context of this bitter contemporary struggle for liberation from oppression and violent resistance to change.

Leonardo Boff and other liberation theologians point out that the historical conditions in which Jesus ministered and died were remarkably similar to those in modern-day Latin America. Palestine was politically and culturally dependent upon the Roman empire. There was economic oppression, for wealthy landowners plundered the peasantry and taxes were heavy. In addition, the Pharisees oppressed ordinary Jews with their demands for scrupulous observance of the religious laws. In this situation of oppression Boff says Jesus sought to free people through proclamation of the absolute utopia of the reign of God and through anticipations of that total liberation in partial liberations in the present. That is, while Jesus preached the coming of perfect harmony in God's reign, he established signs of that future harmony already in the present through reaching out to outcasts and healing the sick. This brought Jesus into conflict with both the religious and political powers of Palestine. Jesus did not seek death, but courageously challenged the authorities. The result was that the religious authorities condemned him for blasphemy, and the political leaders sentenced him to die as a political subversive. Boff calls Jesus' death "judicial murder." Jesus' resurrection vouches for the truth of the absolute utopia that he proclaimed as the reign of God; this hope for ultimate liberation from evil frees people now from despair. Jesus also liberates by generating in believers the strength to strive for partial deliverance from contemporary political, economic, cultural, and religious oppression.[3]

Notice that Leonardo Boff has a different reading of the evil powers than the early church fathers. The fathers sometimes portray the evil powers of sin, death, and the devil as personal beings roaming the world; this often gets branded "mythological." Although the fathers were probably less literal than we might think, these powers seem to be conceived in metaphysical terms somewhat abstracted from historical conditions. In contrast, Latin American and feminist liberation theologians emphasize the concrete, historical forms that sin takes and how these forms of sin, often supported by religious and civil law, produce early and often violent death for the downtrodden. Commonly, the devil is quietly dropped from the picture.

Another difference between Boff's liberation theology and the church fathers is whether they place the accent on the objective or subjective character of Christ's work. Aulén says the church fathers' conception of Christ's work is strongly objective both in the sense that it is done by God and that it has been accomplished primarily outside of human beings today. That is, since in his life, death, and resurrection Jesus really conquered the powerful evil forces that plagued the world like an alien army of occupation, the human

3. Leonardo Boff, *Passion of Christ, Passion of the World*, trans. Robert R. Barr (Maryknoll, N.Y.: Orbis, 1987), 1–4, 9–24, 39–41, 122–35.

situation has been fundamentally changed. What remains is that people should wake up to the fact that evil has been defeated. In comparison, liberation theology puts much more emphasis on the subjective side. Leonardo Boff does place considerable weight on the objective side in this respect: in his life, Jesus established what it means to be truly human, namely, to be fully open to God and to other creatures. But Boff also stresses the subjective aspect that followers of Jesus must also take up this new kind of life, and have their center outside themselves in God and others.

The major limitation of Boff's view, in my opinion, is that he basically ends up with Jesus as the great forerunner who carves out a new way of being human, but now the responsibility rests mostly on the shoulders of other people to fulfill some of that new way of being human in their own lives. What is missing in Boff is Paul's emphasis on the objective within the subjective, that is, the emphasis on Jesus Christ as a living reality who is personally present within persons and human communities *enabling* people to participate in that new mode of human existence. As Paul says about this new life, "It is no longer I who live, but it is Christ who lives in me" (Galatians 2:20). Not all Latin American liberation theologians follow Boff's pattern, however; the most famous of them, Gustavo Gutiérrez, has an extremely strong sense of the presence of Christ today. What is unusual about Gutiérrez's mystical or contemplative awareness of Christ is that, for him, Christ is vividly present in the poor. So to become involved with the poor is to become immersed in the presence of Jesus Christ which nourishes Christian faith.[4]

Now we should ask for ourselves whether victory over evil is still a good metaphor for the work of Jesus Christ. I think it is an excellent metaphor for Jesus' work, but it will be convincing for people only to the extent that they actually experience both the persistent power of evil and the ability of Jesus to combat evil.

Everyone has some experience of evil, but there are widely different interpretations of it. Much of modern Western culture tends to think moral evil can be substantially reduced and eventually eliminated by human efforts, much like medical science has been able to virtually banish the bubonic plague. To this mindset, talk about evil powers holding the world in bondage seems archaic and irrelevant, for humans appear able to push back evil. In opposition, the Christus Victor motif views sin like death; while we may be able to diminish or even eradicate a particular form death takes, we are unable to vanquish death itself. So also we may accomplish a great good by almost eliminating a form of sin such as slavery, but a sharp eye observes other types of enslavement, old and new, that still exist. When one sees this, the picture

---

4. Gustavo Gutiérrez, *The Power of the Poor in History*, trans. Robert R. Barr (Maryknoll, N.Y.: Orbis, 1983), 52, 197, 202.

of evil powers holding the world in bondage takes on more validity. We should not dismiss the insights of the early church fathers simply because they tend to personify these powers. While it is true that few people today think this way, the sometimes colorful personifications point to the persistent force of evil. As we may recall from our discussion of sin in chapter 6, sin is not just this or that individual act of wrongdoing; it is also a blindness that prevents us from seeing much of the evil in ourselves and the world. Communal sin corrupts the institutions of society, and has the ability to shape people's expectations and behavior for generations. The various forms of liberation theology are right to call our attention to the specific shape sin takes in an historical situation. Where I think the church fathers are superior to some versions of liberation theology is the fathers' emphasis that humans on their own are truly in bondage to evil and cannot free themselves. This is the case because sin is essentially alienation from God, and all other aspects of sin are results of that estrangement. Only God is able to set free from the prison of estrangement. On the other hand, the liberation theologies are correct in their concern to combat the concrete evils that sin produces and to build a relatively more just society.

Christ as victor over evil will also be convincing to people insofar as they come to experience the power of Christ to resist evil. Christians are surely not free of trials, but like Paul their faith in Christ may enable them to cope with trial. Christians also do not experience an absence of temptations, for these continue. Christians do not even experience steady personal victory over temptation. The great apostle Paul testified, "I do not understand my own actions. For I do not do what I want, but I do the very thing I hate" (Romans 7:15). The freedom that Christians may know is complex. There is the possibility of facing trials with calm assurance. There is liberation from being dominated by an evil, so that one now battles the temptation rather than consistently giving in to it. There is also partial liberation from the fears and corrupt patterns of behavior that rule in a society. So Latin American peasants in prayer groups frequently change from passsively accepting their poor lot in life to working for greater social justice. Underlying all, there may be liberation from the anxiety of always having to prove one's worth to God and others; instead, there may be the peace of knowing one is loved and accepted by God. This in turn frees one from hatred and bitterness toward those who have done wrong and opens the way to forgiveness and peace among people.

In short, the metaphor of Jesus as the victor over evil expresses some fundamental beliefs of the Christian faith. The metaphor testifies to the enormous potency of evil and the conviction that Jesus overcame evil in his own life and frees believers from domination by sin, death, legalism, and demonic powers.

Doing Justice

A third major metaphor for the work of Jesus Christ uses the courtroom and the notion of justice. While this has been a common arena for images throughout the centuries, different conceptions of justice have produced quite divergent formulations of Christ's work. We shall look at four variations on this theme: Paul, Anselm, Calvin, and some contemporary reflections.

1. *Paul's idea of justification* is the center of his understanding of Christ's work as an act of justice, the most developed in the New Testament. Paul says, "They are now justified by his grace as a gift, through the redemption that is in Christ Jesus, whom God put forward as a sacrifice of atonement by his blood, effective through faith. He did this to show his righteousness" (Romans 3:24-25). The background of this idea of justification is the Jewish law court in which one person accuses another of some wrong and there are no lawyers present to represent either litigant. A judge hears the evidence and gives a verdict. In the situation envisioned by Paul, God is the judge and a sinner is accused. Although the sinner appears doomed to condemnation, God delivers the utterly surprising verdict that the defendant is "justified," that is, found righteous, in the right. How can this be? Paul says the defendant is "justified by his grace as a gift"; the verdict is an act of mercy rather than being deserved. Paul also links this merciful ruling with "the redemption that is in Christ Jesus" and with faith in him. The puzzle for theological reflection is the nature of this linkage between being found righteous and the work of Christ. *How* does the work of Jesus Christ and especially his death bring about God's merciful decision? Assuming that there is a rationality to God's actions, we should be able to have some grasp of the divine rationale. Paul himself does not spell out a rationale, but two later theologians—Anselm and Calvin—have offered influential answers.

2. *Anselm's Satisfaction Theory* of the atonement drew its conception of justice from his feudalistic society in which the overlord is responsible for maintaining order and justice. Here justice is not conceived as an abstract principle of rights, but as a relationship in which vassals render their due to their lord in return for certain privileges granted by the lord. For instance, a duke would be obligated to supply his king with fighting men in time of war in return for certain tracts of land allotted him by the king. Anselm (d. 1109) views God as the overlord of all creatures and interprets sin within this framework: "'To sin,' then, is nothing else than not to render to God His due."[5] What we owe God is that our will be subject to God in all things; this

---

5. Anselm of Canterbury, *Why God Became Man*, Book I, Chapter 11, trans. Joseph M. Colleran (Albany, N.Y.: Magi Books, 1969), 84.

is to honor God as God. Not to render God the honor due is to sin. This is indeed what has happened. Anselm goes on to interpret the human predicament as owing God an infinite debt of honor. This is not a debt of money, but a debt of honor. We humans are unable to pay this debt of honor, for, having dishonored the infinite God, our debt is infinite.

Anselm considers three options open to God. One is to simply forgive the debt of honor out of sheer mercy. After all, Jesus tells us to forgive our neighbor again and again, shouldn't God also generously forgive? Anselm rules out this possibility as unfitting for God on the grounds that God is responsible for order in the universe. That is, while it is good for a sheriff to forgive someone who has hurt him personally by lying, it is wrong for him to simply overlook someone giving false information for a legal contract. The sheriff is sworn to uphold public order, and to forgive all criminals would encourage others to commit crimes and destroy all social order. In similar fashion, God upholds moral order in the universe, so forgiving the debt out of mercy alone would be unfitting.

The elimination of this option brings Anselm to consider two others: punishment or satisfaction. Anselm also rejects the possibility of punishment, because the punishment humans deserve for their sin is so great that they would be completely destroyed. If God were now to annihilate humans, there would have been no point in creating them in the first place. This leaves the alternative of satisfaction. In European feudalistic society, satisfaction was a less harsh choice than punishment. For example, if a member of the Rodriguez family broke the leg of someone in the O'Malley family, a strict rule of punishment would legitimate breaking the leg of the offending Rodriguez or another member of that family in return. This could lead to an endless series of broken legs, however. So another possibility was to make satisfaction by paying money or some other valuable as a way of making compensation for the injury. Notice then that for Anselm it is *either* punishment *or* satisfaction; they are alternatives. God reasonably takes the option of satisfaction as better.

The question still remains of who will make satisfaction to God, for it must cover the infinite debt of honor. No sinful human being is able, yet it must be a member of the human family that does it. Anselm says this is why God became human, so that Jesus Christ could make satisfaction. Although Jesus Christ as human already owes God a perfect life of obedience, he goes beyond that to do what he is not required to do, namely, to die. All sinners deserve to die, but the sinless Jesus voluntarily chooses to die. The death of this sinless God-man is a good deed of infinite worth that Jesus says can be used as satisfaction for the debt owed by all his sinful kinsfolk.

As you can see, this is a complicated understanding of Christ's work that reflects medieval culture. The most important features to remember are Anselm's rejection of forgiving sin by sheer mercy, his strong concern for

God as upholder of order, and the fact that punishment and satisfaction are alternatives. In essence, Anselm argues that God pronounces the verdict of "justified" on believers, because Jesus Christ's infinitely valuable deed of voluntarily dying compensates for the infinite debt of honor that sinners owe to God. In this way justice is done.

3. Another important and still influential interpretation of how the work of Christ links up with God's justification of sinners has been offered by John Calvin (d. 1564), the chief founder of the Reformed/Presbyterian tradition. Calvin's version of Christ's work as an act of justice is commonly called the *Substitutionary Punishment Theory* of the atonement; another name for it is the penal theory.[6] Calvin makes the essential point in his comment on Jesus' death, "This is our acquittal: the guilt that held us liable for punishment has been transferred to the head of the Son of God (Isa. 53:12)."[7] Here sin is understood as breaking the law, which makes the sinner liable for punishment. What Jesus does is take upon himself the punishment that others deserve, and this opens the way for God to announce the verdict "justified" to others. The key biblical text that Calvin finds to support his view is this Old Testament passage which speaks of God's servant,

> But he was wounded for our transgressions, crushed for our iniquities; upon him was the punishment that made us whole, and by his bruises we are healed. All we like sheep have gone astray; we have all turned to our own way, and the Lord has laid on him the iniquity of us all. (Isaiah 53:5-6)

Substitutionary punishment is probably the view of Christ's work most familiar to Christians today, for it is what they were mainly taught while growing up.

There are both differences and similarities between Anselm's satisfaction theory and Calvin's substitutionary punishment theory. A difference appears in what Jesus does to establish the justice of God's acquittal of sinners. According to Anselm, Jesus provides an infinitely valuable deed in compensation for the infinite debt owed to God. For Calvin, Jesus takes the punishment others deserve. Notice that Anselm approves satisfaction as a better alternative to punishment, whereas Calvin thinks punishment is the route Jesus takes. A very important similarity of the two views, however, is that they both place a heavy emphasis on God as guardian of moral order. This is explicit in Anselm, more implicit in Calvin.

---

6. Calvin explains Christ's work in terms of three offices—Christ as prophet, king, and priest. The penal theory is Calvin's rendering of Jesus' death under the priestly work.

7. John Calvin, *Institutes of the Christian Religion*, Book II, Chapter 16, Section 5, The Library of Christian Classics, Vol. 20, ed. John T. McNeill, trans. F. L. Battles (Philadelphia: Westminster, 1960), 509–10.

The crucial thing for both views is that God is able to forgive sinners only after the books are somehow balanced. One result is that for both Anselm and Calvin the generous love of God tends to lose prominence in the work of Christ. While they say that the loving God provides Jesus to meet the demands of justice, love gets overshadowed by the concern to maintain order. This weakness suggests that we should examine the idea of justice and the accompanying response to wrongdoing that is most appropriate for expressing Christ's work.

4. *The Re-creative Approach.* The most common response to wrongdoing is to inflict a penalty on the perpetrater. One reason for this is that the penalty serves justice by deterring the offender and others from committing the deed again. So fines for speeding are meant to discourage drivers from going too fast. In a social setting, this rationale may be combined with others. A second reason for answering an offense with a penalty is retribution. Since this is the motive underlying the atonement theories of both Anselm and Calvin, we must consider it in more detail.

In a penetrating discussion of this issue, British theologian Vernon White says that retribution seeks to do justice by restoring a balance, a balance of rights or benefits or suffering; this is partly expressed in the phrase "getting even." Thus if a thief takes someone's car, it would be appropriate for the thief to return the car undamaged or replace it with a like vehicle. Of course, this alone would not compensate for the distress and inconvenience of having one's car stolen, so in addition a fine might be assessed by a court. This example shows, however, that in most cases it is impossible to strike a balance of exact equivalents. Usually it is necessary to resort to symbolic or compensating penalties such as time spent in prison or a fine. Thus the man who shot and permanently disabled a woman in a convenience store robbery near where I live was sentenced to forty years in prison. While the prison term functions in part to deter this offender and others from robbery (our first reason), there is also a strong sense that the offender must do something to even things up. Since the robber caused the woman great suffering, he deserves to suffer in return. Often this is expressed as the necessity to pay a debt that the offender has incurred. Clearly this idea of retribution underlies Anselm's theory in which the infinite good of Jesus' death pays the debt of honor that sinners owe to God. Retribution also is the basis for Calvin's thinking that Jesus takes the punishment others deserve for their sins.

Retribution seems to be behind some thinking in the Bible about God's dealing with sin, most notably in Isaiah 53, as cited by Calvin; nevertheless, we must ask about the adequacy of this principle for interpreting the work of Christ. The most serious reservation about retribution is that it is a minimal, restraining response that does not aim to improve the relationships in the situation. This is obvious, as Vernon White suggests, if we consider as an example a retributive response to my being unfaithful to my wife. An equivalent retribution would be if my wife then had an affair with another man. A less equivalent action would be if she made me suffer by not speaking to me for six months. Perhaps either of these penalties would make the suffering more even between us. But how would our relationship be improved through any of these efforts to balance things out? Trying to get even would not raise the quality of our love and communication. In fact, the odds are good that such a response would only weaken our relationship more. This raises the question whether another motive may be better for dealing with sin.

Another way of doing justice is to respond to wrongdoing by seeking to reform the offender and re-create a relationship. This is the primary motive that drives some efforts at changing our criminal justice system. This sort of reply to my (entirely fictional) infidelity to my wife would mean that she would seek to use the painful consequences of my action to bring about a stronger relationship between us. Of course, she would still be hurt by my adultery, and our relationship would still have suffered a terrible blow. Yet instead of trying to get even, she would attempt to use my betrayal as an occasion for rebuilding our marriage. This requires that she forgive me for my betrayal without having settled the account between us; she would simply forgive me. Obviously, this approach would finally be effective in re-creating our relationship only if I come to see my unfaithfulness as wrong and turn away from it. Nonetheless, if the re-creative approach is effective, it produces a situation that is better than what previously existed. So we see that while the retributive strategy merely seeks to restore a prior order, flawed as that may be, the re-creative strategy works to improve the situation. Furthermore, justice is served through re-creation, for if my wife and I come through the experience with a stronger, happier marriage, then there is no point in assessing punishment. Thus the re-creative approach is more suited to express God's rationale for the work of Jesus Christ than the retributive motive.

We need to inquire more deeply into what is involved in bringing about redemption through the re-creative approach. I recall watching a television program about a man named Julius working with youth in a poor black neighborhood of Los Angeles that was riddled with crime and drugs and fought over by rival gangs. Julius was not a policeman threatening young people with a nightstick or prison; he was trying to help them lead decent lives and resist the temptations of making quick money by selling drugs. So Julius was engaged in re-creative service to the youth of that troubled neighborhood. How he went about his work is instructive for our purposes. First, it is significant that he shared the life of that neighborhood. He was an African American who knew from his own experience the culture of the people in this area. Although he could afford to live in a much nicer and safer part of the city, he lived in the area he was serving. So daily he shared the world of dirty streets, shabby housing, corner drug deals, thefts, and frequent violence. What made him different was that he represented an alternative way of life to the young; he turned away from the theft, violence, and drugs and led a straight life. He sought to win youth by befriending them, offering constructive activities, encouraging them, standing by them if they got in trouble. Rather than using them, he looked out for their good. In general, Julius was a faithful presence for the young people of that neighborhood. He couldn't compel anyone to follow his way, but he managed to win some with his loyal presence.

Julius's approach is similar to God's re-creative way with humankind. In the re-creative model, God always has a merciful, forgiving attitude toward humans. The obstacle to reconciliation is not in God's anger that must be appeased. Neither is the obstacle in some retribution that must be taken care of, whether it be conceived as debt to be paid or as punishment to be meted out. Rather, the hindrance to reconciliation is in people's persistent trust in themselves or in another creature rather than in God; this is people's lack of faith in God.

How, then, may the life, death, and resurrection of Jesus be considered central to God's re-creative strategy for establishing justice? Paul Fiddes and Vernon White suggest two ways.[8] The first is that Jesus Christ's life and death are God's own movement into the human situation and the very depths of sin. Not that Jesus sinned, but he experienced temptation and the consequences of sin. Since sin is essentially making oneself or some other creatures the center of one's life, it results in isolation from other people and from God as well as a loss of personal meaning. Jesus knew profound separation from other people, for when he was arrested his disciples abandoned him and during his trial and execution he was reviled by others. In the end he also felt distant from God, for he cried out from the cross, "My God, my God, why have you forsaken me?" (Mark 15:34). Although these words from Psalm 22 are an expression of faith in God, it is faith under extreme trial, for what Jesus quotes are the Psalm's opening words of great affliction and remoteness from God, not the concluding words of confident praise and thanks to God. These words from the cross also give voice to a sense of failure and loss of personal meaning. Indeed, Jesus experienced the consequences of sin much more deeply than sinful humans, for one of the effects of sin is blindness to some of its evil; Jesus' deep faith in God made him much more sensitive to the isolation and loss of meaning. While God shares the suffering of every creature, Paul Fiddes and Vernon White suggest that God's own experience of suffer-

---

8. Vernon White, *Atonement and Incarnation* (Cambridge: Cambridge University Press, 1991), 51–61; Fiddes, *Past Event and Present Salvation*, 109–11.

ing in Jesus is the most profound because of the greater openness of Jesus to God and the effects of sin. God's presence in Jesus is the furthest point of God's empathetic entrance into the desolate situation of the fallen world. As we noted in our discussion of providence and evil earlier, God shares in the suffering of the world. What the story of Jesus' life does is entitle us to speak of God's enduring the depths of human suffering. Thus the life and death of Jesus bring a new, deeper experience to God's own life. The movement of Julius into the chaos of his troubled neighborhood mirrors God's entry into the sinful condition of the world.

The second re-creative side to Jesus' work, according to Fiddes and White, is that Jesus' turning away from sin even while experiencing its effects has the power to turn others away from sin as well. The question is how this happens. It is common to think of Jesus as an exemplary human being. There is no doubt that this is true for Christians, for Jesus is their primary model of being human. Yet this is not sufficient for understanding the broader range of what Jesus does to turn others from sin. Think what sort of relationship a devotee usually has with an exemplary figure. A great tennis player such as Martina Navratilova or Steffi Graf can be a model for an aspiring tennis player who is attempting to imitate the aggressive net play of Navratilova and the powerful forehand of Graf. She would have pictures of these tennis stars prominently displayed in her room to remind her of their accomplishments, and she would read articles about them and watch videos of their play. Navratilova and Graf are not friends with our tennis hopeful, however. She has never even met them. The tennis stars are like stars in the sky, sparkling but very remote. This means that our aspiring tennis player bears all the burden to be like them; everything depends on her close observation, good work habits, and desire to perform. If we think of a Christian's relationship with Jesus in this way, then Jesus is also a distant model and everything depends on the believer's commitment to be like Jesus.

Imagine, though, what it would be like if Martina Navratilova were to become the close friend and mentor of our young tennis player. Then Navratilova would not only instruct her as would a paid coach, but would encourage her and be with her through her successes and failures. In fact, their friendship itself would be the chief value prized by both of them, more than whether the younger player ever reached stardom or not. In this case, Navratilova is not a remote figure but an intimate friend whose supportive presence draws the younger person toward greater maturity as a tennis player and a human being.

This is also the kind of relationship that Julius seeks to establish with young people in his neighborhood. He is not a far-off model of a success story, whose steps youth may choose to follow. He is a faithful, encouraging presence who invites youth to accept his friendship as well as his advice and leadership. Such a faithful presence is the heart of the re-creative approach to redemption of life.

This friendship or faithful presence is also the key to understanding the second aspect of Jesus' re-creative work by which he enables others to turn away from sin. For Christian believers Jesus is not a faraway ideal figure, but a faithful presence. Christian faith itself is much more than a set of beliefs, for faith is also trust in God and loyalty to God. The faithful presence of Jesus persistently invites a person to trust and be loyal. For Christians Jesus is the encouraging face of God that gives them the confidence to turn from trusting in themselves or another creature and trust in God. So Jesus re-creates one's relationship with God by winning one's friendship through being a friend.

This understanding of Jesus' re-creative work of redemption requires that Jesus be an actual presence. Thus the resurrection of Jesus is fundamental for his doing justice by his renewing the relationship between people and God. In his life and death Jesus shared the human condition and in so doing turned away from trusting in a creature to fundamental trust in God. In his resurrection Jesus becomes a continuing presence whose depth of experience and faith can draw others also to place their ultimate trust in God.

Interpreting the reconciling work of Christ as a re-creative action of doing justice has support in the New Testament. First, there is the parable of the prodigal son (Luke 15:11-32) in which the younger of two sons asks for his share of his father's property and then goes off to a far country and squanders everything. Finally, in dire poverty, he decides he would be better off as a mere hired hand at his father's place, so he heads for home. While the son is still on his way, the father goes out to him, welcomes him back as a son, not just a hired hand, and calls for a feast to celebrate his return. Then the older son complains to the father that this is not fair, for during all the older son's years of loyal service he has never been given such a celebration. The father defends his generosity as appropriate, for the younger son had been lost and is now found. Notice that the father welcomes back the wayward son without even so much as scolding him or putting him on probation. The father is ready to forgive from the beginning. When the older brother raises the question about fairness, he is really asking for retribution, some sort of balancing of accounts. But the father sets aside any concern for retribution, and simply rejoices in the return of the errant son.

A second scriptural ground for the re-creative interpretation of doing justice is in the Epistle to the Hebrews (2:14-18), where the author talks about the work of Jesus having the same two sides as we found in the re-creative approach. On the one hand, Jesus shares the human condition: "For it is clear that he did not come to help angels, but the descendants of Abraham. Therefore he had to become like his brothers and sisters in every respect." On the other hand, through being so experienced, Jesus is able to help others trust in

God: "Because he himself was tested by what he suffered, he is able to help those who are being tested." A third biblical basis is in Paul's oft-repeated notion of Christians being "in Christ" and Christ being "in" them. Such terminology involves an intimate relationship between Christ and the believer in which Christ is a personal presence. Thus, while the re-creative understanding of Christ's work has not been as widely held in the history of theology as retribution, there are solid biblical grounds for the re-creative way of doing justice.

A further strength of the re-creative interpretation of Christ's work is that it forms a solid foundation for a re-creative ethical approach to social and ecological problems. People may share in Christ's re-creative work by befriending one another and befriending nature. For instance, Charles Colson, who spent time in jail for his part in the Watergate conspiracy, tells of visiting a privately run prison in Brazil that is operated by Christians following the re-creative strategy. In this prison, which has sixty inmates and just two staff, Colson found that the prisoners were regarded as persons who had done wrong but were redeemable. In a context with regular voluntary communal worship, prisoners were treated with respect and given responsibilities. The man with a ring of keys who gave Colson a tour of the prison was a convicted murderer. The prison's single solitary confinement cell was occupied by only a cross. The guide said, "Jesus served time in solitary for all of us." This prison has only 5 percent of its inmates return to Brazil's prisons, whereas the rate for the state system is over 70 percent. A re-creative understanding of Christ's work would also be helpful for the ecological crisis, for the fundamental problem is the domineering attitude of humans toward nature. Seeing Christ's work as retribution, sacrifice, or victory does not seem to speak to the distorted human relationship with nature, but Christ's activity of doing justice by re-creating relationships is pertinent. Justice with nature will in fact be done when people befriend nature, and it is possible for Christians to see such befriending as participation in the befriending work of Jesus Christ.

Demonstrating Love

A fourth metaphor for the reconciling work of Jesus Christ is to interpret his life as a dramatic demonstration of love that changes humans into new persons. This understanding of Christ's work is most closely associated with the theologian who first explicitly taught it, Peter Abelard (d. 1142). Abelard rejected the two major conceptions of the atonement in his day: the early church version of the victory metaphor in which Christ redeems humans from the dominion of Satan and the satisfaction theory advanced by Anselm a generation before Abelard. Most instructive for our purposes is how Abelard's interpretation of the human predicament and of the redeeming work of Jesus

Christ differs from Anselm's. Anselm said human beings were in the quandary of owing God an infinite debt of honor that they were unable to pay, and Christ's voluntary death was an act of infinite value that canceled the debt of honor. Abelard objected that Anselm's view makes God seem to lack generosity, for God appears unable to forgive until the debt is set aside. Anselm's view implies that the obstacle to reconciliation lies in God or in a balance book that God keeps. This is wrong, says Abelard, for God is always ready to forgive. Rather, the obstacle to reconciliation is within people. So it is people that need to be changed.

To be more explicit, Abelard says the human predicament lies in the fact that the human mind is clouded and the will misdirected. He understands sin as consent to wrongdoing. Doing wrong may not be sin, for one could do wrong in ignorance; sin is knowingly and willingly doing wrong. So, according to Abelard, the intention behind an action is what counts most. What has happened to people is that their understanding is confused and their will loves the wrong things. If humans are to be reconciled to God, their understanding of God must be enlightened and their will must be redirected.

How does Jesus bring about this change in people? Abelard gives his answer in his explanation of Paul's remarks on justification in Romans 3:19-26:

> Now it seems to us that we have been justified by the blood of Christ and reconciled to God in this way: through this unique act of grace manifested to us—in that his Son has taken upon himself our nature and persevered therein in teaching us by word and example even unto death—he has more fully bound us to himself by love; with the result that our hearts should be enkindled by such a gift of divine grace, and true charity should not now shrink from enduring anything for him.[9]

Abelard's view has been interpreted differently. Some interpreters believe Abelard is merely saying that Jesus set an example of perfection and it is now up to others to try to follow his example like our aspiring tennis player striving to imitate a distant Graf or Navratilova. These interpreters charge Abelard with having a view of redemption which is subjective in a double sense: redemption takes place both *within* humans and *by* them. God's part in reconciliation is just to send Jesus as a teacher and model human being. Such interpreters often call Abelard's perspective the Moral Influence Theory of the atonement.

I think there is more to Abelard's view than the moral influence interpretation.[10] To be sure, Abelard does say above that Jesus teaches "by word and

9. Peter Abelard, *Exposition of the Epistle to the Romans*, in *A Scholastic Miscellany: Anselm to Ockham*, The Library of Christian Classics, Vol. 10, ed. and trans. E. R. Fairweather (Philadelphia: Westminster, 1956), 283.

10. For this interpretation I am indebted to the insightful lectures of Robert Lowry Calhoun, former professor of Yale University, and to Paul Fiddes, *Past Event and Present Salvation*, 140–47.

example." In his view, a fuller understanding of God is required for reconciliation, for part of the problem is human misunderstanding of the character and will of God. So Jesus shows that God is not a harsh judge but is merciful and loving. Thus the confused human understanding may be illumined. In addition, the misdirected human will needs to be turned to love God. This turning of the will is suggested in the quote above by the expression "our hearts should be enkindled by such a gift of divine grace." What "enkindles" or sets the heart afire is Jesus' act of showing love to the sinner. Love for God is aroused when one truly sees God's love demonstrated in the life and death of Jesus, that is, when Jesus becomes for a person the revelation of God's love. When persons come to love God, there is a reordering of what they care about; their priorities change. They are freed from their old loves and are enabled gladly to follow God's will.

In Abelard's view, the redeeming work of Christ does not happen so much in the years 0 to 30 as in the present when a person comes to know and love God. As Abelard says, "Wherefore, our redemption through Christ's suffering is that deeper affection in us which not only frees us from slavery to sin, but also wins for us the true liberty of sons of God, so that we do all things out of love rather than fear—love to him who has shown us such grace that no greater can be found."[11] Notice that redemption is the deeper affection or love for God within a person now; that is what sets free from sin. So this is certainly a subjective account of Christ's reconciliation in the sense that the redemptive change takes place *within* a person, but the change is not effected merely *by* that person. It is God's act of revealing the divine love in Jesus that ignites or arouses love within the person's heart.[12]

We recognize analogies to this in human relationships. No one can be compelled to love another person, but someone may freely give love in response to being loved. A literary example of the sort of transformation that Abelard has in mind occurs in *Les Miserables*, the classic Victor Hugo novel that has been made into films and a musical. In this story Jean Valjean is released in 1815 from a harsh French prison as a bitter, hardened man after serving nineteen years initially for stealing a loaf of bread to feed his sister's children. After a long day of walking he looks for food and lodging, but all the local innkeepers, warned by the police that he is an ex-con, refuse him a place. Finally, a kind woman directs him to a venerable bishop who invites Jean Valjean to stay for dinner and the night. At dinnertime, the priest even instructs his housekeeper to put out all the silver tableware that they normally use for

---

11. Abelard, *Exposition of the Epistle to the Romans*, in *A Scholastic Miscellany*, 284.
12. As scriptural support for his view, Abelard quotes John 15:13, "No one has greater love than this, to lay down one's life for one's friends." He also cites Romans 5:5-6, "God's love has been poured into our hearts through the Holy Spirit that has been given to us. For while we were still weak, at the right time Christ died for the ungodly."

guests. In the middle of the night while the others are sleeping, Jean Valjean steals the silver plates and departs. The next day on the road he is stopped by police who knows nothing of the theft but discover the silver. Not believing his hastily invented story that the silver is a gift from the bishop, the policemen bring Jean Valjean back to the bishop, whereupon the bishop says he is glad Jean Valjean has returned, for he also wanted to give him the silver candlesticks. This extraordinary, utterly surprising act of mercy and generosity has such an impact upon Jean Valjean that he becomes a changed person. He manifests a deep concern for anyone in need and acts out of mercy rather than strict justice. This transformation of Jean Valjean is like the effect that Abelard sees Jesus' redemptive work has on those who believe in him. Love for God is awakened in a misdirected heart by God's dramatic demonstration of merciful love.

The contemporary theologian Sallie McFague advances a theory of the work of Christ that closely resembles Abelard's while also differing in some respects. Like Abelard and Augustine, McFague sees the heart of our predicament as misdirected love. Humans are loving selfishly. One of her distinctive emphases is that a major result of this selfishness is alienation of humans from nature as well as from one another and God; hierarchical relations destroy mutuality. The work of salvation is also similar to Abelard's idea:

> The heart of salvation in this view is the making manifest of God's great love for the world. . . . The work of salvation is first of all the illumination that all of us are loved by God with the greatest love we can imagine. . . . What this knowledge does is what the announcement of the lover to the beloved at its best always does: it calls forth a response in kind. The beloved, feeling valuable, wants to return the love, wants to be at one with the lover.[13]

How should we evaluate this way of understanding Jesus' work as a demonstration of love? Surely, there is genuine insight in Abelard and McFague, for the story of Jesus' life and death does awaken love for God in many people. Abelard is right to appeal to Scripture in support, for there Jesus' death is taken as the paragon of love. "No one has greater love than this, to lay down one's life for one's friends" (John 15:13). "Indeed, rarely will anyone die for a righteous person—though perhaps for a good person someone might actually dare to die. But God proves his love for us in that while we still were sinners Christ died for us" (Romans 5:7-8). So Abelard has grasped hold of an important truth about the work of Jesus—it is a dramatic expression of love that can inspire a response of love.

---

13. Sallie McFague, *Models of God: Theology for an Ecological, Nuclear Age* (Philadelphia: Fortress Press, 1987), 144.

But there are also some significant shortcomings in many of the formulations of this view. One shortcoming in Abelard's interpretation is that his understanding of the human predicament does not go deep enough. Remember that he interprets sin as consent to evil, that is, knowingly and willingly choosing the wrong. According to him, doing evil out of ignorance is not truly sin. This conception of the human predicament is deficient in two respects. First, while it is appropriate to distinguish various degrees of responsibility depending upon one's knowledge of evil as evil, it is also the case that one of the effects of sin is spiritual and moral blindness that is a mixture of ignorance and deceit, including a measure of self-deceit. Persons avoid facing up to the full extent of the evil in which they are implicated and from which they may receive certain benefits. Thus, ignorant participation in evil is not as innocent as Abelard portrays it. Second, Abelard ignores the fact that sin is not limited to the acts of individuals but gets embodied in human institutions that shape the attitudes and actions of the next generation of individuals. For instance, sexism is not merely the acts of certain individual men and women who treat women as subordinate to men, for sexism is carried in the customs of many families, churches, schools, businesses, and political structures of a society. Individuals who grow up in such institutions are powerfully influenced to consider subordination of women as normal and right.

A second shortcoming in Abelard's conception of the work of Jesus as a demonstration of God's love is that there needs to be a stronger emphasis on the continuing presence of Jesus Christ. There is little doubt that if in a moment of extreme danger my mother had sacrificed her life to save mine, I would be forever grateful to her. And her self-giving would likely inspire me to be generous in giving myself to others as well. Nonetheless, my mother would be dead, and the strength of her influence upon me would depend largely on the vividness of my memory of her. John's Gospel envisions quite a different relationship between Christ and believers when Jesus says to his disciples shortly before his death, "Abide in me as I abide in you. Just as the branch cannot bear fruit by itself unless it abides in the vine, neither can you unless you abide in me" (John 15:4). Here John uses the image of a grapevine and its branches to talk about the relationship between Christ and believers. The main vine has all the nutrients needed for life, and branches can tap into those nutrients only as long as they are connected with the vine. Similarly, Christian believers are able to live the life of love called for by Christ only as long as they are closely linked with Christ. "Abide in me as I abide in you" suggests an intimate personal relationship in which Christ is present in and with believers and they rest in that presence. This continuing presence of Christ has much greater power than the memory of a dead person to enable believers to live the changed life of redirected love.

This second shortcoming is even more pronounced in Sallie McFague's version of Jesus' work as a demonstration of love, for in her view Jesus was not raised from the dead. According to McFague, the role of Jesus in the work of salvation is to be an example of a truly loving person.

> Different phenomena in the world will have different ways of responding to the love of God. Our way is twofold: we are aware, through the illumination of God's great love for us, of a redirection of our love away from self and toward others to the beloved world, and we feel energized to work to overcome alienation, to heal wounds, to include the outcasts. One sees this twofold pattern of awareness of the depths of divine love, and active participation in love's inclusive, healing work, in the destabilizing inclusive, nonhierarchical life and death of Jesus of Nazareth. And one sees it as well in the lives and the deaths of others.[14]

Thus, for McFague Jesus is seen more as an example of a reconciled human being than the continuing agent of God's reconciling action, more as a model of someone redeem*ed* than as the present redeem*er*.

Synthesis

After examining variations on the four major images of Christ's work, our heads may be spinning. Yet it is not very helpful for us just to have a long list of various interpretations. We need to push on toward a personal synthesis in which we at least begin to forge our own understanding of the work of Jesus Christ.

One reason for diverse interpretations of the work of Jesus is that a certain rendering speaks more powerfully to a given situation or person than another view. This is obvious with Anselm's explanation of the atonement, for it spoke so directly to the medieval society of his day. So also with individuals. For a person whose experience is marked chiefly by Christ setting free from bondage to an addiction, the classical image of victory over evil powers may be most convincing. For another person who has been troubled by enormous guilt, Calvin's idea of Christ taking the punishment due others may be most meaningful. So part of coming to a personal synthesis at this time is to see how the several images of Christ's work speak to one's own situation.

The fact that these four images have endured for centuries in the church is testimony that each apprehends some significant aspects of Christ's work; hence no one view of the work of Christ is correct and all the others wrong. Since these are varied perspectives on the same reality, they often complement one another. One view by itself might overlook important aspects of his

14. Ibid.

work. Thus another part of arriving at a personal synthesis is determining whether an interpretation does justice to the full nature of sin and the richness of Christ's work. In other words, not all views are equally comprehensive and profound.

I would suggest three questions to ask in moving toward one's own synthesis. The first question is *whether the interpretation does justice to the human predicament as portrayed in Scripture.* In every construal of the work of Jesus Christ there is a correlation between its reading of the human predicament and its explanation of what Jesus does. We can see this correlation in interpretations of the four images. When Christ is understood as offering himself as a sacrifice for sin, the predicament is that sin is a blemish that must be removed before people can be reunited with God. When Christ is seen as victor, the predicament is that humans and the world are in bondage to evil forces. Behind the several versions of Christ doing justice lies the conviction that humans are caught in a broken relationship with God that they are unable to set right. And the idea that Jesus' work is to demonstrate love is linked with the predicament of a darkened mind and misdirected will. In my own reading of the human situation, the last three of these interpretations give important insights relevant to contemporary experience. I agree with the several visions of Christ as the one who does justice that the root of the human predicament lies in broken relationship with God. The result of this, as Abelard says, is that our minds are darkened about what is good and right and our hearts are attached to many of the wrong things. Our situation therefore is aptly described by the Christus Victor theme as one of bondage to evil powers, social structures, and death.

The second question I would ask about any interpretation of Christ's work is *whether it clearly expresses the generous love of God.* I think that Anselm's satisfaction theory and the substitutionary punishment view are deficient on this score; in both the concern for maintaining order outweighs divine generosity. I believe God freely forgives just as the parable of the prodigal son portrays. God's bountiful love serves justice by striving to recreate the relationships of humans with God, with one another, and with nature. This recreative work involves self-giving sacrifice in the life and death of Jesus Christ, and this sacrificial love has, as Abelard suggests, the power to change the minds and hearts of people. God scored a fundamental victory over evil by enabling Jesus to live a generous, inclusive, faithful life even to an unjust death and by raising him from the dead; victory in this one human life established the beachhead from which other victories could be won.

The third question I would direct to any view of Christ's work is *whether it recognizes the objective presence of Jesus Christ at work within people and the cosmos.* Since reconciliation also means transformation through the gentle yet mighty divine presence rather than through self-improvement schemes, prominent place should be given to that presence of Christ or the Holy Spirit. Most of the traditional images of Christ's work have been weak on this matter. Some have so concentrated upon Christ's work in the past that his present activity gets short shrift. This is especially the case with the sacrifice for sin, Anselm's satisfaction theory, and substitutionary punishment theory, all of which have focused almost exclusively on Jesus' death as the crucial event. Abelard's portrayal of the demonstration of love in Jesus is also strangely silent about his presence today within believers. Nevertheless, several of the traditional images are very accommodating to an emphasis upon the presence of Christ enabling persons and communities to share in a new life. Christ's sacrifice as a self-offering may include a continuing self-giving in his ongoing sacrificial presence. Christ's re-creative work of justice is also a contemporary reality as his presence enables people to forgive one another and to love another into wholesome relationships. The presence of Christ is also an integral part of the victory that Christ wins over evil, for the victory becomes effective in the lives of individuals and communities to the extent that people share in that healing presence.

8

The Church

W hen most of us in the Western world think about the church, we come with preconceived notions that are deeply influenced by our experience with the church. Some people grow up experiencing the church as an integral part of their life, and they never leave it. Others have grown up with some involvement in the church, but have dropped out during their young adult years; they are skeptical about the value of church. Still others have grown up in a family suspicious or even hostile toward the church, and this strongly influences their attitude. Again, others from outside the Christian tradition may see the church as an unknown entity about which they have some curiosity. These preconceptions or initial attitudes powerfully color our thinking about the church.

This chapter falls into two main parts. In the first and larger part, we reflect on five major models of the church in an effort to at least provisionally formulate our own view of the church. In the second part we focus attention on two key issues regarding the institutional structure of the church and the relations among churches: primacy of the pope and infallibility in the church.

As we begin part one, we shall borrow a framework of ideas from the classic book *Models of the Church* by the Catholic theologian Avery Dulles; in this book Dulles distinguishes five models of the church.[1] Each model emphasizes an important aspect of the church's reality, and makes it the key for understanding the church. With some modification of Dulles' terminology, the five models are: (1) the church as institution, (2) as community of the Spirit, (3) as

---

1. Avery Dulles, *Models of the Church* (Garden City, N.Y.: Doubleday, 1978).

sacrament, (4) as assembly of believers in Jesus Christ, and (5) as community of liberation. We will examine these five models, in order to stimulate and guide our reflection on the church.

Church as Institution

Every society organizes and channels basic activities such as sex, education, economics, and politics in certain ways called institutions. For example, part of the American institutionalization of sex is the practice of dating, whereas some other societies have organized courting so that a young man and woman can be together only when an older chaperon is present. Religious activity has also been channeled through institutions that have varied with time and place. Institutional organization of religion in America has been closely associated with certain social groups, chiefly Christian churches and Jewish synagogues, but also mosques and esoteric religious organizations.

While the Roman Catholic Church embraced all of medieval Europe and the Anglican Church enjoyed favored status as the established church of modern Britain, the United States has always had a diversity of churches. Today the two main types of Christian groups in America are the sect and denomination. A *sect* is a close-knit group that sees itself as a purer expression of the Christian faith and plays little role in the larger society. In other words, a sect is sharply distinct from other Christian groups and the surrounding society. A *denomination*, on the other hand, accepts the legitimacy of other Christian denominations, although maybe not their equal value; the denomination also tends not to have a sharp difference with the surrounding society. The general trend has been toward the denominational type. Most large Christian churches in America today are denominations. Even the Roman Catholic Church, which previously saw itself as the one true church, by acknowledging the churchly status of other bodies has come to function in America like a denomination. And many bodies that started out as a sect isolated from the larger society, such as the Assemblies of God, over time have become more like a denomination.

Since the church is a social institution, it can be studied by sociologists just like any other institution. For instance, the membership of American churches reflects social class differences in the society. Using social status indicators such as family income, education, and occupational prestige, the major Christian denominations with the most high-status members are the Episcopal, Presbyterian, and United Church of Christ (Congregational). Their position at the top has remained unchanged since World War II, whereas in the intervening years Catholics have moved up from low- to middle-rank social status. We shall return later to some of these social factors such as social class and race that have been discussed in sociological treatments of the church for over a century.

In order to better understand current attitudes toward the church, we shall focus on three major recent developments of the church as an institution.

1. The most important recent development is that *a greater individualism emphasizes the self's own faith synthesis and has loosened ties to the institutional church.* Americans have always valued individual religious freedom, but commonly it was exercised within the nurturing context of a certain religious tradition. For instance, it was expected that a person reared in the Methodist church would make his or her own affirmation of faith, but for the most part those raised Methodist would continue to identify with the Methodist church. The new individualism has both a greater reliance on the self to fashion its own faith and a looser loyalty to a specific religious denomination.

Individuals do much more picking and choosing of their own beliefs and moral convictions. One study revealed that a substantial number of baby boomers believe in reincarnation, a belief that has no roots whatsoever in the Judaeo-Christian tradition.[2] Greater reliance on the self to produce its own faith was evident in a 1978 Gallup poll in which 81 percent of respondents agreed that one should arrive at one's own religious beliefs independent of a church or synagogue and 78 percent agreed that one can be a good Christian or Jew without attending a church or synagogue.[3] Often implicit in this outlook is the conviction that the individual is prior to the group, and does not need the group except in some secondary way. So it is very common today to hear people say they are spiritual, but they are lukewarm toward what they call "organized religion."

The new individualism is also manifest in a looser institutional loyalty. A sign of this is a much higher rate of switching religious denominations. Whereas a 1955 Gallup poll revealed that only 4 percent of adults in America had moved out of their childhood religious faith, in 1984 about 33 percent had switched.[4] Even among those who have stayed in their denomination, individualism is evident in the nature of their connection; many stay on their own terms and because they feel the institution is satisfactory in meeting their personal needs. Personal choice has influenced the way many Catholics relate to their church. Following the pope's reasserted opposition to artificial means of birth control in 1968, there was a substantial decline in Catholic mass

---

2. Wade Clark Roof, *A Generation of Seekers: The Spiritual Journeys of the Baby Boom Generation* (San Francisco: HarperSanFrancisco, 1993), 125.

3. Wade Clark Roof and William McKinney, *American Mainline Religion: Its Changing Shape and Future* (New Brunswick: Rutgers University Press, 1987), 43–57.

4. Robert Wuthnow, *The Restructuring of American Religion: Society and Faith since World War II* (Princeton: Princeton University Press, 1988), 88.

attendance. Later, when many Catholics returned to regular attendance, they did so on their own terms by disagreeing with their church's teaching on birth control.[5] The facts that the Catholic birth rate in the United States is about the same as that for all Protestants and that mass attendance has leveled off since the 1970s indicate this selective Catholicism continues today. And a great many people who stay in their denomination do so not primarily out of a sense of service to that church, but because they feel the church is doing reasonably well in meeting their personal needs. So for many of those who remain in their denomination, the self is also more important than the group and the group is valued insofar as it serves the self.[6]

What are the sources of this new individualism with its deep confidence in the self and skepticism of institutional religion? One source is the impact of the baby boom generation on American culture. The baby boom generation has been especially skeptical of just about all social institutions. Since they were born during the period from 1946 to 1964, the baby boomers experienced many upheavals that shook American social institutions: the assassination of President John Kennedy in 1963, the Vietnam War, the murders of Martin Luther King Jr. and Robert Kennedy in 1968, Watergate, the resignation of President Nixon in 1974, and the civil rights, ecological, and feminist movements. A 1985 Gallup poll found boomers were more questioning than other age groups of almost every social institution: Congress, the military, public schools, banks, even name brands. It is not surprising that this doubt extended to the church as an institution.[7] Boomer suspicion of many institutions has been communicated to the baby bust generation (born from 1965 to 1976) and the baby boomlet generation (born from 1977 to 1995) through family connections, films, television, and music. Skepticism of religious institutions places the primary responsibility for religious life and development on the individual.

A second source of looser church loyalty is a weaker bond between church and ethnicity. Denominations in America traditionally have been linked partly with ethnicity. A great many American Catholics were Irish, Italian, Slavic, and German. Most Lutherans were Scandinavian and German. Episcopalians tended to be British in origin. Clear boundaries between ethnic groups reinforced the differences among the denominations. As ethnic divisions have lessened, there has been more contact with persons of other ethnic groups and denominations, and there have been many more marriages that have crossed these boundaries. The one ethnic boundary that remains strong is the

---

5. Andrew Greeley, *Religious Change in America* (Cambridge: Harvard University Press, 1989), 52.
6. Roof, *A Generation of Seekers*, 104–9.
7. Ibid, 37–42. See also Roof and McKinney, *American Mainline Religion*, 45–48.

racial border between black and white. Membership statistics reveal that the churches mirror the racial division between black and white in American society. By far most African Americans belong to essentially all-black churches. With the exception of the American Baptists and Seventh-Day Adventists, which both include 27 percent blacks, the other predominantly white churches have only a very small percentage of black members.

A third factor has been less concentration of denominations in certain regions of the country. For instance, the South once had very few Catholics. In 1952 Atlanta had only one Catholic church, but in 1980 it had forty-four. So geographic barriers between members of different denominations have also decreased.[8] A fourth factor contributing to looser loyalty to denomination has been the behavior of the churches themselves. In the twentieth century many churches have sought closer ties with other churches through what is called the *ecumenical movement*. A result of the ecumenical movement has been a widespread attitude of respect for Christians from another denomination. So the churches have lowered the barriers between themselves. They have implicitly communicated the message that the differences between the various Christian churches are not so serious. If one belongs to a different denomination, one has not necessarily compromised the Christian faith. Indeed, even using the term *denomination* for one's own church means that it is one of a number of legitimate Christian churches. So the ecumenical movement has contributed to less denominational loyalty.

Thus several cultural and religious factors have helped produce a new individualism with a looser loyalty to the church as an institution. How this different social climate has affected various denominations is our next subject.

2. There has been a reshuffling of the relative size and influence of certain denominations as some have grown and some diminished. We shall first look at Protestant churches and then at the Roman Catholic Church in the United States. A recent important study by Roof and McKinney divides Protestant churches into four groups—liberal, moderate, conservative, and black. The liberal churches (Episcopalians, Presbyterians, and United Church of Christ) have all reported substantial decreases in membership since 1960. Among the moderate churches there have been mixed results; Methodists and Disciples of Christ have had sizable losses while Lutherans have had a modest decline. Conservative Protestant churches such as the Southern Baptists and Pentecostal churches have announced marked increases.[9] Black Protestant churches have also grown substantially.[10]

8. Roof, *A Generation of Seekers*, 85; Roof and McKinney, *American Mainline Religion*, 117–38.
9. Roof and McKinney, *American Mainline Religion*, 150.
10. Robert N. Bellah et al., *The Good Society* (New York: Random House, 1991), 187.

What accounts for these different fortunes? Four factors are the major influences on the membership of denominations: how many of the denomination's own members stay loyal, how many new members it can bring in, the degree of commitment of these new members, and the birthrate of its members.

a. Protestant denominational loyalty varies greatly, and does not correlate simply with being liberal, moderate, or conservative: 87 percent of black Protestants stay black Protestant, 75 percent of Lutherans remain Lutheran, 73 percent white Southern Baptists are loyal, 70 percent of Pentecostal and Holiness members are loyal, and at the bottom only 37 percent remain in a cluster of small Evangelical and Fundamentalist groups. The other major Protestant churches have about 60 percent loyalty.

b. Another factor affecting membership is how well a denomination attracts new members. In view of the overall drop in the liberal Protestant churches in the United States, it is surprising that they draw somewhat more new people than they lose. This is the continuation of an historic pattern of upward social mobility, for the liberal Protestant churches attract members with high education, income, and prestige. But gains from denominational switching are more than offset by a lower level of commitment and low birthrate among their new members.

c. Measured by regularity of worship attendance, those who switch to liberal bodies are less committed than those who switch to conservative churches. It is likely that in a poll a considerable number of people who identify themselves with a liberal church have such a low level of church involvement that they are not actually counted as members by that denomination.[11]

d. Furthermore, those who switch to a liberal church tend to be older and often beyond childbearing age; this contributes to the fact that liberal churches have the lowest birthrate.

One overall result of these four factors is that the liberal Protestant churches have been decreasing in membership. The moderate Protestant churches (Methodist, Disciples of Christ, Reformed, and Lutheran) as a group lose 5.9 percent more people than the new ones they attract, but the commitment of their switchers and their birthrates are somewhat higher than those of the liberal churches. The outcomes vary from great to modest decline for the different moderate Protestant churches. Black Protestant churches have a high net loss from switching (10.7 percent), but this is offset by a high level of commitment to the institution among their members and the highest birthrate among all church groupings.

When all four of these factors are put together, it is apparent that the large, conservative, mostly white Protestant churches (Southern Baptist, Pen-

---

11. Roof and McKinney, *American Mainline Religion*, 157–81.

tecostal, and Holiness, and so forth) are the biggest winners. The conservative Protestant churches have a rather high loyalty (white Southern Baptists,
73 percent; Pentecostal and Holiness, 70 percent), they appeal to slightly
more new people than they lose, they have the highest level of commitment
to the institution, and they have a higher birthrate than either liberal or moderate churches.

The Roman Catholic Church in America has increased its membership
since 1960. However, polls differ on whether Catholics have increased substantially as a percentage of the total American population.[12] In respect to our
four factors affecting membership, the Roman Catholic Church does very
well on loyalty, for 85 percent of Catholics continue to identify themselves as
Catholic. On the three other counts, though, Catholics are about the same as
moderate Protestants: in their net loss in switching, degree of involvement in
the institution, and birthrate of women under forty-five. Thus, on the basis of
these four factors, it is difficult to account for Catholic growth. What the
studies cited do not take into account, however, is immigration, and it seems
to me that considerably more recent immigrants to the United States have
been Catholic than Protestant or other. In any case, the Roman Catholic
Church has at least kept pace with general population growth in the United
States and probably has done better than that.

So one overall major change in the Roman Catholic and Protestant
churches in America is that there has been a reshuffling in their relative size
and influence in the society. The old WASP (white Anglo-Saxon Protestant)
churches of mostly liberal Protestants have lost numbers and power, while
conservative Protestants and Catholics have increased in both membership
and influence.

3. *There has been a substantial increase in the number of Americans who claim no
affiliation with a religious institution.* A frequently cited statistic is that Gallup
polls show the percentage of the population who say they have no religious
preference increased from 2 percent in 1952 to 9 percent in 1985. The question we need to ask is, What is the meaning of the increase in those who do
not affiliate with any religious institution? One explanation commonly proposed in intellectual circles is secularization, namely, that the darkness of religion is fading under the advancing light of secular, scientific thinking.

There are a couple reasons to pause before jumping to the conclusion of
secularization, however. One reason is that the increase in religious nonaffiliation may not be as dramatic as it first appears when we compare 2 percent in
1952 with 9 percent in 1985. It is not commonly noted that a 1947 Gallup
poll had 6 percent claiming no religious affiliation. This suggests that secu-

12. Greeley, *Religious Change in America*, 24–27.

larization is not some irrepressible force, for rates of nonaffiliation have gone down as well as up. The increase from 6 percent in 1947 to 9 percent in 1985 is also not so dramatic. A further reason to doubt that secularization is leading more and more people to reject religion is the behavior of the religiously unaffiliated. "Persons reporting they have no religious affiliation are a diverse constituency, religiously as well as culturally. Many hold beliefs in the supernatural and the mystical and often show much interest in religious and quasi-religious phenomena. Few are actually militant secularists or committed atheists in their opposition to religion. They simply have little interest in organized religion and lack membership in a conventional church or synagogue."[13] Forty-eight percent believe in life after death, and slightly over half eventually affiliate with some religious institution.

Sociologist Andrew Greeley offers another explanation for the increase in religious nonaffiliation from 1952 to 1985: it was due to the higher proportion of young adults in American society during that time. Religious nonaffiliation can be expected to vary as the proportion of young adults in the population varies, much like the crime rate fluctuates with the numbers of young males in the society. Young adults are the most fluid age group, for they are often uncommitted about career and marriage and have the highest percentage of nonaffiliation with a religious institution or political party. Those who marry later or never marry have higher rates of nonaffiliation; after 1960 the average age of marriage rose and so did the proportion of those never married. The percentage of religious unaffiliates decreases with each decade of life down to 3 percent when fifty or older. So Greeley argues that the rise in nonaffiliation increased when the large baby boom generation became young adults. The baby boom generation was given that name because births averaged four million per year from 1946 to 1964 and then fell off to 3.4 million annually for the baby bust generation. Indeed, Greeley also explains the decline in Protestant church attendance in the same way. People ages 20–29 have generally attended worship at a lower rate than those in their thirties and forties, and the worship attendance rate for twentysomething Protestants in 1980 was virtually the same as in 1940. But in 1980 there were many more in that age bracket.[14] Thus Greeley argues that the higher proportion of young adults is the chief cause of the increased percentage of Americans who are religiously unaffiliated. This may also be a major reason for the surge of greater individualism since the 1960s.

In summary, recent decades have brought major changes in the churches as social institutions. For many years individuals have related to churches in

---

13. Roof and McKinney, *American Mainline Religion*, 99.
14. Greeley, *Religious Change in America*, 28–33; 45–46.

basically three ways: some individuals are continuously loyal church attenders, others drop out of church for a time and then reaffiliate with a church, and still others remain unaffiliated with any church. What has happened since the 1960s with the new individualism is that people have displayed looser ties with Christian groups both in respect to church affiliation and adhering to church teaching. This is evident among the *loyalists* in several ways. Some who have continuously attended church have switched from one denomination or sect to another; perhaps more than once. And among those who remain in the denomination of their birth, many do so with the sense that they *could* be a member of a different denomination without great loss. The individualism is expressed among loyal Catholics by their selective way of relating to church teaching. Those who drop out of any church and then reaffiliate clearly do so by their own choice. In fact, it is common for these *returnees* to drop out and affiliate more than once. The churches that have grown in this fluid situation have been conservative Protestant and Roman Catholic. Finally, there has been an increase in the percentage of those who identify themselves as *unaffiliated* with any religious group. Even among those who affiliate with a church, though, there is commonly a strong emphasis on forming one's own synthesis of faith.

We may recall that when we reflected on human nature, one of the polar realities of human existence is that of the individual and the community. That is, human beings are both distinct individuals and members of communities. What has happened in recent years with the swing toward greater individualism is a decreased emphasis on community, including religious community. Evaluating this shift is complicated. On the positive side, the greater individualism is good in that persons are less likely to remain in a church or other community merely out of inertia, and the community is less likely to have domineering power over the individual. On the negative side, persons are more likely to feel rootless and communities are more apt to be unstable as individuals move from church to church or from one family grouping to another without ever establishing bonds that endure. The extreme example of religious individualism was found by the sociologist Robert Bellah, whose research team interviewed a woman named Sheila who described her faith as Sheilaism; in other words, she saw herself as having her own individual religion.[15] Not many people go so far, for a strictly personal faith is terribly lonely. Yet the current strong emphasis on individual choice raises the question of the significance of the church as religious community.

---

15. Robert N. Bellah et al., *Habits of the Heart: Individualism and Commitment in American Life* (Berkeley: University of California Press, 1985), 221.

Church as Community of the Spirit
and as Sacrament

Since community is a word with many meanings, we will draw first upon sociology and then theology in an effort to understand in what ways the church is a community. The German sociologist Ferdinand Tonnies suggested that there is a range of human groups that can be placed along a continuum from a *pure community* (*Gemeinschaft* in German) at one end to a *pure impersonal society* (*Gesellschaft*) at the other end. In a pure impersonal society everybody is independent; each looks after his or her own interest and does not care about anyone else. People interact only through regulations, laws, and impersonal administrators as individuals exchange goods and services with one another. Although there probably is no entirely impersonal society, people trading on the New York Stock Exchange would approach it. In a pure community the members are closely knit together through shared experiences and strong bonds of common feeling, and members support one another in times of need. A close family and an intimate circle of friends would exemplify many of these qualities.

This distinction between pure community and pure impersonal society is useful in thinking about the church. It is apparent that people's experience of the church differs. Some persons find the local congregation or, more precisely, a subgroup within the congregation rather like a pure community. They have family members and close friends in the congregation, and share with them deep involvement in church activities. If they are ill, these family and friends in the congregation come to their assistance with food, transportation, and visits. Such persons experience the church as a very supportive community to which they have a deep sense of belonging, near to what Tonnies called a pure community.

At the other extreme are those who are very alienated from the church. They have a cynical view of the church, seeing it as a body filled with rules, manipulative leaders, and people too timid to leave or too concerned about making a good impression. The cynic has often been hurt by someone connected with the church, and now feels greatly distanced from it. Such people experience the church quite like what Tonnies thought of as a pure impersonal society.

Most people who identify themselves as Christian have an experience of the church that lies at some point between these two extremes. Although nearly everyone longs for intimate community, only a small minority find it in their congregation. Some congregations today try to meet the desire for close community by offering an array of small groups where intimacy is more likely to occur. In addition to the traditional youth and Bible study groups, these congregations establish groups aimed at people with special interests such as those going through a divorce or parents who have lost a child. Supportive community often does arise in these small groups, yet the groups also have their limitations. There is no long-term commitment to the group, for individuals easily drop out as their life circumstances change or they become dissatisfied. Furthermore, some very effective special groups such as Alcoholics Anonymous are not organized as a specifically Christian community.[16] Thus, in a time when Americans are more than ever exercising freedom of choice vis à vis religious organizations, their deep desire for close, supportive community often is not satisfied or only intermittently satisfied in the church.

Although a congregation gives only some of its members intimate community, it draws many of its people together into an association somewhere between intimate community and impersonal society. We can call this a *community of faith*. Fairly involved members of a congregation share the same symbols that express a common vision of life and reality. These symbols of faith appear in worship with liturgy, hymns, and physical objects; the symbols are also present in small group gatherings where the Bible is read and Christian prayers are uttered. To the extent that individuals resonate to these symbols, they feel they belong to this community of faith. Yet a congregation functions in some respects like a more impersonal society, for it provides services such as religious education and the rites of baptism, confirmation, marriage, and burial, which are sometimes used by people otherwise uninvolved with church. Yet these very services may build community by bringing people together with Christian symbols at critical points in their lives.

The denomination is further toward the society end of the spectrum than a congregation, for individuals are related through a denominational bureaucratic structure often similar to those in government and large corporations. Yet the individual can identify with the denomination rather like identifying with a nation. There is the sense that one belongs to a big, often diverse group that shares a common history and set of symbols. So the denomination may have the character of a large community of faith. The denomination often links together people from different nations and cultures with a shared denominational history and common symbols. In our transient society, a denomination also provides mobile individuals with continuity in familiar patterns of worship and church organization.

Much of what we have said so far from the sociological perspective about the church as community could be said about other groups, such as a national college sorority or the Elks Club. The theological perspective goes further by speaking of the church as a community of the Holy Spirit. This is a state-

---

16. Wuthnow, *Restructuring of American Religion*, 121–31. See also Robert Wuthnow, *Sharing the Journey: Support Groups and America's New Quest for Community* (New York: Macmillan, 1994), 11–28.

ment of faith grounded in people's experience of God touching their life in and through the church. Out of this faith experience many in the Christian tradition say that God is especially present and active in the church. A Christian may believe that God can also touch people in a given gathering of a sorority or Elks Club, since God is present throughout the world building up human life. Yet Christians generally claim that God is active in the church in a way unlike God's presence in a sorority or Elks Club, for only the church is explicitly dedicated to the worship and teaching of God as made known in Jesus Christ. That God may work through some sorority event is entirely incidental to the goals of a secular sorority, whereas the central purpose of a church is to witness to God. One biblical way of expressing this special presence of God in the church is to call it the *community of the Spirit.*

A closely related way of affirming God's special presence in the church is through this New Testament metaphor: the church is the *body of Christ.* When Paul speaks of the church as the body of Christ in Romans 12 and 1 Corinthians 12, he is using a biological metaphor. One of his main points is that as the human body has many different parts which all help in the proper functioning of the body, so also the church has diverse members each of whom make their own contribution to the well-being of the Christian community. One might say something similar about a sorority or Elks Club. But Paul goes further by saying that the various church members' contributions are gifts of the Holy Spirit. So the Holy Spirit is at work building up the church as a supportive community of Christian faith. He calls this community the body of Christ, for Christ is especially present in this particular social group and its varied gifts of leading, healing, teaching about Christ, speaking in tongues, and so forth. As Christ once acted in and through his own physical body, so now Christ also acts in and through this social body. Thus Paul's image of the church as the body of Christ emphasizes the immediate presence of Christ and the Spirit within this group enabling it to be a supportive community of faith.

A variation on this theological theme occurs in two other New Testament letters, Ephesians and Colossians, which speak of Christ as the head of the body. Perhaps employing an ancient biological theory that views the head as the source of the whole body's nourishment and harmony, the author says to the Christian community in Ephesus, "We must grow up in every way into him who is the head, into Christ, from whom the whole body, joined and knit together by every ligament with which it is equipped, as each part is working properly, promotes the body's growth in building itself up in love" (Ephesians 4:15-16). The standard of maturity is Jesus Christ with his faith in God and care for others, and the growing up is a corporate rather than an individualistic enterprise. As an arm or a leg matures along with the whole body rather than separately, so persons in the church need others and their spiritual gifts in order that both person and community can become more mature. To the extent that this Christlike maturity occurs, the church will approach being a pure community in which "the members may have the same care for one another. If one member suffers, all suffer together with it; if one member is honored, all rejoice together with it" (1 Corinthians 12:25-26).

Thus in the New Testament the image of the church as the body of Christ is used to suggest at least three things about the church: that the Holy Spirit is especially active in this community equipping it with particular functions and gifts, that God intends the church to be a community of Christlike maturity, and that human maturity in considerable measure is communal, not simply individual.

Roman Catholic thinking about the church in most of the twentieth century gave very serious attention to the special divine presence in the church by emphasizing the image of body of Christ or the mystical body. In its *Dogmatic Constitution on the Church* (Latin title *Lumen Gentium*), the Second Vatican Council (1962–1965) ratified this trend by choosing as its first affirmation that the church is a mystery, for the mystery is God present in the church.

A question hangs like a dark cloud over all this talk about the church as community in which God is especially present: How can one make such an exalted claim about the church when it is deeply flawed just like any other human community? Sexism, racism, and differences between social classes are generally reflected in the church. It is far from uncommon to hear news reports about sexual abuse of children or vulnerable women by clergy. Conflict and bitter dissension often riddle church life. Skepticism toward the church seems warranted in any age, but it is particularly prominent today when a great many people in America are suspicious of just about all social institutions. So unqualified claims for the church as community of the Holy Spirit sound hollow.

Honest recognition of sin in the church must lead to a qualified interpretation of the church as community of the Spirit. One must avoid the notion that the Holy Spirit's presence in the Christian community is unambiguous. Three qualifications are essential. One qualification emphasizes the role of the Holy Spirit in battling sin. Before Paul calls the church in Corinth the body of Christ, he chastises them for quarreling and for a case of sexual immorality (1 Corinthians 1:11; 5:1; 12:27). In other words, it is not a flawless communal life that causes Paul to call the church the body of Christ and to affirm the Holy Spirit's presence in equipping church members. The church is a community of sinners. Yet the presence of the Holy Spirit is marked by *struggle against* evils, such as quarreling and sexual immorality. Rather than such evils being accepted as normal or unavoidable, in the church the Holy Spirit leads the struggle against them. Admittedly, the battle is not always won. What counts, though, is the struggle against moral evil.

A second very important qualification views the church within the context of Christian eschatology. As we have noted before, the term *eschatology* comes from a Greek word, *eschaton,* which means last things; so eschatology is literally thinking about the last things. In other words, eschatology has to do with the future and especially the ultimate future of the world and humankind. Remember that Christian faith is grounded in a story. This story tells of what God has done in the past in creation, providence, and reconciliation. But the story also looks to the future when God's work of creation, providence, and reconciliation will be completed. One of the key biblical symbols for this fulfilled future is the reign of God. The church must be understood within this eschatological framework. That is, the church is not to be equated with the ultimate reign of God in which all sin and evil will be overcome and perfect harmony will exist. On the other hand, the church is a foretaste and anticipation of that reign of God, for the church is the particular community that explicitly proclaims the presence of that reign in Jesus and expressly hopes for the final fulfillment of God's reign through Jesus.

A third qualification recognizes that experience of God's presence in the church is never obvious and publicly accessible, no more than the skill of Beethoven or the Beatles is perceived by everyone who happens to hear their music. As we noted in chapter 3 on the reasonableness of belief in God, just as some training in music or art is necessary in order to experience some of what an expert musician or artist experiences, so it is also with Christian experience of God. Learning biblical stories, Christian teachings, and hymns will not automatically give one a Christian experience of God's presence any more than studying music theory will inevitably make one appreciate Beethoven's music. Nonetheless, some training in Christian things is needed.

In any case, when we take into account these three qualifications of the Spirit's role in battling sin, the place of the church in Christian eschatology, and the hiddenness of God's presence, then it is clear that the claim of God's special presence in the church is not a simple, unambiguous assertion. Nevertheless, the Christian tradition has consistently affirmed God's special presence and activity in the church.

With what we have said so far about the church as an institution and as a community of the Spirit, we are now in position to ponder the mystery of the church. On the one hand, the church is a social institution that behaves in ways akin to other social groups, so that sociologists can gather data on it. On the other hand, the Christian tradition claims that God is especially present and active in this human group. This claim that the church is the community of the Spirit runs counter to our culture's new individualism in which 78 percent of Americans say one can be a good Christian or Jew without attending a church or synagogue. The new individualism assumes that God's presence is generally available and is not in any way particularly linked with a Christian community. This individualism believes that God first meets independent individuals apart from any group, and then individuals may or may not choose to join a church. In contrast to this, the Christian tradition asserts that God's goodness and mercy are especially manifest in a community where the biblical story is regularly rehearsed.

What is the church? We begin to see the real theological issue at stake here only when we start to grasp both sides of this question. If we pay attention only to the human, social side of the church, then the church is just like any other social institution and can be adequately explained in those terms. If we attend only to the theological affirmations about the church as the body of Christ and the community of the Spirit, then our understanding of the church tends to become divorced from the hard realities of life. But as the body of Christ, the church resembles Jesus Christ. Both Christ and the church have a clear, human reality, and it is possible to say that this is all there is. Yet for most of the Christian tradition, Jesus Christ and the church, each in a distinctive way, have a special divine presence.

Now we turn briefly to the third model of the church, which seeks to hold together both sides of the mystery of the church; this model is the *church as sacrament*. This requires some understanding of the idea of sacrament. An ancient definition associated with St. Augustine is that *a sacrament is a visible sign of an invisible grace*. For example, the eucharist or holy communion has bread and wine as visible, tangible elements, yet the bread and wine are not ends in themselves, but signs of an invisible, gracious presence of Christ. In an extended sense, it is possible to speak of Jesus Christ as a sacrament, since there is a visible human life, but this visible humanity points beyond itself to an invisible divine presence. In another extended sense, the church can be called a sacrament, for the church is a visible human institution which is a sign of God's invisible grace. Since the 1950s the sacramental model of the church has been widely used in Catholicism where the sacraments are so central to the spirituality. The Second Vatican Council used this model (along with others) when it spoke of the church as "a kind of sacrament or sign of intimate union with God" and "as the universal sacrament of salvation."[17]

The chief strength of the sacramental model is that it is able to hold together in one symbol the institutional and spiritual community aspects of the church. A sacrament must have both a visible sign and an invisible divine grace. For those with a good understanding of sacrament and deep spiritual bond with sacraments, this model is a very significant way of understanding

---

17. *Dogmatic Constitution on the Church* (*Lumen Gentium*), Articles 1 and 48, in *The Documents of Vatican II*, Walter M. Abbott, ed. (New York: Guild Press, 1966), 26, 79.

the church. The main weakness of this model, as Avery Dulles points out, is that it assumes a fairly sophisticated understanding of sacrament. Thus it has appealed more to professional theologians and clergy than to laity.

Church as Assembly of Believers

Since the model of church as *assembly of believers* has been most prominent among Protestants, we shall begin by looking at the first official Protestant statement of it. In the Augsburg Confession (1530), Lutherans defined the church as *the assembly of all believers among whom the gospel is preached and the sacraments administered*.[18] There are two things to notice about this conception of the church. One is that the church is understood as the assembly of believers, that is, as the gathering of those who believe in God as revealed in Jesus Christ. This is in accord with the basic meaning of the Greek word for church in the New Testament: *ecclesia*. The Greeks used this term for an official town meeting of citizens and the Christians applied it to their faith communities. Thus in theology thinking about the church is called *ecclesiology*. In any event, the church or *ecclesia* is first of all not a building or an ideal, but a human group, the company of believers in Jesus Christ. Paul distinguishes between the church and a building when he says to the Christians in Rome, "Greet also the church in their house" (Romans 16:5). Since the empirical church is a mixture of believers and unbelievers that is beyond human ability to separate, emphasis falls on what God does to create the company of believers. Thus, the other thing to notice in the Augsburg Confession statement is that two activities are highlighted as essential to the church: preaching of the gospel and administration of the sacraments. The reason for stressing these two activities is that they are the essential means for creating faith in Jesus Christ. Lutherans believe that wherever the gospel of Jesus is preached and the sacraments administered God will bring about faith in Jesus Christ and thereby create the assembly of believers that is the church. John Calvin and many other Protestants share these convictions about the church.[19] Basic to this view is the idea that the church arises out of God calling and people responding in faith.

The biblical image that most directly supports this model is the church as the people of God. When we speak of "a people," we mean one group dis-

---

18. The Augsburg Confession, Article 7, in *The Book of Concord*, Theodore G. Tappert, ed. (Philadelphia: Fortress Press, 1959), 32.

19. John Calvin, *Institutes of the Christian Religion*, Book IV, Chapter 1, Section 9; The Library of Christian Classics, Vol. 21, ed. John T. McNeill, trans. F L. Battles (Philadelphia: Westminster, 1960), 1023.

tinguished from others; when we say "my people," we refer to a particular group with whom we are identified. So in the Old Testament when it is often said that Israel is "God's people," this means both that Israel is a particular group distinguished from others and the group with whom God is particularly identified. This terminology is rooted in the Old Testament story of *covenant*. God called Abraham to set out on a journey and promised to give him a land, to make him the father of a great nation, and to bless all people through him (Genesis 12:1-3). Then in Moses' time, God declared Israel to be God's people and called them to be faithful to the law (Exodus 24:7-8). Unlike other peoples who have their source in a human factor such as common language or history, Israel became the people of God through God's free choice and call. God's call is primary, Israel's response is secondary. In fact, many Christian theologians today say that Israel remains the people of God through God's faithfulness even though Israel has in some respects been unfaithful.

What the early Christians did was to apply this language of God's people to the church. So the basis of the church's unity as a group is also not to be found in any human commonality such as ethnicity, social status, or personal decision, but in God's call to faith in Jesus Christ. Thus the church is viewed as having a special relationship with God founded on God's call given in the proclamation of Jesus.

While Protestants for a long time have favored this image of the church, part of the major shift in Catholic thinking about the church at the Second Vatican Council was expressed by giving a prominent place to the church as the people of God. For about four hundred years Roman Catholic ecclesiology was dominated by a certain institutional model of the church that emphasized the church hierarchy. In responding to the challenges of Protestantism and later of secularism, Catholic theology stressed the hierarchical structure of bishops in communion with the pope as the distinguishing mark of the true church. Part of the Vatican II effort to produce a more balanced view of the church was to give prominence to the church as the whole people of God in which the laity also play an active part.

One strength of this assembly of believers model is that it holds up a clear notion of the church's identity and mission. While the church is often tempted to be relevant by latching onto some current movement, this model says the church's identity lies in its faith in Jesus Christ. To compromise that is to lose what is basic to the church's being. Seeing the church as assembly of believers in Jesus Christ also lays out a clear mission of communicating the message of Jesus Christ. A commonly voiced criticism of this model is that its heavy emphasis upon proclamation tends to downplay the importance of active service in the world. This is the primary concern of our next model of the church.

Church as Community of Liberation

Our fifth model is the church as *community of liberation*. There is emphasis here both upon community and liberation. That is, community is found in close, supportive human bonds within the church as its members contend with social oppression. Liberation is also vital, liberation both within the church and in society. The accent falls both upon the church as a nurturing sanctuary of freedom within an oppressive society and as a vanguard dedicated to transforming that oppressive society.

A favorite biblical passage among those who see the church as liberation community is a portion of the Old Testament prophet Isaiah that Jesus quoted at the synagogue in Nazareth: "The Spirit of the Lord is upon me, because he has anointed me to bring good news to the poor. He has sent me to proclaim release to the captives and recovery of sight to the blind, to let the oppressed go free, to proclaim the year of the Lord's favor" (Luke 4:18-19). As Jesus proclaimed the nearness of the reign of God, worked among the poor, and sought the liberation of all people, so the church should be an agent of liberation today.

Liberation theologians—African American, Third World, and feminist—are the foremost exponents of this view of the church. James Cone, a contemporary African American theologian, emphasizes that a sound understanding of the church must begin with sociological analysis of how the church relates to realities such as race and social class. Over the years, white church members have tended to simply reflect the racist attitudes in American society generally. So white slave owners used the Bible to justify slavery, and most white church members in the 1960s were very cautious about integration. It is necessary to recognize injustice in the church and society if the church is to fulfill its proper role of being a servant of Jesus and the reign of God that he lived and proclaimed. James Cone says, "The task of the church is more than preaching sermons about justice and praying for the liberation of all. The church must be the agent of justice and liberation about which it proclaims."[20]

The Brazilian theologian Leonardo Boff includes elements from all five models in his conception of the church, yet the liberationist model predominates. Boff sees the beginnings of the liberating church already in base Christian communities in which people experience intimate, democratic community. He realizes that community cannot exist over time without structure, so institutionalization is necessary. What is needed at this point in history, says Boff, is a fundamental conversion from the traditional church as

20. James H. Cone, *Speaking the Truth: Ecumenism, Liberation, and Black Theology* (Grand Rapids, Mich.: Wm. B. Eerdmans, 1986), 124–25.

institution of dominating power to an institutional church with structures that embody democracy and care for the poor. He sees the church not as a hierarchical body, but as the whole people of God, the assembly of believers. But above all, the church seeks to transform the society in which it exists. Christians nurture hope for the utopia of God's reign and strive to improve life for everyone now by working with others for greater political, economic, and social justice.[21] For Boff the church is fundamentally a community of liberation.

Whereas male African American liberation theologians focus on overcoming racism and male Latin American liberation theologians stress liberation from poverty, feminist theologians emphasize liberation from sexism and patriarchy. Feminist theology has been deeply critical of the language and institutional structures of the church for legitimating patriarchal subordination of women. Since we have elsewhere touched on the issue of language, we shall focus here on church structures. Feminists point out that traditionally the churches have been controlled by men. Only males could be priests or ordained ministers, and nearly all other leadership positions were filled by men. To be sure, women have had some distinct groups of their own such as religious orders for women (nuns) and specific women's organizations. In these groups women have exercised decision making and leadership, and performed extremely important work for the church. Yet these women's organizations have been encompassed by a larger church structure controlled by men. Thus among the demands of the early women's movement in America was the call for the ordination of women and the right of women to vote on church decisions. These demands have finally been met in many Protestant churches, yet feminists have seen that ordination and the ecclesiastical vote do not solve the deeper problem of hierarchy in the church.

Hierarchy often involves relations of dominance and subordination, inequality of decision making and power. Hierarchical relations persist in churches, for clergy generally have greater influence within the congregation and denomination than lay people. Clergy are commonly viewed as authoritative teachers and church leaders, laity as learners and followers. There are also differences of power within the clerical ranks, since bishops or other ecclesiastical supervisors have a certain control over priests or ministers under their authority. So to have women become a minister or bishop does not automatically change the quality of the relationships; it may only mean that someone with a female body has hierarchical control over others. In those churches that do not have female clergy, ordination of women still is an

---

21. Leonardo Boff, *Ecclesiogenesis: The Base Communities Reinvent the Church*, trans. Robert R. Barr (Maryknoll, N.Y.: Orbis, 1986), 1–9; *Church: Charism and Power: Liberation Theology and the Institutional Church*, trans. John W. Diercksmeier (New York: Crossroad, 1985), 1–11, 47–64.

important symbol of the subordination and exclusion of women; nevertheless, most feminists realize that ordination alone does not solve the fundamental problem of hierarchy in the church. Although radical feminists such as Mary Daly, formerly a Roman Catholic, have decided the church is so patriarchal that it cannot be transformed, there are many Christian feminists who believe the church can be reformed.

Anne Carr, a feminist who clearly identifies with the Roman Catholic Church, calls for major changes in the church. While she sees value in all models of the church except the hierarchical, institutional model, fundamentally she regards the church as a community of liberation with a mission to the world. She asks, since God's grace is everywhere, why do we need the church? She answers, "There is need today for a model that . . . clearly shows the purpose of the church, not as service to itself, but for the world to which it is sent." So Carr agrees with the Vatican II *Dogmatic Constitution on the Church* that the church is a mystical communion in which the Holy Spirit is present, that the church is a sacrament, and that it is a people nurtured by prayer and worship. Nevertheless, Carr's overriding image of the church is as a pilgrim people struggling toward the reign of God in which justice and peace will prevail. Basic to God's reign are relations of equality, so the church should be striving for greater equality in its internal life as well as in society. That is, the church is properly a community of liberation.

Carr says the hierarchical character of the church's institutions and its exclusion of women from ordained ministry make the church an ambiguous sign of God's gracious reign. Thus transforming church institutions to make for equal participation by all members will enable the church to be a clear sacrament of the reign of God and an effective agent for liberation in society. In the present, patriarchal situation, Carr endorses the participation of women (and men) in small feminist groups, often called "women-church," as a way of meeting the need for egalitarian, Christian community without necessarily abandoning the larger church.[22]

One's Own View of the Church

Now we can pause and look back over the five models of the church that we have considered: institution, community of the Spirit, sacrament, assembly of believers, and community of liberation. It would be a mistake to pick one

22. Anne E. Carr, *Transforming Grace: Christian Tradition and Women's Experience* (San Francisco: Harper & Row, 1988), 194–200; 36–40. A very similar view of the church is presented by Mary E. Hines, "Community for Liberation," in *Freeing Theology: The Essentials of Theology in Feminist Perspective*, Catherine Mowry LaCugna, ed. (San Francisco: HarperSanFrancisco, 1993), 161–84.

model as the right one and reject the others, for each model highlights an important aspect of the church's reality. In coming to one's own theological understanding of the church, it is wise to ask what insights in each model ought to be incorporated into an adequate view of the church. Nevertheless, all the various insights cannot have the same weight; some will be more important than others. Hence, in sorting out your own perspective on the church, you should seek to identify what is most central. To aid you in this process, I will explain my own understanding of the church. This will give you a conversation partner as you sort out your own thinking.

1. I think the primary feature of the church is that *the church is the assembly of believers in Jesus Christ*. The church is first of all the very human company of people whose being revolves around the gospel of Jesus Christ made known in word, sacrament, prayer, and deeds of love. The most relevant biblical metaphor for this is the church as the people of God, the people responding to God's call to faith and service. There are several significant points involved here.

One is that the church is founded on the story of Jesus Christ and is charged with the task of proclaiming that story. There are any number of groups devoted to a worthy cause and composed of good, sincere people. But that does not make them a church. The specific term *ecclesia* or church has its source in the group of disciples that Jesus called together and that proclaimed him as messiah to others. Out of enthusiasm for a worthy cause, it is easy to lose this focus on Jesus and make another cause the center of attention.

It seems to me that this is what has happened with Rosemary Radford Ruether's conception of the church. While she understands the church as a community of liberation, Jesus has only a secondary role as one of an indefinite number of exemplary figures committed to justice in human life. So Ruether gives a chapter-length discussion of the church in which Jesus is only mentioned twice and then only in passing. Jesus is entirely missing when she gives the identifying marks of the authentic church: "The Church is where the good news of liberation from sexism is preached, where the Spirit is present to empower us to renounce patriarchy, where a community committed to the new life of mutuality is gathered together and nurtured, and where the community is spreading this vision and struggle to others."[23] The gospel (good news) of liberation from sexism is substituted for the gospel of Jesus Christ. Every conception of church implies a distinction between true church and false church, between what is genuine and what is counterfeit church. According to Ruether's view, the church exists most clearly in feminist

23. Rosemary Radford Ruether, *Sexism and God-Talk: Toward a Feminist Theology* (Boston: Beacon, 1983), 213.

groups, whereas many communities that gather in the name of Jesus are effectively not considered church. There is no doubt that sexism is a tremendous evil that should be overcome, but all those who fail to fight sexism should not be written out of the church. The group called church has its center in the gospel of Jesus Christ.

Another element in understanding the church as the assembly of believers in Jesus Christ is that the existence of the church is not simply an accident of history but is an essential part of God's redemptive activity. The point is that Jesus could not be the Christ (Messiah) without the existence of the church. That is, if there were no company of followers who believed in Jesus as the Messiah and proclaimed him so to others, Jesus would not be remembered and revered by later generations. Without an assembly of believers to pass on the message, it would not matter what Jesus had said or done. Without the church, Jesus could not be the Christ. Thus the church is an integral part of God's work of reconciliation through Jesus. Of course, this does not mean that First Baptist Church on the corner of Grove and Fifth is indispensible nor does it mean that any church is without flaws. But it does mean that *some* assembly of believers in Jesus is essential to the divine activity of reconciliation through Jesus.

2. The church is a pilgrim people journeying toward the reign of God and as such is a cloudy sign of that future harmony and an unsteady servant of Christ. The church must be viewed within the context of eschatology, that is, within the framework of Christian hope for the future. Following in the tradition of Jesus, Christians look forward to the reign of God in which God will finally overcome all evil and achieve harmony based on perfect justice and love. The church is a company of people that is journeying toward God's reign, but has not reached that perfection. The church is therefore a group of pilgrims. Early in the biblical story, Abram and Sarai were called to leave their comfortable home in Haran and venture toward a distant promised land, so also today the church is called repeatedly to sever comfortable ties and journey in the direction of God's reign. Yet like Abram and Sarai, the assembly of believers today is a mixture of faith and unbelief.

As a pilgrim people, the church is an ambiguous reality. On the one hand, the church is a sign of the future reign of God in which love and justice prevail. By the grace of God, the church is like a sacrament that truly makes present what it signifies. In the church there are always persons and groups that manifest trust in God, compassion, generosity, self-giving, and fairness—qualities that resemble Christ and life in God's reign. Also in the church there are always persons and groups that reach out to the world and serve the needs of that world. For instance, church agencies such as World Vision, Catholic Charities, Church World Service, and Lutheran World Relief are models of efficient, dedicated service to suffering people around the world. In more grass roots fashion, many American congregations and parishes have been instrumental in resettling many thousands of refugees from Southeast Asia and elsewhere. So by being a community of liberation, which in its own life exhibits some qualities of God's reign and strives to improve life for others, the church is also a sacrament of God's future reign.

On the other hand, the church is a sinful community that is a countersign to God's grace in Jesus Christ and an accomplice in the injustice of the world. Liberation theologian James Cone asks, "How can one speak about the church as the body of the crucified Jesus of Nazareth when church people are so healthy and well-fed and have no broken bones? Can we really claim that established churches are the people of God when their actions in society blatantly contradict the one who makes that identity possible?"[24] Critics pick up on the church's ambiguity when they speak about hypocrisy in the church. What they are identifying is the inconsistency between the perfect love and justice in God's future reign and the injustice and selfishness present in life today. The church is definitely part of the corrupt world, and this should not be quickly glossed over.

Social analysis helps identify the church's implication in the evils of the world such as racism and poverty. Social studies of American society reveal clearly the lower average status of blacks from that of whites in great differences in average income, level of unemployment, quality of housing, scores on college entrance exams, and out-of-wedlock births. The situation is complex, for the departure of many middle-class blacks from the urban ghettos has left those areas with a lack of good black leaders and role models. The general result, though, is clear: there is a large, poverty-stricken, black underclass racked with extremely high unemployment and having few prospects for improvement. There is also a much larger white underclass, although smaller as a percentage of all whites. So severe poverty and deprivation exist on a massive scale in America, and it is distributed disproportionately by race.

How do the churches relate to these problems of poverty and race? Sociological studies show that the churches generally reflect the divisions of social class and race in America. Membership of churches tends to fall along lines of social class. The division is more sharp in respect to race. Blacks are heavily concentrated in overwhelmingly black churches. There are no easy answers or quick solutions to these divisions of social class and race. Black churches have historically been the center of the black community's struggle for freedom and the birthplace of many other black cultural institutions.[25] For the

24. Cone, *Speaking the Truth*, 114.
25. C. Eric Lincoln and Lawrence H. Mamiya, *The Black Church in the African American Experience* (Durham: Duke University Press, 1990), 2–10. For social class divisions and black membership statistics, see Roof and McKinney, *American Mainline Religion*, 110, 142.

most part, though, white churches and white Christians have largely ignored divisions by social class and race. It would be easy to go on to talk about the church's involvement in other evils, but the point is clear: the church is a sinful community.

The church is a cloudy sign of God's reign and a halting servant of Christ. This is always true. Does this mean that we cannot distinguish between better and worse? Is this a night in which all cats are grey? Not at all, for it matters greatly in what direction a church is leaning. Paul advises the church in Rome, "Do not be conformed to this world, but be transformed by the renewing of your minds, so that you may discern what is the will of God—what is good and acceptable and perfect" (Romans 12:2). Is a church mainly conforming to this world? Or is the church seriously seeking God's will and resisting the ways of the world?

It would be convenient if we were able to agree on how to grade churches on some scale of conformity-nonconformity with the world, but real life is not so simple. Since modern cultures are complex, a church can conform to certain strands of a culture and not to others. For example, when the United Church of Christ approved ordination of persons who are practicing homosexuals, the church was agreeing with many social liberals in the society and disagreeing with conservatives. Many other churches have rejected ordination of practicing homosexuals. Which side is pointing toward the reign of God and which is conforming to this world? That is a question on which Christians honestly disagree. Nevertheless, it is incumbent upon churches and their members to continually ask whether their ways of living and operating point in the direction of God's reign of justice and love or basically conform to sinful ways of the world.

It is possible to dismiss such issues. The following is the statement of faith by Joe, a white, middle-class college student who attended twelve years of Catholic schools, but now believes there is no God in the Christian sense: "The faith I have focuses on the concrete aspects of my life. I try to do and think what I want to regardless of whether people say it is right or moral. I place a lot of emphasis on succeeding and advancing personally even if it means looking past issues that affect other people or groups." Joe is not concerned about an underclass of whites and blacks. He looks past such issues.

But if one takes seriously the calling of the church to be a sacrament of the future reign of God and a community of liberation, then identifying with the church is a very unsettling thing. One cannot knowingly look past issues that affect other people. Of course, if one is absolutely sure about being on the right side of all the issues, then one will remain untroubled while criticizing the sins of others. But it is highly doubtful that any person or group is truly without reservation on the side of God's reign. All groups and individuals suffer at various points from conformity to this world. Since much of the time we are blind to our own conformity to the world, it is vital to pay special attention to those who suffer. The liberation theologians are right when they say that the voices of the oppressed should have a privileged hearing amidst the swirl of competing opinions, for the oppressed call attention to what the comfortable overlook. So to take seriously the call to represent God's reign is to expose oneself and one's church to the searching, unsettling light of divine love and justice.

3. *The church is the community of the Spirit, the body of Christ.* The church is a community. This too must be understood within the context of Christian eschatology's hope for the reign of God. Saying the church is a community is both a description of what the church to some extent already is and a goal that the church is called to approach more closely. As we noted earlier, the church in America provides intimate community for only a minority of its members, yet to some degree the church is already a community of faith that binds its members together with a shared vision of life and with a web of supportive relationships. The church as community of faith is basically the same as the assembly of believers. On the other hand, the church also needs to become a more caring and inclusive community. We have seen that people in the church are often divided by social class and race, and now we can add division by ethnic group and sex. The church falls short of Paul's view of community in which "there is no longer Jew or Greek, there is no longer slave or free, there is no longer male and female; for all of you are one in Christ Jesus" (Galatians 3:28). So the church is already a partial realization of community and yet falls far short of the perfect community in the future reign of God.

It is especially important to emphasize the church as community in a time of greater individualism. We have seen that the new individualism has both good and bad sides to it. A bad effect is to foster a consumer attitude toward the church. Just as individuals shop around for clothes and buy from those stores that satisfy their taste, so some people shop around for a church and join the one that suits them best. Then they often stay in a church only as long as it meets their needs; they have little commitment to a particular ecclesial community. Such individuals may move from church to church rather like some people go through a series of sexual partners. So in this respect the strengthened individualism erodes church community. On the other hand, individual choice in belonging can strengthen church community if that choice involves a deep commitment to the community.

Nevertheless, even as individuals today exercise more freedom of choice about whether to join a church and which church to join, the factor of community plays a significant role. Sociologists distinguish three categories of people in regard to church membership: loyalists, dropouts, and returners.

Loyalists are those who consistently identify themselves with the church. Roof's study of baby boomers found 33 percent of its sample in this category. *Dropouts* are those who say they are unaffiliated with a church at the time of the survey. Disengagement from any institutional religion is a common phenomenon in America; some research indicates that about one-half of Americans drop out of organized religion for at least two years sometime during their lifetime. Dropouts often have a high interest in religion and explore other faiths through means such as books and lectures that do not commit them to membership in a community. *Returners* are those who drop out of the church for a while and then return.

Recent sociological research identified a person's communal bonds, especially family ties, as the most significant social influence on church affiliation. One study interviewed about a thousand baby boomers in 1965 when they were high school seniors, and interviewed them again in 1973 and 1982. Family considerations were the main social influences on their church affiliation. One very important family factor was relation with parents. Those who were close to their parents and had developed religious habits as teenagers were most likely to be loyalists. Among the dropouts, those who were close to parents in high school and in later years were more likely to return to the church. Those who were distant from parents were most likely to remain dropouts over the whole period of the study.

Other family influences on religious affiliation are marriage and having children. Those who marry between the ages of 18 and 25 are less likely to drop out of church, but if they do, they are more apt to return. Those who married after the age of 25 were also more likely than the unmarried to be loyal or return. People who remained unmarried into their thirties were the most apt to remain unaffiliated with a church. Parenthood had a similar effect to marriage. Those who were single and childless were most likely to have remained a dropout.[26] Another study of baby boomers confirmed that family was the most frequently cited reason for returning to the church, but also reported a personal quest for meaning and the importance of belonging to a community of faith as additional reasons.[27]

Thus those individuals who are closely integrated into a family community are more likely to affiliate with a church community, while those who are least integrated into a family are least likely to join a church. In this age of individualism, people may not admit a need for community. Yet communal bonds are a very significant influence on the choices individuals make regarding the church.

---

26. John Wilson and Darren E. Sherkat, "Returning to the Fold," *Journal for the Scientific Study of Religion* 33 (June 1994): 148–61.
27. Roof, *A Generation of Seekers*, 154–61.

Not only is the church a community, it is a community of the Holy Spirit; it is the body of Christ. These biblical images—community of the Spirit and body of Christ—basically affirm a special presence of the divine in the church. We have seen earlier that in the Bible, the Spirit (literally *breath*) is closely associated with life and with the renewal and fulfillment of life. When we assert that the church is a community of the Spirit, it means that human choices are not the most fundamental reality about the church; more basic is the Holy Spirit engendering a renewal of human life. And the renewal that the Holy Spirit brings in the church is participation in the life of Christ. The life of Christ is not merely an ideal, an abstract goal that people can project for themselves. Christ is a living presence, and others are brought to share in his presence and life. Christ is not a secondary reality that must wait upon our decisions to have existence; rather, Christ exists prior to people's choice. What the Holy Spirit does in the church is to enable people to participate in Christ's life and presence. So Paul says believers are "in Christ," for it is as if they exist within an atmosphere pervaded by Christ.

In addition to bringing about a renewal of life as life in Christ, the Spirit is building community. So when Paul talks about the church as the body of Christ with many members, he speaks of the members' contributions as gifts of the Spirit (Romans 12:4-8; 1 Corinthians 12:4-31). The gifts of the Spirit to the various members are given for the common good of the church. This is quite a different outlook than is generally fostered in contemporary American culture where the premium is placed on actualizing all one's potential whether that benefits others or not. As our college student Joe put it, "I place a lot of emphasis on succeeding and advancing personally even if it means looking past issues that affect other people or groups." As the community of the Holy Spirit, the dynamic of the church is toward building mutual support, service, and caring for one another. What we would want to add today in our modern social situation where the church has considerable influence in society is that the gifts of the Spirit are given also for strengthening mutual care throughout society.

Christ and the Spirit are also present throughout the world building community, for God is not confined to the boundaries of the church. Yet there is a special presence of Christ and the Spirit in the church, for there the Spirit works in and through the various means by which the Christian community witnesses to what God has done in Jesus. That is, I believe that the Holy Spirit is present when representatives of two governments reach a just peace agreement, for the Spirit is surely a Spirit of peace. But when a Christian community gathers for the eucharist, the Spirit's inner prompting is connected with the church's explicit testimony that God is the ultimate source of peace and in Jesus has even suffered to bring about peace in the world.

Building community is integral to God's activity. The trinitarian under-standing of God that I have advanced in this book suggests that in the amaz-ingly complicated and lengthy activity of creating and guiding the world, God is leading creatures toward ever-richer unity. Of course, the movement is not simple and linear. For instance, there are all sorts of dead ends in extinct life forms. Human history is also a confused mixture of community and disunity. Nonetheless, the overall trend of evolution appears to be toward more complex forms of community, and Christian faith hopes for the perfect community of God's reign. This means that building community is basic to God's activity throughout the course of creating and reconciling the world.

Now let us pause and briefly compare my view of the church with other views. By taking as my primary model the church as assembly of believers in Jesus Christ, I have followed the main tradition in Protestant thinking about the church. This agrees with elements of the idea of the church as the people of God, which was a strong emphasis of the Vatican II *Dogmatic Constitution on the Church* and its second main image for the church. There is considerable overlap here as well with the image of community of disciples proposed by the Catholic theologian Avery Dulles as a sixth and more satisfactory model than the five he had earlier identified.[28]

In treating secondly the church as a pilgrim people that is a cloudy sign of God's reign and halting community of liberation, I have given the models of sacrament and community of liberation a somewhat ambiguous, betwixt-and-between status. I affirm the church as sacrament of God's reign and as com-munity advancing toward that reign. Yet I have placed considerable stress on the sinful character of the church. Here I agree with liberation theologian James Cone that discussion of the church should give important place to analysis of the church's position in society. This involves a forthright recogni-tion of the church's sin, which is consistent with classical Protestant thinking and present but less prominent in the *Dogmatic Constitution on the Church*. By subordinating the community of liberation model to that of the assembly of believers, I produce a view of the church that gives a lower profile to the church's role in transforming society than most liberation theologians do.

It is significant that I place the affirmation of the church as the communi-ty of the Spirit third. Here I differ with the *Dogmatic Constitution on the Church*, which makes the mysterious divine presence in the church its first affirmation. I agree with Avery Dulles that a more modest way of speaking about the church is appropriate, and assembly of believers is modest. Fur-thermore, while the Spirit's presence in the church is more fundamental than the power of sin and so has a priority over sin, I think the affirmation of God's

28. Avery Dulles, *A Church to Believe In: Discipleship and the Dynamics of Freedom* (New York: Crossroad, 1983), 7–11.

special presence is more likely to gain a hearing *after* a straightforward acknowledgment of the sin and ambiguity of the church.

Finally, I have so far omitted any treatment of the organization of the church. This is a major question: Is a certain structure of the church willed by God? We will turn our attention next to this issue in part two of this chapter. But the fact that I have delayed discussion of this matter until last is in itself significant; not every theologian would do so.

The Church's Structure

As we begin part two of this chapter, we note that in the Nicene Creed Christians confess faith in "one, holy, catholic, and apostolic church." These four terms—one, holy, catholic, and apostolic—have been variously interpreted by different Christian traditions. One of the key differences of interpretation has centered on church structure. Is a specific church structure an essential feature of the church being one, catholic, and apostolic? This question has been discussed by representatives of different Christian traditions in the *ecumenical movement*.

The term *ecumenical* comes from a Greek word meaning the whole inhabited world, and in practice the ecumenical movement has promoted better relations among separated Christian bodies. We can refresh our memory on the major Christian traditions with this Christian family tree (Figure 1):

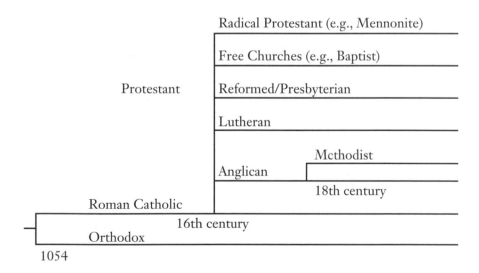

Figure 1
The Major Christian Church Families

The ecumenical movement was initiated by Protestant foreign missionaries who were trying to avoid imposing divisions created in Europe on Christians in other areas of the world. The movement was born at a conference of mission societies in Edinburgh, Scotland in 1910. After further meetings, 146 Protestant and Orthodox churches formed the World Council of Churches in 1948. Fruits of the ecumenical movement have included a number of church mergers, mostly within Christian families, as well as friendlier ties among churches from different families.

The Roman Catholic Church remained basically uninvolved in ecumenical activities until Pope John XXIII called Catholic bishops together for the Second Vatican Council (1962–1965) and invited the major Protestant and Orthodox bodies to send observers. Since the Second Vatican Council, many discussions between representatives of the Roman Catholic Church and those bodies belonging to the the World Council of Churches have helped produce much more cordial and cooperative relations at every level. Numerous theological issues have been addressed in these dialogues, but we will look at only two of the most difficult questions bearing on the church and its structure—papal primacy and infallibility of the church.

Papal Primacy

The office of the pope or papacy is the occasion for both unity and disunity among Christians today. There is little doubt that the papacy has been a major factor in unifying the Roman Catholic Church, the world's largest and ethnically most diverse church. While Protestantism has produced a bewildering proliferation of separate churches, Roman Catholicism under the pope's headship has maintained amazing unity. At the same time, different attitudes toward the papacy have divided Roman Catholics from Orthodox and Protestant Christians. At the heart of the difference in attitude is the issue of papal primacy.

Papal primacy means a certain preeminence belongs to the position of the pope, the bishop of Rome. Whether there is a proper papal preeminence and of what it consists are the debated questions. The *Dogmatic Constitution on the Church* of Vatican II views the papacy within the context of the entire college of bishops, and sees the pope as the head of that college. The rationale given for this was stated already by Pope Leo I (d. 461) and was affirmed by several medieval church councils. The traditional rationale is that when Jesus commissioned the original disciples, he appointed Peter as their head. Further, Jesus intended that the bishop of Rome be the successor of Peter as head and that bishops be the successors of the original disciples. "Just as the role that the Lord gave individually to Peter, the first among the apostles, is permanent and was meant to be transmitted to his successors, so also the apostles' office of nurturing the Church is permanent, and was meant to be exercised without interruption by the sacred order of bishops."[29] Thus by divine institution the church has a definite structure that includes papal primacy: a college of bishops headed by the pope. In ecumenical discussions, four major views of papal primacy have emerged.[30]

1. A *conservative Catholic defense of papal primacy* accepts both the traditional rationale for papal primacy and the form that primacy has taken in the modern era. Joseph Ratzinger, a German theologian and cardinal working as a top administrator of the Roman Catholic Church in the Vatican, is an articulate spokesperson of the conservative Catholic outlook. Ratzinger sees a danger in those who emphasize the church as the people of God; he thinks the distinctive character of the church is more adequately expressed as the body of Christ. He emphasizes the divine presence in the church. So he says that while we as individuals sin, the church does not sin. Although humans organize the external face of the church, Ratzinger says its fundamental structures are willed by God.

> But the Church of Christ is not a party, not an association, not a club. Her deep and permanent structure is not *democratic*, but *sacramental*, consequently *hierarchical*. . . . Here authority is not based on the majority of votes; it is based on the authority of Christ himself, which he willed to pass on to men who were to be his representatives until his definitive return. Only if this perspective is acquired anew will it be possible to rediscover the necessity and fruitfulness of obedience to the legitimate ecclesiastical hierarchies.[31]

During most of the modern era, the papacy exercised strong central control over the Roman Catholic Church. Vatican Council I (1869–1870) represented the culmination of this centralization with the promulgation of papal infallibility. Because of the Italian civil war, Vatican I was suspended before it could address the role of the bishops. Vatican II took up this theme and recognized that bishops have a responsibility for the whole church as well as their own diocese. While maintaining papal primacy among the bishops, the council approved a more collegial relationship between papacy and bishops without specifying how this collegiality should be carried out. In the first decade or so after Vatican II there was rather wide-open discussion in Catholic theological circles about what direction the church should take. But since then there seems to have been a *restoration* of more centralized control

29. *Dogmatic Constitution on the Church*, Article 20, p. 40.

30. A clear, helpful book on the issue is J. Michael Miller's *What Are They Saying About Papal Primacy?* (New York: Paulist, 1982).

31. Joseph Cardinal Ratzinger with Vittorio Messori, *The Ratzinger Report* (San Francisco: Ignatius, 1985), 49.

under the papacy. This has been manifested by papal appointment of many conservative bishops and disciplinary actions taken against some vocal, liberal Catholic theologians including Swiss Hans Küng, Brazilian Leonardo Boff, and American Charles Curran. As head of the Vatican's Congregation for the Doctrine of the Faith, which is charged with deepening and guarding the church's doctrine, Joseph Ratzinger has played a key role in the restoration. Consistent with this conservative Catholic perspective, Ratzinger affirms in the quote above both the traditional idea that papal primacy is grounded in Christ himself and the centralized form of papal primacy that stresses obedience to the church hierarchy.

2. A *moderate defense of papal primacy* holds that the pope's preeminence has come about by guidance of the Holy Spirit and that papal leadership should be exercised with strongly collegial relations with other bishops. This outlook is held by many Roman Catholic theologians such as Avery Dulles, Karl Rahner, and J. M. R. Tillard as well as by some non-Catholics. It has become common to distinguish between the question of Peter's primacy among the original disciples and the question of successors to Peter's primacy. On the first issue, it is difficult to deny that Jesus looked to Peter as the leader of the original disciples (Matthew 16:18-19; John 21:15-17). Biblical evidence also indicates that Peter was a prominent leader in the early church, although James has the last word in the so-called Council of Jerusalem (Acts 15:6-22) and Paul does not appear to be under Peter. These moderate Catholic theologians are convinced that Jesus did indeed regard Peter as the leader of the disciples, but they doubt that Jesus himself envisioned the bishops of Rome as successors to Peter. In fact, they point out that the earliest Roman bishops themselves did not even claim to succeed to Peter's primacy; such a claim developed over several centuries. Nevertheless, moderates believe that papal primacy is not merely an historical accident, for the Holy Spirit guided the church in this development. So even though the moderate defense of papal primacy does not accept the traditional rationale, it endorses that primacy as a permanent church structure willed by God.

The major difference between moderate and conservative defenders of papal primacy comes in the form primacy should assume. Whereas conservatives support a strongly centralized mode of operation, moderates want greater collegiality among bishops and more open discussion. J. M. R. Tillard represents this moderate Catholic perspective when he says the pope has become "more than a pope" by seeking to control the church like a monarch. Tillard favors a view in which the purpose of papal primacy is to foster unity and communion among the churches by using all available means of consultation with fellow bishops; further, rather than frequently and consistently intervening in local church affairs, the papacy would better serve unity by leaving a large number of matters under the control of local churches or conferences of bishops and intervening only in extraordinary situations when local or regional direction fails. For example, rather than the pope routinely appointing every bishop around the world, there should be a return to the practice of the first millenium when local churches selected their own bishop and the pope accepted that person unless there were exceptional reasons.[32]

3. A *functionalist view of papal primacy* rejects the idea that papal preeminence is willed by God; papal primacy arose because it was functional for the church, so it can in principle be dropped or reformed if it becomes a hindrance. Functionalists may well think Jesus saw Peter as the leader of the disciples, but they do not believe God has willed the pope to be Peter's successor as head over other church leaders. While this view has been most common among non-Catholic Christians, it also has been held by some Catholic theologians such as Hans Küng. The functionalist outlook has a basically positive attitude toward the papacy, for the papacy is regarded as having some possible useful function in the life of the church.

4. *Papal primacy is contrary to the gospel*. This is a view that has been held by many Protestants since the Reformation. As early as 1519 Martin Luther denied the traditional claims for the divine institution of papal primacy, but for the sake of church unity he was willing to recognize a certain papal preeminence subordinate to the Word of God. But in his late-life treatise, "Against the Roman Papacy, An Institution of the Devil," Luther saw no legitimacy to the papacy. This final opinion has been held by many Protestants ever since.

Having distinguished these four views of papal primacy, we may now consider the issue of the papacy in future relations among the churches. If there are going to be closer relations of the Roman Catholic Church with other major Christian churches, then what role will the papacy have? Two of our views bar any progress toward closer relations. The view that papal primacy is contrary to the gospel allows for no common ground on this issue with Roman Catholics. The conservative Catholic view also eliminates any common ground by insisting on a degree of papal control that is fundamentally objectionable to Orthodox and Protestant Christians. However, the moderate defense of papal primacy and the functionalist approach make possible some degree of agreement on papal primacy between Roman Catholics and other Christians. In fact, participants with these views in a Lutheran-Catholic dialogue in America found a considerable measure of convergence, although not full agreement.

32. J. M. R. Tillard, *The Bishop of Rome* (Wilmington, Del.: Michael Glazier, 1983), 182–84.

The fundamental concern of those in the Lutheran-Catholic dialogue on papal primacy was for some visible means of fostering unity in the church worldwide. While nearly all Christians share one baptism, the Bible, certain creeds, and the ancient ecumenical councils, the dialogue participants thought it desirable to have a contemporary office dedicated to unifying the church. The question is whether the papacy might fulfill this role in the universal church today. For instance, it is a fact that the pope is the only figure that is widely recognized as an important spokesperson and representative of the Christian faith. When the pope visits anywhere in the world, large crowds turn out, and the crowds are not only composed of Catholics. The Orthodox Churches have no one of comparable status. The archbishop of Canterbury, the head of the Anglican Communion, is not nearly so widely recognized. And no Protestant leader, other than a prominent evangelist such as Billy Graham, even begins to draw worldwide attention. So would not a papal office able to serve as a voice for all Christians be beneficial for the unity of all the churches and for their ministry to the world?

Both sides in the dialogue agreed in calling for a renewal of papal operations that allowed legitimate diversity, collegiality, and local control whenever possible (called the principle of subsidiarity). This was possible because the Catholic participants had a moderate view of papal primacy that avoids centralization and the Lutherans had a functional view that sees a possible positive role for the papacy. One of the major points on which they disagree is whether the papacy is part of God's permanent will for the church.[33] The open question is whether it is possible and desirable for Catholics and other Christians to recognize the pope as the preeminent Christian leader even though they differ on the necessity of the papacy.

In his 1995 encyclical on ecumenism, *Ut Unum Sint*, Pope John Paul II expresses a desire "to find a way of exercising the [papal] primacy which, while in no way renouncing what is essential to its mission, is nonetheless open to a new situation." To this end he sets forth broad guidelines for fulfilling the papacy's mission of promoting unity in the church. He emphasizes that the authority proper to the papacy is not power over people, but an authority of leading toward unity and peace. In communion with bishops, the pope also has responsibility to keep watch over all major aspects of church life. "He has the duty to admonish, to caution and to declare at times that this or that opinion being circulated is irreconcilable with the unity of faith."[34] The encyclical does not take any startling new position, but it is nonetheless

---

33. Paul C. Empie and T. Austin Murphy, eds., *Papal Primacy and the Universal Church* (Minneapolis: Augsburg, 1974), 9–23.

34. John Paul II, *Ut Unum Sint*, in *Origins: CNS Documentary Service* 25, no. 4 (June 8, 1995): 93–95.

significant that the pope explicitly puts on the table for ecumenical discussion the issue of *how* papal primacy might be exercised in a united church.

One's conception of the church plays a very important role as background for considering the question of papal primacy. For instance, a significant modification of the Catholic understanding of church took place at Vatican II. The conviction that had prevailed in modern Catholicism until Vatican II was that the church *is* the Roman Catholic Church. It was recognized that there are other Christians, but they were "separated brethren" outside the church. In a crucial vote at Vatican II, instead of saying the church is the Catholic Church, the council approved the more vague wording, "This Church . . . subsists in the Catholic Church, which is governed by the successor of Peter and by the bishops in union with that successor."[35] The terminology "subsists in" implies that the church is centered in but not limited to the Catholic Church. Vatican II recognizes different degrees of incorporation into the church. Those who accept the entire Catholic structure are fully incorporated into the church. So papal primacy belongs to the full being (*plene esse*) of the church. Those who take a functional view of the church do not agree that the papacy is essential to having the full reality of church, but today some Protestant and Orthodox theologians think a reformed papal primacy would be for the well-being (*bene esse*) of the church.

Another extremely significant element in one's conception of church is how one understands the relationship of the Holy Spirit with the church. Here a fundamental difference appears between mainstream Roman Catholic and Protestant notions of the church. The dominant Catholic perception is that the Holy Spirit dwells in and is deeply identified with the institutional structures of the church. So there is a Catholic confidence that the Holy Spirit guides the pope and bishops in leading the church. To be sure, mistakes and corruption have occurred, but there is a deep sense that the Holy Spirit guides the church in its overall course through history. This confidence is evident in Joseph Ratzinger's conservative Catholic belief (quoted above) that although individuals sin, the church does not sin. It is also manifest in the moderate defense of papal primacy, for this rests on the conviction that the papal primacy is a fruit of the Spirit's guidance. On the other hand, Protestants generally see a more dialectical relation between the Holy Spirit and the institutions of the church. So Protestant affirmations of the influence of the Holy Spirit are strongly tempered by admissions of sin in the church. However, in recent decades the two traditions have moved somewhat closer together. Many Catholic liberation and feminist theologians stress the pilgrim character of the church, touched upon by the *Dogmatic Constitution of the*

---

35. *Dogmatic Constitution on the Church*, Article 8, p. 23.

Church. Feminists are especially sensitive to sinful collusion of the church with sexism in nearly all church institutions from early on. For their part, discussions with Catholic theologians has led many Protestant theologians to reexamine their traditional rejection of the papacy as thoroughly corrupt. Nonetheless, a difference in emphasis still tends to exist between Protestants and Roman Catholics on their basic attitude toward the Holy Spirit's relation to the church.

Infallibility in the Church

The underlying issue in all discussions about infallibility in the church is the issue of authority in the church's teaching. There are two main meanings of authority. One is that authority means legitimate power; the other that an authority is a trustworthy source. Since authority in the church is properly derived from Jesus, we must first attend to the authority of Jesus. In the New Testament Jesus has authority in both senses of the word. On the one hand, Jesus has power over the demons (Mark 1:27) and the authority to forgive sins (Mark 2:5-12). At the end of Matthew's Gospel, Jesus says, "All authority in heaven and on earth has been given to me. Go therefore and make disciples of all nations . . . teaching them to obey everything that I have commanded you" (Matthew 28:18-20). In these contexts Jesus is seen as having legitimate power given from the final authority, God. It is important to notice that Jesus' legitimate power is never used to control or dominate people, but is always used to serve people and set them free from some bondage. On the other hand, Jesus is also pictured as one who teaches with authority (Matthew 7:28-29), and this involves both having a God-given power to teach and being a trustworthy guide. Ever since Jesus departed from this world, Christians have faced the question of where they can find a God-approved, trustworthy guide for what they teach; that is, to what authority should Christians look in settling disputes over teachings?

There is a range of answers to this question, but we can uncover most of the key issues by distinguishing four views on authoritative teaching in the church. The first two positions are held mostly by Roman Catholics, the last two are held chiefly by Protestants. In the Roman Catholic tradition, there is a teaching authority (*magisterium* in Latin) composed of pope and bishops who are in communion with the pope. Modern Catholic doctrine goes on to say that under certain conditions, pope and bishops teach infallibly, that is, their teaching is immune from error. The prematurely adjourned Vatican Council I in 1870 defined papal infallibility in these terms:

> It is a divinely revealed dogma that the Roman Pontiff, when he speaks *ex cathe-dra*, that is, when acting in the office of shepherd and teacher of all Christians,

he defines, by virtue of his supreme apostolic authority, a doctrine concerning faith or morals to be held by the universal Church, possesses through the divine assistance promised to him in the person of Blessed Peter, the infallibility with which the divine Redeemer willed His Church to be endowed in defining the doctrine concerning faith or morals; and that such definitions of the Roman Pontiff are therefore irreformable of themselves, not because of the consent of the Church.[36]

Vatican Council II (1962–1965) reaffirms Vatican I on papal infallibility, but emphasizes that the gift of papal infallibility is given within the context of an infallibility promised to the whole church and adds that bishops in council with agreement of the pope may also define a teaching infallibly. "The infallibility promised to the Church resides also in the body of bishops when that body exercises supreme teaching authority with the successor of Peter. To the resultant definitions the assent of the Church can never be wanting on account of the activity of that same Holy Spirit, whereby the whole flock of Christ is preserved and progresses in unity of faith."[37]

All agree that infallibility of the magisterium must be carefully understood. One must avoid the popular misconception that papal infallibility means the pope can never be wrong. Vatican I clearly states that papal infallibility applies when the pope is engaged in the formal act of defining a doctrine and only a doctrine concerning faith or morals. So the pope's opinion about who will win the next soccer World Cup is no more reliable than anyone else's opinion. Furthermore, the Catholic affirmation of infallibility of the magisterium under these certain conditions is grounded not in the virtue of those men, but in the profound confidence that, as Christ promised, the Holy Spirit guides the church (John 14:25-26). Thus on those rare occasions when an infallible doctrine is defined, the pope or bishops with pope do not set forth some idea that just popped into their heads; they are articulating a belief that will elicit widespread assent among the Catholic faithful. Beyond these basic points, however, there is a lively debate among Catholics over how to interpret infallibility of the magisterium. We can get some feel for that discussion if we distinguish between a conservative Catholic view and a moderate Catholic view of infallibility.

1. *A conservative Catholic view of infallibility of the church and its hierarchy.* One common mark of this outlook is that a conservative Catholic is likely to recognize more infallible teachings than the three that nearly all Catholic theologians accept: the Vatican I statement on papal infallibility, the Immac-

---

36. J. Neuner & J. Dupuis, eds., *The Christian Faith in the Doctrinal Documents of the Catholic Church* (New York: Alba House, 1982), 234.
37. *Dogmatic Constitution on the Church*, Article 25, p. 49.

ulate Conception of Mary defined in 1854, and the Assumption of Mary defined in 1950. A conservative Catholic is likely to regard a long standing, consistent teaching of the magisterium for all practical purposes as infallible. Even though such teachings have not been explicitly defined as infallible in an extraordinary papal act of defining a dogma, they have been a constant and ordinary teaching of the magisterium.

A second and related mark of a conservative Catholic view is that in matters on which the pope has clearly expressed a position, even though it does not claim to be infallible, the appropriate Catholic response is submission. Conservative Catholics have a rather strict interpretation of this paragraph in the *Dogmatic Constitution on the Church*,

> In matters of faith and morals, the bishops speak in the name of Christ and the faithful are to accept their teaching and adhere to it with a religious assent of soul. This religious submission [*obsequium* in Latin] of will and of mind must be shown in a special way to the authentic teaching authority of the Roman Pontiff, even when he is not speaking *ex cathedra*. That is, it must be shown in such a way that his supreme magisterium is acknowledged with reverence, the judgments made by him are sincerely adhered to, according to his manifest mind and will.[38]

They tend to agree that the Latin term *obsequium* above should be translated as submission, and in practice they support the Vatican policy of discipline against theologians such as Charles Curran, who publicly endorsed some views on sexual issues that ran counter to consistent teaching by the magisterium.

2. A moderate Catholic view of infallibility of the church and its hierarchy. One major feature of a moderate Catholic position is its emphasis on the limitations of the doctrine of infallibility. Moderates generally limit the number of recently enunciated infallible doctrines to the three that explicitly claim to be such. They also underscore the limits on the adequacy of any teaching about divine things, including infallible teachings, for God transcends human words and every doctrinal statement bears the constraints of its own historical context. Thus, moderates stress the limits of infallibility. To be infallible does not mean to fully grasp the truth; it only means to be immune from falling away from the truth. In this basic sense, the whole church is infallible in its *belief*. Because of Christ's promise to teach them through the Holy Spirit, the church will not fall away from the gospel of Jesus Christ. This or that person, this or that group may fall away, but the Christian church as a whole will not fall away. This restricted meaning of infallibility also applies to the magisterium in its *teaching*.

38. Ibid., 48.

The magisterium in its ordinary week-by-week teaching can have various shortcomings in what it says or does, but it cannot entirely fall away from the gospel. And in the extraordinary act of defining a doctrine, the magisterium again cannot fully fall away from the gospel. So one group of Catholic scholars said, "Even while true in the technical sense, a dogmatic statement may be ambiguous, untimely, over-bearing, offensive, or otherwise deficient."[39] Infallibility is a limited notion, but a valuable one, for it affirms the fundamental faithfulness to the gospel of the church and its teaching authority.

A second feature of the moderate infallibility view is a strong desire to encourage free debate of issues that have not been definitively settled by the magisterium. In the passage quoted above from the *Dogmatic Constitution on the Church*, moderate Catholics generally prefer to translate the key Latin term *obsequium* more softly as deference rather than as submission. Moderate Catholics take comfort in the fact that an earlier papal prohibition on public debate of issues settled by the pope was not reasserted at Vatican II even though it had been in the preliminary draft. Moderate Catholics such as Avery Dulles want to broaden the scope of legitimate discussion in the Catholic Church.

A third mark of the moderate Catholic outlook on infallibility is that it stresses that infallible teaching by pope and bishops occurs within the context of the whole church's infallible faith. Thus an infallible teaching by the magisterium will reflect what the whole church believes. This point, which was also highlighted by Vatican II, is important, for it suggests that a papal teaching such as that on birth control ought not be considered infallible, because the vast majority of Catholics in industrialized countries dissent from it.

A fourth feature of a moderate Catholic position is that it deals gently with those—both Catholic and non-Catholic—who dissent from the Catholic doctrine of infallibility of the magisterium. Avery Dulles says dissenters may be more aware than others of the inherent limitations of any attempt to articulate the transcendent mystery of God. And the whole Catholic team involved in the Lutheran-Catholic dialogue on papal infallibility point out that the dogma of papal infallibility and the two modern dogmas concerning Mary that were defined with the gift of papal infallibility are not core Christian beliefs; so it is possible to be a Christian and question or deny these dogmas.[40]

3. *The conservative Protestant view that the Bible is the only infallible authority for the church.* Conservative Protestants regard any talk about infallibility of pope and bishops with deep suspicion, and may appeal to a tradition in which

39. Paul C. Empie, T. Austin Murphy, and Joseph A. Burgess, eds., *Teaching Authority and Infallibility in the Church: Lutherans and Catholics in Dialogue VI* (Minneapolis: Augsburg, 1980), 45.

40. Ibid., 93, 53–55.

leaders such as Luther and Calvin at times referred to the papacy as the antichrist. For most conservative Protestants the only fully trustworthy guide for Christian teaching is the infallible Bible.

Actually there are differences among conservative Protestants in how they refer to the reliability of the Bible. Fundamentalists generally speak of the Bible as *inerrant*, while many Evangelicals avoid the language of inerrancy and prefer the term infallibility. Even though these two terms may appear identical, they are not. Those who call the Bible inerrant insist that the biblical text has no errors even in apparently insignificant details. Such folks will work to reconcile little discrepancies in the Bible, such as when Numbers 25:9 says 24,000 died in one day, whereas when Paul mentions this event in 1 Corinthians 10:8 he says 23,000 died. One solution is to say about 23,500 died, so the figure could be rounded down or up. Conservative Protestants who speak of the Bible as infallible are often willing to admit there are errors in some minor details, but they stress the Bible is "the only infallible rule of faith and practice." In other words, the Bible may *contain* some errors, but it does not *teach* any errors. In what it as a religious book affirms or teaches, the Bible is entirely trustworthy.[41]

Among conservative Protestants there is no commonly recognized church structure looked to for guidance in interpreting the Bible. In practice, conservative Protestantism has experienced many conflicts over questions of doctrine and morals that have often produced divisions in church bodies.

4. *The moderate Protestant view that affirms the indefectibility of the church, but rejects infallibility of the Bible and church hierarchy*. This outlook introduces us to a new term—*indefectible*. Obviously this term is based on the word *defect*, but there are several meanings of defect. Moderate Protestants do not believe the church is without any defect, flaw, or blemish. Rather, indefectibility is related to the verb *to defect*, which in the Cold War meant to desert one's country for another. To defect means to abandon one's allegiance to something and give it to another. So to say that the church is indefectible means that the church cannot cease to believe and proclaim the gospel of Jesus Christ. To be sure, individuals or groups of Christians may defect, but the church as a whole cannot abandon the faith. The ground of this confidence is trust in Christ's promise to preserve the church (for instance, "the gates of Hades will not prevail against it," Matthew 16:18).

During the twentieth century moderate Protestants generally came to reject the idea that the Bible is infallible or inerrant. Like their more conservative sisters and brothers, moderate Protestants regard the Bible as the high-

---

41. Robert K. Johnston, *Evangelicals at an Impasse: Biblical Authority in Practice* (Atlanta: John Knox, 1979), 18–35.

est authority in matters of faith and morals, but they see that authority in the Word or message that God communicates in and through the biblical text. Convinced that the language of infallibility tends to confuse and mislead people about the true nature of biblical authority, they have turned away from it.

Both Roman Catholic positions discussed above agree that the church is indefectible, so there is substantial overlap between the church's indefectibility and what Catholics call its infallibility in believing and teaching. That is, the church will continue in the faith, because until the end of time the gospel will be taught and people will have faith in it. And for both Catholics and moderate Protestants, this indefectibility is based on Christ's promise to protect and guide the church through the Holy Spirit. So it was that in their dialogue on this issue, Catholic and Lutheran theologians both said at times they could not identify any more than a verbal difference between their positions.

Of course, the big difference that remains between the Roman Catholics and moderate Protestants is that the Catholics go on to specify a structure (bishops in communion with the pope) within the church that can be counted upon to follow the Holy Spirit's guidance in articulating and defending authoritative teachings. Here long-term differences between Catholic and Protestant become visible. In large part because of their stronger emphasis on the damaging effects of sin in all areas of human life, Protestants believe that on occasion popes and councils can be deceptive guides. For their part, Catholics share a confidence that special gifts of the Holy Spirit to bishops and pope will sufficiently override their sin, so that under certain conditions their teaching may be considered infallible.

Here again we can focus our attention on the larger issue of church structure, for the question of where Christians may find authoritative teaching raises the issue of church structure very strongly. As we have seen, Catholics hold that the church structure of bishops in communion with the pope is essential. Protestants tend to be suspicious of giving too much power to any person or group. Nevertheless, ecumenical discussions have revealed that there may be less of a gap between Catholic and Protestant than has been commonly thought.

The gap between a conservative Catholic view of church authority and a conservative Protestant view remains wide indeed. While the conservative Catholic insists upon submission to the magisterium, many conservative Protestants think the Roman hierarchy has on occasion been dreadfully wrong and unbiblical in their teaching (for instance, when it proclaimed certain dogmas about Mary).

The gap between moderate Catholic and moderate Protestant views of church authority, however, is not so great. Indeed, the moderate Lutheran and moderate Catholic theologians involved in the dialogue on teaching authority discovered a convergence in their views, although not full agreement. In addition to the common affirmation of the church's indefectibility, moderate Catholics say that differences on papal infallibility and the Marian dogmas need not be church dividing, since these teachings are not core Christian teachings. On the other hand, moderate Protestants in the Lutheran-Catholic dialogue found themselves longing for some sort of universal church structure which would enable all Christians to speak with one voice on certain matters. These moderate Protestants became painfully aware of the fragmentation among Christians and especially among Protestants. Both the Catholic and Lutheran participants in this dialogue proposed that their churches explore ways to have mutuality in the teaching function; for example, the Lutherans suggested this might involve participation in a truly ecumenical council that included bishops or leaders from all churches.

As we look back over this chapter, we can see that in many ways the church is a controversial topic. In part one of this chapter we thought about the highly debated issue of what the church is and ought to be. We reflected on five models of the church and considered my own view of the church as a way of sparking your own thinking about the church. In part two we thought about two disputed issues in ecumenical discussions regarding the structure of the church: primacy of the pope and infallibility in the church. Nevertheless, the church is not an end in itself, for Christians generally believe that the Holy Spirit is at work in special ways within the church to bring about salvation. Thus, we must turn our thoughts next to the Holy Spirit and salvation.

9

The Holy Spirit and Salvation

The title of this chapter, "The Holy Spirit and Salvation," may not immediately grab your attention, but the subject matter raises some very interesting and important questions. The chapter is divided into two parts, the first on the Holy Spirit and the second on salvation, and we will discover that the two topics are very closely related.

We have our work cut out for us when we try to understand what Christians mean by the Holy Spirit, for the Spirit of God is elusive and Christian reflection on the Spirit has been far less developed than on God the Father/Mother and Jesus Christ. The Christian understanding of the Holy Spirit is grounded chiefly in the intersection of the Christian tradition about the Spirit and contemporary Christian experience of God's presence. Thus it is essential to look at the Christian tradition regarding the Spirit, and then examine contemporary experiences of God's presence. We shall begin with biblical stories and teachings.

The Spirit in the Bible

The Hebrew word for spirit (*ruach*) also means wind or breath. Since many life forms live by breathing, *ruach* is closely associated with life. God's Spirit gives life to all creatures. The Greek translation of the Old Testament, called the Septuagint, used the word *pneuma* for most uses of *ruach*. And in the New Testament, which was written in Greek, *pneuma*, Spirit has the same linkage with wind, breath, and life. The purpose of this little word study is to point out that the Spirit is the presence of God in the creation, a presence that gives life to all living things. So fundamentally the biblical writers knew God's Spirit as God present and active in the world granting life.

This life-giving activity of the Spirit sometimes includes bestowing an ecstatic experience in which a person is given a special gift beyond his or her normal capabilities. For instance, one time the Old Testament character Samson was going to a Philistine town when a young lion roared at him. Then the Bible says of Samson, "The spirit of the LORD rushed on him, and he tore the lion apart barehanded as one might tear apart a kid [lamb]" (Judges 14:6). Some of the prophets also speak of their message as given by the Spirit. So Isaiah 61:1 says, "The spirit of the LORD God is upon me, because the LORD has anointed me; he has sent me to bring good news to the oppressed, to bind up the brokenhearted, to proclaim liberty to the captives, and release to the prisoners." Sometimes a prophet exhibited unusual behavior such as the frenzy in which the Israelite king Saul danced with other prophets (1 Samuel 19:24), but more often there was no such extraordinary activity. Indeed, there seems to have developed some suspicion that the prophets who behaved wildly often did not speak for God.[1]

In the New Testament, Jesus has an intimate relation with the Spirit. On the one hand, Jesus is the *bearer of the Spirit* who is given a full measure of the Spirit. The Synoptic Gospels (Matthew, Mark, and Luke) call attention to the Spirit's presence at several key points in Jesus' life, but the pivotal event is the baptism of Jesus. "And just as he was coming up out of the water, he saw the heavens torn apart and the Spirit descending like a dove on him. And a voice came from heaven, 'You are my Son, the Beloved, with you I am well pleased'" (Mark 1:10-11). This portrays the commissioning of Jesus as God's Son or special representative on earth. With this divine commission comes the Spirit descending like a dove on him. The book of Acts especially emphasizes that the Spirit empowers Jesus to do what he needs to do as God's representative. Luke, the author of Acts, points out "how God anointed Jesus of Nazareth with the Holy Spirit and with power; how he went about doing good and healing all who were oppressed by the devil, for God was with him" (Acts 10:38). Notice that the Spirit is God present, "for God was with him," and this divine presence empowers Jesus for his mission.

On the other hand, in the New Testament Jesus is also pictured as *giver of the Spirit*. The Gospel of Luke, Acts, and the Gospel of John all portray Jesus as bestowing the Spirit on his followers: "When he had said this, he breathed on them and said to them, 'Receive the Holy Spirit'" (John 20:22). The significance of this is that from now on for Christians the Holy Spirit is closely connected with Jesus. Now Jesus Christ is not limited to one time and place

---

1. Alasdair I. C. Heron, *The Holy Spirit* (Philadelphia: Westminster, 1983), 14.

in history, but through the Spirit is present in all times and places. Furthermore, God's presence and activity in the world (the Spirit) takes the form of making others like Jesus Christ. So, in his letters, Paul can speak interchangeably of the Christian being "in Christ" or "in the Spirit." Now to participate in the Spirit is in some way to participate in Christ.

There are interesting differences of perspective on the Holy Spirit within the New Testament writings. The main difference is between Acts and Paul. In Acts Luke paints a rather idealized picture of the early church, and part of that picture is an unambiguous presence of the Spirit. That is, in Acts it is generally outwardly obvious when a person or group receives the Holy Spirit. On the day of Pentecost when all the disciples were gathered in a house, "All of them were filled with the Holy Spirit and began to speak in other languages, as the Spirit gave them ability" (Acts 2:4; cf. 8:16-18; 10:44-46). Other signs of the Spirit are prophecy, bold proclamation of the gospel, and guidance for individuals or the church. Since most of these signs can be heard and seen, it was obvious when the Holy Spirit was at work. This is the biblical tradition that is emphasized in the contemporary Pentecostal-charismatic movement.

In Paul's letters, however, the presence and activity of Spirit is less self-evident. Paul thinks of two ways of living human life, and one of his characteristic usages for designating these is to speak of living according to the flesh or according to the Spirit. To live according to the flesh does not mean merely following physical desires; it means human beings living as though they are the masters or mistresses of their own lives and not responsible to God. To live according to the Spirit is to live with trust in and loyalty to God and Christ. Whether someone is living according to the Spirit must be discerned rather than being plain to all. Paul recognizes that extraordinary phenomena such as speaking in tongues may come from the Spirit, but he does not see tongues as an unambiguous divine blessing. One should ask, for instance, whether speaking in tongues builds up the community of the church or is disruptive.[2] Despite their difference over the self-evident character of the Spirit, however, Paul and Luke agree that the Christian life is an existence lived in the Spirit of God.

Another matter on which Acts and Paul agree is that the Spirit builds up the community of believers, the church. Acts presents the Pentecost day outpouring of the Spirit on Jesus' followers in Jerusalem as the birthday of the church and its mission. Continuing on from that day, the Acts account of the expanding church sees the Spirit vitalizing the church's worship and public witness and guiding its life. Although Paul does not even mention Pentecost,

2. Ibid., 43–46.

he understands the Spirit as the One who equips the various members of the church with special gifts that are intended to build up the church's common life (1 Corinthians 12:12-31).

When we look back over the testimony about the Spirit of God in the diverse writings of the Scriptures, we find a comprehensive view of the Spirit's involvement in the world. Remember that the basic understanding in the Bible is that the Spirit is God present and active in the world. But the nature of this divine presence and activity varies considerably, so that we need to distinguish different spheres and modes of the Spirit's presence.

1. *The Spirit's presence in the universe is suggested by the basic biblical association of Spirit with breath and life.* There is a sense then in which all living things, microscopic and macroscopic, participate in the Spirit of God. In the second creation story humans also derive their life from God's *ruach* or spirit: "Then the LORD God formed man from the dust of the ground, and breathed into his nostrils the breath of life; and the man became a living being" (Genesis 2:7).

There are Old Testament hints, but only hints, of an even-wider presence of the Spirit throughout the inanimate as well as animate universe. The very opening verse of the Bible says, "In the beginning when God created the heavens and the earth, the earth was a formless void and darkness covered the face of the deep, while a wind from God swept over the face of the waters" (Genesis 1:1). While *ruach* is here translated as "a wind from God," the alternative and traditional translation is "the Spirit of God." No particular role or activity is ascribed to the Spirit in creation, for in this creation story it is the Word that is the creative agency. The presence of the Spirit in all reaches of the universe is also explicitly affirmed in Psalm 139:7-10:

> Where can I go from your spirit?
> Or where can I flee from your presence?
> If I ascend to heaven, you are there;
>   if I make my bed in Sheol, you are there.
> If I take the wings of the morning
>   and settle at the farthest limits of the sea,
>   even there your hand shall lead me,
>   and your right hand shall hold me fast.

Again no specific activity in the inanimate creation is assigned to the Spirit. Here and in Genesis 1:1 the point seems to be simply that God is present throughout time and space; there is no moment and no location in which God is absent.

Hellenistic Judaism in the centuries just preceding the time of Jesus developed this idea of the Spirit in all the world by linking Spirit with the Old Testament notion of Wisdom. In the Old Testament book of Proverbs, Wisdom is not just a quality of some people but is God's Wisdom. Further, this divine Wisdom helps create the world. So Proverbs 8:29-30 says, "When he [the Lord] marked out the foundations of the earth, then I [Wisdom] was beside him, like a master worker." What some later Jewish authors did was to connect the Spirit with Wisdom, so that the Spirit is understood as having a creative function. This identification of Spirit with Wisdom is seen in some books called apocryphal or deuterocanonical.[3] An example of this is found in the Wisdom of Solomon 7:24-25, "For wisdom is more mobile than any motion; because of her pureness she pervades and penetrates all things. For she is a breath of the power of God."

Today with our understanding of matter as energy and thoroughly dynamic, I like to speculate on the Spirit's role in a broader meaning of animation. That is, analogous to the Spirit's role in giving life to living beings, might not the Spirit be the source of the energy that takes form in physical things? Although I cannot point to an Old Testament or New Testament text in support of this idea, it does seem to be a reasonable extension of biblical thought.

2. The Spirit's presence in human life. This is a complex subject, for we need to make distinctions between several modes of divine presence in human life.

a. The Spirit is present to all people simply by the fact that they are human beings. In fact, Scripture speaks of human beings as spirit (small s). This spirit seems to refer to the capacity of humans to transcend their circumstances and ask questions about where they have come from and where they are going. But being spirit is more than just some hardware built into humans like a heart or lungs. Being spirit comes from a relationship with God; we are spirit because we are met and addressed by the absolute Spirit in a way different from other creatures on earth. The great twentieth-century Catholic theologian Karl Rahner emphasizes that as humans encounter the world, we also encounter God. Not that we meet God as one object alongside others; rather, God or infinite being is the *horizon* within which we meet anything in the world. This is not first of all a conscious encounter, but a preconscious meeting that creates a longing or hunger in the human for infinite being. Thus, like Augustine long ago who prayed, "Thou hast made us for thyself and restless is our heart until it comes to rest in thee," Rahner says that humans have

---

3. These writings were included in the Greek translation of the Hebrew Bible (the Septuagint), but they were eventually not accepted by Jews as part of their Scripture. Protestants followed this later Jewish practice, so these books are not part of the Protestant Bible. Protestants refer to these books as apocryphal writings. Roman Catholicism followed the Septuagint that accepted these writings within the biblical canon. Today Catholic scholars refer to them as deuterocanonical writings, that is, those recognized later as canonical.

a deep longing for God.[4] Very often people do not realize this, and try to satisfy this longing for infinite being with finite things such as human relationships, achievements, power, or possessions. In any case, the Spirit of God is present to all human beings, although they may not recognize it.[5]

The fact that human beings are spirit does not mean that they have an unfailing pipeline to God. God is never under human control. God seeks a personal relationship with people, and a personal relationship must involve freely given loyalty on both sides. What is especially significant about saying humans are spirit is that God is always present to them and inviting their participation in a relationship of mutual loyalty.

b. The Spirit in the people of Israel. Here experience of God's Spirit becomes conscious and testimony to the Spirit explicit. We have touched on just a few of the many references to the Spirit in the Old Testament and Apocrypha. Here we find profession that the Spirit is omnipresent, the source of life, and the giver of special life-enhancing gifts such as prophecy and wisdom.

Is God's Spirit still with Israel? This is a difficult question for many Christians. Since the New Testament generally sees a close bond between the Spirit and Jesus Christ, many Christians think the Spirit is given only to those who believe in Jesus. Yet in Romans 9–11 Paul, a Jew who has faith in Jesus, wrestles with the question of whether those Jews who do not believe in Jesus are cut off from God. His thoughts on the matter are convoluted, yet he ends up affirming that God's election of Israel is not nullified and "all Israel will be saved" (Romans 11:26). He does not know *how* this salvation of all Israel will happen, for he concludes his reflections on the issue with praise of the mysterious ways of God. While Paul does not mention God's Spirit in his discussion, it is difficult to conceive of the election of Israel being maintained and the salvation of all Israel happening without the presence and activity of God's Spirit.

c. The Spirit in and through Jesus. Whereas other people may receive special gifts from the Spirit sporadically and the presence of the Spirit in their life is always contested by the counterforce of sin, Jesus is portrayed in the New Testament as one whose special gifts from the Spirit abided and whose life is without sin. For instance, the special power to heal appears to have rested on the adult Jesus. Frequently he is inundated with people seeking healing, yet we have no account of his failing to heal except where people's unbelief blocked it. Some people are even healed by merely touching him. Jesus is also without sin. He is said to experience strong temptations, yet the Gospels say

4. Augustine, *Confessions*, Book One, Chapter 1 in *Augustine: Confessions and Enchiridion*, trans. and ed. Albert C. Outler, The Library of Christian Classics, Vol. 3 (Philadelphia: Westminster, 1955), 311.

5. Karl Rahner, *Foundations of Christian Faith*, trans. William V. Dych (New York: Seabury, 1978), 31–34.

he overcame them. Such qualities testify to a potent, enduring presence of the Spirit in Jesus.

As we have already noted, the New Testament also tells us that after his resurrection Jesus gave the Spirit to his followers. The Spirit not only is *in* Jesus, but also comes to his disciples *through* Jesus. Thus to participate in the Spirit is also to participate in some way in Jesus Christ.

d. The Spirit in the church. Several New Testament writers hold that the Spirit enables people to have faith in Jesus. Jesus says, "Very truly, I tell you, no one can enter the kingdom of God without being born of water and Spirit. What is born of the flesh is flesh, and what is born of the Spirit is spirit" (John 3:5-6). And Paul says, "No one can say, 'Jesus is Lord' except by the Holy Spirit" (1 Corinthians 12:3). Thus the Holy Spirit gives life to the church by creating faith in its members.

The Holy Spirit goes further by producing Christlike character in believers who live by the Spirit rather than by the flesh: "The fruit of the Spirit is love, joy, peace, patience, kindness, generosity, faithfulness, gentleness, and self-control" (Galatians 5:22-23). In addition to bringing out faith in Jesus, the Spirit fashions Christlike character in Christians.

The Spirit also supplies the church with a diversity of gifts for building up community. Paul emphasizes this: "Now there are varieties of gifts, but the same Spirit, and there are varieties of services, but the same Lord, and there are varieties of activities, but it is the same God who activates all of them in everyone. To each is given the manifestation of the Spirit for the common good" (1 Corinthians 12:4-7).

In summary, the life-giving Spirit in the church grants new life to human beings. Not only is the Spirit of God the source of animation and life in all the universe, the Spirit also gives new life to those in the church. This new life goes beyond merely existing and brings humans closer to the fulfillment God intends for them in the harmony of the reign of God.

e. The Spirit is especially present also in some people outside the church. This presence of the Spirit goes beyond the general presence to all people simply as human. To assert a special presence of the Spirit of God to some people outside the church is controversial, for the New Testament concentrates its witness on the Spirit's activity within the Christian community. Scriptural testimony to God's presence with someone outside the covenant community is sparse, although the ancient figures of Melchizedek and Abimelech are examples (Genesis 14:17-20; 20:1-18) and Jesus commends a Canaanite woman for her great faith (Matthew 15:21-28). There are also two indirect arguments in favor of my assertion. One is the argument above: Paul's belief that all Jews will eventually be saved seems to require the activity of the Spirit at least among Jews at some point in time. The other argument uses Paul's statement in Galatians 5:22-23: "The fruit of the Spirit is love, joy, peace, patience, kindness, generosity, faithfulness, gentleness, and self-control." Our contacts with people in the world tell us that these qualities are not limited to Christians. Since Paul says the source of these characteristics among Christians is the Spirit, it is reasonable to think that wherever such qualities are found in human beings, the Spirit has been at work. So to participate in the Spirit is to share in Jesus Christ. This participation in Christ may not be an explicit faith in Jesus, but it may be participation in a Christlike life. In other words, the gifts that God's Spirit gives to people, no matter what their religion or philosophy of life, resemble the qualities of Jesus.

This concludes our look at the biblical witness to the Spirit. Now we must consider what the postbiblical Christian tradition said about the Spirit. This could be a long exposition indeed, but we will limit our discussion to the Spirit in the doctrine of the Trinity.

The Spirit in the Trinity

When the Nicene Creed was first approved in 325, the Council of Nicea had only the barest confession to make about the Spirit. After its affirmation of faith in God the Father and Jesus Christ, the creed simply added "And [we believe] in the Holy Spirit." There was no statement about what the Spirit did. The 381 revision of the creed expanded somewhat on the role of the Spirit, but thought about the Spirit was still spare. This read, "And [we believe] in the Holy Spirit, the Lord and life-giver, Who proceeds from the Father, Who with the Father and the Son is together worshiped and together glorified, Who spoke through the prophets." The creed's affirmation of the divinity of the Spirit is made somewhat indirectly, for the Spirit is not explicitly called God. Instead, the Spirit is called by the divine name, Lord, and is said to be worshiped; worship is rightly given only to God. The Spirit is distinguished from the other two persons of the Trinity by the affirmation that the Spirit "proceeds from the Father." The only two functions of the Spirit that are mentioned are giving life and speaking through the prophets. Although rather scanty attention to the Holy Spirit has been the case throughout most of Christian history, Western and Eastern Christianity developed different conceptions of the Spirit in the Trinity.

When we discussed the Trinity in chapter 2, I suggested that the doctrine of the Trinity testifies to both the relatedness and the vitality of God. On the one hand, we may speak of the relatedness and vitality within God's eternal being, the *immanent Trinity*. The relatedness within God is most clearly expressed in family metaphors that involve personal relations. So traditionally it was said that eternally there is the relation of Father and Son in God. God does not exist in solitary isolation, for to be father/mother implies a son or daughter, and to be son/daughter implies a father/mother. Furthermore, the Holy Spirit is understood widely in traditional Western Christian theology as the bond of love between Father and Son. That is, not only are Father and Son related as begetter and begotten, but they are related also in mutual love, each giving Godself to the other and receiving the other in love. Augustine says this bond of love between Father and Son is the Holy Spirit.[6] So in this tradition, the three persons of the Trinity are understood as relations rather than as individual realities. Thomas Aquinas later spoke of the three persons of the Trinity as "subsisting relations." I must confess that I find the idea of the Spirit as the bond of love between Father and Son unbalanced, for Father and Son seem to refer to individuated realities who are inseparably related. That is, both the categories of individual and relation can be referred to Father and Son, but the Spirit seems to be no individuated reality, only a relation. This is evident in one of the analogies of the Trinity that Augustine favored: lover, beloved, and love itself. A similar analogy would be husband, wife, marriage. It appears that marriage is not individuated in the way that husband and wife are. That is, lover and beloved, husband and wife, suggest a reality that is like a person, whereas love itself and marriage are abstractions of a personal relationship.

The Eastern Orthodox way makes more sense to me; it distinguishes the Spirit by its "procession" from the Father, whereas the Son is "begotten" by the Father. This term *procession* comes from the Greek in John 15:26, which the New Revised Standard Version of the Bible translates this way: "'When the Advocate comes, whom I will send to you from the Father, the Spirit of truth who comes from the Father, he will testify on my behalf.'" Older versions generally translated the key Greek term as "proceeds from" rather than as "comes from." To be sure, we cannot know what "proceeds from" means *for God*, anymore than we know what "begotten" means for God. Yet they are biblical ways of distinguishing the Spirit and Son from the Father. Whether one follows the Western or Eastern view, they share the notion that there are relations within God eternally.

Since there are distinctions and relations within God's own being, there is also vitality and activity within the divine being. In chapter 2 I characterized this activity as a double movement of going forth and advancing toward a richer unity within God. This double movement is suggested by the Son being begotten and responding to the Father/Mother in love. The Spirit also

6. My struggle here with the dominantly male metaphors of the theological tradition is, I hope, evident. The main barrier I feel is with talking about the second person of the Trinity as Daughter, since that seems awkwardly linked with Jesus Christ. It is easier to use female metaphors if one shifts to Wisdom as does Elizabeth A. Johnson in *She Who Is: The Mystery of God in Feminist Theological Discourse* (New York: Crossroad, 1992), but in her own trinitarian formulation she simply refers to the second person as Jesus Christ (213–14). We are still groping.

comes forth or proceeds from the Father/Mother like a breath and also responds to the Father/Mother and Son with love.[7]

So far we have discussed the relatedness and activity within God's eternal being, the immanent Trinity. Now we must turn to God's relatedness and activity in relation to the world, the *economic Trinity*. God's relation with the world and all its creatures is an *internal or real relation*. In a merely external relation between two beings, changes in one do not affect the other. For instance, you may have two pens sitting side by side on your desk. You may pick up one of the pens, but that does not influence the other pen. The pens have an external relation to each other as well as probably an external relation to you. That is, you probably do not grieve when you lose one of the pens or it ceases to function; you just get another. In an internal relation, what happens to one affects the other. We have held all along that God has an internal or real relation with the world. So the stupendous project of creating and guiding a world to its fulfillment in the reign of God affects God; God grows in experience and will find satisfaction in achieving her goal. This internal relation includes God's participation in the suffering of all creatures in the universe. Whereas you and I share in the suffering of a few other creatures significant to us, God participates in the suffering of all. This means that the creative process is immensely costly to God. All this we have discussed previously. The important new point is that it is God's Spirit that is present in and to all creatures, so the Holy Spirit is vital to making God's relation with creatures an internal relation. Indeed, Scripture speaks of the Spirit having a more intimate relation with us than anyone else. God knows us far better than even our very best friend, for God knows our thoughts before we utter them (Psalm 139). And Christian mystics have witnessed to "experiences" of union with God, times of such intimate communion with God that the usual barriers between knower and what is known are overcome. The central way in which the biblical and Christian tradition speaks of this profound presence of God is to say Spirit.

We must also talk about the shape of God's activity in relation to the world. Not only is God eternally active, but God is also living and active in relation to the universe. In fact, the economic Trinity faithfully reflects the

---

7. The Eastern and Western Christian churches have had different views of the Spirit's relation with the Son. The West has held that the Spirit proceeds from the Father *and the Son* (Latin *filioque*), while the East holds to the 381 Nicene Creed view that the Spirit proceeds from only the Father. The idea of *filioque* surfaced in the fifth century and its insertion in the Nicene Creed for liturgical use was approved by the Pope in 1014. The Eastern churches objected both to the idea and the unilateral manner in which the Nicene Creed was altered. The difference was one major factor in the formal division in 1054 of the Eastern and Western churches. For further comment from a Western perspective see Ted Peters, *God—The World's Future* (Minneapolis: Fortress Press, 1992), 249–52; for an Eastern perspective, see Vladimir Lossky, *The Mystical Theology of the Eastern Church* (Crestwood, N.Y.: St. Vladimir's Seminary Press, 1976), 56–62.

immanent Trinity. That is, the way God appears in relation to us in time is a faithful reflection of what God is eternally.[8] I have said that the shape of God's activity eternally and in time is a dance with a richly varied double movement of going forth and then achieving a richer unity within God. The Word goes forth into the world even to the point of becoming incarnate in Jesus, and is now involved in the lengthy enterprise of bringing the fallen and imperfect world to the wholeness and harmony of the future reign of God. Our attention now is focused on the Spirit's double movement of going forth into the creation and also renewing creatures by forming individuals and communities that will eventually be suited to the reign of God. So the double activity of the Spirit in the world is (1) to be intimately present in creatures and (2) to draw them toward greater unity and wholeness. Thus the Spirit seeks to lead creatures toward their fulfillment, but this fulfillment is not an individualistic actualization of all one's potential. With the Holy Spirit, fulfillment is understood both as greater unity of creatures with one another and with God and as wholeness or healing of the physical, interpersonal, and spiritual brokenness present in the world. In short, this unifying, healing work of the Holy Spirit is salvation.

I said at the start of this chapter that Christian understanding of God's Spirit occurs at the intersection of the Christian tradition about the Spirit and contemporary Christian experiences of the Spirit. So far we have examined the Christian tradition about the Spirit; now we must look at some contemporary experiences of the Spirit. One important form of experience of the Spirit comes to those involved in the Pentecostal-charismatic movement, which is the Christian movement that most consciously and directly focuses on the Holy Spirit. This is the topic to which we will now turn.

The Pentecostal-Charismatic Movement

Imagine that you have accepted an invitation from a friend to attend her Pentecostal church, although you have never been to such a church before. As you enter the church and make your way to the sanctuary, people are friendly. Several persons greet your friend by name, and a couple shake your hand and welcome you as well. The service opens with singing several songs to the accompaniment of both organ and a piano that provides various embellishments. While there is the customary substantial Protestant sermon, other features of the worship service catch your attention. At one point, a man in the congrega-

---

8. So with proper qualifications, I agree with Karl Rahner's rule that, "The Trinity of the economy of salvation *is* the immanent Trinity"; *Theological Investigations*, IV (Baltimore: Helicon Press, 1966), 94.

tion makes strange sounds out loud; it is as though he is speaking a foreign language that you cannot understand. Silence follows and then a woman speaks in English, beginning with, "Thus says the Lord," and the whole message is presented as a communication directly from God. Your friend tells you that this was first a person speaking in tongues and another giving an interpretation of the tongues message. At another point, everyone begins to sing, but there are no common words; everyone sings their own words that again seem to be in foreign languages. Your friend says this is singing in tongues. Throughout the service you hear frequent reference to the Holy Spirit and to something called baptism in the Spirit. At the conclusion of the service, people are invited to the front of the church, in order to have prayer for conversion, receiving baptism in the Holy Spirit, or healing. As you leave the church, you are puzzled by much that you have observed, but you also have the sense that these people believe God is very much alive. In attending this church, you have had contact with one of the most influential twentieth-century church movements, the Pentecostal-charismatic movement.

There are two main points that we should notice about the Pentecostal-charismatic movement. The first is the Pentecostal understanding of the Christian life. When the Pentecostal movement began in 1901 at a small Bible college in Topeka, Kansas, the students and faculty at the Bible college were all from the revivalist tradition that taught a two-stage view of the salvation of an individual. The first stage is conversion or being born again; here a person comes to faith in Jesus Christ and receives forgiveness of sin (justification) and the beginnings of sanctification. The second stage is sometimes called *entire sanctification*, which means that a person is so holy that one no longer consciously sins. John Wesley, the founder of Methodism, had said persons with entire sanctification might make mistakes, but they would not deliberately sin. Another common name for this second great experience is *baptism in the Holy Spirit.* The basic idea of baptism in the Holy Spirit is that while the Holy Spirit is present in every converted Christian, being *baptized* in the Holy Spirit is a deeper experience like being immersed or dunked in the Spirit. So baptism in the Spirit is understood as a deeper presence of the Spirit in a person's life. Many Pentecostals do not agree with Wesley that those with this deeper involvement of the Spirit are without deliberate sin, but all Pentecostals strongly maintain that baptism in the Spirit brings a considerably deeper commitment to God. Thus, the revivalists at the Bible college in Topeka in 1901 thought of a person's salvation as focused on two experiences. The first experience was conversion to a conscious Christian faith. The second experience that usually comes later in time was baptism in the Holy Spirit with its deeper faith commitment. The second experience was not considered necessary for going to heaven, but it made one a much more dedicated follower of Jesus.

The question that occupied the attention of the people at this Bible college was, How can we *know* whether we have received the second experience of baptism in the Holy Spirit? What *outward evidence* is there of this second great experience? The answer they arrived at was that *speaking in tongues* is consistently the initial outward sign of this inner religious experience. Here emerged for the first time the *Pentecostal doctrine of salvation*: conversion brings reconciliation with God, but baptism in the Holy Spirit, as evidenced by speaking in tongues, makes a person more committed and more bold in witnessing to others. These two experiences may occur almost simultaneously, but usually they are separated in time, often by many years. This distinctive doctrine of salvation is the first major point about Pentecostalism.

The second main point about the Pentecostal-charismatic movement is that it stresses the manifestations of the Spirit in extraordinary phenomena such as speaking in tongues, healing, and prophecy. The Pentecostal movement took its name from the biblical day of Pentecost, fifty days after Easter, when the Holy Spirit was poured out on the first community of Christians in Jerusalem and they spoke in tongues; the early Christians also made public testimony to their faith and gained many converts. While ecstatic gifts such as speaking in tongues and prophecy were common in the early years of the church, gradually they were pushed to the margins of church life. For centuries there were only occasional outbursts of these phenomena. The Pentecostal movement made these phenomena central to its life. However, from 1901 until the late 1950s, these extraordinary manifestations of the Spirit remained confined largely to separate Pentecostal churches that catered mostly to lower economic groups. Then in 1959, through contact with Pentecostal Christians, people in mainstream churches began to have Pentecostal experiences. Most of these people chose to remain in their mainstream churches rather than join a Pentecostal church. This movement involving mainstream church people with Pentecostal experiences is commonly called the *charismatic movement*, coming from the Greek word *charis*, which means gift.[9] While the growth of the charismatic movement seems to have leveled out in the United States, the worldwide Pentecostal-charismatic movement as a whole is fast growing.

All Pentecostals and charismatics place great emphasis upon the nine gifts of the Holy Spirit mentioned by Paul in 1 Corinthians 12:4-10: prophecy, speaking in tongues, interpretation of tongues, healing, a word of wisdom, a word of knowledge, faith to work miracles, miracles, and discernment of spirits. Since the four gifts of prophecy, speaking in tongues, interpretation of

---

9. Sometimes the term "charismatic movement" is used in a broader sense to include the Pentecostals as well as those in mainstream churches. Other times the distinction is made between classical Pentecostals and Neo-Pentecostals; the latter are what I call charismatics.

tongues, and healing are most conspicuous, they deserve a short explanation. A prophecy is considered to be a direct communication from God. Speaking in tongues is most often used in private prayer, but when it occurs in public worship and then is interpreted so that people can understand the message, the message, like prophecy, is regarded as an immediate word from God. Prayer for healing is very prominent in Pentecostal and charismatic worship services and prayer meetings. Many in the Pentecostal-charismatic movement feel that their teaching on salvation and on the Spirit's manifestation in extraordinary gifts constitute the *full gospel*, and this name has been taken up by the active Pentecostal-charismatic organization Full Gospel Businessmen's Fellowship International.

There are some variations in this large movement. A good number of charismatic Christians have modified the classical Pentecostal teaching on salvation, in order to fit better into their own church tradition. For instance, some charismatics do not insist on speaking in tongues as the failsafe outward sign of baptism in the Spirit. Nevertheless, Pentecostal and charismatic Christians agree that Christians should seek baptism in the Holy Spirit as a highly significant deepening of one's faith. Again, some charismatics do not insist upon a distinct conversion experience as does revivalism. In general, though, we can say that most Pentecostal-charismatic Christians hold these two major teachings: first, a two-stage view of salvation consisting of conversion and baptism in the Holy Spirit, and second, the Spirit's manifestation in extraordinary gifts such as speaking in tongues. It would be a mistake, though, to think these Christians are chiefly interested in unusual, ecstatic experiences. While this is surely high-voltage religion, the central reality of the Pentecostal-charismatic movement is a profound and vivid sense that God is present and active in today's world. Indeed, this strong sense of God present is exactly what one would expect from a movement that emphasizes the Holy Spirit, for the Spirit is the presence of God in the world.

The Pentecostal-charismatic experience is one form of the more widespread experience of salvation. Thus we must examine in some detail the saving work of the Spirit. In so doing, we find that the experience of salvation and interpretation of the Spirit's part in salvation are closely interwoven.

Salvation

We should recognize from the beginning that we may have an uphill battle with the Christian understanding of salvation, for most of us come with two preconceptions that are at odds with a biblical understanding of salvation: first, we usually equate salvation with life after death, and second, we tend to think of salvation as entirely spiritual and not at all physical or worldly; for instance, salvation is restricted to the individual "getting right with God." However, the Bible and much of Christian tradition conceive of salvation more broadly as an event of deliverance that certainly has a spiritual center in an individual's life, but also embraces the whole physical and communal dimensions of human life. Furthermore, salvation begins to take place in this life on earth and is completed after death. Thus salvation takes place both in the present and the final future. The usual theological way of stating this present-but-also-future character of salvation is to say that salvation is *eschatological*, for biblical eschatology involves beliefs about life after death, but it also refers to present existence. This broad meaning is suggested by the origin of the English word *salvation* in the Latin *salvus*, which means healed. To be saved is to be healed in some way. So from the start we need to reorient our thinking; salvation is not limited to some purely spiritual event after death, but also includes occurrences of healing that touch spirit and the body during our present life.

The chief biblical words for saving (Hebrew *yasa* and Greek *sozo*) generally mean to rescue or deliver from some threat. In the Old Testament to save most often means to rescue from some earthly, physical danger that has a spiritual dimension. That is, the danger may be an enemy (Psalm 60:11) or an illness (Psalm 6:4), but the relationship with God is at the heart of it. The greatest saving event of the Old Testament is the exodus in which God delivers the people of Israel from slavery in Egypt. The nation's later release from captivity in Babylonia is regarded as a new saving exodus. While human beings might be the agents through whom salvation comes, it is ultimately God who saves.

In the New Testament Jesus and the message about him are the center of God's work of saving. Sometimes to save means to rescue from imminent physical danger such as during a storm on the Sea of Galilee when Peter awoke the sleeping Jesus, saying, "Lord, save us!" (Matthew 8:25). In the accounts of Jesus' healings, the word *save* is often used. Whether it is saving from a storm or from a disease, the faith of the one seeking help is a key factor. Peter also speaks of a spiritual and physical salvation when he is questioned by religious authorities about his healing of a lame man and testifies to Jesus by saying, "There is salvation in no one else" (Acts 4:13). In Paul's writings the emphasis on salvation in this life shifts more clearly toward the spiritual, but in the final future he looks forward to the redemption of our bodies (Romans 8:23). Thus in the Bible salvation has its center in the spiritual dimension of relationship with God, but it also includes physical and communal dimensions. That is, salvation normally involves a healing of relationship with God, but eventually and perhaps presently will include healing of one's body and relationships with other creatures as well.

Differences in contemporary interpretations of present salvation arise in part over whether salvation is limited to healing of the individual's relationship with God or salvation is taken to include the transformation of some physical or social disorder. Traditionally Christian theology has for the most part focused on the former; the various forms of liberation theology today emphasize the latter.

In my view, the primary focus of salvation should be on being right with God, for frequently in the New Testament salvation is explicitly understood as forgiveness of sins or being justified before God (Luke 1:77; Acts 10:43; Romans 1:16-17). Salvation in this sense is peace with God and can be counted upon. Nevertheless, there is a secondary place for salvation as healing of the body or healing of relationships with other creatures. But salvation in this secondary sense is always partial and imperfect in this life.

The biblical story of Zacchaeus, a rich tax collector in Jericho, illustrates this complex character of salvation. Tax collectors in the Israel of Jesus' time were hated and despised people, because they were Jews hired by the Roman empire to extract taxes from their own people and in the process they routinely cheated their fellow Jews. Jesus went against prevailing social conventions by reaching out to this outcast and having a meal at his house. At the meal Zacchaeus announced, "Look, half of my possessions, Lord, I will give to the poor, and if I have defrauded anyone of anything, I will pay back four times as much." Jesus replied, "Today salvation has come to this house" (Luke 19:1-10). Notice that salvation has come to Zacchaeus "today." Notice also that the salvation consists fundamentally in the forgiveness that Jesus conveyed by seeking out this social outcast, but it is also manifest in the tax collector's new attitude of faith and his just relations with other people.

There are a number of images and concepts in Scripture and the history of theology for various aspects of salvation; I will focus on two that have dominated: justification and sanctification.

Justification

We sometimes say that someone tried to justify herself/himself or to justify an action. We mean that the person is claiming to be in the right. This is the main thrust of the biblical usage of justify and justification, for in Scripture these words mean being in the right with God. This terminology occurs most often in Paul's letters, but it also appears less frequently elsewhere in Scripture. Justification is actually a metaphor that uses legal terminology to apply to the relation with God. The basic picture is a law court in which a person appears before a judge who renders a judgment in the case. To be justified is to receive a favorable judgment, to be considered in the right. Although it is not apparent in English, in the Greek the word closely related to justification (Greek *dikaiō*) is righteous (*dikaos*). The connections are that the justified person is considered righteous before God, and that in justifying a person, God is also righteous.

One of the classic texts in which Paul speaks of justification is Romans 3:20-25:

> For "no human being will be justified in his sight" by deeds prescribed by the law, for through the law comes the knowledge of sin.
> But now, apart from law, the righteousness of God has been disclosed, and is attested by the law and the prophets, the righteousness of God through faith in Jesus Christ for all who believe. For there is no distinction, since all have sinned and fall short of the glory of God; they are now justified by his grace as a gift, through the redemption that is in Christ Jesus, whom God put forward as a sacrifice of atonement by his blood, effective through faith.

This passage asserts three things with which all major Christian traditions agree. First, Paul says that one cannot be justified before God on the basis of one's actions in following the Jewish law. Christians have generalized from this to say that one cannot be justified through following any laws or moral principles whatsoever. Their point and Paul's point is that no one *deserves* to be justified by God. Justification cannot be earned, "since all have sinned and fall short of the glory of God." Second, justification before God comes as God's pure gift. As Paul emphasizes, "They are now justified by his grace as a gift." Since grace means gift, Paul underscores the point with a redundancy, "by his grace as a gift." So justification is by grace. Third, this gift of being right with God is received by faith in Jesus Christ. That is, a person knows and acknowledges the pure gift of justification through having faith in Jesus.

These basic points about justification are agreed upon by all major Christian traditions—Orthodox, Roman Catholic, and Protestant. However, justification became a major point of contention at the time of the Protestant Reformation in the sixteenth century, and it has remained a teaching over which Christians have differed. The difference becomes evident when we look at two major interpretations of justification; we shall call them the transformationist interpretation and the classical Protestant interpretation.

a. The *transformationist interpretation* of justification is clearly articulated by Augustine (d. 430), whose formulation of it has been very influential in the Roman Catholic tradition, but in its basic thrust is also affirmed in Eastern Orthodox theology. The primary emphasis of Augustine's interpretation is that grace is transforming grace. That is, God's fundamental grace or gift to human beings is to transform their thinking, willing, and valuing. God's grace changes people so that they reorder their priorities; loving God becomes primary. So God's transforming grace is the driving force of what especially the Orthodox call *theosis*, becoming like God. God's grace remolds human beings to be more like God's own being.

In this transformation process, the central response of humans is *repentance* so as to love differently. Repentance is a biblical term that was prominent in Jesus' message. Jesus' preaching is summed up by Mark this way, "The time is fulfilled, and the kingdom of God has come near; repent, and believe in the good news" (Mark 1:15). To repent means literally to change direction, and in the New Testament it means to change the direction of one's life. To repent means to recognize that one has been (negatively) headed down the wrong path, but now one (positively) shifts to the right path. Like the Gospel of John, Augustine sees the redirection of repentance to lie chiefly in a change of one's priorities, that is, a fundamental alteration in what one loves. Instead of loving some creaturely thing most of all, God's grace turns a person's primary love toward God.

While the primary stress in Augustine's interpretation of grace is on transformation, the secondary emphasis is on the forgiveness of God. Not only does God transform people, God also forgives the sin that they have committed. Both these elements are present in the Zacchaeus story, for his salvation consists in being forgiven by Jesus who seeks him out and in being transformed in his priorities to the extent of amply repaying those whom he has wronged.

b. In the *classical Protestant interpretation* of justification, the order of emphasis is exactly reversed. The chief emphasis here is upon grace as sheer mercy that forgives the sin of people. The reason for the shift in emphasis was that a concern arose in the late Middle Ages of whether one could be *sure* of being right with or accepted by God. Martin Luther (d. 1546) was the one who first pressed this question vigorously. Asking the question led him to reflect on the *grounds* of being acceptable to God. At first he followed Augustine's transformationist interpretation, but he came to believe that the transformationist path could not provide assurance of being acceptable to God. The reason is that while God's grace does indeed transform people, the transformation during this lifetime always remains incomplete, unfinished. The Christian on earth is always a sinner and a saint, a mixture of good and evil. If the *ground or basis* of being acceptable to God is the transforming grace of God, then one could never be sure of being acceptable to God since that grace has only partially done its work while we are on earth. One might continue to ask, Am I adequately transformed so as to be acceptable to God? At what point has transforming grace done its work sufficiently to assure God's acceptance?

Luther's answer to this question was to turn to another conception of God's grace, namely, grace as sheer mercy. That is, even though one is always a sinner during this life and never fully devoted to God, God mercifully forgives that sin. The primary emphasis of Luther was on grace as God's mercy. Justification or being righteous before God is now first of all understood as the forgiveness of sins. The appropriate human response to the gospel message of God's mercy is faith in Jesus Christ, and faith is understood by Luther as principally trust in Christ or clinging to Christ as a drowning person clings to his or her rescuer. Consequently, in addition to saying justification is by *grace alone*, as many theologians agreed, Luther added that justification is by *faith alone*. The point of the faith alone is that justification or forgiveness is given not because of any merits of the person; it is a complete gift given to those who trust in Christ, not in the quality of their life even partially transformed by grace. Thus Luther's doctrine is often called *justification by grace through faith*, and it is understood to mean by grace alone and through faith alone.

Luther recognized that Christians are also transformed by the grace of God so as to change their priorities, but he underscored the partial, incomplete character of this transformation. Repeatedly in his writings and lectures he hammered away at the need for a clear distinction between these two kinds of righteousness, the righteousness of Christ ascribed to the believer through God's mercy and the righteousness of Christ that begins to transform the believer.

Notice that both kinds of righteousness are understood by Luther as the righteousness *of Christ*. This righteousness never *belongs* to a person on his or her own right, but is always a righteousness in union with Christ. Luther stressed that faith unites the believer with Christ like the close union of bride and bridegroom.[10] The other premier reformer John Calvin also placed great weight on this union of the believer with Christ. Calvin says,

> First, we must understand that as long as Christ remains outside of us, and we are separated from him, all that he has suffered and done for the salvation of the human race remains useless and of no value for us. Therefore, to share with us what he has received from the Father, he had to become ours and to dwell within us.[11]

Luther essentially agrees with Calvin that it is the Holy Spirit who brings about this union of Christ and the believer.

Luther's interpretation of justification was basically adopted by John Calvin and most other major Protestant reformers, although Calvin managed to strike a more even balance between the two kinds of righteousness in his understanding of the life of the Christian. Calvin and many other Protestant theologians after Luther distinguished between these two kinds of righteous-

---

10. Timothy F. Lull, ed., *Martin Luther's Basic Theological Writings* (Minneapolis: Fortress Press, 1989), 603.

11. John Calvin, *Institutes of the Christian Religion*, Book III, Chapter 1, ed. John T. McNeill, trans. F. L. Battles, The Library of Christian Classics, Vol. 20 (Philadelphia: Westminster, 1960), 537.

ness by designating the righteousness given in forgiveness as justification and the righteousness that transforms a person as sanctification.

Sanctification

Sanctification comes from the Latin term *sanctus*, holy, so sanctification means to make holy. Terms often used relatively interchangeably with sanctification are regeneration and new life. In a Catholic or Orthodox context, sanctification is equivalent to the primary meaning of justification as transforming grace. In a Protestant context, justification has the restricted sense of full forgiveness of sin, while sanctification is always in this life a partial transformation of sinners. If you are confused, perhaps you can see why Catholics and Protestants have often misunderstood one another on this issue.

Mutual recrimination and mutual misunderstanding over justification and sanctification was the order of the day between Catholics and Protestants from the sixteenth century until quite recently. Mutual recrimination occurred, because each side stressed the potential corruption of the other's position. Protestants argued that the Augustinian view of the Roman Catholics readily led to "works righteousness" and an uneasy conscience. There was some truth in the first charge, for when the Catholic view became corrupt, it almost always degenerated into works righteousness. This is the idea that one will be approved by God and go to heaven only if, for example, one goes to mass regularly, prays frequently, and obeys the basic rules of morality. Salvation is no longer God's pure gift, but something one at least in some measure has to earn. There was less truth in the charge of an uneasy conscience. To be sure, Catholics were taught that it is presumptuous to claim assurance of acceptance from God, but few Catholics seemed deeply troubled by that. They simply did not seek for assurance.

The official Catholic answer to the Protestant understanding of justification was given at the Council of Trent, the gathering of Catholic bishops that took place on and off from 1545–1563. Trent charged the Lutheran conception of justification with producing lazy Christians who are nonetheless presumptuously confident that their sins are forgiven.[12] There was some truth in this charge as well, for a common corruption of Lutheranism has been a slack belief that since God freely forgives sins, people can simply conform to the ways of the surrounding society. Two of the greatest Lutheran theologians, Søren Kierkegaard (d. 1855) and Dietrich Bonhoeffer (d. 1945), attacked the easy, conformist Lutheranism of their day.

---

12. *Canons and Decrees of the Council of Trent*, Sixth Session, Chapters 7–10, trans. H. J. Schroeder (St. Louis: Herder, 1950), 33–36.

Mutual misunderstanding over justification was fostered by the fact that often the same term meant something different to the two parties. As we have seen, the chief misunderstanding was often about the meaning of justification itself. What classical Protestants in the Reformed and Lutheran traditions meant by justification was the mercy by which God forgives sin, and commonly they came to refer to God's gracious transformation of people as sanctification. But for Catholics, justification *was* primarily sanctification. Another point of frequent misunderstanding was that Catholic and Classical Protestant tended until recently to understand the concept of faith differently. Catholics generally followed Thomas Aquinas and the Council of Trent in interpreting faith as belief, that is, holding something to be true. Obviously, such faith is not sufficient for a right relation with God, for a good many people hold Christian beliefs about God yet do not trust in God or love God above all things. The Council of Trent also gave considerable weight to the Epistle of James which has a similar conception of faith and which takes quite a different view of justification than Paul, on whom the Protestant reformers chiefly relied.

> What good is it, my brothers and sisters, if you say you have faith but do not have works? Can faith save you? If a brother or sister is naked and lacks daily food, and one of you says to them, "Go in peace; keep warm and eat your fill," and yet you do not supply their bodily needs, what is the good of that? So faith by itself, if it has not works, is dead.
> . . . Was not our ancestor Abraham justified by works when he offered his son Isaac on the altar? You see that faith was active along with his works, and faith was brought to completion by works. . . . You see that a person is justified by works and not by faith alone. (James 2:14-24)

The Council of Trent feared that justification by faith alone was a dangerous doctrine that promoted a lax faith. The Catholics said that love needs to be added to faith. Protestants such as Luther, however, understood faith to be a living trust in Christ. So Protestants rejected the Catholic emphasis upon faith formed by love, because that seemed to imply humans had to do something to contribute to their salvation. Then salvation would at least partially be earned rather than a pure divine gift.

Great strides have been taken toward better mutual understanding since Catholics and Protestants became deeply involved in the ecumenical movement in the 1960s. Progress toward better understanding is reflected in the U.S. Lutheran-Catholic dialogue on justification by faith, which speaks of a substantial convergence of views on justification, although no full agreement. Both Catholic and Lutheran theologians in the dialogue agreed that justification is by grace alone, but they had some disagreements over saying it is by faith alone. They credit the remaining disagreements mainly to an abiding difference in their principal *concerns*. Lutherans still are chiefly concerned to proclaim God's unconditional promise of complete acceptance; that is, they wish to stress the full forgiveness of sins purely through God's mercy. Catholics continue to be primarily concerned with highlighting the transforming power of God's grace in people. Using the later Protestant distinction between justification and sanctification, we can say that Lutherans stress justification, while Catholics stress sanctification. Largely because of this difference in concerns, they continue to voice worries about the other position. Catholics worry that justification by faith alone fosters lazy believers with an ill-founded confidence of being right with God. Lutherans in the dialogue still are troubled by the Catholic stress on doing good works, especially when it is linked with talk about human cooperation with God in justification and with human merit. While theologians in the dialogue recognize these differences, they go on to say that the differences of emphasis on justification do not require separation of Catholics and Lutherans. Catholics and Lutherans could be united in one church and retain their characteristic emphases on justification.[13] So far, however, the two church bodies have not followed the recommendation and remain separate.

c. As you think through this issue and try to establish a view of your own on justification, you should know that there is another outlook on salvation from the revivalistic tradition. This view in various forms is held by most Evangelicals as well as by Pentecostals and most charismatics. We shall call it the *revivalistic interpretation of salvation.*

We can capture the thrust of this outlook in this statement by a revivalistic theologian, "Regeneration and justification are terms that denote God's part in transforming an individual, while the words faith, repentance, and conversion are used to express man's necessary response to Christ and God, if regeneration is to be experienced."[14] There are two things to notice in this statement. First, certain aspects of salvation are credited to God, while other aspects are what humans do in response. Regeneration and justification are "God's part," whereas faith, repentance, and conversion are "man's necessary response." This distinction reflects the revivalistic tradition which places great importance on the "decision" of faith. The great revivalist Billy Graham always calls upon the unconverted to make a conscious "decision for Christ." Of course, someone who makes this first decision of faith remembers when

13. *Justification by Faith: Lutherans and Catholics in Dialogue VII*, H. George Anderson, T. Austin Murphy, and Joseph A. Burgess, eds. (Minneapolis: Augsburg, 1985), 51–55; 70–73. See also the *Catechism of the Catholic Church* (Mahwah, N.J.: Paulist, 1994), 481–90 for a brief, clear explanation of justification in the Catholic perspective.

14. Julius R. Mantey, "Repentance and Conversion," in *Basic Christian Doctrines*, Carl F. H. Henry, ed. (Grand Rapids, Mich.: Baker, 1962), 193–94. A similar statement that speaks of the divine side and human side of salvation appears in the Baptist theologian Morris Ashcraft, *Christian Faith and Beliefs* (Nashville: Broadman, 1984), 242.

and how it took place, so it is a memorable experience that one can look back upon years later. Second, you should notice that transformation is the primary concern. This is evident in the quote, for the author has a clear preponderance of terms associated with transformation: regeneration, transforming, repentance, and conversion. Whereas most Evangelicals focus on the conversion experience as the central transforming experience, Pentecostals and charismatics place more weight on the transformative power of the experience of baptism in the Holy Spirit.

The revivalistic view of salvation is a middle position between the classical Protestant view of Luther and Calvin on the one hand, and the transformationist view on the other hand. Like classical Protestants, revivalists distinguish justification from sanctification or regeneration and they say justification is by faith alone, yet like the transformationist position the main emphasis is on sanctification or the transformative power of God's grace. Distinct from both the Catholic and classical Protestant views is the revivalist stress on the turning point experience of conversion or the double turning points of conversion and baptism in the Holy Spirit.

The major criticism of this outlook is that the revivalist's strong emphasis on a person's conscious decision of faith arises from an overly individualistic understanding of the Christian life. That is, the revivalist thinks of human beings as first of all distinct individuals, and the church is created by a number of individuals choosing to gather together in a community. The individual is clearly primary, the community secondary. Catholics and classical Protestants in the Reformed and Lutheran traditions put much more weight on the prior influence of the Christian community that makes an individual's choice of faith in Christ possible.

Your task as a student of Christian theology is not only to understand these three major historic positions, but at least to begin to form your own view on the issue. Many students have grown up in one of these three traditions—the transformationist, the classical Protestant, or the revivalist—and have been taught the position of their tradition. If that is your situation, you may end up either affirming your own tradition's viewpoint or differing from it. In either case, you will have grown by thinking through the issue on a more mature level. As an example of this assessment process, I will set forth my own view. You may not agree with me, but I hope you can learn from watching how someone else sorts out the relevant questions. I will explain my position in three points.

First, there is the question of whether justification is primarily transformation or forgiveness. It is probably not surprising that I as a Lutheran have a strong affinity with the classical Protestant position on this matter. But this affinity has been confirmed in my own life experience. As someone who has had a cancerous tumor removed and who now lives under the threat of another tumor appearing elsewhere in my body, the *assurance* that God accepts me without qualification is a tremendous comfort. As a justified child of God, a person is reconciled and united with God. The peace this reconciliation with God brings has profound significance, for now one is united with the loving Source of oneself and all reality. Rather than being alienated and separated from the Ground of reality and life, now one is at home with God. Just as in Jesus' parable there was great joy when the prodigal son came back home to the open embrace of his father, so there is tremendous joy and peace in coming home to God. Justification as forgiveness is an amazing gift.

I think this position also finds strong support in Scripture even outside of Paul's letters. The biblical portrayals of Jesus accepting Zacchaeus and other sinners clearly suggest that God's forgiveness is either complete or not at all. God does not say, "I forgive you for this, but I don't forgive you for that." As the father in the parable of the prodigal son (Luke 15:11-24) opens his arms for his wayward son without conditions or limitations attached, so I believe God welcomes the sinner. To be sure, someone may not repent and ignore or reject God's unconditional acceptance. Then God's acceptance remains ineffective for that person, but it does not make God's acceptance conditional. As a good parent who loves an estranged child will go on loving that child and working for his or her return even though rejected by the child, so God lovingly pursues the alienated with open arms, not with conditions. Thus, on the question of whether justification is primarily transformation or forgiveness, I come down definitely on the side of forgiveness.

Second, a transformation of a person's priorities, words, and actions begins to take place; this is sanctification. This transformation is always partial on earth and takes place in and through the events of our life process. While Paul met Jesus in a vision on the road to Damascus, afterward Paul spent several years apparently sorting things out before he emerged as a Christian missionary. John Newton, the author of the widely used Christian hymn "Amazing Grace," had a conversion experience while he was captain of a ship bringing slaves from Africa to the new world, but it was some time before he actually quit the slave trade. Faith in God involves a person in a lifelong process of sifting through one's attitudes and behavior as new experiences prompt reexamination and changes. In Paul's imagery, faith in Jesus Christ involves one in an ongoing process of dying with Christ (dying to sinful ways) and rising with Christ to a new life with changed priorities and actions.

It appears obvious when we look at Christians around us that this transformative work of sanctification takes place at different degrees in people. At this point in their life, some Christians are kind, caring, humble people who are generous with their time, money, and self toward all whom they meet. Other Christians at this point may be kind and generous toward their family and selected others, but they may be closed to the needs of many others at a distance and spend their money much as the majority do in our society. But the transforming power of God's grace is always ready to bring about deeper changes in a person's life.

I find my own Lutheran tradition rather weak on the matter of sanctification. To be sure, there has been *Pietism*, an evangelical movement among Lutherans that began in 1675 and actually made sanctification its principal concern. But on the whole, Lutherans have been so concerned to stress the forgiveness of sins, that sanctification has often been regarded as a dangerous topic and given minor treatment. Here I find attractive Calvin's even balance of attention to justification and sanctification. Admitting this, of course, makes me immediately suspect by many other Lutheran theologians.

Frequent exposure to Roman Catholic and Anglican worship and devotional life has also brought me to greatly value many of their religious practices as excellent ways by which God furthers sanctification. For instance, most of what I have learned about prayer has come from Catholic, Anglican, and Orthodox sources, and I have benefited in some small measure from Hindu meditational practice. However, my interest in prayer practices as an intentional means for fostering sanctification has been met with suspicion by some Lutherans, since they worry that it is a form of trying to earn salvation through one's own deeds. Granted, occasionally in a Catholic setting I encounter a troubling step in the direction of works righteousness, but on the whole I find there a deeply shared sense of salvation by grace.[15]

A point at which many Protestant and Roman Catholic interpretations of sanctification are faulty is that they too readily identify holiness with an individual's middle-class morality. A deeper understanding of holiness would have compassion as a key virtue, especially compassion for the poor, marginal, and outcast. Here, privileged first world Christians have a great deal to learn from Latin American liberation theology, which begins with identification with the poor. Not merely identification with certain ideas about poverty, but a personal involvement and solidarity with the poor themselves. Such compassion and solidarity with the marginal is surely consistent with Jesus who reached out to Zacchaeus as well as to women and the poor. For us today compassion and solidarity should also be extended to nature, whose welfare is so often overlooked in our calculations about comfort and profit. In short, the sanctifying work of the Holy Spirit is not confined to making this or that individual good according to middle-class standards. The Spirit aims to save the entire world in keeping with Jesus Christ.

---

15. An example of a troubling step toward works righteousness may be seen in the books and tapes of Anthony DeMello, which are much admired at some Catholic retreat centers.

This brings us back to the question of whether salvation is limited to one's relationship with God or includes transformation of some physical or social disorder. I think the core of salvation proclaimed by Christians is reconciliation with God through Jesus Christ. This is primary. Yet the salvation that Christ brings also affects human relationships and bodies. When Jesus says to Zaccheaus, "Today salvation has come to this house," it is not altogether clear what is included under salvation, but at least reconciliation with God and some more just human relationships are involved. I think it is sound to have this clear center and rather open boundary to our notion of salvation, for while it is possible to have peace with God now, God ultimately intends the salvation of all dimensions of existence.

Third, while I admire the revivalists' earnest quest to reach the unconverted in our world, I think their accent on the decision of faith as the key to being born again is too individualistic. A human being seldom, if ever, stands alone. We exist within a communal context of family, friends, nation, and perhaps church. Many Americans who make a "decision for Christ" have grown up within a situation where they had some previous involvement with Christianity through family and church. They may have taken that involvement for granted and seen no value in it. Yet that contact with the Christian tradition undoubtedly influenced them more than they realize.

Recall our thought experiment in which I asked you to imagine how very different you would be if you had grown up in a fundamentally dissimilar culture infused with another religion. Not only would you have a different name, you would also speak a different language, hold another set of values, and probably have other life goals. The beliefs, values, and goals of our community influence and shape us in ways of which we are usually not conscious, unless we move into a truly different culture. If you had grown up in a Muslim culture, your adult decision of faith would be in reference to Islam. If you had been reared in a Hindu culture, your decision of faith would very likely reflect Hindu elements. Contemporary Western societies have a variety of faith communities within them, yet Christianity is by far the largest and most influential. In any case, an individual always exists within a broader social environment that subtly influences his or her thinking on matters of faith. So in my opinion, the revivalistic emphasis on a person's decision of faith is often too individualistic and does not sufficiently recognize the contributions of community to this decision.

My main point in regard to this third issue is that the importance of an individual's decision of faith should not be allowed to overshadow what the Holy Spirit does through human communities to bring about justification and sanctification in persons. One's faith decision as an adult is always a response to the intricate workings of the Spirit using elements of the Christian tradition and other people to touch one's life. This difference from revivalism's individualism is also very pertinent to the subject of our next chapter on the role of sacraments and devotional practices in salvation.

Grace and Human Freedom

An issue underlying this whole discussion about salvation is the nature and extent of human freedom in salvation. To what extent is salvation a gift of God's grace and to what extent is human freedom involved? These have been disputed questions in the history of Christian theology. Since the issue is complex, we shall devote this section to it.

The issue of the relation between human freedom and divine grace first emerged in a heated dispute that erupted in the early fifth century between Augustine and another theologian named Pelagius. Out of this dispute and its aftermath emerged three positions that, with some variations, are still with us today. Pelagius and Augustine represent two of these positions, for they had very different understandings of free will and grace and sharply contrasting notions of the role of humans and God in salvation.

1. *The Pelagian view says that the human will is not seriously damaged by sin, so is free to choose faith or unfaith.* According to Pelagius and two other theologians who supported him, the human will is healthy, so that when a person is confronted with moral and religious choices, the person is fully able to select either the good or the evil. One reason Pelagius held this was because the frequent exhortations and commands in Scripture seem to imply that people have the ability to either obey or disobey. Otherwise, he said, the exhortations and commands are empty. According to Pelagius, God's grace is evident in two ways: first, the natural human abilities of intelligence and free will graciously given in creation, and second, the grace of moral and religious instruction that God has provided in the Ten Commandments, the example and doctrine of Jesus, and other biblical teachings. Thus by God's grace human beings have the natural capability to choose a life of faith and moral uprightness, and God graciously assists them in this choice by providing guidance.

2. *Augustine said the human will is in complete bondage to sin and is set free only by grace.* First, Augustine argued that *original sin seriously damages the human will* so that it is unable to love God above all things and unable to do truly good deeds. Left to ourselves, we would simply remain in bondage to sin. Thus grace is necessary for salvation. Second, Augustine believed that *grace is a divine gift that goes beyond what was given in the natural, created powers of humans.* Grace liberates the human reason and will from the power of sin and

enables persons to commit themselves to God in faith and love and to do truly good deeds.

Third, Augustine taught the *sovereignty of grace*. God's grace is sovereign or all-powerful both in deciding who receives grace and in the irresistibility of grace. Augustine believed that grace must be freely given, otherwise it is not grace. Thus there can be no respect in which the people who are liberated from sin *achieve* it by their own ability. The only ground for liberation from sin lies in God. This led Augustine to affirm a doctrine of *predestination* in which prior to the creation of the world God decided to free certain human persons from sin and leave the rest to their just punishment as sinners. It is not that God *foreknows* who will believe and chooses them for salvation accordingly. Then, said Augustine, salvation would be given to those who in some sense had earned it. Rather, the basis for salvation lies solely in God's free and sovereign decision to save some people.

Fourth, the sovereignty of grace is also apparent in Augustine's teaching of the *irresistibility of grace*. That is, if God has predestined Lisa Somebody for salvation, God's grace will certainly be effective in bringing her to faith. Lisa will not reject salvation, for grace is so attractive and effectual that she will surely come to faith. The irresistibility of grace is also evident in Augustine's conviction that those who receive grace will not fall away; they shall surely persevere in faith.

3. *The human will is damaged by sin, but still has a limited power to accept or reject grace.* A middle position on the issue of grace and human freedom was upheld by John Cassian and others, but as a middle position it leans much more toward Augustine than Pelagius. John Cassian largely but not entirely agreed with Augustine on the first two points above, and clearly disagreed on the sovereignty of grace in predestination and irresistibility of grace. That is, Cassian firmly dissents from Pelagian teaching and supports the Augustinian doctrine with some exceptions. So Cassian agrees to a great extent with Augustine about the negative impact of original sin on human reason and will, although unlike Augustine Cassian says there still remains a limited human freedom to accept or reject grace. And Cassian, like Augustine, affirms that divine grace beyond the gifts in creation is necessary to set the human reason and will free from sin.

However, Cassian objects to Augustine's doctrine of predestination on the grounds that it makes empty Jesus' universal invitation, "Come to me, all you that are weary and are carrying heavy burdens, and I will give you rest" (Matthew 11:28). Cassian also points to 1 Timothy 2:3-4, "God our Savior, who desires everyone to be saved and to come to the knowledge of the truth." God's universal will that everyone be saved appears to be contradicted by Augustine's teaching on predestination. Cassian criticized Augustine's view of predestination and irresistible grace as fatalistic and deterministic, that is, everything is determined by God in advance. In essence, Cassian says there is a paradox of inescapable human involvement in sin and human responsibility; that is, the overpowering tendency of humans to sin makes grace absolutely necessary for salvation and yet humans are responsible for what they do with their life. To Cassian's mind, Augustine had resolved this paradox of grace and freedom by overglorifying grace, while Pelagius had resolved it by overemphasizing human freedom.

The Pelagian view was decisively rejected by the early church, most authoritatively at the Council of Ephesus in 431. The whole church—East and West together—has never made a definitive ruling between the other two positions. However, a regional gathering of Western bishops at the Synod of Orange in 529 basically approved Cassian's view. In this way, Augustine's teaching on grace was largely but not wholly approved, and his doctrine of predestination was definitely rejected by the Synod.

The issue of grace and free will continued to occupy the attention of theologians throughout the Middle Ages and was the subject of heated dispute between Martin Luther and Erasmus during the Reformation in the early sixteenth century. Luther firmly upheld the bondage of the will position; however, he makes some additional points. First, Luther clearly affirms what we might call *psychological freedom*. This is our freedom to make both minor choices such as choosing which cereal to eat for breakfast or what clothes to wear today and major choices such as what career to pursue or whom to marry. We certainly *feel* free in making these decisions, and Luther says we are. Luther also endorses what we can call *freedom in civic morality*. This is the ability of humans to choose to obey or disobey civil laws and moral injunctions such as state laws and moral principles about stealing property. So unbelievers may be admirably moral persons. However, Luther's second point is that human beings do not have the freedom to turn their life toward God and salvation. In this arena the human will is in bondage to the forces of evil, and cannot of its own volition turn to God in faith. Third, conversion to faith in God is entirely the work of God. To support this, Luther relies upon a doctrine of predestination, much as did Augustine. Luther says,

> His will is eternal and changeless, because His nature is so. From which it follows, by resistless logic, that all we do, however it may appear to us to be done mutably and contingently, is in reality done necessarily and immutably in respect of God's will . . . what is done cannot but be done where, when, how, as far as, and by whom, He foresees and wills.[16]

Luther sees in this doctrine a firm foundation for the believer's confidence

---

16. "The Bondage of the Will," in *Martin Luther: Selections from His Writings*, ed. John Dillenberger (Garden City, N.Y.: Doubleday, 1961), 181.

that salvation is completely the gift of God. When asked why God gives the gift of faith to some and not to others, Luther answers that we should not dwell on this unrevealed, secret will of God, but on God's revealed intention that all should be saved. As a result, predestination was not a central teaching in most of Lutheran history. In any event, for Luther conversion to faith is completely God's free, unmerited gift.

Luther's most renowned opponent in the debate over grace and human freedom was the celebrated humanist Erasmus (d. 1536). The humanist took a middle position rather like Cassian's but softer on grace. Erasmus said the human reason and will have been weakened by sin, so that the will "could not improve itself by its own natural means."[17] Erasmus assigns the greater role in conversion to grace, but also says human free will plays a subordinate but necessary part. People must have the ability to accept or reject God's grace, otherwise they cannot be held responsible. It appears that Erasmus thinks of this relationship as one in which God makes the offer of salvation and the person accepts or refuses the offer. "The mercy of God offers everyone favorable opportunities for repentance. One needs only to attach the rest of one's own will to God's help, which merely invites to, but does not compel to betterment."[18] Erasmus strongly rejects Luther's doctrine of predestination as depriving humans of responsibility, for it makes absolutely all events in human affairs happen by necessity.

A middle position more like that of Cassian than Erasmus was taken by the Council of Trent in its 1547 decree on justification. Grace is the primary mover in conversion, yet the person must also consent or refuse. Trent holds that justification in adults is derived from the prevenient grace of God that calls the person to conversion. This means

> that they who by sin had been cut off from God, may be disposed through His quickening and helping grace to convert themselves to their own justification by freely assenting to and cooperating with that grace; so that, while God touches the heart of man through the illumination of the Holy Ghost, man himself neither does absolutely nothing while receiving that inspiration, since he can also reject it, nor yet is he able by his own free will and without the grace of God to move himself to justice in His sight.[19]

In this view, the human will has been so damaged by sin that it is unable on its own to turn toward God; yet when God's grace does call a person to conversion, the will may persist in its sin by refusing or, helped by grace, accept con-

---

17. Erasmus, "The Free Will," in *Erasmus-Luther: Discourse on Free Will*, Ernst F. Winter, trans. and ed. (New York: Frederick Ungar, 1961), Chapter III, Article 16, pp. 22–23.
18. Ibid., Chapter III, Article 20.
19. *Canons and Decrees of the Council of Trent*, Sixth Session, Chapter 5, 31–32.

version. While salvation is mostly a divine gift, Trent holds that the transforming power of grace in a person makes it legitimate to speak of the grace-filled believer as also meriting an eternal reward from God. The middle positions of Trent and Erasmus were branded by Protestant reformers with the unsavory name of *semi-Pelagian*.

The great Protestant reformer John Calvin (d. 1564) clearly sided with Augustine and Luther on this issue. Calvin said the human will is in such bondage to sin that it is totally unable to contribute anything toward conversion. Salvation is entirely God's gift. Why then do some people believe and others do not? Calvin's answer is a doctrine of double predestination; that is, before the foundation of the world, God chose some people to salvation and assigned others to damnation. The primary function of the doctrine of predestination is that it may give assurance to believers that their salvation comes entirely from God's mercy and in no way is dependent on their own virtue. Whereas Luther gave a low profile to the mysterious decree of predestination and stressed God's revealed will that all be saved, Calvin said the doctrine should be taught as comfort for the elect.[20] Since Calvin is the most influential of the founders of the Reformed tradition, the doctrine of predestination has received much attention in this tradition.

The issue of grace and free will is very much alive today as well. Although few Christian theologians in church circles support the Pelagian position, there are others who teach something like it. For instance, for many people today humanistic psychology serves as a substitute religion, and at their core most forms of humanistic psychology hold that human beings are entirely free to change the fundamental direction of their lives. No talk of God's grace even enters the picture. Among American church folk a middle position like that of Erasmus seems most prevalent. In this view, God is understood to be like a car salesperson who puts an offer on the table and wants people to take it, but leaves it up to people to accept or reject the offer. The least common view today is the Augustinian position that emphasizes bondage of the will to sin and salvation as entirely God's gift. What you need to consider is which of these views is closest to the truth. Do you agree most with a Pelagian position? Or one of the middle views of Cassian, Erasmus, or Trent? Or with the bondage of the will position that salvation is wholly God's gift?

To further stimulate your reflection on this issue, I will explain my own view, which is somewhere between the middle position of Cassian and Trent on the one side and the bondage of the will position on the other side. One of the advantages we have today is that we clearly distinguish between persons

20. John Calvin, *Institutes of the Christian Religion*, Book 3, Chapter 21, The Library of Christian Classics, Vol. 21, pp. 920–32.

and things. This was not the case for all the earlier views that we have discussed, so they often used mechanical analogies to talk about human freedom; as a result, it was difficult for Augustine and his followers to avoid the implication that the destiny of a person is determined. I will begin with a story drawn from personal relationships.

Imagine that you have come to know an eleven-year-old girl who was rejected by her own parents and then shuttled from one foster home to another. This girl has also been sexually abused. Now you want to help and befriend the girl. But you soon discover that she does not trust anyone. After all, life has taught her not to trust, for she has repeatedly been abandoned and abused by others. The question you face is how to get her to trust you. I would say that at this point the girl is *unable* to trust you. She cannot simply *decide* to trust you, because trusting or not trusting are not controlled by our volition, no more than feeling anxious or not feeling anxious are subject to choice. If you face a very stressful situation and someone says to you, "Don't worry," can you simply *decide* not to worry? No. There are some fundamental attitudes or orientations of the self that are not subject to our conscious, deliberate control. We are unable to turn them on or off just by making a conscious decision. Trusting is one of these fundamental stances of the self. Because of her past experience, the young girl is truly unable to trust. It is not merely that she is *unwilling* to trust, for that implies trusting is something we can decide to do. Rather, at this point in her life she is strictly *unable* to trust, even though she desperately longs to have friends and family that she can trust. How can you win her trust? Only by being steady, reliable, always worthy of trust. Over the course of time and only after repeated testing of your reliability, the girl may come to trust you. In a personal relationship, one person's behavior may *enable* the other to trust. Your trustworthy behavior may enable the girl to do what she was previously unable to do.

This story makes three points which are relevant to the grace–free will debate. First, there are some basic stances of the self that are not subject to our volition; we cannot simply decide to do or not do them. This is what the Augustinian position says about faith in God. Faith is the most fundamental orientation of the self, for it involves trusting in God above all else and committing one's self to God above all else. I think that the four theological greats Augustine, Aquinas, Luther, and Calvin are right in saying that in regard to this radical reorientation of the self, the human will is truly unable to bring it about on its own. Another way of saying this is that the will is in bondage to sin, much like the young girl on her own is in bondage to distrust.

The second point of the story is that what is impossible for a person to do alone becomes possible in a good relationship with another person. What happens in conversion to faith in God is that over the course of time, God *wins* the trust and commitment of the person. That is, through the Christian message experienced in dramatic or undramatic fashion, a person discovers that God is steadfast and true. It is the message of God's kind, generous, steady character that now makes it possible for that person to respond in faith.

Third, if you treat distrustful people in reliable, trustworthy ways, you do not always and automatically evoke trust from them. Some will come to trust you, but others will persist in their distrust. Here, I think, we see the "freedom" of the human will at work. But this is not a sovereign, I'm-always-in-control freedom such as we have when we decide which breakfast cereal to eat or which college to attend. The freedom to trust or distrust the ever-faithful God is much more like the feeble ability of alcoholics in a treatment program either to affirm or reject the sobering-up program. Left to themselves, alcoholics are powerless and lost. And even when they have sobered up, alcoholism is not simply left behind; the addiction clings to the person as a dreadful, self-destructive power that still tempts. So also sin is the persistent tendency to trust in a creature rather than in God. Believers who truly grasp the nature of their situation before God will therefore never tout the great achievement of their own will. They know that they have been *set free*. They know that their very response of trust and commitment *has been made possible* by the message of God's generous, steadfast love. They clearly realize that salvation is God's free gift.

How does this view of the issue compare with the major traditional and contemporary views? I said at the start that my outlook is between the middle position of Cassian-Trent and the bondage of the will view of Augustine. I am close to the Augustinian position in that I strongly emphasize that God sets the will free, so salvation is overwhelmingly God's gift. Yet I dissent from the double predestination doctrine in the Augustinian tradition. The doctrine of predestination is unavoidable unless one makes humans responsible for accepting or rejecting God. So like Cassian and Trent I recognize a minor role for the human will. But since I use the analogy of personal relationships to treat the issue, I am much better able than they to explain how the will is in bondage to sin, but may be liberated to accept God's grace. Furthermore, I disagree with Trent's affirmation of human merit in relation to God. The whole idea of merit, however carefully nuanced, is questionable because it is so easily misunderstood and corrupted. Further still, my view does not lay as much weight on the decision of faith as revivalism. Rather, my primary emphasis is on the mysterious grace of God seeking the lost and ultimately enabling them to trust God. In my opinion, revivalism puts the accent in the wrong place. Finally, I heartily disagree with the common view that God makes people an offer and then leaves it up to them to accept or reject it. Such an outlook does not do justice to the subtle and obvious ways God seeks to win the trust of a person. The Holy Spirit is active in preparing and enabling a person to trust in God. This is my view on grace and free will. You must sort out the issue for yourself.

Summary and Conclusions

Now it is time to recall the main emphases of this chapter, in order to clearly organize our thoughts. I shall begin with the second theme, salvation, and then return to our initial theme, the Holy Spirit. Earlier I said that most people come to the discussion of salvation with two false preconceptions: that salvation is equated with life after death and that salvation is entirely spiritual, not physical. We have seen that a biblically based understanding of salvation sees it as a reality of both present and future existence. In this chapter we focused on salvation or healing in the present life. We looked at three major ways of conceiving salvation. One is the classical Protestant understanding that I followed in interpreting salvation as justification (forgiveness) and the partial transformation of sanctification. A second way of conceptualizing salvation is the transformationist approach that places the primary emphasis on the transformation of a person's priorities. Although these two ways of interpreting salvation have been a source of division between Protestant and Catholic in the past, today many see them as two legitimate patterns of thought that share many overlapping ideas but are not identical.[21] The third way of understanding salvation is the revivalistic approach that puts primary stress on a conscious decision of faith as the beginning of personal salvation. The Pentecostal-charismatic version of revivalism modifies this interpretation to add a second decisive stage in salvation which they call baptism in the Holy Spirit.

It is clear that present salvation is a healing that includes various physical as well as spiritual dimensions. Salvation not only affects one's inner thoughts and priorities; it also changes one's relationships, how one spends money, how one treats nature, and maybe brings healing to one's body. Christians are also called to work for changes in social institutions such as government, schools, and family, so that greater justice exists. Thus salvation influences the external world as well as a person's inner life.

One of the issues debated in Christian history and today is the relative roles of God's Spirit and humans in salvation. Three main positions have appeared. First, the Pelagian view says that humans are free enough to have

---

21. A fine example of this convergence is Roger Haight's discussion of grace that seeks to incorporate Luther's insights on justification into a Catholic, Augustinian framework. See Roger Haight, "Sin and Grace," in *Systematic Theology: Roman Catholic Perspectives*, Vol. 2, Francis Schüssler Fiorenza and John P. Galvin, eds. (Minneapolis: Fortress Press, 1991), 107–39.

the primary responsibility for redirecting their lives toward God. Second, there is the Augustinian outlook that stresses the human will's bondage to sin, so that God alone can set the will free to have faith and to do good. Third, several forms of a middle position have held to some combination of divine grace and human responsibility for salvation.

Most Christian theologians have agreed that the Spirit of God is the primary mover in the healing of human life. The Spirit is God present in the world, but we saw reason to distinguish various modes of the divine presence: God's presence in the whole creation, in all humans, in Israel, in Jesus, in Christians, and in non-Christians who manifest fruits of the Spirit. The Spirit who is present in the world is the same Spirit who, eternally within God's inner trinitarian life, is engaged in an ever-new two-step dance of going forth and achieving a richer unity. So the Spirit's activity in salvation is part of this divine movement, for in salvation the Spirit goes forth into various people and brings them into a richer, more harmonious unity with God, other people, and other creatures.

There are significant differences among Christians on which gifts of the Spirit to focus their expectations. Along with the basic work of salvation, Pentecostal-charismatic Christians dwell on the gifts of extraordinary phenomena such as speaking in tongues and physical healing. Again, as part of the basic work of salvation, mainstream Protestants, Catholics, and Orthodox focus on the Holy Spirit producing moral-spiritual growth as evident in the fruit of the Spirit such as love and generosity. Nevertheless, Christians share in common their confidence that the Spirit as God present brings about fundamental healing in human life.

10

Sacraments and Devotional Practices

This chapter will have three parts. First, since sacraments and devotional practices make extensive use of symbols, we shall begin by considering the role of symbols in human life. Second, we shall examine certain religious rituals that many Christian churches call sacraments. Third, we shall look more at several Christian devotional practices.

Symbols

We shall start by looking at symbols from the perspectives of anthropology and psychology; this will illuminate the use of symbols in religion and theology. Symbols are often distinguished from signs, although no single way of making the distinction has won universal support. Sometimes *sign* is used in a generic sense to include all marks or gestures that refer to some meaning or thing beyond themselves. For instance, the anthropologist Raymond Firth uses sign as a general category that includes several subtypes: index, signal, icon, and symbol. It is common to distinguish between sign and symbol, however, and a clear way to do so is on the basis of their relative complexity of meaning. This is the practice that I will follow. Thus a *sign* is relatively straightforward in its meaning. For instance, traffic signs are simple and direct in their significance: stop, do not pass, steep hill ahead, and so on. There is little or no surplus of meaning beyond the direct message of the sign. Much language functions also as sign in conveying unambiguous information. For example, a sentence such as "The street in front of our house is deteriorating" in most contexts supplies rather straightforward information.[1]

---

1. Raymond Firth, *Symbols: Public and Private* (Ithaca, N.Y.: Cornell University Press, 1973), 74–75.

Symbols are more complex in their meaning and therefore more ambiguous; they contain a surplus of meaning that is more difficult to define exactly. For instance, nouns such as democracy, freedom, love, and cross all suggest meanings so complex that one can identify some aspects of their meaning and yet feel that one has not exhausted their significance.

There are three major types of symbols. As we have noted, there are *linguistic* symbols, for sometimes language functions symbolically. For Americans to say the pledge of allegiance or to sing the national anthem before a ball game are symbolic. There are also *physical objects* that operate as symbols. At the conclusion of athletic tournaments, it is common to present a trophy to the winner. When we give a gift to a family member or friend, the physical object is a symbol of our affection. Sometimes the human body functions symbolically. This is true of whole body movements such as Americans standing up to say the pledge of allegiance. Gestures with parts of our body also may be symbolic—putting one's hand over one's heart for the pledge of allegiance, saluting, waving the hand, kissing—these are all bodily symbols. In addition to linguistic and physical symbols, *social arrangements* also work as symbols. Who does what often is symbolic of relative power between persons or groups. The mayor of a city does different things than a city garbage collector. Physical and social symbols overlap, for who possesses what is also symbolic; what housing or car one has says something about one's social status.

Rituals are standardized patterns of behavior that commonly involve all three types of symbols—words, physical objects and bodily movements, and social arrangement. For instance, every society has ritualized, standardized patterns for exchanges of food. In most of North American society it is customary to have a dinner for the wedding couple, the wedding party, and the families on the evening prior to the wedding. The dinner is usually paid for by the groom's family, and often during the dinner the best man stands up to offer a toast to the wedding couple. Unlike invitations to dinner among friends, there is no obligation for the guests at this prenuptial dinner to reciprocate in the near future, unless there is a wedding in a guest's family. The location of the prenuptial dinner and the food eaten are also symbols of the social position or aspirations of the groom's family. Obviously, the dinner is much more than a pragmatic way for people to obtain food needed to sustain life.

Societies also have rituals for greeting people. In Western society it is common for men to stand up when greeting a new person, but it is permissible for a woman to remain seated. A third party may facilitate the meeting by identifying the two people by name and provide other relevant information such as workplace, home, school, or family. Words are also exchanged between the people meeting for the first time. Customary words of greeting are usually used, words that vary according to the social position of the persons involved. A college student will speak differently when meeting another college student than when meeting the parent of a friend. In addition to the exchange of words, often some form of touching occurs between the two persons. Men generally shake hands with another man. It is customary for a man to shake hands with a woman only if she offers her hand. A gesture that often accompanies the greeting is a smile. The whole ritual of greeting is altered considerably if one is meeting a person who holds an important position. The exchange of words would be initiated by the person with the important position, as would any touching. In such cases a physical object is often given as a token of good will. The object may be a gift from the person of lower status to the one of higher status or it may be some object given by the higher status person that recognizes certain contributions of the lower status person. In any case, greeting rituals are highly symbolic. Much more is being communicated than straightforward biographical information. Greetings convey good will or hostility, openness or closure, as well as relative social position and power.

Anthropology looks at the social functions of symbols. We can distinguish three social functions of symbols: to communicate, to shape knowledge, and to express relative power. First, symbols enable us to communicate with one another about complex and more transcendent ideas. If our communication were limited to the straightforward ideas shared through signs and signals, life would be flat and uninteresting. But we use symbols to convey our thoughts about rather transcendent matters that are less amenable to precise formulation, yet are often much more important—subjects such as peace, love, eternal life, God. Second, symbols play a major role in shaping our knowledge. Our knowledge of the world is a complex act of interpretation. We do not read off the character of the world in some simple act of one-to-one correspondence between reality and our thought. We are always interpreting reality; we contribute something to the final product as well as receive input from external reality. But none of us starts from scratch in this process of interpreting the world around us; we exist in a society and culture that provides us with the tools for interpretation and tries to teach us how to use those tools. The particular language we employ from childhood is one of the basic means for interpreting reality, and each language reflects its culture. For instance, since Tibet is a Buddhist country that highly values certain forms of meditation, the Tibetan language has many terms for distinguishing different aspects of our thinking processes. The English language that comes from a more pragmatic culture has only a few such words. In addition to language, a culture's religion, art, literature, and science all use symbols to interpret the more transcendent, difficult-to-grasp dimensions of reality. Thus symbols are very significant in shaping our understanding of reality. Third, symbols express relative power in human relations. As we have noted, who does what and who possesses what are indications of people's positions in society. By performing these three functions, symbols express a certain culture's way of making sense of life in the natural, social, and spiritual world. In other words, *symbols are a culture's vehicle for expressing the meaning of life.*

When some individuals encounter the symbols of their culture, however, it may be that they will interpret the culture's dominant symbols differently than is generally the case. Given the imprecision of symbols, it is very possible for one person to interpret a symbol differently than most others. In other terms, a person may "decode" the symbol in another way than the person who "encoded" the message of the symbol. It may be that some individuals will experience certain symbols of their society as inadequate or repressive. Hence, in addition to examining the role of symbols in society, we must also look at how symbols work in the life of the individual. This is one of the tasks of psychology.

The individual human being is involved in a life process in which it is vital to come to some understanding of the self and its place in the world. Another way of saying this is that the individual is striving to find his or her personal identity and meaning in life. In this process symbols play a dual bridging function. On the one hand, symbols form bridges between a person's unconsciousness and his or her consciousness. For instance, we all have dreams when we sleep. The psychologist Rollo May says, "The dream is an 'answer' from unconscious levels to a 'question' posed by the patient's immediate existence."[2] That is, the conscious mind is wrestling with the question of what way to go in life at this point, and the dream gives an answer to that question. The dream provides its answer in the form of symbols whose meaning is not always obvious. On the other hand, May also says that symbols form bridges between the individual's conscious existence and transcendent reality, the ultimate, or God. Transcendent reality cannot be grasped in direct signs, but can only be understood in part through symbols. In all of this bridging activity through symbols, the individual is searching for self-identity and meaning in life.

A huge problem in contemporary Western culture is that some individuals find few symbols that are convincing to them. Unable to affirm any deep meaning in life and unable to find a solid personal identity, such individuals often seek answers in what is straightforward—signs and techniques, rather than in symbols. For example, they may engage in sex merely for the pleasure, but it is sex without a deep symbolic meaning of love and commitment. Other individuals alienated from the symbols of Western culture seek for meaning in the symbols of non-Western religion. It is not uncommon for teenagers and young adults, at least for a while, to feel that the symbols that have guided their parents are empty and to search for other symbols that can shape their life.

2. Rollo May, *Symbolism in Religion and Literature* (New York: George Braziller, 1961), 19.

Christian symbols are the way that the Christian community has found meaning, and it offers these symbols to individuals searching for self-identity and meaning. Christian symbols do not come as a cluster of entities isolated from one another; rather, two ways the symbols are frequently joined together are stories and rituals. A *story* involves characters and a plot with some sort of movement of events. A story such as the fall into sin of Adam and Eve in the garden of Eden contains many symbols. The garden itself is a symbol of paradise. The serpent is a symbol of cunning wile. The forbidden fruit represents every enticing temptation. The man and woman are symbolic of every human being, and the story as a whole is symbolic of human sinfulness in any era. To read the story as straightforward, literal information is to misread it.

A *ritual* is a customarily repeated action or series of actions; words, objects, or bodily movements are employed in routinized fashion. As we have seen, the words, objects, or bodily movements of a ritual are symbolic. Since some people in contemporary Western culture commonly express disenchantment, even contempt, for some secular and religious rituals, in the popular mind ritual is often equated with empty, insincere ceremony. Ritual is thus often understood as mere outward forms lacking inward conviction. We have seen, however, good reasons to believe that no human being lives without ritual, for everyday behavior such as greeting and parting, sharing a meal, and giving of gifts is ritualized by everyone, albeit in different ways. Even the most outspoken rebels in America have their standard ways of greeting and parting and they are likely to eat a Thanksgiving dinner gladly, exchange gifts at Christmas or Hanukkah, and send birthday cards to family and friends. Those who protest against the emptiness of certain rituals, however, raise the important, perennial issue of the relation between external rite and interior intention. Thus the question is not whether to use ritual, but rather which rituals to use and how to use them.

Christians observe a number of rituals. Every group worship—whether informal or formal—involves ritual. In the United States a church potluck or picnic is a ritual. We will now focus our attention on those specific rituals that many churches call *sacraments*. Christian sacraments are rituals that take place during worship; indeed, sacraments *are* a form of worship. Thus we must first briefly consider Christian worship before we turn to sacraments.

Christian worship is essentially praise and thanks to God. That is, Christian worship praises and glorifies God simply for what God is. Christian worship is properly not a means to another end; it is neither a tool to propitiate an angry deity nor a means to obtain favors from God. Rather, Christian worship is an end in itself. It is appropriate for Christians to express appreciation, reverence, and admiration for God. In worship Christians also express thanks to God for what God is and for what God has done.

Some scholars say that the first Christians took over four basic forms of Jewish synagogue worship and added to them Christian rituals such as the eucharist and baptism. These four worship forms today are almost universally present in Christian worship: reading from Scripture, giving a sermon, singing of hymns, and praying. Central to all these activities is recalling the biblical story of God and especially the story of Jesus. Story is another word for what anthropologists call *myth*; the word *story* is preferable, since in our culture myth so often carries the negative connotation of falsehood, which is not intended by anthropologists.

Christians find meaning in life as they interpret their life story and the story of their community within the context of the larger Christian story. The Scripture reading, sermon, hymns, and prayers all use key symbols to evoke memory of the Christian story. This combination of praise, thanks, and recollection of the Christian story is illustrated in the first stanza of Charles Wesley's hymn "Love Divine, All Loves Excelling":

> Love divine, all loves excelling,
> Joy of heaven, to earth come down.
> Fix in us thy humble dwelling,
> All thy faithful mercies crown.
> Jesus, thou art all compassion,
> Pure, unbounded love thou art;
> Visit us with thy salvation,
> Enter every trembling heart.

This hymn largely praises Jesus as "love divine, all loves excelling" and "all compassion, pure, unbounded love." The story of the incarnation is alluded to in "Joy of heaven, to earth come down." And the petition "Fix in us thy humble dwelling" implicitly rests on the story of Jesus' resurrection and the accounts of Paul and others who speak of Jesus as a living personal presence.

Theologians commonly identify certain media by which the Christian story is communicated and call them the *means of grace*. Theologians who train people for ordained ministry frequently focus on just two means of grace: the word of God (which then is often quickly reduced to preaching), and the sacraments.[3] In other words, a highly clericalized understanding of the means of grace emerges, for in most churches it is almost exclusively the clergy who preach and administer the sacraments. I think this clerical conception of the means of grace is a mistake. Over a period of about fifteen years I have asked many students to write a paper telling about the most important

---

3. Two recent examples of this are Daniel Migliore, *Faith Seeking Understanding* (Grand Rapids, Mich.: Wm. B. Eerdmans, 1991), 206; and Ted Peters, *God—The World's Future* (Minneapolis: Fortress Press, 1992), 269–70.

influence on their own faith. Most of the students speak of their faith as some form of Christianity, and I would estimate that about 85 percent of them identify their parents as the chief influence on their faith. Seldom has the key person been clergy, except for those students who are children of clergy.

I think this data is good reason to open up the notion of means of grace. Of course, word and sacrament should be counted among the means of grace, but word should not be narrowed down to preaching. Much more influential is the lived word, the Christian message in the lives of people. In addition, prayer in the name of Jesus and Christian hymns should be considered means of grace. In fact, the whole concept of means of grace should be open and flexible, since an indefinite number of things may serve God as means of communicating grace. Many Christians would want to count icons and nature in conjunction with the Christian word as means of grace for them.

Since the specific means of grace used in Christian worship are too varied for us to survey, we will focus attention on those rituals that at least some churches call sacraments.

Sacraments in General

Probably your first question is, "What is a sacrament?" That is not an easy question to answer. In fact, Christianity existed for more than a thousand years before a clear definition of sacrament won wide support. During those years Christians certainly enacted rituals that came to be called sacraments, but they did not sharply define a sacrament and so distinguish a sacrament from other rituals. Indeed, the word *sacrament* does not occur in the New Testament. The earliest Christians referred to certain sacred rituals as *mysteries*, and this is still the preferred usage in the Orthodox Church. It was the Latin-speaking Cyprian (d. 258), bishop of Carthage in north Africa, who translated the Greek word for mystery with the Latin word *sacramentum*, yet he did not try to define a sacrament. As Jaroslav Pelikan says, the first task was to develop teachings about the specific sacraments of baptism, eucharist, and penance before going on to the general question of what constitutes a sacrament.[4] Four men stand out in the historical effort to establish a definition of sacrament and to settle the closely related question of the number of sacraments.

1. *Augustine* (d. 430) addressed this more philosophical issue in connection with the practical issue of countering a schismatic movement called Donatism. Following a period of Roman persecution of Christians, the

---

4. Jaroslav Pelikan, *The Emergence of the Catholic Tradition (100–600)*, Vol. 1 of *The Christian Tradition* (Chicago: University of Chicago Press, 1971), 163.

Donatists argued that those people, baptized or ordained by a priest or bishop who had lapsed from the Christian faith under persecution, had not received genuine baptism or ordination to the priesthood. In other words, the Donatists said that a sacrament is effective only when the person administering it is holy. Those priests and bishops who had renounced the Christian faith under persecution and then retracted their renunciation were guilty of the mortal sin of apostasy, and any sacraments performed by them were not effective sacraments.

This controversy prompted Augustine to reflect on the nature of sacraments and especially on the relation between the one who administers the sacrament, the outward ritual of the sacrament, and the inward benefit to the recipient. Augustine was the first person to attempt to define a sacrament, but he never settled on a consistent definition. One of Augustine's formulations used two key phrases that were widely used by later theologians: a visible sign and invisible grace. Later theologians put these together to define a sacrament as *a visible sign of an invisible grace*. Here Augustine uses the generic idea of sign as something that points to another reality beyond itself. He noted that in addition to natural signs (for instance, smoke is a sign of fire) and conventional signs like language, there are sacred signs that point beyond themselves to a higher reality, an invisible grace. Augustine also distinguishes between literal signs and figurative signs. For instance, the English word *ox* literally refers to a certain animal, but ox may also have a figurative meaning that goes beyond referring to this animal. When people call a football player an ox, they are suggesting something about his great strength. The figurative sign is what we usually call a symbol. In Christian sacraments, Augustine says there is an outward, visible, figurative sign or symbol and an invisible spiritual reality to which the symbol points. Furthermore, word and physical symbol are united in a sacrament, for water alone does not make a baptism; there must be both water and the appropriate words of baptism together.

In opposition to the Donatists, Augustine taught that God's grace is objectively present through the sacrament regardless of the holiness of the one who administers it, for it is the sacrament of God and the church, not of the presiding priest. Yet he knows it is possible for people to go through a sacramental ritual with its visible signs and because of their lack of faith they do not receive the invisible divine gift. So Augustine's understanding of the symbolic character of sacrament enables him to affirm that God's grace is present and available in the sacrament without turning the sacrament into a magical rite in which humans automatically receive a spiritual benefit.

While Augustine offered several definitions of sacrament, he never specified a certain number of sacraments. In fact, he identified an indefinite number of sacraments, including not only baptism and eucharist, but also making the sign of the cross, the salt used in baptisms at that time, the baptismal font, the creed, and the Lord's Prayer. So for Augustine an indefinite number of figurative signs could be symbols of divine grace.

2. The second influential person to try to define a sacrament was the medieval theologian *Peter Lombard* (d. 1160). Lombard builds on Augustine's foundation when he defined a sacrament as "a sign of the grace of God and a form of invisible grace, so that it bears its image and exists as its cause."[5] In addition to Augustine's basic idea of a sacrament as a visible sign of invisible grace, Lombard adds two points. One is that the sacramental sign bears a likeness to the reality it signifies; for example, the water of baptism that can physically wash a person is a symbol of spiritual cleansing. The second point is that the outward sacramental symbol is a *cause* of the invisible grace symbolized. With this more precise definition in hand, medieval theologians proceeded to work out a full sacramental theology with complex distinctions.

Lombard listed seven sacraments: the chief sacraments of baptism and eucharist and the other sacraments of penance, confirmation, anointing of the sick (extreme unction), marriage, and ordination. Partly because Lombard's *Sentences* quickly became the standard theological textbook, by about 1200 it was common for Western theologians to identify these seven rituals as sacraments.

3. *Thomas Aquinas* was the third major theologian to shape Western Christian thinking about the sacraments. Besides agreeing that there are seven sacraments, one of his major contributions in this area was to apply the philosophy of Aristotle to sacramental thinking. For example, he used the Aristotelian concept of matter to refer to the physical symbol, the concept of form such as the words "I baptize you . . ." in the sacrament of baptism, and described a sacrament as the "instrumental cause" of the grace symbolized. Distinguished from the sacraments were the *sacramentals*, which are an indefinite number of religious practices that may bring a spiritual benefit to those persons who use them with faith, but there is not the same certainty of an objective presence of divine grace that a sacrament has. Thus many rites, such as making the sign of the cross, that Augustine called sacraments were now set on a lower level as sacramentals. The teachings of Thomas Aquinas on sacraments by and large received official Catholic endorsement at the Council of Florence in 1439 and the Council of Trent (1545–1563).

The contemporary Catholic theologian Regis Duffy remarks that during the medieval period there was a pronounced concentration on the question

---

5. Peter Lombard, *The Four Books of Sentences*, Book IV, Distinction I, Chapter IV in *A Scholastic Miscellany: Anselm to Ockham*, ed. and trans Eugene R. Fairweather, The Library of Christian Classics, Vol. 10 (Philadelphia: Westminster, 1956), 339.

how a sacrament works rather than *why* it is given. There was an allied focus on what was absolutely essential to have an effective sacrament; the result was a minimalist approach to sacraments. That is, what was the minimum required for the sacrament to effectively convey grace to a person? Thus, while complicated theological explanations of the sacraments were developed, actual participation in the eucharist declined. By the late medieval period people customarily attended church regularly to observe the mass, yet only received communion once a year at Easter, which was the minimum required by church law. Another aspect of this minimalist attitude was the teaching that a sacrament effectively communicates grace to a person as long as he or she does not place an obstacle to it. That is, rather than putting the emphasis on the positive stance of faith as the suitable response to a sacrament, the teaching stressed the negative standard of not preventing the sacrament from being effective through committing a mortal sin.[6]

4. The fourth chief person influential in shaping church doctrine on the definition and number of sacraments was *Martin Luther* (d. 1546). In keeping with his emphasis on having biblical authority for theological statements, Luther insisted that there be a clear biblical warrant for counting a ritual as a sacrament, namely, that a sacrament is instituted by a command and promise of Jesus. So Jesus instituted the eucharist by commanding his disciples to "Do this in remembrance of me" and giving the promise that "This is my body that is for you" (1 Corinthians 11:24). By this standard Luther clearly recognized two sacraments—baptism and eucharist. He wavered for several years about penance, for in John 20:23, "If you forgive the sins of any, they are forgiven them; if you retain the sins of any, they are retained," Jesus authorized penance. In the end, though, Luther recognized just the two sacraments of baptism and eucharist, because penance lacked a distinctive physical sign. Nearly all Protestants have agreed with him on the number of sacraments. Only two later Protestant groups, Quakers (Society of Friends) and the Salvation Army, acknowledge no sacraments whatsoever.[7]

As a result of study of the early centuries of Christianity, many recent scholars have reopened the issues of the definition and number of sacraments. Many scholars now say that there is no certain definition of a sacrament, for sacramental rituals are too mysterious to be so precisely pinned down. For example, Luther's definition of a sacrament leaves us wondering about the status of penance, and would seem to authorize ritual footwashing such as Jesus did to his disciples at the last supper (John 13:1-17). Many experts—

6. Regis A. Duffy, "Sacraments in General," in *Systematic Theology: Roman Catholic Perspectives*, Vol. 2, Francis Schüssler Fiorenza and John P. Galvin, eds. (Minneapolis: Fortress Press, 1991), 195–97.
7. James F. White, *Introduction to Christian Worship*, rev. ed. (Nashville: Abingdon, 1990), 179.

both Catholic and Protestant—also agree that the number of sacraments should be more indefinite. In other words, the boundary between sacrament and sacramentals should be more elastic. For instance, Methodist scholars Robert Browning and Roy Reed say,

> [Joseph] Martos, and many others, are aware that so-called "sacramentals" or "devotions" like the "Way of the Cross" or the Rosary may be more spiritually powerful in the lives of Christians than the official sacraments. Why would we not be better served if the idea of sacrament, instead of being official and legal, were more a matter of Spirit power and the reality of God's *mysterion* among us as we in fact experience it?[8]

Browning and Reed go on to propose that the number of sacraments be expanded to include the rite of footwashing, which some churches already use. So at present we have a somewhat fluid situation regarding the number of sacraments. The churches still maintain their historic positions: Roman Catholics and Orthodox have seven sacraments, most Protestants have two. Nonetheless, many scholars are saying that the whole matter should be reopened.[9] In any case, Catholic, Orthodox, and Protestant Christians agree that the chief sacraments are baptism and eucharist, and it is to these two that we now turn.

The Chief Sacraments: Baptism and Eucharist

Baptism

Baptism is the Christian rite of initiation into the church. In this unrepeated rite the visible symbol is water in which one is immersed or with which one is sprinkled along with words that the person is being baptized in the name of the Trinity. Our reflection on baptism will be divided into two sections: first, we will consider what invisible grace is given in baptism by examining the meaning of the ritual, and second, we will look at various practices in connection with baptism.

The Meaning of Baptism

Baptism is a ritual with rather rich meaning, so we will distinguish five aspects of meaning delineated in the ecumenical study *Baptism, Eucharist, and Ministry,* issued by a World Council of Churches commission that included Roman Catholics.

8. Robert L. Browning and Roy A. Reed, *The Sacraments in Religious Education and Liturgy: An Ecumenical Model* (Birmingham: Religious Education Press, 1985), 294–95.
9. In addition to Browning and Reed, see also James F. White and Regis Duffy, both cited above.

1. *Baptism involves participation in the death and resurrection of Jesus Christ.* This meaning is stressed by Paul in several of his New Testament letters.

> Do you not know that all of us who have been baptized into Christ Jesus were baptized into his death? Therefore we have been buried with him by baptism into death, so that, just as Christ was raised from the dead by the glory of the Father, so we too might walk in newness of life. (Romans 6:3-4)

Paul is saying that baptism symbolizes a dying or drowning of the old, sinful self and a rising of a new self dedicated to God. This symbolism is most profoundly expressed by the action of fully immersing a person in water and then coming up out of the water, for water has the power both to drown and to sustain life. This dying and rising of the self is not merely a moral imperative that the Christian ought to follow (although it is that too). Since Christ is a living, present reality, Christ draws the Christian into sharing the quality of his life. This dying and rising are not accomplished in a moment, but take place over the entire life of the baptized person. Over the years, as a person dies and rises again and again with Christ, the person's life takes on greater resemblance to the life of Jesus with its deep trust in God and compassionate love for others. The fruits of this identification with Christ are sanctification and freedom from sin (Romans 6:22).

2. *Baptism cleanses from sin.* Part of the natural symbolism of water is that it may wash away dirt and make a person clean. Baptism also brings about a spiritual cleansing by forgiving sins. Because forgiveness of sin is intimately involved in justification for all Christian traditions, albeit in various ways, then the cleansing power of baptism bestows justification.

3. *With baptism comes the Holy Spirit.* The New Testament book of Acts recounts a number of incidents of baptism, and the Holy Spirit is normally given to those baptized. Sometimes there was a lapse of time between the act of baptism and the giving of the Spirit, however; on occasion baptism comes first and on another occasion the Spirit is received first (Acts 8:12-17; 10:44-48). The presence of the Spirit in a person's life does not instantly make him or her mature in the faith, but the Spirit is given as a first installment on the spiritual and moral fulfillment that will eventually come in God's reign. The presence of the Spirit may take different forms. In some people the giving of the Holy Spirit is a discrete, ecstatic experience accompanied by speaking in tongues. In others the Spirit may work unobtrusively over time through family and church members to awaken faith in the baptized person. In still others the work of the Spirit may be frustrated by a baptized person's resistance (for instance, Simon in Acts 8). In any case, the Spirit is normally associated with the ritual of baptism, although not in a mechanical or magical way that binds God's Spirit to the ritual. The gift of the Holy Spirit is powerful testimony to the fact that God and the awakening of faith are not under human control.

4. *Baptism is a powerful symbol of inclusion in the church and its ministry.* Baptism not only links baptized persons to Christ and the Holy Spirit, but also to the community of believers who are the church. This inclusion in the church is past and present fact as well as future possibility. That is, baptism is the rite of initiation into the present fellowship of the church, so that it is a fact that the baptized are recognized by the community as members of the church. Furthermore, baptism also symbolizes the commissioning of new members—even infants—to the general Christian ministry of service to others. Yet Christian sharing in the one rite of baptism is also a call to actualize in the future deeper and fuller dimensions of inclusion in the church. For instance, Paul connects baptism with breaking down all social barriers and divisions in the church.

> As many of you as were baptized into Christ have clothed yourselves with Christ. There is no longer Jew or Greek, there is no longer slave or free, there is no longer male and female; for all of you are one in Christ Jesus. (Galatians 3:27-28)

5. *Baptism is a symbol of the future and present reign of God.* In baptism we encounter the eschatological dimension just as we do in the eucharist, for eschatology pervades Christian faith and practice. You recall that eschatology has to with the ultimate future of the world, but that ultimate future reality of harmony and justice can be partially actualized in the present as well. In God's reign people will live with perfect trust in God and perfect love for their fellow human beings and creatures. Baptism is an anticipation and foretaste of that future unity and wholeness, for in this ritual people confess their faith in the triune God, bring another person into the community of believers, commission that new member to serve all people and creatures, and employ the natural symbol of water to proclaim this renewal of life. Faith in God, human community, and unity with nature are fundamental to the rite of baptism and to the future reign of God. In baptism a natural substance, human gestures, and words are used to express and declare the Christian vision of what God has in store for the world.

Baptismal Practices

The paramount issue regarding baptismal practices is whether to limit baptism to people old enough to make an informed decision to receive baptism or whether to baptize infants as well as adult converts. On this matter the churches are divided. The vast majority of Christians belong to churches that baptize both infants and adults, for this is the custom in the Orthodox, Roman Catholic, Anglican (Episcopal), Lutheran, Methodist, and most of the Reformed churches, among others. Yet there is a significant minority of Christians who belong to churches that only baptize persons old enough to make a responsible decision; Baptist, Pentecostal, and many Evangelical churches observe this practice.

In the background of this discussion are different emphases on two matters: individual and community, divine grace and the human response of faith. Those who follow the practice of *believer baptism* (that is, who baptize only those old enough to confess their personal faith) place the primary emphasis of baptism on the individual and his or her response of faith. They view baptism as the public testimony of a person's inner faith; hence they baptize only when someone is ready to make a public confession of faith. Those who also baptize infants put the main stress on the Christian community and the priority of God's grace. What counts most for them is that the baptized person is placed within the community of faith where the Spirit makes use of word, sacrament, prayers, hymns, and Christian lives to bring about faith in the individual. They emphasize how the Christian community influences the individual.

While these differences in emphasis exist, each tradition also gives subordinate recognition to the other factor in each pair. On the one hand, most of those who put the accent on community and God's grace by baptizing infants also have the ritual of confirmation, which usually comes some years later and allows for the more mature individual to make his or her own confession of faith. On the other hand, those who practice only believer baptism usually have a ceremony of dedication in which parents pledge to rear their young child within the church community, and they acknowledge in their teachings that God's prior grace makes possible a person's confession of faith.

It is difficult to settle this difference in practice through evidence from Scripture and Christian tradition. Most biblical texts that tell of a baptism recount the baptism of adults. Yet those who practice infant baptism point to several New Testament passages that strongly suggest that infants were also baptized in the first century of Christian history. There are three references to baptism of a whole household (1 Corinthians 1:16; Acts 11:13; 16:15). Peter's words on the day of Pentecost also suggest the baptism of infants as well as adults, "Repent and let each of you be baptized. . . . For the promise is for you and your children" (Acts 2:38-39). The testimony of Irenaeus, Origen, and Hippolytus indicate that infants were also baptized during the second and third centuries. This practice increased in frequency as the numbers of Christians rose, and more and more Christian parents wanted their children brought into the full fellowship of the church. Nevertheless, from the second to the fifth centuries, the ancient church also had a rigorous program of preparation for adults seeking to join the church; this program was called the *catechumenate*. This program normally lasted three years, and involved study and gradual inclusion in Christian worship life. After a final examination of their spiritual and moral life along with prayer and fasting, the participants received baptism, the laying on of hands, anointing by the bishop, and participated for the first time in the eucharist.

The debate over infant baptism ignited during the sixteenth-century Reformation when some Protestants insisted upon only believer baptism; by their opponents they were dubbed Anabaptists, that is, rebaptizers, since they baptized people as adults even though those people had been baptized as infants. The issue has been a lively topic also in the twentieth century. The great theologian Karl Barth went against most of his own Reformed tradition when he argued for only believer baptism, partly on the grounds that the practice of infant baptism has diluted the significance of church membership, for in a secular age many of those baptized as infants never participate in the church or come to faith in Jesus Christ. Undoubtedly this is a weakness in the way infant baptism has been practiced, for often children have been baptized whose parents have virtually no involvement in the church. On the other hand, a criticism of believer baptism is that it often results in baptism—and sometimes of sacraments generally—losing importance. For example, note how the meeting places of television evangelists who practice only believer baptism are commonly designed like a theater; that is, the focus is entirely upon the preached word and sacraments are ignored. Ecumenical discussions, such as the World Council of Churches deliberations on baptism, have brought some measure of better understanding and mutual respect for each other's position on this practice, yet those churches that have historically baptized infants persist in doing so and traditional believer baptism churches continue their practice.

What you need to decide is which practice you think is more sound. For myself, I find it difficult to see the difference to be of highest significance, because it appears that God honors both practices; churches in both traditions endure as vital Christian communities. Nevertheless, I definitely think infant baptism is the better approach, as long as it is not done for those families without any living involvement in the church. The reason for my position is that I think the proper priority of emphasis should be given to God's grace working in and through the Christian community as it influences children growing up within its midst. The human response of faith is important, but as a response it is secondary to grace.

The best analogy that I know for baptism is adoption; perhaps this is because I have an adopted son. When Kim came into our family at age four-and-a-half, he had almost nothing to say about it. The decision for the adoption was made by my wife and me as well as by the adoption agency. Nevertheless, the adoption made a major change in Kim's life. Up to that point, he knew only the customs and language of Korea, and he was without a family. Within a relatively short time Kim was Americanized and knew the love and support of parents and siblings. Today as a young adult living and working in

New York City, Kim is curious and respectful of his Korean roots, but he is thoroughly an American who subsists on bagels, deli sandwiches, yogurt, and pizza. Being placed in a new community has had a profound affect on Kim, even though he did not participate in the original decision to join this community.

I remember Kim's baptism very clearly. The deepest moment came just after the baptism with water when the pastor made the sign of the cross on the young boy's forehead and said, "You are marked with the cross of Christ forever." I thought how profoundly true those words are. Because Kim was now living within the context of a Christian family and church, the religious faith to which he must respond would be the Christian faith. Even though later in life he might conceivably reject the Christian faith, it would be Jesus Christ that he would be rejecting. If he had stayed in Korea, he might have responded to Gautama Buddha or Confucius. In other words, the social context in which he grew up would powerfully influence him. Of course, his baptism would lose some of its significance if our family had never prayed in the name of Jesus or never attended Christian worship. And, naturally, years later Kim had to make his own adult affirmation of faith in Christ. But even if he had come to renounce Christ, that would not nullify baptism's good news of God's love for him. The situation is similar to that in which Kim might possibly have rejected our family and said he wanted nothing more to do with the Hanson clan. That rejection would not stop his mother and me from persisting in our love for Kim and seeking for reconciliation with him. Just so, baptism is primarily a symbolic expression of God's love and acceptance, a love that perseveres in its quest for our answering love.

A second issue to think about in connection with baptismal practices is how baptism may be an ongoing part of Christian experience and not merely a distant event in one's past. In some respects Martin Luther led the way on this by emphasizing the apostle Paul's idea that Christians are baptized into Christ's death and resurrection. Luther suggested that each day Christians should remember their baptism, for they need daily to die to sin and rise to the new life of trust in Christ. A liturgical form for remembering baptism occurs for some Christians during the Easter vigil liturgy when the congregation is sprinkled with water in memory of their baptism. Another liturgical reminder happens when a baptism takes place within the context of congregational worship and the congregation is invited to reflect on the meaning of their own baptism. The common Catholic practice of dipping one's hand in water and making the sign of the cross on oneself when entering church may be another excellent way to remember one's baptism. The issue underlying all of these practices is how baptism may be enduringly integrated into everyday Christian experience.

Eucharist

The eucharist is a ritual in which Christians eat small portions of bread and wine in conjunction with a corporate recollection of Jesus' life, death, and resurrection and with a repetition of Jesus' words of blessing the bread and wine during the last supper with his disciples. Partly because the eucharist is a repeated sacrament and baptism is not, the eucharist is the central sacrament among Christians. While it is possible to devote considerable attention to the history of the eucharist, our focus will be upon its contemporary meaning for Christians. Because the eucharist is so full of symbols, time and again it rewards with fresh insights those who carefully reflect upon it.

The eucharist is like a rich fabric with complex patterns and ever interesting detail. When a fabric is woven on a loom, one set of threads goes vertically or lengthwise on the loom (the warp) and another set of threads goes horizontally or crosswise (the woof). In the eucharist we can distinguish two warp threads of meaning and five woof threads of meaning (Figure 1).

WARP Threads

Figure 1

Just as in cloth the warp threads are interwoven with all the woof threads, so in the eucharist the warp threads of meaning interlace with all the woof threads.

Warp Threads of Meaning

I. THE EUCHARIST AND ITS VARIOUS MEANINGS ARE INTIMATELY RELATED WITH ALL THREE DIMENSIONS OF TIME: PAST, PRESENT, AND FUTURE. The eucharist has all sorts of connections with past events: the life, death, and resurrection of Jesus, the meals in which Jesus participated, his stories about meals, the Passover meal and other sacred meals celebrated in Judaism, God's past activity of creating the world, and God's providential guidance of history. These are only some of the links with the past in the eucharist; we will find others as we proceed. These multitudinous ties with the past help us understand and appreciate what is going on in the eucharist today.

The eucharist also has many references to the future, for the eucharistic meal should be understood within the context of Christian eschatology. You may recall that eschatology concerns the last things or the ultimate future. The eucharistic meal is an anticipation of the fellowship of the heavenly banquet in the kingdom or reign of God. Similarly, the eucharist now should reflect at least some of the justice and love that will exist in that future reign of God.

The present is also a powerful dimension of meaning in the eucharist. Above all, the eucharist is an experience of the presence of Christ, a presence both in space and time, here and now. There is also a presence of people with one another, an openness and caring for one another. Thus present as well as past and future run throughout the diverse meanings of the eucharist.

2. THOSE WHO CELEBRATE THE EUCHARISTIC MEAL PARTICIPATE IN THE TRINITARIAN LIFE OF GOD. As we have noted before, there is a pattern in God's trinitarian life: the Father/Mother is the source, the Word or Wisdom is an Other that comes forth as an articulate expression of God, and the Spirit is the bond that unites them. The eucharist reflects the pattern of this trinitarian life, for God is the Source who takes bodily form in bread and wine and the fellowship of believers, all for the purpose of fashioning a richer, fuller unity of nature, people, and God.

Woof Threads of Meaning

1. THE EUCHARIST IS THE MEAL OF THE REIGN OF GOD. The eucharist is first of all a *meal*. This may not be obvious, since the amount of bread and wine consumed is so small. Yet Jesus instituted the eucharist at what is called the last supper, the last meal that he ate with his disciples before being arrested and killed. His actions of blessing the bread and wine and passing them around were part of a full Jewish meal, and for a time the earliest Christians continued to celebrate the eucharist in connection with a complete meal. Although quite soon the eucharist was separated off as a special, sacred rite, it still has its roots in the action of a community eating together.

Commonly in human cultures a meal is much more than the obtaining of physical nourishment for one's body; it takes on symbolic meanings. One such meaning is that a meal has very important social significance as a symbol of personal bonds of common values and good will; a meal together in a home or restaurant is often an occasion for personal sharing among family or friends. Another meaning is that some meals are regarded as festive occasions: weddings, anniversaries, Christmas, and Easter dinners are times of celebration. Still another meaning is that a meal is sometimes associated with a critical event in history; Thanksgiving Day in the United States is an example. Other cases are the Jewish Passover meal that remembers the deliverance of ancient Israel from slavery in Egypt and the Christian eucharist that commemorates Jesus' death and resurrection. A further meaning of a meal is that it may be linked with the recurrent patterns of nature. This was common in traditional agrarian societies in which animal or fruit offerings were made to deities and sometimes accompanied by a meal. For Christians the use of bread and wine in the eucharist is a significant bond with God-given processes of nature by which all life is sustained.[10] Yet another meaning in the eucharistic meal is that Jesus is both the host of this repast and the one who serves it. No wonder then that one of the common names for this meal is the *Lord's Supper*, a name that calls attention to the fact that this is a meal or supper hosted by the Lord Jesus. Thus the fact that the eucharist is a meal has multiple meanings.

Now we must call attention to the fact that the Lord's Supper is *a meal of the reign of God*. The kingdom or reign of God is a symbol for a situation in which God's rule is no longer opposed but is fulfilled in perfect harmony, peace, and justice. Obviously, this perfect harmony lies in the future, the ultimate future; nevertheless, this reign of God is also present to the degree that life in the world is marked by harmony, peace, and justice. Jesus proclaimed the nearness of the reign of God in his ministry and person. So the reign of God is past and present as well as future.

To be mindful of the Lord's Supper as a meal of the reign of God would include awareness of the following meanings. Looking to the past, there would be remembrance of the joy and peace that those who ate with Jesus knew, a joy and peace grounded in Jesus' open acceptance of disciples and marginalized folks that broke bread with him. It was no accident that Jesus was criticized for eating with disreputable "tax collectors and sinners" (Mark 2:15-17). Such open fellowship at table was a symbol of the reign of God. Someone aware of the eucharist as a meal of the reign of God would also look to the future when the reign will come in fullness. This too will lend a festive air to the occasion, for the eucharist is an anticipation of the time when all suffering will be swallowed up in joy. Furthermore, mindfulness of the reign of God will include a challenge to the present life of the church and world to more fully manifest the harmony and justice of God's reign. This consciousness involves both a recognition of God's judgment upon current injustices and an invitation to strive for a better world and church. The one loaf and the one cup from which all communicants eat and drink are material symbols of this unity remembered, anticipated, and fragmentarily experienced now.

10. F. W. Dillistone, *The Power of Symbols in Religion and Culture* (New York: Crossroad, 1986), 37–41.

When the Lord's Supper is seen in eschatological perspective, its mood is happy. Most contemporary Christians think of the eucharist as a somber event in which one should ponder one's sins and the awful sufferings and death of Jesus. In effect, in the eucharist many contemporary Christians tend to ignore the resurrection of Jesus and to dwell only on his death. When the Lord's Supper is experienced as also a promise of the future reign of God, then both Jesus' death and resurrection receive their due. His resurrection opens the way to future fulfillment, but his death manifests the costliness of God's identification with the world and human suffering. Sorrow and joy, penitence and hope coexist.

2. THE EUCHARIST IS THANKSGIVING TO GOD. Indeed, the term *eucharist* comes from a Greek word that means thanksgiving. It is well to remember that the fundamental character of worship is to give thanks and praise to God; the name *eucharist* captures this thanking, praising spirit of worship. The entire eucharistic liturgy is meant to be thanks and praise to God: the initial movement of people gathering for worship, the songs, prayers, sermon, the sacramental meal, and return to service in the world. Perhaps the high point of this thanks and praise comes in the eucharistic prayer, generally called The Great Thanksgiving, that comes shortly before receiving communion. The heart of The Great Thanksgiving is a rather extended prayer that recounts God's work in creation and reconciliation, recalls Jesus' words of institution for the eucharist, and asks the Holy Spirit to be present.

3. THE EUCHARIST IS A MEMORIAL OF JESUS CHRIST. The key word here is memorial or the Greek term *anamnesis*. Clearly it has to do with remembrance, but what sort of remembering is meant? Recent study in the history of liturgy has emphasized that the remembering intended in the eucharistic liturgy is not merely the recollection of a past historical event. In historical remembering, the past event is present now only insofar as it is subjectively in a person's thoughts. So Napoleon may live in the thoughts of a contemporary historian, but there is no doubt that Napoleon is dead and buried. However, when Jews are urged to remember in the Passover meal their people's exodus from slavery in Egypt over three thousand years ago (Exodus 13:3), the God whom they remember is alive and present today as well. The liberating God of the exodus is the same God who is at work liberating people from oppression today and promises ultimate liberation in the future. Similarly, when Christians are invited to recall what God has done through the life, death, and resurrection of Jesus Christ, that same God and that same Jesus Christ are alive and present on the contemporary scene. So the remembrance of the eucharist has the meaning of being mindful of what God has done in the past, is doing in the present, and promises to do in the future. Of course, this rich

recollection goes on in the hymns, prayers, Scripture readings, and sermon or homily as well as in the eucharist; remembrance of the Christian story is basic to all Christian worship. What is unique about the eucharistic memorial is that the remembering of Jesus Christ in the past, present, and future takes place in the context of a special meal with its actions of eating and drinking.

4. THE EUCHARIST IS A RE-PRESENTATION OF CHRIST'S SACRIFICE. This is one of the topics on which Christians have heatedly differed, and on which much effort has been expended in recent ecumenical conversations to reach more agreement. First, a few words about the historical differences that erupted during the sixteenth-century reformation. Very early in the reformation movement (1520), Martin Luther objected to the eucharist being considered a *propitiatory sacrifice* and other Protestants came to agree. To propitiate God means to gain the favor of God, to be reconciled to God after the breach of sin. It had become common practice in the medieval church to regard the eucharist as a sacrifice offered to God for sin, a sacrifice that could obtain God's favor. You may recall that in our discussion of the work of Christ as a sacrifice, we noted the distinction in Old Testament sacrificial practice between a sin offering and a thank offering. That is, a sacrifice of thanks is an offering of the self to God in gratitude for what God has done. Luther and other Protestants approved of viewing the eucharist as a sacrifice in this sense of thank offering. What they objected to was thinking of the eucharist as a sin offering or propitiatory sacrifice, a sacrifice that wins God's approval. Their objection was that Jesus Christ had already made the one necessary propitiatory sacrifice long ago in his life and death. To the Protestants, offering the eucharist as a propitiatory sacrifice seemed to suggest two things: that Christ's sacrifice is inadequate and that people today are trying to do something to earn their own salvation. The Roman Catholic response at the Council of Trent was to uphold the legitimacy of the eucharist or mass as a propitiatory sacrifice. Trent insisted that the same Christ who made a bloody sacrifice long ago is offered again in the eucharist in an unbloody manner.[11]

Roman Catholics and Protestants were at loggerheads over this issue until recent ecumenical discussions have made some progress toward resolving it. The main advance has been to link the eucharist as sacrifice with the biblical understanding of remembrance or *anamnesis* that we just discussed. As we saw, the heart of biblical remembrance of Christ is not limited by time, so that Christ is present today. To remember Christ is to be mindful of what he has done in the past, is doing now, and will do in the future. So the Vatican-

---

11. *Canons and Decrees of the Council of Trent*, Twenty-second Session, Chapter 2, trans. H. J. Schroeder (St. Louis, Herder, 1950), 145–46.

approved *Catechism of the Catholic Church* (1994) says, "Because it is the memorial of Christ's Passover, the Eucharist is also a sacrifice" and "The Eucharist is thus a sacrifice because it *re-presents* (makes present) the sacrifice of the cross, because it is its *memorial* and because it *applies* its fruit." The catechism explains that because Christ is not limited by the division of past and present in time, the sacrifice of the mass is not *another* sacrifice than that one offering long ago. The mass simply makes present (re-presents) the one sufficient sacrifice of Christ.[12] While this new approach has made it possible for Catholic and Protestant views on this subject to converge, that is, move toward agreement, full agreement has not yet been reached. Many Protestant theologians still are afraid that calling the eucharist a propitiatory sacrifice readily lends itself to misunderstanding the ritual as a human effort to mollify God.

5. THE EUCHARIST AS COMMUNION WITH JESUS CHRIST, WITH OTHER PEOPLE, AND OTHER CREATURES. The word *communion* literally means union with; more generally it means sharing. There are different degrees of sharing ranging all the way from having certain beliefs and values in common with persons whose names we do not know to a very close, personal bond. This entire range of communion takes place in the eucharistic ritual that is also called *Holy Communion*, sharing in the holy. We shall distinguish three dimensions of Holy Communion: communion with Christ, communion with fellow Christians, and communion with the whole world of people and creatures.

a. Communion with Christ. The entire Christian life is a sharing in the life of Christ. This is a prominent motif in the New Testament. As we have noted before, the apostle Paul frequently speaks of Christians as being in Christ and as dying and rising with Christ; both notions assume a profound sharing of the Christian in the living Christ. The Gospel of John speaks of this communion with the image of grapevine branches (Christians) that must remain attached to the main vine (Christ) if they are to live and flourish (John 15:1-12). Christ is present to Christians in many ways: in the Christian message or word, in communal worship "where two or three are gathered in my name" (Matthew 18:20), in the poor and needy, in the person of the minister who presides at Christian worship, and in the sacraments. Holy Communion is often experienced by Christians as an especially intimate moment of commu-

---

12. *Catechism of the Catholic Church* (Mahwah, N. J.: Paulist, 1994), 343–44. See also the World Council of Churches document from an ecumenical commission that included Roman Catholics, *Baptism, Eucharist, and Ministry*, Faith and Order Paper No. 111, Eucharist, II (Geneva: World Council of Churches, 1982; special U.S. Lutheran reprint edition), 8–10 which emphasizes Christ's continuing intercession and memorial as the basis for viewing the eucharist as sacrifice.

nion with Christ, because here the presence of Christ is made more vivid through the physical symbols of bread and wine. However, the presence of Christ in Holy Communion has been a subject of dispute among Christians.

We can distinguish four traditional ways of interpreting Christ's presence in the eucharist.

(1) *The bread and wine are permanently changed into Christ's body and blood.* This is the central affirmation of the Roman Catholic understanding. Since 1215 the authoritative way to express this realistic presence of Christ has been the idea of *transubstantiation.* As formulated by Thomas Aquinas, transubstantiation relies upon a philosophical distinction between substance and accidents. Substance refers to the inner reality of a thing, whereas accidents are the outer appearances of a thing. One could speak of the substance and accidents of anything, so that the substance of a dog is its essential being as a dog and its accidents are characteristics such as its fur, coloring, and weight. The dog's substance is the "subject" to which the accidents belong. In the eucharist, according to this interpretation, the substance or inner reality of the bread and wine are changed into the inner reality of Christ's body and blood (hence tran-substantiation), yet the outer features of the bread and wine such as its color and taste (the accidents) remain unchanged. The essential point for Catholic teaching is that the bread and wine are changed or converted into Christ's body and blood. The Thomistic interpretation using the concepts of substance and accidents has been considered by Catholics as especially appropriate, because it affirms the essential point while avoiding a crude literalism that would see the Christian literally chewing on Christ's body and drinking his blood.

Since contemporary people seldom think in ancient Greek philosophical categories, however, some Catholic theologians in recent decades have sought other concepts for expressing the mystery of Christ's special presence in the eucharist. One suggestion has been to speak of *transignification.* In this view the significance or meaning of a thing is part of its reality, and a change of its significance may occur. For instance, my wedding ring is much more than its physical characteristics of gold composition and specific design. These physical features have remained relatively constant throughout its existence, but at my wedding ceremony its significance changed. Prior to my wedding, the meaning of the ring was chiefly that of a product to be sold by a jeweler. But at my wedding, the ring took on a new meaning as a symbol of my marriage to Marion. A tran-signification took place. Similarly, in the eucharistic ritual bread and wine take on a new significance as the body and blood of Christ. While this interpretation has not been formally rejected by the Catholic teaching authority, it also has not been officially approved. So transubstantiation remains the authoritative interpretation of Christ's presence in the eucharist.

The Roman Catholic understanding of a permanent change in the bread and wine has resulted in certain devotional practices. Consecrated bread (called the host) that is not consumed at a eucharist is saved or reserved in the *tabernacle*, a special container placed at the front of the church building. Since Christ is believed to be uniquely present in this host, many Catholics show adoration and respect by genuflecting or bowing deeply as they enter and leave the sanctuary. Other associated practices are exposing the host in a special container (a monstrance) for adoration and carrying the host in solemn procession for adoration, such as is sometimes done on Corpus Christi Day.

(2) *The body and blood of Christ are present in, with, and under the bread and wine during the eucharistic action.* This is the Lutheran understanding of Christ's presence. *Real presence* is the preferred term among Lutherans for expressing their understanding of Christ's presence in the eucharistic elements of bread and wine, but the term is also used at times by other Christians. The Lutheran view differs in two major ways from transubstantiation: in the Lutheran conception there is no metaphysical change in the bread and wine, and Christ's body and blood are not permanently present in the consecrated bread and wine. Sometimes the Lutheran view has been described in Aristotelian terms as consubstantiation, that is, the inner reality of Christ's body and blood are present with (the prefix *con*) the bread and wine, but real presence is the designation preferred by Lutherans. Belief in the real presence of Christ brings a strong sense of reverence that Lutherans commonly express by kneeling to receive Holy Communion.

(3) *The Holy Spirit makes Christ's body and blood present to those who participate in the Lord's Supper.* This is the interpretation offered by John Calvin, one of the two major founders of the Reformed tradition. Whereas both the Roman Catholic and Lutheran conceptions involve a spatial, local presence of Christ's body in the eucharist, Calvin rejected such a localized presence as repugnant, for it seemed to imply that in the eucharist Christians literally chew Christ's body. In Calvin's understanding, Christ's body is located in heaven, but the Holy Spirit bridges this great distance and offers the benefits of Christ's body and blood to all who share in the Lord's Supper, although only believers actually receive those benefits. "What, then, our mind does not comprehend, let faith conceive: that the Spirit truly unites things separated in space."[13] We may call this the idea of *spiritual presence*.

While the Orthodox Church has a realistic understanding of Christ's presence that is close to that of Roman Catholicism, the Orthodox share with the Calvinist tradition a strong awareness of the Holy Spirit's role in the

---

13. John Calvin, *Institutes of the Christian Religion*, Book 4, Chapter 17, Section 10, ed. John T. McNeill, trans. F. L. Battles, The Library of Christian Classics, Vol. 21 (Philadelphia: Westminster, 1960), 1370.

eucharist. The Orthodox stress the importance of the ancient Christian *epiklesis*, a eucharistic prayer for the Holy Spirit to enter both the people and the elements of bread and wine.

(4) *Christ is present in the eucharist as Christians remember the sacrifice of his life.* This is the view of Ulrich Zwingli (d. 1531), the second major founder of the Reformed tradition, although he preceded Calvin in time. Like Calvin, Zwingli also objected to the idea of localized presence involved in the Catholic and Lutheran outlooks, for it seemed to imply a physical eating of Christ's body and blood. Zwingli emphasized the eucharist as a memorial and we can call his view *memorial presence*. This has generally been understood as an occasion to recall what Jesus did long ago. The bread and wine are symbols that help one remember Jesus' sacrifice; the eucharist, so to speak, jogs the memory. This is the view most widely held in Reformed and Evangelical churches today. Indeed, polls show that this is the view actually held by many Catholics and Lutherans even though it is not the official teaching of their churches.

Some scholars argue that this popular interpretation is not really what Zwingli taught. These scholars say that Zwingli actually saw the eucharist as a memorial in the deeper sense that we discussed earlier, namely, that by the Holy Spirit Jesus Christ is not subject to the limitations of time, but is present as well as past and future. In this interpretation Holy Communion is not just an exercise in calling to mind a dead figure of the past, as we do in historical remembrance. Rather, eucharistic remembrance is awareness of the Christ who by the Spirit bursts the boundaries of time to be past, present, and future.

If we look back over these four conceptions of Christ's presence in the Lord's Supper, we can see that transubstantiation, real presence, and spiritual presence share a common belief in an *objective* presence of Christ. What is meant by this becomes clear when contrasted with the common understanding of remembrance as merely recalling what a past historical figure did. This popular remembering is purely *subjective*; that is, Christ is present only insofar as a person has him in mind at the eucharist. This would mean that if people have their mind on something else, then Christ is not present to them. But the other three views all teach an objective presence of Christ. In the eucharist Christ is truly present to everyone who participates even though some of them may be thinking about other things. So while these three views of Christ's presence differ in how they talk about it, they all agree on this very important point: Jesus Christ and the grace of God are objectively present and offered to everyone who receives the eucharist. If some scholars are correct, Zwingli himself also taught a form of Christ's objective presence. In any case, all these views agree that only those who have faith actually receive the benefits of the eucharistic grace. Thus in varying formulations all these interpretations prevent the eucharist from becoming a magical rite by which humans manipulate God to produce automatic benefits.

Ecumenical conversations have produced significant advances over the animosities and sharp divisions between the traditional conceptions of Christ's presence. First, fuller knowledge of ancient church practice has made contemporary theologians aware that the views of Christ's eucharistic presence held since the Middle Ages have focused too exclusively on Christ's presence in the bread and wine. Now there is recognition that Christ is present throughout the eucharistic ritual in several other ways as well: in the reading and preaching of the word, in the assembled community, and in the presiding minister who represents Christ. Second, study of ancient Christian thinking has also recovered the profound understanding of remembrance as mindfulness of the past, present, and future Christ. This may bring those who identify with Zwingli to a deeper, less subjective understanding of Christ's presence. Third, while the several church traditions have continued to affirm the heart of their historic positions regarding Christ's presence, a number of ecumenical dialogues have suggested that some differences in an objective understanding of Christ's eucharistic presence need not continue to divide the churches. In other words, it may be possible to allow a certain diversity of opinion on this question within a united church.

b. Communion with other Christians. Holy Communion is also an occasion for communion with other Christians. This begins with one's own congregation or parish. Paul speaks of the church as the body of Christ, and this social body of Christ is first of all the local church. Many Christians and perhaps especially many young adult Christians are highly critical of the local church of their family. They see the foibles and petty behavior of these people whom they have observed for several years, so they do not admire many of these local people. Yet the eucharist is an event that reminds Christians that their local church with all its faults is still the body of Christ, and this implies a presence of Christ among them. So one of the many threads of meaning in Holy Communion is that the ritual enacts and strengthens the common bond of participation in Christ.

Communion with Christians beyond the local church is especially manifested in the prayers that immediately precede the reception of the elements. At this point intercessions commonly are offered for church leaders and for Christians around the world. Probably the worldwide character of the Christian community is experienced most powerfully when a person or group has Holy Communion in a foreign land.

c. Communion with all people and other creatures. The bond of Christians with all humans is also expressed in the intercessory prayers just prior to receiving the elements, for the usual practice is to pray for persons and groups in need all around the world, regardless of their religious affiliation. The link with other people and creatures is also symbolized in the bread and wine. Both elements come from natural products of grain and grapes which are then fashioned by human labor into bread and wine. Indeed, the transformation of bread and wine that takes place in Holy Communion is a powerful symbol of the eschatological transformation of the entire universe in the ultimate future of God's reign.

By now your head may be swimming from the many meanings of the eucharist that we have discussed. And these are not all the possible meanings associated with this ritual. Christians cannot entertain all these meanings simultaneously or even on one occasion of receiving Holy Communion. However, awareness of the richness of significance in this sacrament may certainly enhance participation in the eucharist.

Other Sacraments or Rites

As we saw in our discussion of sacraments in general, there are differences among Christians over the number of sacraments. Orthodox and Catholic Christians recognize seven sacraments, while Protestants generally acknowledge only two sacraments—baptism and eucharist. Nonetheless, the other five sacraments accepted by Orthodox and Catholic are often observed by Protestants as sacred rites, even though they are not called sacraments. These other five rituals are confirmation, penance or reconciliation, ordination, marriage, and anointing for healing. It is to these that we now turn our attention.

Confirmation

Confirmation is a Christian ritual that is looking for a meaning; indeed, its meaning today is far from clear. This fact will become evident if we first quickly sketch out the history of this rite and then go on to ask the question about its meaning.

The historical development of confirmation begins with the New Testament. The central gesture underlying confirmation is *laying on of hands* for the person being initiated into the church. In the Book of Acts, when it tells of someone being baptized, it is sometimes (but not always) said that hands were laid on the person (for instance, Acts 9:17-18, but see Acts 8:38). It soon became customary when baptizing to also lay hands on the person. Before long the practice emerged of also anointing the baptized with oil; this was called *chrism*. Originally the laying on of hands and anointing were done simultaneously with baptism by the bishop. Thus a person being initiated into the church was baptized, had laying on of hands, and participated in the eucharist all on the same occasion. This is still the practice of the Orthodox Church, which thereby admits infants and very young children to Holy Communion. The initiation need not be done by a bishop, however; the usual Orthodox custom is for a priest to do it, although using anointing oil consecrated by the bishop.

Development in the Western church proceeded differently. Here during the early Middle Ages, confirmation and first communion became separated from baptism mostly because of practical difficulties in celebrating them together. The difficulty was that as many people in rural areas of Europe converted to Christianity, it was impossible to continue with the ancient custom of having a bishop present to do confirmation. So the practice arose in the Roman Catholic Church of delaying confirmation for both baptized infants and adults until the bishop could get to the local church. Participation in Holy Communion was then also delayed. The Protestant churches that emerged since the sixteenth century followed what had become the custom in the West by delaying confirmation for those baptized as infants, although adults were confirmed at the same time as being baptized. Following the Second Vatican Council, the Roman Catholic Church has revived a shorter form of the ancient catechumenate in its Rite of Christian Initiation of Adults, which normally concludes on Easter with baptism, laying on of hands, and the eucharist. However, when baptizing infants the prevailing practice in the Catholic Church and most Protestant churches is still to delay first communion and confirmation until some years after baptism. So in these churches, the meaning given to confirmation has assumed that the rite most commonly occurs some years after baptism.

We will briefly examine three major meanings advanced for confirmation. One meaning suggested has been that confirmation *bestows the Holy Spirit.* In several New Testament passages the laying on of hands is associated with conferring the Holy Spirit. The problem is that baptism itself is also commonly believed to be a sign of the Spirit's presence. So how can confirmation give what has already been given in baptism? A second proposed meaning attempts to deal with this problem by saying that confirmation *strengthens the baptized for Christian living with an extra measure of the Spirit.* This makes sense if confirmation comes some considerable time later than baptism, but it does not appear appropriate for those baptisms that are immediately followed by laying on of hands and anointing. A third meaning that has wide support is that confirmation is the sacrament or rite in which *the baptized now make their own mature affirmation of faith.* Obviously this meaning also presumes the practice of a confirmation that is substantially separated in time from an early-age baptism. But again the meaning does not fit the Orthodox practice or the initiation of adults in Protestant rites and the Catholic Rite of Christian Initiation of Adults, for in these cases baptism and confirmation are given almost simultaneously.

Today there is considerable divergence between prevailing church practice of confirmation and the opinions of many theologians about the rite. On the one hand, the prevalent procedure in the Catholic Church as well as most Protestant churches is to baptize infants and delay confirmation until the teenage years. Of course, for those Protestant churches that use only believer baptism, the problem of what to do with confirmation's laying on of hands does not even arise. On the other hand, many theologians, both Catholic and Protestant, are painfully aware of the inconsistencies between confirmation practice and the proposed meanings of the rite. Catholic theologian William Bausch favors restoring the unity of confirmation and baptism either by doing both in infancy or by enrolling infants in a catechumenate that would last for some years and end with baptism, confirmation, and first communion.[14] Protestants Browning and Reed recommend that for children of practicing Christians baptism, confirmation, and first communion should be given all at once. They go on to say that confirmation should be a repeatable ritual, repeated at those times in a person's life when his or her faith goes through a major reformulation that results in a renewed commitment.[15] This approach is one way of restoring the original unity of the three rites and yet recognizing the practical wisdom of having some ritual in which a person baptized as an infant may declare his or her faith. I myself think that the laying on of hands closely associated with baptism should never have developed into a distinct sacrament or rite; this laying on of hands should be as much an integral part of baptism as making the sign of the cross. However, I agree that there is wisdom in having a distinct ritual of another laying on of hands linked with the continued work of the Spirit in baptized persons' lives and their own expression of Christian commitment; it would be appropriate to call this ritual confirmation. Whatever the opinions of individual theologians on the matter, church practices of confirmation are not likely to change soon. Hence, confirmation will still be searching for a consistent meaning.

Penance or Reconciliation

The spiritual concern underlying any rite of penance is repentance or conversion of someone within the Christian church; that is, when a Christian sins, especially in a serious way, then she or he needs to turn away from that sin and return to unity with God and the church. Penance is the sacrament or rit-

14. William J. Bausch, *A New Look at the Sacraments*, rev. ed. (Mystic, Conn.: Twenty-Third Publications, 1983), 122.
15. Browning and Reed, *The Sacraments in Religious Education and Liturgy*, 139, 192.

ual that deals with repentance and conversion from sins after baptism. Penance has gone through some major changes in form during its history. In recent years the Roman Catholic Church has made important revisions in the sacrament, although frequency of participation of Catholics in the sacrament has declined. Meanwhile, among Protestants, who had largely abandoned any rite of private confession, many are feeling the need for such a rite. As I explain these ideas in this section, we will see that there has been and continues to be considerable ferment going on in regard to penance. We will begin by distinguishing four stages in the historical development of penance.

The first stage is what is called *canonical penance*, which existed in a rather fluid, informal way in the first churches during New Testament times and in a more formal way from the second century until about the seventh century. The author of the New Testament Letter to the Ephesians exhorts Christians to be "kind to one another, tenderhearted, forgiving one another, as God in Christ has forgiven you" (Ephesians 4:32). Provision for dealing with the sin of another member of the church also appears in the New Testament. Christians should talk to the one who has sinned against them; if reconciliation is not reached, then other members of the church should be called in and, if need be, the entire congregation. If the offender refuses to listen even to the whole congregation, then he or she should be excluded from the church. "Truly I tell you, whatever you bind on earth will be bound in heaven, and whatever you loose on earth will be loosed in heaven" (Matthew 18:18). These words have often been taken as Jesus' authorization of the church's practice or sacrament of penance.

The close link seen here between reconciliation with God and reconciliation with the church is one of the hallmarks of canonical penance. In other words, it was not enough just to make peace with God inwardly, subjectively, for a serious sin was also an offense against the church. The church was meant to be holy, and a serious, public sin detracted from that holiness. What was considered a serious sin? Lists of grave sins from various early church documents indicate considerable diversity, but it was generally agreed that apostasy (denying the Christian faith), adultery, and murder were grave sins that required special reconciliation with the church as well as with God.

Another closely related feature of canonical penance was that the discipline of reconciliation with the church took a public form. That is, at least by the second century the person who had committed the serious sin was excluded by the bishop from Holy Communion, in a word, *excommunicated*. The sinner became part of a group of penitents who received special instruction and observed some disciplines aimed at furthering a deeper conversion of life. Those who had committed serious sin underwent this penitential discipline for some years, perhaps even until their deathbed before being readmitted to the eucharist as the outward sign of reconciliation with the church.

A further characteristic of canonical penance was that it could only be done once in a person's life. Of course, baptism forgave any sins committed up until that point and ordinary or venial sins were not subject to this rigorous discipline, but after baptism, there was only one opportunity given for repentance from a grave sin.

It is obvious that only people who had a very deep commitment to the Christian faith would undergo canonical penance. In fact, the practice became less and less common as time passed. Many delayed the sacrament or rite of penance until they were close to death; this meant that one would not prematurely use up the single chance for repentance from grave sin and also that one could avoid the rigors and embarrassment of that public penitential process.

By the end of the sixth century, Irish missionaries brought to the European continent another form of penitential practice called the *Irish tariff penance*, which rather quickly replaced the by-then almost unused canonical penance. Irish tariff penance had its origin in the many Irish monasteries in which a monk would discuss his spiritual life and failings with another monk, who would then suggest a penitential discipline and pray for God's forgiveness. This custom was soon extended to people outside the monastery. What evolved was a practice of penance that was private rather than public; that is, it involved individuals confessing their sins in private to a priest. Then the priest assigned a penance or discipline to be performed and announced absolution or forgiveness. The penance assigned was customarily taken from one of a number of books written by monks which listed various sins and for each sin gave the appropriate penitential discipline. This assigned penance was the penalty or tariff for the sin; hence the system has been called the Irish tariff penance.

The Irish tariff penance differed from canonical penance in several respects. Whereas the canonical penance was public, the Irish penance was private. While canonical penance emphasized the role of the church in reconciliation, the Irish approach put the stress on the individual's role. Whereas canonical penance could only be given once, Irish penance was repeatable many times. And while canonical penance dealt only with grave sins, Irish penance covered less serious, venial sins as well. Furthermore, whereas canonical penance envisioned the renewed conversion of the sinner as a long-term process that lasted many years, the Irish system viewed conversion of the sinner in a relatively short time frame, the time from one confession until the next. In the high Middle Ages to the Irish practice of penance was added a rather sophisticated theology of penance. Penance was understood to have four parts: contrition (sorrow for sin), confession of sin to a priest, penance or satisfaction for the sin (for instance, fasting or saying so many prayers), and absolution (the announcement of forgiveness by a priest). Private penance according to the Irish pattern prevailed in Catholicism until the Second Vatican Council (1962–1965).

The third major development regarding penance to which we should attend is that the Protestant Reformation launched several criticisms of Catholic penitential practice and over time the practice of private penance died out in most Protestant churches. Martin Luther started the Reformation discussions of penance by questioning some popular ideas of contrition, confession, and the necessity of receiving forgiveness through this sacrament. In respect to contrition, Luther insisted that genuine sorrow over one's sin was necessary; mere fear of future punishment in hell for one's sin (called attrition) was not sufficient. In regard to confession, Luther attacked the practice of *integral confession*, which was the obligation of the penitents to list in confession all their sins and the circumstances of them. Luther claimed that it is impossible for a person to be recall every specific act of sin, and to insist upon this is to place an undue burden on the Christian's conscience. Luther also rejected the idea that God's forgiveness was obtainable only through the sacrament of penance; what brings forgiveness is faith in God's promise of mercy, which is not limited to this sacrament. Finally, although Luther eventually did not recognize penance as a sacrament, he thought it was important to retain it as a church rite. While private penance was observed as a rite among some Protestants well into the seventeenth century, in the end the practice virtually disappeared from Protestant churches; what commonly remained was a purely group confession of sin and general announcement of absolution in Sunday worship.

The fourth stage of development with penance is recent reform of the rite. Reform of penance was initiated by the Second Vatican Council and resulted in a new Rite of Penance that has been operative in Catholicism since 1976. This rite offers three forms of penance. First, there is a reformed rite of individual penance. While this is done in privacy, the penitent generally has the option of either following what had become the traditional pattern of making confession with a screen between the penitent and the priest or of a face-to-face meeting with the priest like the Irish custom long ago. Second, there is a communal rite which includes a time for individual, private confession and absolution. This rite puts a clear emphasis on reconciliation with the church as well as with God, an emphasis that was prominent in the ancient canonical penance. Third, provision is made for a purely communal confession and absolution; this is reserved for very special situations such as in the military when a priest might give penance to a large group of men and women about to go into battle.

These revisions in the Rite of Penance are the fruit of considerable rethinking of the whole practice. One new emphasis in Catholic thinking has been to view the Rite of Penance within a larger context of occasions of reconciliation. That is, reconciliation with God and the church should not be confined to the sacrament of penance. For instance, the *Catechism of the*

Catholic Church (1994) calls attention to many forms of reconciliation in Christian life: informal reconciliations with family, friends, neighbors, and co-workers; concern for reconciliation in society through working for justice and the poor; and seeking reconciliation through the eucharist, prayer, and meeting privately with a spiritual director. The sacrament of penance should be the high point of experiences of reconciliation, rather than the only occasion for it. Another, related emphasis in recent Catholic thinking about penance has been to put a stronger accent on the primary concern of the ancient canonical penance—reconciliation with the church community.[16] The ritual option of setting private confession in the context of a community worship occasion is a clear expression of this emphasis.

In spite of the liturgical reforms in the Rite of Penance, actual use of the sacrament has fallen off considerably among Catholics. In part, this can be attributed to a decline in the social cohesiveness of the average Catholic parish. As William Bausch says, "It will be difficult to gather a sense of community concerning reconciliation when people really don't feel a part of their parishes to begin with."[17] There probably is more to it than that, for this does not account for the drop in private confessions. It would seem, though, that a decline in use of the sacrament of penance is also in part a consequence of the new emphasis on reconciliation in the whole of the Christian life. If the Rite of Reconciliation is meant to be the peak of reconciling experiences for the Christian rather than the only occasion, then it seems reasonable that faithful Catholics would make use of such a peak experience less frequently than before.

There has also been some rethinking of penance in Protestantism. Many Protestants feel that the community confession and absolution that is common in Protestant worship does not enable the Christian message of forgiveness and reconciliation to penetrate the hearts and minds of church members. While Protestants may frequently hear the gospel of reconciliation, many of them do not *feel* forgiven and reconciled with God and other people. Thus there have been some attempts to revive a ritual of private penance which would meet this need. The *Book of Common Prayer* of the Episcopal Church has two rites of private confession, and the *Lutheran Book of Worship* has a rite of Individual Confession and Forgiveness. In addition, many Protestant pastors find that what often happens informally in pastoral care and counseling is that they hear a person's confession and speak the message of forgiveness to that person. It is obvious to many that there is a widespread need for some private form of reconciliation with God and others that is not met by the standard public confession. Thus there is a good deal of ferment regarding penance in both Protestant and Catholic circles.

16. *Catechism of the Catholic Church*, 360–61.
17. Bausch, *A New Look at the Sacraments*, 187.

Ordination or Orders

While this topic often draws a big yawn from lay Christians, it is a hot issue among those engaged in ecumenical discussions among churches. Different conceptions of ordained ministry remain major points of division between churches. In this very brief treatment, we can only touch on some of the issues.

Recent scholarship in the Bible and early Christianity has altered the arguments used in defense of a particular conception of ordained ministry. Previously it had been common for some churches such as the Presbyterian and Roman Catholic to argue that their understanding of ordained ministry was solidly grounded in the Bible and very early church. Now scholars have shown that there was no single pattern of church organization in the New Testament. Rather, there was a variety of patterns. For example, the Jerusalem church at first was led by the remaining original eleven disciples of Jesus now called apostles (those who are sent), who were assisted in caring for the needy by seven elders. But some different offices are mentioned by Paul in his letter to the church at Corinth in Greece, "And God has appointed in the church first apostles, second prophets, third teachers" (1 Corinthians 12:28). He then goes on to mention other spiritual gifts; apparently in the churches Paul knew, the positions of prophet and teacher had influence second only to that of an apostle. Furthermore, there is strong evidence that women as well as men filled important leadership positions in the church of Paul's time and earlier; but soon thereafter women were excluded from such positions.[18] Although we cannot clearly trace any uniform church order back to Jesus and the first Christian churches, it is clear that Jesus did establish *some* sort of designated persons for leading the mission and life of the community that followed him.

By the beginning of the second century, a threefold pattern of church order was emerging in some areas: a single *bishop* (coming from the Greek *episcope*, overseer) presided over a local town church and was assisted by a group of *presbyters* and some *deacons*. But elsewhere such as in mid-second century Rome, the church was governed by a group of presbyters. By the third century the *monarchical episcopate*, in which a single bishop was overseer of a region containing many churches, each with its own presbyter or priest, had become the prevailing pattern. In these early centuries bishops played an important role in keeping the churches faithful to the apostolic tradition and separate from aberrant religious movements. In the Latin-speaking West a person was said to be ordained to a certain position or order in the church—bishop, presbyter/priest, deacon; hence the name, the sacrament or rite of orders.

18. Elizabeth Schüssler Fiorenza, *In Memory of Her* (New York: Crossroad, 1983), 264–66.

Passing over other developments in later centuries, we will focus on contemporary ecumenical discussions regarding ordination or the sacrament of orders. Ecumenical discussions have recognized considerable common ground on ordained ministry. One point of agreement is that the ordained ministry is now viewed within the context of the ministry or service of all Christians; all the laity or nonclergy are initiated by baptism into the *general ministry* of the church. A second common point is the recognition that some form of special, public ministry has always been present in the church. The usual ritual for appointing someone to this *ordained ministry* is the rite of ordination that consists centrally of invocation of the Holy Spirit and laying on of hands. A third point of agreement is that an ordained minister at the local level (what was once called the presbyter) has three basic responsibilities: proclaim the word, administer the sacraments, and give pastoral care. Thus the ordained ministry is often called the ministry of word and sacrament.[19]

Several differences over orders remain among the churches. First, there is the question of what form the ordained ministry should have. The predominant pattern, followed by Orthodox, Roman Catholic, and Anglican churches, is a threefold pattern of bishop, presbyter (priest, pastor), and deacon in descending order of authority and dignity. But many Protestant churches do not have bishops or ordained deacons, and if a Protestant church does have bishops or bishop-like figures, they are usually just regarded as a presbyter or pastor with a special function.[20]

Second, there is the question of *apostolic succession*. All churches claim to be faithful to the apostolic tradition, that is, to the teachings and practices of the apostles, who were the initial leaders of the Christian movement. But some churches have emphasized the importance of bishops as guardians of the apostolic tradition. The Orthodox, Roman Catholic, and Anglican churches also stress having bishops that are in apostolic succession. In my opinion, however, it is no longer clear what apostolic succession means. Once it was thought that bishops in apostolic succession could trace an unbroken historical link with the apostles; that is, that an apostle ordained bishop A who in turn ordained bishop B and so on down to bishop Z today. However, historians express considerable skepticism about the unbroken character of such links. The core of the idea seems to be that the apostles appointed leaders to assume oversight of the church after the apostles were dead, and that bishops are these successors to the apostles. But recent scholarship has demonstrated that there was a variety of patterns in church leadership in the initial centuries

19. Richard P. McBrien, *Catholicism*, rev. ed. (San Francisco: HarperSanFrancisco, 1994), 874–76.

20. For a defense of a single or twofold pattern of ordained ministry, see Ted Peters, *God—the World's Future*, 303–4.

of Christian history. As we noted earlier, the Roman church itself was led in its early years by a group of presbyters, not a bishop. Nevertheless, today the Anglican, Orthodox, and Roman Catholic churches say that their bishops are in apostolic succession, and they question the validity of ministry in churches without bishops in apostolic succession. This difference is an obstacle to further movement toward reunification of Christians.

A third difference among the churches over ordination is whether to ordain women as well as men. The Anglican (Episcopal) Church and many Protestant churches now ordain women, while the Roman Catholic, Orthodox, and other Protestant churches exclude women from the ordained ministry. The chief reasons given for not ordaining women are that Jesus selected only men to be the twelve disciples, that church tradition continued to ordain only men, and that women and men have significantly different natures. One of the main reasons given in support of ordaining women is that in the church human barriers should be broken down; in Christ there is neither male or female (Galatians 3:28). This difference in practice, however, is an obstacle to mutual recognition of ordained ministries as valid.

Marriage

A common thread running through the complex history of marriage is this: while nearly every authority in the biblical/Christian tradition has consistently viewed marriage as symbolic of some deeper meaning, many Christians also call marriage a sacrament.

First, marriage is often seen as symbolic of a deeper meaning, but authorities differ on precisely what that meaning is. The Bible does not present a well-developed, unified interpretation of marriage, but offers scattered insights on it. The two accounts of creation in Genesis 1–3 do not present a full symbolic interpretation of marriage. They are content to ground the distinction between female and male in God's creative will, so the sexuality underlying marriage is not merely an accident of human development. Genesis 1 emphasizes having children as the purpose of marriage, while the Genesis 2–3 story of Adam and Eve in the Garden of Eden portrays companionship as the fundamental purpose of marriage. An important symbolic rendering of marriage occurs later when some Old Testament prophets regard marriage as being symbolic of God's covenant relationship with Israel. In the New Testament also there are diverse comments on marriage. Jesus underscores the sanctity of marriage by taking a strict stand against divorce (Mark 10:1-12). Paul says that in light of the nearness of the reign of God, it is preferable to be celibate; yet marriage may be a practical necessity (1 Corinthians 7:1-9). And in what became a highly influential text, Ephesians 5:21-33 says marriage is symbolic of Christ's covenant relationship with the church.

An ambivalent attitude toward marriage was promoted by Augustine and many other Christian teachers until modern times. In the church traditions of both East and West, it was common to view marriage as a lower, less holy condition than the chaste single life of celibacy. Augustine (d. 430), on the one hand, regarded human sexual desire as deeply corrupted by the power of sin, yet said involvement in sex is permissible if done within the bounds of marriage. So sex even in marriage is not celebrated so much as a good, but as a tainted, dangerous necessity for continuing the human race. On the other hand, Augustine saw three important values in marriage. One value of marriage is that it produces children. Augustine saw this as the primary, but not the only purpose of marriage. Another value is the faithfulness of the married couple to one another and to their children. The third value of marriage is that the indissoluble bond between the spouses is a symbol of the future communion of all people in eternity. Augustine calls marriage a sacrament in the broad sense of a visible sign of eternal human community. We recall that Augustine believed there is an indefinite number of such sacraments. Since every faithful marriage, whether of Christians or not, is such a visible sign, Augustine does not think of marriage as a specifically Christian means of grace.

Theologians in the eleventh and twelfth centuries began to count marriage as a sacrament in the restricted sense of a means of grace for Christians. Marriage was officially counted as one of seven sacraments by the Council of Florence (1439) and again by the Council of Trent in the sixteenth century. Trent's position was taken in opposition to Martin Luther's denial of marriage as a sacrament in the restricted sense. In many respects Luther reaffirmed Augustine's teaching on marriage as a restraint upon sinful lust, yet having three values. However, Luther rejected the idea that marriage is less holy than celibacy, and saw profound positive significance in marriage as a Christian calling to serve God and others through the relationships of marriage and family.

The Roman Catholic understanding of marriage was significantly modified by the Second Vatican Council, yet maintains important ties to the tradition. One major modification is that marriage is no longer viewed as a less holy way of life than celibacy; so marriage is held in very positive light. A second shift is that the propagation of children is no longer given as the primary purpose of marriage; indeed, in the treatment of marriage in the *Constitution on the Church in the Modern World* (Latin title *Gaudium et Spes*) conjugal love is discussed first and then comes the matter of children. This shift is in keeping with a generally more interpersonal approach to the topic, rather than the legal emphasis on marriage as a contract with certain rights that had become predominant in recent centuries. Nevertheless, in continuity with a long tradition going back to Paul, the marital relationship is seen as a symbol of Christ's relationship with the church.[21] The contemporary Catholic theologian Francis Schüssler Fiorenza criticizes this Pauline tradition, though, for inculcating patriarchal attitudes in the family, since Paul compares the husband to Christ and the wife to the subordinate church. Following suggestions of his wife, the New Testament scholar Elisabeth Schüssler Fiorenza, Francis Schüssler Fiorenza argues that marriage is symbolic of the egalitarian community of the earliest Christian community and the future reign of God.[22]

Ecumenical discussions between Orthodox and Roman Catholic theologians found agreement on considering matrimony a sacrament. Protestant views of marriage converge but do not fully agree with the Orthodox and Catholic views. Part of the difficulty is semantic. Mostly what Catholic scholars Francis Schüssler Fiorenza and Richard McBrien mean by the "sacramentality" of marriage is that marriage is a visible sign or symbol of the wholesome community of the reign of God.[23] Protestants fully agree with Catholics and Orthodox on this score, for all it entails is the broad Augustinian meaning of sacrament. All agree, therefore, in rejecting the popular notion that the fundamental meaning of marriage consists in a couple's romantic love; not only do Christian theologians understand true marital love to be deeper than romantic love, but the couple's love should be understood as a symbol and foretaste of the loving community that will embrace all people in the reign of God. A difference persists, though, on whether marriage should be counted as one of the church's official sacraments. Differences between Catholic and Protestant also exist on the permissibility of divorce and the use of artificial means of birth control in marriage.

Anointing of the Sick

There are two New Testament texts that are commonly appealed to as scriptural precedents for the rite of anointing the sick. The main text is James 5:14-15, "Are any among you sick? They should call for the elders of the church and have them pray over them, anointing them with oil in the name of the Lord. The prayer of faith will save the sick, and the Lord will raise them up; and anyone who has committed sins will be forgiven." Here we see the physical act of anointing with oil linked with prayer for healing. Similarly, when Jesus sent out his twelve disciples to do ministry in Israel, the description of their ministry includes this remark: "They cast out many demons, and

---

21. *Constitution on the Church in the Modern World* in *The Documents of Vatican II*, Walter M. Abbott, ed. (New York: American, 1966), sections 47–50.

22. Francis Schüssler Fiorenza, "Marriage," in *Systematic Theology: Roman Catholic Perspectives*, Vol. 2, 330–32.

23. Ibid.; see also McBrien, *Catholicism*, 856–63.

anointed with oil many who were sick and cured them" (Mark 6:13). Again healing is linked with anointing with oil. We do not know whether anointing of the sick was practiced during the first four centuries of Christian history, since there is no documentary evidence of it. The initial written testimony of it appears around 400, and other evidence follows.

At the beginning of the ninth century a major shift in the practice of anointing took place in Western Christianity. At this time anointing came to be understood as the "last rites" for the dying. Several centuries later Peter Lombard called the rite *extreme unction*, that is, the last unction or anointing. This conception of the rite was officially approved at the Council of Florence in 1439. The Council of Trent modified this slightly by not limiting it to the dying, yet said anointing was "particularly" for those near death. So the practice of making anointing the last rite for the dying prevailed in Catholicism until the Second Vatican Council.

Vatican II restored the practice of the early church and underscored this understanding by recommending that the sacrament be called Anointing of the Sick rather than Extreme Unction. In other words, anointing of the sick is for any seriously ill or infirm person, not just those close to death. Indeed, Vatican II also restored a final eucharist as the last rite for the dying, a rite commonly called *Viaticum*, which means provisions for a journey.[24]

While anointing of the sick recently has undergone extensive revision in Roman Catholicism, the rite is receiving more attention in many Protestant churches. In the sixteenth-century Protestant Reformation both Martin Luther and John Calvin denied that anointing of the sick was a sacrament, because it had only been instituted by an apostle (James) rather than by Christ himself. Calvin also said that Christ and his apostles healed in other ways besides anointing; they healed by having a person bathe in a pool or by using mud made with spit or simply by speaking. So why weren't these actions also sacraments? Both Calvin and Luther certainly approved of the practice of praying for healing, but did not want to limit it to last rites for the dying as in extreme unction or to a rite of anointing. In the last several decades many Protestants have shown renewed interest in a rite of anointing the sick. Anglican/Episcopalian and Lutheran worship books now have both a private and public rite for anointing of the sick. And as many scholars recommend that the number of rites called sacraments be more open and indefinite, Protestant liturgical scholars such as Methodists James White, Robert Browning, and Roy Reed say anointing of the sick, as well as the funeral rite, should be recognized as a sacrament.[25]

24. McBrien, *Catholicism*, 843–48; Regis A. Duffy, "Anointing of the Sick," in *Systematic Theology: Roman Catholic Perspectives*, Vol. 2, 253–56.

25. White, *Introduction to Christian Worship*, 263–68; Browning and Reed, *The Sacraments in Religious Education and Liturgy*, 267–69, 281–85.

The resurgence of interest in anointing of the sick is coupled with revitalization of a healing ministry in general among Christians in recent years. Certainly the many accounts of healing in Jesus' life story testify to the importance he placed on this ministry to the whole person. The Pentecostal/charismatic movement and greater awareness of body and mind unity have both contributed to a strengthened healing ministry. In any event, concern for healing and attention to a rite of anointing the sick is consistent with the effort to incorporate all aspects of human experience into the Christian story. So anointing of the sick encourages Christians to see their illness as having profound meaning through participation in the death and resurrection of Jesus Christ.

Having completed our examination of sacraments and sacred rites, in the third part of this chapter we shall turn to a discussion of several Christian devotional practices.

Devotional Practices

Prayer

Prayer is the most prevalent devotional act among Christians. Polls show that even most of those people who drop out of corporate Christian worship and its sacraments continue to pray. So prayer deserves our thoughtful attention.

Participating in the very act of prayer says a great deal about one's conception of ultimate reality. For instance, ardent Zen Buddhists spend much time in meditation to train their mind, but they do not pray. The act of praying assumes that ultimate reality is an Other to whom one can speak and from whom a response may be sought. Underlying the practice of prayer is the belief that our relationship with ultimate reality is something like an interpersonal relationship. Furthermore, a person's actual practice of prayer accurately discloses what his or her relationship with God is like. It shows the degree to which one's relationship with God is characterized by trust or distrust, devotion or convenience, living faith or mere inertia, love or fear. It reveals whether one thinks of God as kindly or severe, merciful or demanding, awesome or under human control, working with nature or intervening in nature.

Prayer is both a simple act that children do and a profound mystery that engages the deepest reflection of a Christian saint. One of the theological issues raised by prayer, especially prayers asking God to do something for oneself or others, is the issue of divine providence. You may recall that providence has to do with God's guidance of events in personal lives, history, and nature. The question that prayer raises is how is God related to events within the world. You may wish to look again at chapter 5 on providence and especially at the first three sections of that chapter.

We can begin to grasp some of the richness and depth of prayer if we think of it as an activity or relationship with four dimensions. These four dimensions of prayer are not stages which one goes through consecutively; rather, they may all be present simultaneously as aspects of one's whole communication with God.

One dimension of prayer is *speaking to God*. This is the most common aspect of prayer, for it is what children and adults do when they say their bedtime prayers, what families do when they pray before a meal, and what a Christian congregation does at various points in its worship services. When Christians speak to God, they express their thoughts in words either out loud or silently. Quite often people equate prayer with speaking to God, as though this were the only aspect of prayer. But this is a mistake, since speaking to God is simply the most commonly recognized form of prayer.

A second dimension of prayer is *listening to God*. Another name for this is *meditation* or *meditative prayer*. Christian meditation also involves the use of words and thoughts as a person reflects on his or her life in relationship to God. Common forms of Christian meditation are to ponder a passage in Scripture, some event in the life of Jesus, or some personal experience. Of course, scholars also ponder these things, but there is a big difference between such scholarly analysis and meditative prayer. The scholar is active in probing and asking questions; in fact, the scholar assumes a posture of control and dominance over the subject matter being queried. In contrast, the person engaged in meditative prayer is more receptive, relatively more passive. The stance of the meditator is openness to God, letting God speak through a Scripture passage, an event, or experience. It is appropriate to think of Christian meditation as listening to God. Listening is not the same as hearing, for listening is the endeavor to hear. The heart of Christian meditation is the endeavor to hear God speak in and through one's reflections on some portion of Scripture or another writing, an event, or some experience. Naturally, listening to God is interspersed with speaking to God, so that conversation and two-way communication are established.

Contemplation or *contemplative prayer* is the third dimension of prayer. This is more subtle and difficult to talk about, for the other dimensions of prayer more closely resemble our ordinary modes of awareness. The heart of contemplative prayer is awareness of God's presence. One analogy to this consciousness of God's presence is what sometimes happens between two very close friends when one is aware of the other's presence, although little or nothing is said. In this form of prayer, words recede and may cease altogether, yet there is consciousness of the presence of God. Paradoxically, contemplative prayer may also include awareness of the absence of God. As one who longs for and perhaps at times knows the immediate presence of God, the contemplative is also unusually sensitive to the absence of God and the human inability to grasp God in human ideas and words. Another name for contemplative prayer is mystical prayer, for the essence of Christian mysticism is consciousness of God's presence.[26]

The fourth dimension of prayer is *the communal dimension* in which humans support and teach one another. While prayer is chiefly a relationship with God, it also includes relationships with other people. This communal aspect is obviously expressed in intercessory prayer, in which the person praying beseeches God on behalf of others, but community is also manifested in corporate prayer, in which the words uttered by one person become the prayer of all. In less obvious ways, all prayer has a communal dimension, for even when a solitary person prays in the name of Jesus, she or he has learned to pray in this manner from other Christians.

Remembering that these four aspects of prayer are not successive stages and may be part of the total prayer experience of any one person or group, we will now consider two specific examples of Christian prayer: the Lord's Prayer and the Jesus prayer.

The *Lord's Prayer* is the most widely used Christian prayer, and it is a clear example of both speaking to God and communal prayer. Here is a contemporary translation of the Lord's Prayer, which is also called the Our Father:

> Our Father in heaven,
>   hallowed be your name,
>   your kingdom come
>   your will be done,
>   on earth as in heaven.
> Give us today our daily bread.
> Forgive us our sins
>   as we forgive those
>   who sin against us.
> Save us from the time of trial
>   and deliver us from evil.[27]

Three short comments on this prayer. First, the opening address to God as Father is characteristic of Jesus. Although Jesus may not have been the first Jew to address God as Father, he makes it his central way of speaking to God. We have already seen that this language is problematic for some people, for it is possible to construe the word *Father* in a patriarchal way. But to do so is

26. This understanding of contemplative prayer is primarily based on my own experience, but it has been confirmed recently by the monumental study of Bernard McGinn, *The Foundations of Mysticism*, Vol. 1 of *The Presence of God: A History of Western Christian Mysticism* (New York: Crossroad, 1992), xvii–xx.

27. This follows the reading in Matthew 6:9-13. A somewhat shorter version appears in Luke 11:2-4. Christian tradition has also added a conclusion to the prayer: "For the kingdom, the power, and the glory are yours, now and forever. Amen." Some such ending would have been customary in Jewish prayers.

clearly to misunderstand Jesus, for in his original language of Aramaic Jesus uses the intimate term *Abba*, which is closer to dad than to the more formal father. The essential point is that this Father "in heaven" transcends the domineering ways of an earthly patriarchal father.

Second, the nonpatriarchal nature of the Father in heaven is indicated by that fact that this Father creates genuine community among people; God is addressed as *Our* Father. God is understood as the Father of all people and perhaps as Father of all living things. No person is excluded when asking God to give "us" our daily bread or to forgive "our" sins. The Our Father is a *we* prayer.

Third, eschatological expectation of the ultimate future pervades the prayer. This is most evident in the petition, "Your kingdom come," for this expresses longing for God's reign to come with full justice and peace. But this is not a hope that seeks escape from the present world; rather, this hope for God's perfect justice and peace generates the desire that God's will be done now on earth as it is in heaven. Such a hope inspires people to live trusting in God for their *daily* bread, rather than anxiously trying to fortify themselves against the threats of the future. Such a hope also leads people to establish peace now through mutual forgiveness.

The *Jesus Prayer* is a form of devotion that has been nurtured especially in the Orthodox tradition. The standard words of this prayer are: "Lord Jesus Christ, Son of God, have mercy on me"; however, shorter and somewhat longer versions are also used. During the period of the fifth to eighth centuries, the Jesus Prayer emerged in Eastern Christianity as a specific spiritual way or practice. The goal of following this way has been restful awareness of Christ's presence beyond words and thoughts. So the goal is contemplative prayer. A Greek word for this quiet state of resting in God is *hesychia*, so the tradition that has cultivated the Jesus Prayer is called *hesychasm*.

In the tradition of hesychasm, the recommended way to contemplative union with Christ is frequent repetition of the Jesus Prayer. It has been common also to urge correlation of the prayer with one's breathing, so that one says or thinks "Lord Jesus Christ, Son of God" while inhaling and then "have mercy on me" while exhaling. This breathing pattern fosters stillness of body, mind, and heart. Ordinarily it takes years of using the Jesus Prayer to be given the gift of contemplative prayer.

While the Jesus Prayer has been nurtured by the Orthodox Church and especially among its monks, during the last forty years the Jesus Prayer has been used by many Roman Catholics and Protestants. So today it is likely that the Jesus Prayer is more widely used than at any time in its history.[28]

---

28. Kallistos Ware, "Ways of Prayer and Contemplation—Eastern," in *Christian Spirituality: Origins to the Twelfth Century*, ed. Bernard McGinn, John Meyendorff, and Jean Leclercq (New York: Crossroad, 1988), 395–410.

Devotion to the Saints and Mary

The word *saint* is used among Christians in several ways. Saint may refer to any Christian; so Paul addresses all the members of the church in the region of Corinth as saints (2 Corinthians 1:2). Saint may also designate any of the dead who have entered into eternal life. Or saint may mean someone who is an example of holiness, some of whom have been widely recognized as such either by custom or by a formal church process called *canonization*. Among Orthodox and Roman Catholics Mary, the mother of Jesus, is regarded as preeminent among the saints. Devotion to saints involves various practices expressing veneration or reverence of Mary and the other saints in heaven. The nature of these devotional practices has developed over time, and the validity of some practices and related teachings has been a matter of dispute among Christians. First, we shall look briefly at the historical development of devotion to saints and Mary mainly in the Roman Catholic tradition. Second, we shall consider the role of this devotion in Orthodoxy, Protestantism, and contemporary Catholicism.

Veneration of saints has some precedent in scriptural passages that hold up various Old Testament figures as models of faith (Hebrews 11:4—12:1; Romans 4:13-25). However, veneration of saints took new forms in the second century when it became common to show special reverence to Christian *martyrs* (those who died for the faith) by visiting where they had lived or were buried and by praying to them to perform miracles for the living; before long their relics were also venerated. After legalization of Christianity in the fourth century when there were few new martyrs, veneration was extended to other heroes of the faith such as confessors (those who suffered but did not die for the faith), ascetics, as well as outstanding teachers and leaders. Following the Roman system of patronage, saints came to be seen as heavenly patrons of certain individuals, groups, or endeavors. The saints therefore were viewed as standing *between* God and those on earth; people on earth would then petition the saints to intercede for them with God. In 787 the Second Council of Nicea sought to curb abuses by distinguishing between *worship* which is due to God alone and *veneration* which is properly given to the saints. During the Middle Ages veneration of the saints flourished in both the Eastern and Western churches. One significant development in the West was the frequent portrayal of Christ as a strict judge, so then people looked to the saints as more accessible.

In the early sixteenth century, Protestant reformers criticized certain abuses such as collecting more and more relics of saints, but went further by rejecting invocation of (praying to) saints and Mary. Catholic leaders also sought to correct abuses, but responded to basic Protestant objections by strongly encouraging veneration and invocation of the saints as a badge of Catholic identity clearly distinguishable from Protestantism. Until the Second Vatican Council, Catholics commonly understood their relationship to the saints as that of earthly petitioners and heavenly patrons.

Vatican II brought about an important shift in thinking about the saints; rather than the traditional way of seeing the saints being *between* earthly believers and God, now the saints were envisioned as being *with* believers in one vast communion with Christ that spans time and eternity. This shift was accomplished in part by placing the Council's main teaching about saints toward the end of the *Dogmatic Constitution on the Church*. Thus the Council underscored the fact that the saints in heaven are also part of the one church whose head is Christ. Rather than being viewed as highly placed patrons who can put in a good word for people with a remote deity, the saints are now seen as forerunners and companions in the total church.

Veneration of Mary followed a development roughly similar to that of the saints, although there were differences in detail and especially in doctrine. In the New Testament Mary is directly mentioned in all four Gospels and Acts, but Mary was not prominent in the preaching and teaching of Paul who refers to her only once indirectly when he says, "God sent his Son, born of a woman" (Galatians 4:4). Testimony in the Synoptic Gospels (Matthew, Mark, and Luke) varies considerably. Matthew says little about Mary other than to affirm her virginity prior to Jesus' birth (Matthew 1:25). Luke depicts Mary in very favorable light as a faithful and obedient hearer of God's Word who is highly favored by God to be the mother of the Messiah. In her song of praise, called the Magnificat, Mary speaks as one of the marginal of society (Luke 1:26-56). On the other hand, twice Mark says that when Jesus visited his hometown of Nazareth, his family did not believe in him; Mary is not singled out for exception from this (Mark 3:21; 6:4). Devotion to Mary has focused upon the favorable picture of her in Luke and the latter part of John, which says she was present at the crucifixion (John 19:25-27).

Mary is hardly mentioned in the existing second-century Christian sources. When celibacy became a highly valued state of life in the third century, the belief that Mary was a *perpetual* virgin was almost universally accepted. Devotion to Mary gained a big boost when the Council of Ephesus in 431 approved the title of her as "Mother of God" and not merely "Mother of Christ." Veneration of Mary followed the same pattern that we observed with the saints in general: she came to be thought of as a powerful heavenly patron standing between God and people on earth. Germanus (d. 733) and others called her Mediatrix and held that she was able to turn away God's wrath from sinners. The great Bernard of Clairvaux (d. 1153) said that God's grace is channeled not only through Christ but also through Mary; his phrase "everything through Mary" became a widely held principle.

There was long discussion of two beliefs about Mary that eventually became official doctrines of the Roman Catholic Church. One of these Marian teachings is the doctrine of the *Immaculate Conception*. This is often confused with the virginal conception of Jesus, but the doctrine deals with the idea that Mary was free of sin (immaculate) from the very moment of her conception. Some major medieval theologians opposed the teaching: Anselm of Canterbury, Bernard of Clairvaux, Peter Lombard, and Thomas Aquinas. Bernard and Thomas both thought Mary was made free from sin after her conception while still in her mother's womb. So they too thought she was sinless, but Thomas opposed the idea of her being sinless at conception on the grounds that she would then not have needed redemption by Christ. Later in the Middle Ages this objection was countered by Duns Scotus (d. 1308) who argued that Christ redeems from both actual sins and from original sin, and in the singular case of Mary redeemed her from original sin at her conception. The sixteenth-century Council of Trent excluded Mary from its teaching of the universality of original sin. Finally in 1854 Pope Pius IX defined the Immaculate Conception as an infallible dogma.

The second Marian dogma is the *Assumption*, which declares that Mary was assumed body and soul into heaven. In other words, Mary does not need to wait until the general resurrection; because of her unique role in the economy of salvation, her sinless life, and her fullness of grace, she has been assumed into heaven and glorified. This is a relatively old Marian belief, for from about A.D. 700 various churches in Eastern and Western Christianity celebrated a feast of Mary's bodily assumption. One might ask, On what grounds was this belief arrived at? Catholic scholar Richard McBrien says,

> By now theology in the West had become increasingly divorced from the Bible. A rational, deductive kind of argumentation prevailed. One form . . . was known as the argument from convenience. Its structure was simple: God (or Christ) *could* do something; it was *fitting* that he should; therefore, he *did* it. *Potuit, decuit, fecit*. This principle would play a large role in the development of medieval Mariology.[29]

In 1950 Pope Pius IX defined the Assumption as an infallible doctrine. Both Marian dogmas flowed out of Marian piety, and in turn reinforced it.

The Second Vatican Council brought about a shift in thinking about Mary rather like it did with the saints. Whereas the traditional model had been of Mary as a powerful patron standing between God (Christ) and believers, Vatican II changed the emphasis. Again, this was done by placing the discussion of Mary as the last chapter in the *Dogmatic Constitution on the Church*. Here Mary is placed in close yet clearly subordinate relation to Christ, and she is seen in close relationship to all the faithful in the church. Mary has preeminence as the foremost model of what the church should be in its faith, love,

29. McBrien, *Catholicism*, 1086.

and hope and as the paradigm of what God's grace can do in people. Yet Mary's preeminence is set within her solidarity and community with all believers in the church. In the years since Vatican II, feminist and Third World liberation theologians have especially highlighted Mary's role as an advocate of the marginal and poor.[30]

What role does veneration of saints and Mary have in Orthodoxy, Protestantism, and contemporary Catholicism? Look again at this chart of church families (Figure 2). In general, those church families closest to the bottom of the chart are most deeply committed to veneration of saints and Mary, while those nearest the top are strongest in their reservations about the practice.

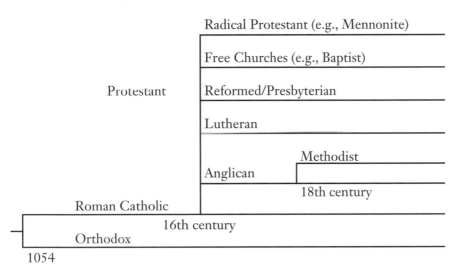

Figure 2
The Major Christian Church Families

Orthodox Christianity has long observed devotion to the saints and Mary. It believes in the Assumption, although Orthodoxy objects to the unilateral manner in which the papacy defined this dogma. The Orthodox believe that Mary was sinless, but they do not think she was free of original sin; thus they dissent from the Immaculate Conception.

There is a range of opinion among Protestants on these questions. Anglican and Lutheran reformers did not entirely reject honoring the saints, but they objected to *invocation* of the saints, that is, asking the saints for their help and prayers. The Lutheran Augsburg Confession (1530) says, "It is also

30. Elizabeth A. Johnson, "Saints and Mary," in *Systematic Theology: Roman Catholic Perspectives*, Vol. 2, 146–64. McBrien, *Catholicism*, 1077–1117.

taught among us that saints should be kept in remembrance so that our faith may be strengthened when we see what grace they received and how they were sustained by faith. Moreover, their good works are to be an example for us."[31] Martin Luther had a warm regard for Mary that even included endorsement of the Immaculate Conception as a likely opinion, but not as an essential article of faith.[32] The relatively positive attitude toward veneration of saints is evident in the common Lutheran and Anglican practices of naming churches after saints, remembering a certain saint on a specific day, and including in the liturgical calendar certain days such as the Annunciation in which Mary figures prominently in connection with Christ. Devotion to Mary and the saints has been especially cultivated by high church Anglicans, but addressing prayers to saints is rejected by the Anglican Articles of Religion. Lutherans and Anglicans do not necessarily deny that the saints and Mary pray for the church on earth, but they have persistently questioned asking for their intercessory prayers for two reasons: the practice detracts from Christ as sole mediator and it does not rest on any biblical command or promise. Today they generally reject the Assumption and Immaculate Conception as well as the sinlessness of Mary, because there is no explicit support for these teachings in the Bible.

John Calvin was more fully opposed to veneration of saints and Mary, because he was concerned that the practice fostered belief in their merit, which detracted from relying only upon the merit of Christ. Thus one does not find Reformed encouragements to keep the nonscriptural saints in remembrance nor does one ordinarily find a church in the Reformed tradition named after a saint. The same beliefs and practices are followed in the Free Church traditions.

In Catholicism one especially important form of Marian devotion has been the rosary. The *rosary* is a form of meditative prayer that has been widely used among Roman Catholics. The rosary had its origin in the twelfth century with devotions using the Our Father and prayers to Mary, and soon strings of beads were used to count the prayers. The devotion was called in Latin a *rosarium* (a rose garden), which was a common term for a collection of similar material. By the fifteenth century the rosary was employed in nearly its modern form.

A modern string of rosary beads looks like this (Figure 3, p. 309):

---

31. The Augsburg Confession, Article 21, in *The Book of Concord*, ed. Theodore G. Tappert (Philadelphia: Fortress Press, 1959), 46; cf. in the same volume Melanchthon's Apology of the Augsburg Confession, Article 21, 229–36.

32. Eric W. Gritsch, "The Views of Luther and Lutheranism on the Veneration of Mary," in *The One Mediator, The Saints, and Mary: Lutherans and Catholics in Dialogue VIII*, ed. H. George Anderson et al. (Minneapolis: Augsburg, 1992), 236–41.

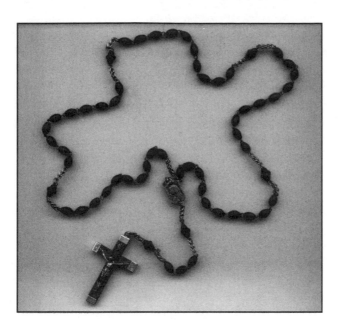

Figure 3

One begins by reciting the Apostles' Creed while holding the cross, and then saying the Our Father on each of the single, separated beads and a Hail Mary on each of the beads clustered together in groups. The Hail Mary goes:

> Hail Mary, full of grace,
>   the Lord is with thee;
>   blessed art thou among women,
>   and blessed is the fruit of thy womb, Jesus.
> Holy Mary, Mother of God,
>   pray for us sinners now
>   and at the hour of our death. Amen.

The Hail Marys are in groups of ten or decades, and each decade ends with saying another prayer called the Glory Be (Glory be to the Father and to the Son . . .). Thus, on one level the complete rosary, whether said publicly or privately, consists in three rounds of the beads, that is, a series of 150 Hail Marys divided into decades that begin with the Lord's Prayer and end with a Glory Be.

On a deeper level, though, the rosary is a meditation on the lives of Jesus and Mary. This takes the form of meditating on certain events in the lives of Mary and Jesus that are called *mysteries*. There are fifteen mysteries set in three groups of five: the joyful mysteries that deal with the birth and boyhood of Jesus, the sorrowful mysteries that concern the suffering and death of

Jesus, and the glorious mysteries that treat the glorification of Jesus and Mary. Thus while people are saying the vocal prayers, they are to be pondering the meaning of these mysteries and listening for what God has to say through the mysteries.

Protestants do not use the rosary, for as we have seen they object to prayers directed to Mary on the grounds that such prayers detract from Christ's position as mediator and they lack explicit biblical support. Catholic and Orthodox Christians who pray to Mary answer that they are really praying to Jesus Christ through Mary. They also say that asking the saints and Mary to pray for people on earth does not detract from Christ's role as mediator, just as asking a friend to pray for you does not undermine Christ's position. For reasons that are not altogether clear, since Vatican II use of the rosary as well as veneration of saints and Mary have greatly declined among most Catholics in Europe and North America, although the practice remains strong among Hispanic American, Third World, and Eastern European Catholics.

It appears that Protestant differences from Catholicism and Orthodoxy over invocation of saints and Mary will remain for the foreseeable future, for these dissimilarities reflect variations in the understanding of grace and in the relative weight of Scripture and church tradition. So the attitude toward these particular devotional practices becomes a symbol of a whole way of relating to God. The question is whether such differences in devotional practices need bar these churches from a greater degree of unity with one another. When Catholic and Lutheran theologians addressed this question in a dialogue, their answer was no. The Lutherans pointed to their Augsburg Confession and Apology of the Augsburg Confession as precedents for merely seeking their freedom from the *obligation* to invoke the saints and Mary—a freedom that Roman Catholics themselves already have. The Catholic theologians said Catholics could live in fellowship with Lutherans if Catholic invocation practices were respected. In short, both could recognize that this is a permissible difference consistent with fundamental agreement in the Christian faith.[33]

Differences over the Immaculate Conception and Assumption will also remain for some time. While the differences between Orthodox and Catholic on these matters are probably not great enough to bar eventual full union, their disagreements with Protestants are much greater. Here the issue becomes the relative importance of these two doctrines. If the two Marian dogmas are regarded as truly essential to the faith, then closer unity is not possible. But if the doctrines are not of central importance to the faith, then the door would be open to fuller unity without consensus on these points.

---

33. "Common Statement: The One Mediator, the Saints, and Mary," in Anderson, ed., *The One Mediator*, 56–58.

There is some precedent for this in the fact that Vatican II allowed limited eucharistic sharing between Catholics and Orthodox even though the Orthodox do not accept the Immaculate Conception. This point is also relevant for those Roman Catholics who dissent from either the Immaculate Conception or Assumption. Richard McBrien argues that such dissent by an otherwise faithful Catholic does not necessarily amount to lapsing from the Roman Catholic Church.[34]

This brings the chapter to a close. In this chapter we have dealt with three main topics: symbols, religious rituals that at least some churches call sacraments, and several Christian devotional practices. It is evident that when one grasps their meaning, Christian sacraments and devotional practices are far more than empty routines; they are powerful symbols that express and inculcate a rich understanding of human life in relationship to God and the divine purpose.

34. Ibid., 58–59; McBrien, *Catholicism*, 1102–1104.

11

Christianity and Other Religions

Throughout their history Christians have been aware of other religious people who were not Christian. Most first-generation Christians were Jews who had relatives and friends who did not believe in Jesus. During the next several centuries Christians lived among a host of other religious faiths in the Roman Empire. In the medieval period when Christianity dominated Europe, they lived with small communities of Jews and became mindful of the Muslims who conquered many ancient Christian territories and threatened the heart of Europe. When Europeans established colonies in the Americas and Far East, they encountered still other religions. And today as Christians travel throughout the world and at home meet people from other cultures, they often come into contact with different religions. So the issue of how Christians should view other religious faiths and relate to their adherents is not new.

Another part of this history of Christians interacting with people of other religious faiths is that frequently Christians have persecuted and discriminated against those with a different religion. Of course, Christians have not been the only ones to do this, and at times they themselves have known costly persecution. Nevertheless, the truth is that Christian history is blemished with oppression of other religious believers. The sorriest record concerns treatment of the Jews. Anti-Jewish statements by such Christian leaders as Martin Luther are an embarrassing reminder that the persecution was not merely the work of an ignorant few. Another sad chapter of Christian history is that conquest and colonization in the Americas and elsewhere was often justified in part by the claim of spreading Christianity. To be sure, most Christian missionaries were not out for personal gain. As an African Christian friend once said to me, "The missionaries were the best of the whites who came to Africa." Nonetheless, the Christian faith was mixed up with Western imperialism. So over the centuries the attitude of Christians toward other religious believers has often served as a legitimation for oppressing them.

With this history in mind, we must now turn our attention to the contemporary issue of Christianity and other religions, or what is today often called a theology of religions. That is, how should Christians understand the relationship between themselves and other believers, between their Christian faith and other religious faiths? We should be clear that here we are not talking about the relationships between Catholic and Protestant or Episcopalians and Baptists, for these are all groupings within the one religion of Christianity. Our focus is on how Christians should relate to Jews, Hindus, Muslims, Buddhists, and so forth. People of other religions must consider the issue from their own perspective, but those of us who are Christian must look at it from our point of view.

Three Views

Although there is a spectrum of opinion on this issue among Christian theologians today, three main views appear: exclusivism, inclusivism, and theological pluralism. It will help us think through the most important questions if we examine each of these positions.

1. *Exclusivism* has taken various forms down through history. Ever since the third century one form of exclusivism has stressed belonging to the Christian community, as expressed in the principle: outside the church there is no salvation. While this principle has been interpreted in several ways, at least it has meant that only those participating in the Christian community receive salvation. Today an exclusivist position most commonly regards salvation as dependent on an individual's faith in Jesus Christ. The most influential voice for Christian exclusivism in the last one hundred years has been the great Swiss Protestant theologian Karl Barth (d. 1968).

Karl Barth's view of Christianity and other religions is difficult to understand at first, because he uses the term *religion* in an unconventional way. To Barth, religion is a negative, ungodly activity, for in the many religions of the world he thinks humans are attempting to create their own pictures of God and seeking to justify themselves. This applies not only to the rituals and institutions of the major religions, but also to atypical forms such as the religion of social activism and the individualized religion of those who prefer their own personal beliefs to any religious institution. What makes all these instances of religion ungodly, according to Barth, is that in them humans try to remain in control. Humans produce their own concept of God or ultimate reality and try to justify themselves as worthy people. This is true of Christianity as a religion as well as other religions. So Barth agrees with the church's critics who see considerable pretense and external show in church life. But Barth goes further and attacks these critics for their own self-righteousness and unwillingness to listen to God. As Barth sees it, the many forms of personal and institutional religion, whether hypocritical or sincere, are all efforts of people to escape from God and manage their own lives. Barth sums it up by saying religion is unbelief.

Barth says that God is the only one who can provide a way out of the prison of religion through revelation. Karl Barth has made an important contribution to the understanding of this major theological concept of revelation. To reveal something is to make it known, to uncover what was previously covered. Barth emphasizes that what God reveals is primarily God's own self. God is Lord of all things and, thus, rightly the Lord of people's lives; this revelation comes as judgment upon people's efforts to direct their own existence, and thus as judgment on religion. Revealed also is God's mercy, whereby God reconciles humans to himself through Jesus Christ. The only revelation of God is given through the biblical history and above all in Jesus Christ. Since Christianity carries the biblical message, God can use some of its forms to break through the human-centeredness of religion and bring about revelation, but this always depends on a new action of God and is not under human control.

The only appropriate response to divine revelation is faith and, according to Barth, this means faith in Jesus Christ and the triune God. Having faith in Jesus Christ is an "event," that is, it is actually living right now with trust and obedience to God. The moment people trust in their own piety, respectability, or unconventionality, they have turned away from faith into the unbelief of religion.[1]

Now we can see why Karl Barth's view of the religions is an example of exclusivism. According to Barth, the only genuine revelation of God is given through the biblical history and especially Jesus. To be sure, Barth finds fault with all religions including Christianity, so Christianity as religion is not better than other religions. Yet there is an exclusivity about God's revelation. Another exclusive element is that salvation comes only through faith in Jesus Christ. However, here Barth surprises us. Whereas we might expect him to say that only genuine Christian believers will be saved and the great mass of non-Christians damned, Barth so emphasizes the priority of God's will to save all people that he hopes beyond death God will save everyone through Jesus Christ. On this point many other exclusivists criticize Barth.

---

1. Karl Barth, *Church Dogmatics*, Vol. I/2, trans. G. T. Thomson and Harold Knight (New York: Scribner's, 1956), 297–325.

The exclusivist outlook is very strong in conservative Christian circles, which include but are not limited to Evangelicals and Fundamentalists. The exclusivist position is clearly stated with only slight variation from Barth by the contemporary Evangelical theologian Donald Bloesch:

> Christianity will not tolerate the view that there are many revelations or various roads to salvation. . . . In the Christian perspective God has revealed himself fully and definitively in the person of Jesus Christ and has through his work made available to humankind an all-sufficient redemption. The truth of creation is indeed reflected in all world religions, but the saving Gospel of reconciliation and redemption is to be found only in Christianity. There are many roads by which man seeks to come to God, but there is only one road by which God comes to man, namely, Jesus Christ.[2]

2. *Inclusivism* is exemplified by another giant of Protestant theology in the twentieth century, Paul Tillich (d. 1965). Tillich also has an unusual concept of religion, for he understands religion very broadly as ultimate concern. The ultimate concern of a person or community is whatever concerns them most of all; it is their highest priority. The ultimate concern of many people is directed toward God or a higher principle; these are commonly called religions. But secular "quasi-religions" such as communism also involve an ultimate concern.

Tillich also has a very broad concept of revelation, for he thinks there is a revelation of God present within all cultures and religions. Every revelation has elements that are universal (for people in all times and places) and elements that are particular (pertaining to a specific time and place). There is no revelation in general, for we human beings always exist in a specific cultural situation. Since Tillich believes some revelation of God is grasped within each religion and quasi-religion, he denies that Christianity has the one true revelation and all other religions are false. Yet Tillich does not say that all religions are equally valid. The criterion by which all the religions, including Christianity, are to be judged is Jesus as the Christ. Obviously he says this as a Christian.

One might ask, "By what right does he claim that Jesus as the Christ is the standard for evaluating all religion?" Part of Tillich's answer is that there is no such thing as a purely universal perspective for any human being, for we always exist in a particular time and place within a particular tradition. Thus the Christian must appeal above all to that which lies at the base of Christianity, Jesus as the Christ. He expects faithful Buddhists or Hindus will look to their own foundation.

---

2. Donald G. Bloesch, *Essentials of Evangelical Theology*, Vol. 2 (San Francisco: Harper & Row, 1979), 248, 249.

Has Tillich fallen back into Christian exclusivism by insisting on Jesus Christ as the criterion? Tillich denies this, for instead of exclusivism's outright rejection of other religions, he endorses a dialectical relation between the religions, which includes both acceptance and rejection.[3] Tillich argues that throughout its history, Christianity has confronted other religions predominantly in this dialectical manner. Of course, this has been true of Christianity's relation with Judaism, for Christians have treated the Hebrew Bible as Holy Scripture and taken over some of the ritual and terminology of Judaism while insisting, contrary to Judaism, that Jesus is the Messiah. Christianity also borrowed from the mystery religions in the ancient Roman world as well as later from the religious practices of the Germanic tribes. For example, the evidence strongly suggests that although the specific day of Jesus' birth is not known, it came to be observed on the winter solstice (December 25 in the old Julian calendar, January 6 in the Egyptian calendar), the day many pagans celebrated the start of their sun god's return. Yet Christian acceptance of this festival date was combined with rejection of worshiping the pagan deity. Christians began to call Jesus Christ the "Sun of Justice." Christians subjected the pagan practice to their criterion of Jesus as the Christ.

Tillich favors this dialectical approach today as Christians encounter people of other religions. On the one hand, he rejects exclusivism, for he believes dialogue should replace the effort to convert other believers. On the other hand, he opposes trying to mix the religions to form some supposedly common, universal religion, which would be merely a lifeless concept. The universal can only be found by plunging deeply into the particulars of a specific tradition.

Not all inclusivists agree with Tillich on everything, yet he exemplifies the principal points that can be identified as Christian inclusivism. First, many religions involve a faithful response to God, so Christians may discover in them some insight into God. Second, the Christian operates with faith in God as understood in Jesus and with the presumption that this tradition is fundamentally true. Third, if a conflict in basic belief appears between Christian faith and another religion, one begins with the presumption that the Christian belief is more true. While this is Christian inclusivism, one could also speak of Muslim or Buddhist inclusivism. For instance, a Muslim inclusivist would value some insights of other religions, yet give priority to God as understood in the Koran. The basic stance of inclusivism is an open attitude toward other religions, yet a firm commitment to one's own religious tradition and the presumption that it is more true than conflicting beliefs.

---

3. Paul Tillich, *Christianity and the Encounter of the World Religions*, Fortress Texts in Modern Theology (1963; Minneapolis: Fortress Press, 1994), 28–30.

3. *Theological Pluralism* is a third major view of the relations among the religions that has emerged quite strongly in the last two decades. Everyone must recognize what we might call social pluralism, that is, the obvious fact that there is a plurality of religions in the world and a plurality of perspectives within each religion. But theological pluralism goes further to argue for a certain way of understanding the relationships among these various religions and the claims to truth that they make. The foremost spokesperson for theological pluralism is the British philosopher of religion John Hick. Among the family characteristics of religion, Hick focuses on two features: that religion is a response to a transcendent reality, which he refers to as the Real or Ultimate Reality, and that the great world religions are deeply concerned with transformation of human life. Hick makes important claims about both of these features of religion when he proposes,

> the pluralistic hypothesis that the great world faiths embody different percep-
> tions and conceptions of, and correspondingly different responses to, the Real
> from within the major variant ways of being human; and that within each of
> them the transformation of human existence from self-centeredness to Reality-
> centeredness is taking place. These traditions are accordingly to be regarded as
> alternative soteriological "spaces" within which, or "ways" along which, men
> and women can find salvation/liberation/ultimate fulfilment.[4]

We can distinguish four points in John Hick's theological pluralism. First, the religions of the world are diverse responses to the Real. The differences among religions derive from the diverse cultures and situations in which humans live. For instance, some religious traditions think of the Real as a personal God, while other traditions conceive of the Real as impersonal. Hick rejects both the exclusivist view that only one of these beliefs is true and the skeptical, naturalistic view that all beliefs about a transcendent are merely human fantasies. He thinks that the Real is the ground of all such beliefs about the transcendent.

Second, the Real in itself remains unknown and unknowable. Here Hick draws on the great German philosopher Immanuel Kant (d. 1804), who distinguished sharply between a thing in itself and our experience of that thing. For example, while we experience the chair on which we're sitting as a solid object, the chair in itself is not necessarily solid. Indeed, physicists tell us that the apparently solid chair is mostly empty space and energy, although we must remember that the physicists' view is also an interpretation and does not grasp the reality of the chair in itself. According to Kant, the thing in itself is beyond our reach, unknowable; all we have are our interpreted experiences of it. John

---

4. John Hick, *An Interpretation of Religion: Human Responses to the Transcendent* (New Haven: Yale University Press, 1989), 240.

Hick applies this idea to the Real and our experience of it. Hick says the Real in itself is unknowable. All we have are our experiences of the Real, and these experiences vary in the different religions. Not all pluralists follow Hick in saying the Real is completely unknowable, but they all strongly emphasize that the Real is highly mysterious and very little can be said about its character.

John Hick's third major claim is that within the great world religions transformation or salvation is taking place to about the same extent. Whereas the earliest, primal religions emphasize stability, all the great world religions, which emerged roughly in the period about eight hundred years before Jesus until several centuries after him, stress transformation of human life. Hick knows that conceptions of salvation often differ radically in these religions, yet he sees the crucial factor as changing persons from self-centeredness toward Reality-centeredness, especially as this is expressed in compassionate love. On this score of moving people toward compassionate love, all the great religions are about equally effective.

The fourth point in Hick's theological pluralism is his conclusion from the preceding, namely, that the great world religions should be regarded as equally valid paths to follow.

In summary, exclusivism, inclusivism, and theological pluralism are the three main positions taken on this issue. As we have noted, there are some differences among the proponents of any one of these positions. That is, not all exclusivists fully agree on every point, nor do all inclusivists or pluralists. Yet supporters of each view share enough in common to warrant grouping them into these three positions.

Evaluating Exclusivism and Theological Pluralism

When the issue of Christianity and other religions is presented in one of my college classes, usually the students who have the most vocal opinions take either the exclusivist or the pluralist position. We will evaluate each of those positions in turn.

The strongest argument made by the exclusivists is that the New Testament makes some absolute claims for Jesus: "Jesus said to him, 'I am the way, and the truth, and the life. No one comes to the Father except through me'" (John 14:6); "There is salvation in no one else, for there is no other name under heaven given among mortals by which we must be saved" (Acts 4:12). These and other New Testament texts appear to support exclusivism, and should be carefully considered by anyone seeking to carry on Christian theological reflection. Nevertheless, I will argue that such biblical passages may properly be understood in a way that retains high claims for Jesus Christ without insistence on conversion of everyone to Christianity.

This touches another powerful exclusivist argument, namely, that the missionary effort has been an integral part of Christianity since its beginning and has been commanded by Jesus when he said, "Go therefore and make disciples of all nations, baptizing them in the name of the Father and of the Son and of the Holy Spirit" (Matthew 28:19). This too is a point that should not be ignored. Christianity has indeed been a missionary religion with a message that Christians have felt would benefit the salvation of every person. Theological pluralism effectively wipes out any endeavor to win people to the Christian faith, for it views all religions as equally good paths to salvation. While Christianity without a missionary thrust would probably continue to exist, a vital Christianity seems to include the missionary belief that it has something unique to offer people.

Although the exclusivist outlook has some strong points, I think it is unsatisfactory for at least two reasons. First, exclusivism tends to make overly harsh judgments on the religions, including Barth's condemnation of Christianity. While it is indeed true that humans continually bend religions to their own ends, is it really the case, as Barth asserts, that religion is *merely* the human attempt to escape God? When one meets people from various religions who have deep moral wisdom, spiritual insight, and perhaps a profound understanding of God, it is very difficult to write them off as thoroughly mistaken. There seems to be more going on in the religions than simply escape from God (Barth) or a rebellious misreading of a general revelation given in nature (Bloesch).

Another major weakness lies in the popular exclusivist view that all those without personal faith in Jesus Christ are condemned to eternal hell. To be sure, not all exclusivists hold this. Karl Barth tends toward a hope that God's love will finally win all people. Donald Bloesch says that only those who actually reject and deny Jesus Christ will be placed in hell by God and further that hell is not a concentration camp but "a sanatorium for sick souls who are ministered to by Jesus Christ."[5] Thus Bloesch holds out the possibility of persons reaching salvation through accepting Jesus Christ after death. Yet the much more common opinion among exclusivists is that those without faith in Jesus in this life on earth will be eternally rejected by God. Such a view conflicts with the idea of a God of love and justice. How can God condemn the vast majority of people in the world for not having faith in Jesus when such a faith is not a live option for them?

For their part, the theological pluralists in my classes are most strongly motivated by the desire to avoid compulsion and pressure in matters of personal faith. While pluralistic scholars think especially of examples in history

5. Bloesch, *Essentials of Evangelical Theology*, Vol. 2, 225.

of one religious group using force and legal penalties to bring about religious conformity, students often have in mind the subtle pressures that families and communities sometimes exert on young people to believe and act as their elders do. Both the scholars and the students have a legitimate concern, for religious faith must be freely given, not in any way coerced. Nevertheless, there is a better way to give people psychic space for their own faith affirmation without falling into the difficulties of pluralism. I shall identify three major weaknesses in the position of theological pluralism.

The first weakness is that theological pluralism is inconsistent with some core beliefs of Christian faith. Members of other religions will see that pluralism conflicts with some of their central beliefs, but here our focus is on Christian faith. Surely Jesus is central to the Christian faith. The life, death, and resurrection of Jesus have been seen by Christians as the key to understanding God and genuine humanity. This perspective need not mean that Jesus is the *only* source of insight into God and human destiny, but it does mean that Jesus is the decisive source. For Christians Jesus is not just one among a number of equal religious leaders. Nevertheless, John Hick has spearheaded a theological drive to reject the traditional Christian belief in Jesus as the incarnate Son of God and endorses the idea that Jesus is one of a number of great spokespersons for the Real.[6]

Another core Christian belief is that salvation is primarily a gift of God; in other words, salvation is by grace. For biblical authors and nearly all other Christian theologians of note, the initiative for salvation lies with God. God comes to people and they respond to that initiative. They did not think of God as totally hidden, leaving humans on their own to search the darkness and create images and concepts of the divine. They believed that God took the initiative: that God called Abraham and Moses, that God sent prophets to Israel, that God chose Mary to give birth to the Savior, that God commissioned Jesus at his baptism, that the risen Christ halted Paul in his tracks. Throughout the story, the action begins with God. However, in John Hick's pluralistic view the Real is shrouded in complete darkness while people construct their own images and concepts of it. The Real is passive, humans are active. There is no revelation from God. There is no grace.

The second weakness in theological pluralism is that its account of what we can know about Ultimate Reality is seriously inconsistent. John Hick asserts that the Real is unknowable, for none of the concrete descriptions of our experience can be appropriately applied to the Real in itself. He says, "Thus it [the Real in itself] cannot be said to be one or many, person or thing, substance or process, good or evil, purposive or non-purposive."[7]

6. John Hick, ed., *The Myth of God Incarnate* (Philadelphia: Westminster, 1977), 179–84.
7. Hick, *An Interpretation of Religion*, 246.

There are serious problems with this view. If the Real is utterly unknowable by us, then we cannot say anything about *what* it is. As Hick says, "It cannot be said to be one or many, person or thing, substance or process, good or evil, purposive or non-purposive." In spite of this statement, Hick refers to the Real as "it", that is, as one Real rather than many. He defends his practice on the practical ground that it is more economical, and he does not rule out the possibility that the Real is indeed plural. There is a more serious difficulty, though, with his idea that by aligning people with the Real all the major religions are equally effective in transforming people from self-centeredness to Reality-centeredness as manifest especially in unselfish love. But how can "alignment with the Real" bring about such a movement toward good if the Real cannot be said to be either good or evil; in other words, if it is not more appropriate to say that Reality is good rather than evil? Surely alignment with an evil Real would not produce good in people.

The third major flaw of theological pluralism is that it actually tends to undermine dialogue and cooperation among followers of different religions. Interreligious dialogue and cooperation involve more than formal discussions by theologians; more important are respectful, mutually beneficial relations between members of different religious faiths living side by side not only in North America but in such places as Lebanon, Palestine, Malaysia, and India. In addition to exploring another religion's unfamiliar ways, interreligious cooperation must involve efforts to overcome prejudice and to build peace and social justice. Is pluralism the best view for promoting such interreligious dialogue and cooperation?

At first glance pluralism's apparent toleration of differences might seem to be the best alternative to an exclusivism in which each religious group regards itself as in the right and all other groups as in the wrong. When one examines theological pluralism more closely, however, it turns out to be far less tolerant than it appears. Pluralism's apparent toleration comes from the fact that it seems to stand above every particular tradition; it seems to adopt a purely universal perspective that is not limited by a particular culture. The truth is, though, that Hick's theological pluralism is also rooted in a particular tradition, the Enlightenment, a powerful eighteenth-century cultural movement in France, Germany, England, and America that has been very influential until today. One of the greatest representatives of the Enlightenment was Immanuel Kant, who called for religious toleration. But Kant's toleration of religious differences was grounded in his conviction that the particular beliefs and practices of a religion are of merely minor importance (at least for intellectuals), because what really matters are universal principles of morality. For example, the universal elements in Jesus' moral teachings are what count, while the particular events of his life and death are valuable merely as illustrations of those general principles. Kant's Enlightenment outlook has a condescending attitude toward the distinctive beliefs and practices of religious groups; while most ordinary folk need those particular images and rituals, informed people regard such things as peripheral to the universal principles of morality. Indeed , in actual practice Kant was not so tolerant, for he harshly criticized contemporary pietistic forms of religion in Germany as fanatical.

John Hick's version of theological pluralism is similar, although not identical, to Kant's view. According to Hick, the particular beliefs of the various religions are certainly important to their adherents as the way they interpret human destiny and the Real, but these beliefs are secondary. What counts is whether people's lives are being transformed toward agape or compassionate love. In fact, Hick argues that certain distinctive religious beliefs should be discarded for the sake of greater harmony among the religions. As we noted above, Hick has led a theological movement within his own Christian tradition to reject its traditional belief in Jesus as the incarnate Son of God. Hick supports the idea that Jesus is one of a number of great spokespersons for the Real. Since the Christian understanding of God as triune is closely tied to the traditional view of Jesus Christ, the doctrine of the Trinity would also have to be discarded. It is logical that the same principle should be applied to other religions. Muslims should give up their convictions about Muhammad as the final prophet and the uniqueness of the Koran, and Buddhists should relinquish their belief that the doctrine of the Buddha brings the highest wisdom.

Now back to the question whether theological pluralism is the view that best fosters dialogue and cooperation among followers of different religions. We will use Lebanon as an example, simplifying the situation by focusing only on the relations between Muslims and Christians there. Would it promote greater understanding and mutual acceptance to ask the Muslims and Christians in Lebanon to give up some of those central beliefs that have defined them as Muslims and Christians and, in effect, adopt a new outlook grounded in the European Enlightenment? I think not. One of the prerequisites for better understanding of others is to allow them to be truly themselves and not immediately try to change them. Naturally, for dialogue and cooperation, we must also look for common ground, but it should be common ground that can be discovered in the depths of each particular religious faith. Theological pluralism fails in this respect, for essentially, it asks each religion to become something else.

In this section we have evaluated both exclusivism and theological pluralism. I think exclusivism's emphases on the centrality of Jesus Christ and the missionary task of winning others can be better incorporated within an inclusivist stance. Two serious flaws of exclusivism are that it takes an overly pessimistic view of the religions and that in popular form it threatens the love and justice of God by consigning all non-Christians to hell. I also argued that theological pluralism has three damaging weaknesses: it contradicts some core beliefs of Christian faith, its account of what we can know about Ultimate Reality is fatally inconsistent, and it actually undermines interreligious dialogue and cooperation. Now I will proceed to make a case for a form of inclusivism.

A Case for Inclusivism

Inclusivism has four strengths. The first is that inclusivism preserves the integrity of Christian faith by basing constructive interreligious encounters on specifically Christian beliefs such as the doctrine of the Trinity. As we saw in a previous chapter, Christians can speak of God as Father/Mother, Word or Wisdom, and Holy Spirit. In relation to the world, Father/Mother refers to God as the source of all existence; thus every human being, all living things, and everything in the universe ultimately owe their existence to God.

God the Word or Wisdom is the rational expression of God that gives order and meaning to the world. Obviously the universe is not chaos, for it has structure and order that we depend upon everyday and that scientists study. But according to Christian faith the order of the universe is not finished, for the universe is moving toward an order even more in accord with the Word or Wisdom of God. This Word or Wisdom is also Jesus Christ who was born of Mary, carried on a public ministry in Palestine, was crucified under Pontius Pilate, and was raised from the dead. As the Gospel of John says, "And the Word became flesh and dwelt among us, full of grace and truth" (John 1:14). For Christian faith the goal of all people is to become like Christ and the goal of the whole world is to become the realm of God that Jesus proclaimed. As the Letter to the Colossians says of Jesus Christ, "All things were created through him and for him. He is before all things, and in him all things hold together" (Col. 1:16-17). In other words, the destiny of all people and of the world is to become like Christ, for all things were created *for* him.

The triune God is also the Holy Spirit, the active divine presence within the universe, the source of life and the source of people's ability to respond to God. The Holy Spirit is at work throughout the world seeking to draw creatures toward their fulfillment in the realm of God. This means that the Holy Spirit strives to lead all humans to become persons like Christ and to form ever-wider bonds of community. In fact, there is good reason to regard current efforts at interreligious dialogue and cooperation as part of this Spirit-led movement toward greater unity in the creation.

For Christians, the fact that there are signs of Christlike humanity in persons of other religions indicates that the Holy Spirit is also at work within those people and cultures. God's active presence is not limited to the sphere of Christianity but is universal. This universal divine presence is not John Hick's vague, utterly unknown Real, however, but is the God who makes herself reliably known in the particular history of Jesus and is at work moving the creation toward Christlikeness. This is a specifically Christian understanding of the world's religions and of God's relationship with them. Thus inclusivism can enter into dialogue with other religions without sacrificing Christian beliefs. The expectation is that followers of other religions will talk about ultimate reality and the significance of interreligious dialogue in their own ways.

This Christian conception of God and of the religions is a solid foundation for constructive interreligious encounters. In a formal dialogue between theologians or an informal dialogue between acquaintances, members of different religions discuss their faith with one another. Whereas theological pluralism seeks to ground dialogue in a supposed universal perspective that relegates each religion's particular beliefs and practices to secondary status, an inclusivist approach recommends that religious believers enter into discussion from the core convictions of their own religious faith. Christians come with their understanding of the triune God and the decisiveness of Jesus Christ; other believers such as Muslims and Hindus come with their own faith perspectives. To proceed in this way is not arrogance on the part of Christians or Muslims or Hindus. In part it comes from the humble recognition that as limited human beings we must view things from our own concrete perspective in history. In this way the particular integrity of each religion is acknowledged.

The second strength of inclusivism is that its approach to interreligious encounters turns out in practice to be the most fruitful. M. M. Thomas, one of the small minority of Christians in India (2–3 percent), says Christians have had a powerful influence on Indian culture in the twentieth century precisely because they did not minimize specifically Christian teachings but emphasized the centrality of Jesus Christ. The Christian interpretation of Jesus' life and death as revelation of God's identification with suffering humanity moved Mahatma Gandhi and many other Hindu leaders to reexamine their own tradition and its justification of suffering such as that borne by the untouchables in Indian society. "For them the renewal meant digging into the Hindu tradition to bring out what was like Jesus and transforming that tradition in the light of Jesus."[8] More recent dialogues between Christians and followers of secular ideologies in India have confirmed the fact that Christians were able to contribute most to the dialogues when they did not deemphasize their distinctive Christian teachings. The German theologian Jürgen Moltmann also found this to be true in dialogue between Christians

8. M. M. Thomas, "A Christ-Centered Humanist Approach to Other Religions in the Indian Pluralistic Context," in *Christian Uniqueness Reconsidered: The Myth of a Pluralistic Theology of Religions*, Gavin D'Costa, ed. (Maryknoll, N.Y.: Orbis, 1990), 53.

and Marxists in the 1960s: "Our dialogues began in Prague with Marxist philosophers inviting the Protestant theologian Joseph Hromadka for a discussion. He was prepared to speak about justice and peace on earth, but the Marxists preferred to have the meaning of Christian prayer explained to them."[9] Christians will also be able to learn most from interfaith discussion when their dialogue partners are deeply rooted in their own tradition and represent its beliefs and practices.

One aim of interfaith dialogue is to learn more about reality. For instance, listening carefully to American Indian religions has helped many Christians rethink their view of nature. Similarly, attention to non-Christian radical feminism has opened the eyes of many Christians to sexism in Christianity. In both cases a virtual blind spot in Christian awareness has been discovered. Thus, for both Christians and their dialogue partners, interfaith discussions can be genuine learning experiences about the nature of reality. Interfaith dialogue can also be a learning experience by strengthening and confirming conviction of one's own religion. But this learning is most likely to take place when the dialogue partners stand firmly in their specific tradition.

Another aim of constructive interreligious relationship is cooperation in the struggle against injustice, violence, and suffering. When Muslims, Jews, and Christians in the Middle East come together, interreligious dialogue must be joined with peacemaking. This should also be true of Christians in North America. An inclusivist perspective grounded on faith in the triune God not only permits but urges Christians everywhere to this active cooperation in building a better world. Working to combat evils such as poverty, violence, racism, sexism, and abuse of nature certainly is integral to Christian faith, for that faith says the destiny of the world is to become the realm of God where justice and harmony prevail. An inclusivist outlook enhances the chances for interreligious cooperation in the work of justice and relieving suffering, for it expects other believers to have their own religious reasons for participating in the work.

Does this emphasis on learning through interreligious dialogue and practical cooperation mean that inclusivism has abandoned the missionary thrust of Christian faith? Not at all.

The third strong point of my form of inclusivism, unlike Tillich's, is that it gives a prominent place to explicit Christian witness as well as to meeting other human needs. Christians are sent both to announce the Christian message and to serve the concrete needs of others, even as Jesus did in his ministry. In this way Christians are called to serve people as whole persons with physical, social, and spiritual needs.

9. Jürgen Moltmann, "Is 'Pluralistic Theology' Useful for the Dialogue of World Religions?" in ibid., 153.

Explicit Christian witness takes place in many ways. It occurs when people are inquiring about Christianity. It may happen when Christians encounter people who are alienated from their religious background, have a merely nominal connection with it, or are without any religious ties. Christian witness occurs as well when friends and neighbors, who are firm adherents of different religions, talk about their respective faiths. Mutual witness also happens in a formal interreligious dialogue, say, between Muslim and Christian scholars. The Christian does not necessarily assume that the other person is in total darkness about God, but the Christian is called to give testimony to what God has done in Jesus. It seems to me that the unique message the Christian brings is that with amazing compassion God in Jesus has shared the depths of human alienation and freely gives reconciliation. This message of the free mercy and grace of God is truly good news. In situations involving firm believers of different religions, there may be no overt attempt to convert the other. This is all right. After all, conversion is not in human hands; the Christian's responsibility is to give witness in word and action to what God has done in Jesus.

I disagree with those exclusivists who say that salvation is only for individuals who have faith in Jesus Christ. The testimony of the New Testament on this issue is not entirely clear, for in various passages three different scenarios are suggested.[10] One set of passages says that salvation is only for those with faith in Jesus Christ (John 3:16; Romans 1:16). A small but not insignificant group of passages envision a final judgment on the basis of a person's deeds (Matthew 25:31-46; Romans 2:6-8; 2 Corinthians 5:10; 1 Peter 1:17). A third set of passages suggests that all people will eventually be saved (Romans 5:18; 11:32). On the basis of this diversity, it is best to refrain from rigid pronouncements about who will not be ultimately saved. Perhaps part of the answer to the puzzle is to view faith in Jesus as a blessing rather than as a requirement. Faith is often seen as the required entrance ticket for heaven. It is better to regard faith in Jesus as a blessing, for it can bring assurance that God is merciful. So the aim of the Christian mission is to make known this blessing that is the core of present salvation.

Seeking to win people to faith in Jesus Christ is definitely part of the Christian mission, but so are witness through interreligious dialogue and cooperation in the work of peace, justice, and mercy. In practice this means that the Christian does not actively recruit converts among other believers whose lives already manifest Christlike qualities. There are more than enough alienated, hurting people in the world that Christians should seek to help without pursuing those in whom God's Spirit appears already to be working.

---

10. See Ted Peters, *God—The World's Future: Systematic Theology for a Postmodern Era* (Minneapolis: Fortress Press, 1992), 352–53.

So far I have argued for three strengths of inclusivism. One is that unlike theological pluralism, which either sets aside or relegates to peripheral status a religion's distinctive beliefs in an effort to find common ground with other religions, an inclusivist position affirms the Christian doctrine of the Trinity and finds in it the basis for constructive interreligious relationships. The second is that interreligious dialogue is in fact most beneficial for all when the parties represent the particular beliefs and practices of their own tradition, rather than following the pluralist strategy of minimizing their distinctive beliefs. The third strength is that inclusivism has a comprehensive understanding of the Christian mission to whole persons that includes winning others to the Christian faith. Now I wish to discuss a fourth reason for adopting inclusivism—that inclusivism takes seriously the question of truth in religion.

The theological pluralism of John Hick evaluates religions strictly on their moral effects, whether they produce compassionate love in their adherents. He says that nearly all the great questions of truth on which religions differ cannot be settled. We cannot have any knowledge of the Real, which will remain unknown and unknowable probably even in heaven.[11] Hick concludes that all the religions that have positive moral effects are "equally valid." A less sophisticated but more popular view would say that all the religions are "equally true" or that each person's religion is "true for that person."

Undoubtedly it is very difficult to resolve the differences in truth claims among religions, yet there are serious consequences when we set aside altogether the question of truth in such matters. There are several different conceptions of truth, but probably the most basic is that truth has to do with what is the case. If on a very cloudy day I say, "The sun is shining brightly today," my statement does not represent what is the case. It is a false statement. Of course, the nature of ultimate reality is not a simple matter of fact like whether or not the sun is shining. Yet there is a significant difference between believing ultimate reality is loving and believing that no such quality as love can be ascribed to ultimate reality. As a Christian I truly believe that ultimate reality is loving; indeed, I stake my way of life on it. So personally, existentially I live with the conviction that God is love. On the other hand, a wise Zen Buddhist roshi once replied to my question whether Buddhists had something like the Christian belief in divine creation with these words, "There is something that gives rise to the world." And then he refused to take any further questions. The use of the term *something* expressed the roshi's reluctance to ascribe to ultimate reality qualities or character such as intentional creation, love, or even "Godness." I suspect that in further discussion the Buddhist roshi and I would find a degree of agreement in our thinking about ulti-

---

11. C. Robert Mesle, review of Hick, *Interpretation of Religion*, in *Journal of the American Academy of Religion* 58, no. 4 (Winter 1990): 713.

mate reality, but it seems foolish to ignore the significant differences in our convictions and truth claims.

The result of setting aside the whole issue of truth regarding ultimate reality is that views about ultimate reality take on the status of mere personal preferences such as individual taste in clothing styles. There is no question of truth in matters of personal taste. If you like one style of clothes and I like another, we can discuss whether the styles are in fashion or out of fashion, but we would not ask whether our liking of either style is true or false. Now when beliefs about God or Reality are treated as personal preferences, religion is purely subjective. There is no sense of God *having expectations* or Reality *making a claim* upon people. What is objectively ultimate makes no claims upon us, for it is utterly unknowable. What people believe about the Real are entirely human constructions. Whatever a person believes is acceptable as long as it meets the practical standard being applied. Admittedly, Hick's standard of compassionate love is lofty. But why is this standard appropriate if Reality cannot be said to be either good or evil? Hick's absolute relativism simply lends support to a more popular form of relativism whose only standard is that a person feels "comfortable" with their beliefs.

When religion is just a subjective matter, it is also a purely private concern. The highest virtue becomes tolerance, in the sense of every individual leaving everyone else to do their own thing as long as they do not infringe on one's own choices. When we are trying to arrive at our own identity in relation to our family and community, some toleration of differences is valuable. But regarding religious belief as a purely individual matter exacts a high price. As Jürgen Moltmann says, "There are benefits to such tolerance, of course, but religion inexorably loses its social character and becomes purely private. Different religious traditions lose their capacity to be the binding element of societies and become instead mere options for religious consumers to select for their own private reason, reasons which are not to be argued about. Thus 'democratized,' religions enter the marketplace as objects of subjective choices in much the same way as brands of toothpaste and laundry soap. . . ."[12] When religion becomes merely a private affair, human life becomes fragmented. There is nothing substantial to bind us together into a community. We are left with only readily changeable common loyalties to sports teams and music groups and loyalties to our ethnic group or nation, which also divide and arouse group conflicts.

When religion is viewed as a purely subjective, private commitment, then the importance of interreligious dialogue is also undermined. Just as discussing different preferences in clothes styles or toothpastes has no weight

12. Moltmann, "Is 'Pluralistic Theology' Useful?" in D'Costa, ed. *Christian Uniqueness Reconsidered*, 152.

or urgency about it, so comparing different tastes in religious belief and practice becomes idle conversation. Interreligious dialogue takes on the character of a style show. There is nothing to debate, nothing to challenge one another. Religions become, as Moltmann says, "Mere options for religious consumers to select for their own private reason, reasons which are not to be argued about."

Whereas theological pluralism dismisses the question of truth in most religious issues, inclusivism takes the quest for truth very seriously. Without claiming to have all the truth about ultimate reality, inclusivist Christians believe that God has given a reliable revelation of himself and his intentions in the biblical history and especially in Jesus. They do not think ultimate salvation is limited only to Christians, but they do believe that the likeness of people's lives with Jesus' character and message will be decisive for all people. In this sense the inclusivist can agree, "There is no other name under heaven given among mortals by which we must be saved" (Acts 4:12). Jesus' parable about the last judgment of all the nations in Matthew 25:31-46 strongly suggests this centrality of a Christlike humanity, for what counts at the judgment is whether a person has fed the hungry, given drink to the thirsty, and welcomed the stranger. The Christian inclusivist asserts that there is one criterion for human wholeness, and it is the life and message made known in Jesus Christ, although many follow the essence of that life and message through another religious tradition. Thus the inclusivist Christian makes some very significant truth claims.

Again, this is not an arrogant assertion that Christians have all the truth, but it does recognize that Christian faith involves truth claims just as do Muslim faith and Buddhist faith. Whenever there is a conflict of central truth claims between religions, inclusivists—whether Christian, Muslim, or Buddhist—will begin with the presumption that their tradition takes priority. As limited beings, we all have a specific perspective on ultimate reality.

Discussing truth claims can be fruitful if we are willing to genuinely listen to one another by searching for the deep concerns underlying the theological formulations. We may find that some different truth claims are not contradictory but complementary. For instance, as Christians listen to representatives of Native American religion, we may discover truths about our relationship with nature that will lead us to reexamine our Christian tradition much as Mahatma Gandhi rethought his Hindu tradition in the light of Christian teaching. As we investigate other religious teachings we will also meet truly conflicting truth claims. But that does not mean that we should persecute one another; we may agree to disagree. But in our very disagreement, we show respect to other religious believers by regarding their beliefs as real assertions about what is the case, just as they do. In the end, it may turn out that Buddhists or even atheists are nearer the mark than Christians. That is a risk we all take in believing and dialoguing. In the meantime, though, we honor one another most by treating our various views as including some genuine alternatives.

One reason why theological pluralism has wide appeal today is that many are reacting against pretensions to having all the truth in religion. While it is a mistake to claim to know too much about God, it is also an error to claim too little. The medieval theologian Thomas Aquinas is a good example to follow on this score. Aquinas says that God is ineffable, incapable of being expressed in words, yet he does not mean that God is utterly unknowable. Indeed, Aquinas asserts that God is one, simple (without parts), infinite, good, powerful, knowing, and wise. To be sure, he says that these things are true of God by analogy. For instance, when it is said that God knows, this does not mean that God knows in the same way that we humans know. Although we can rightly say that God knows, we cannot say *in what way* God knows. This is rather like saying that a dog perceives things, even though we are unable to know *how* a dog perceives since we are not dogs.[13] In short, while Aquinas realizes our words cannot apply to God in the same way that they apply to finite things, he does not think God is completely unknowable, for he makes some very significant assertions about God even within his natural theology. In similar fashion, inclusivist Christians affirm that Jesus has highest priority as revelation of God, yet they do not pretend to understand all that this means for the being and intentions of God.

In conclusion, whenever we think about the relationships among the religions, it is wise to remind ourselves that we are limited beings who cannot stand above time to survey the whole sweep of world history. We have access to the universal presence of God only in and through a particular tradition in history. In good part because it recognizes this, inclusivism has four strengths to commend it: inclusivism affirms central Christian teachings, it approaches interreligious encounters in the most fruitful way, it understands the Christian mission comprehensively, and it takes the question of truth seriously.

13. Keith Ward, "Truth and the Diversity of Religions," *Religious Studies* 26 (March 1990): 7.

12
Eschatology

The subject matter of this final chapter is eschatology, a word that comes from the Greek *eschaton*, meaning last, final, or end thing; hence, eschatology literally means thinking about the end. There are two major meanings of end. One meaning is to be last in a series. So in this sense eschatology would be reflection on the end of time, the last events in the history of the world or of an individual's life, and then the possible entry into eternity. Another meaning of end is that of goal or purpose; in this same sense we also speak of something's goal as its finality. Eschatology as a theological study usually involves both of these meanings.

As reflection about goal and what is last, eschatology includes thinking about the future and the impact of the future on the present. We should note that there are two types of future, however. On the one hand, we have plans and dreams for tomorrow, next month, and probably for ten years from now. Our plans for the near future may be quite specific: the courses we will take next semester, a trip that we intend to take, or the resumé that we want to produce. We also may have dreams about romance, sex, work, family, and politics. All such plans and dreams deal with what we may call the *secondary future*. On the other hand, we move to a different level of concern when we ask, Toward what are we moving in and through all the specific plans and dreams that fill day-to-day life? Even though our plans and dreams for such things as romance and work may be fulfilled, those happy conditions will eventually be taken away by the passage of time. So we ask, Is this all there is? Or is there a fulfillment that cannot be taken away? Is there an absolute fulfillment for us humans beings and our world? To ask this question is to be concerned about the *ultimate or absolute future*. This question about the ultimate future and its impact on the secondary future is the central concern of eschatology.

Since the heart of eschatology is concern about the ultimate future for human beings and the universe, eschatology enters into many areas of Christian teaching. For example, we could not adequately talk about the doctrine of creation without introducing the issue of the ultimate purpose or goal of God's creation of the world. We also found that Jesus could not be properly understood unless we took into account the eschatological ideas so fundamental to his teaching and ministry. Eschatology is connected with the doctrine of the church as well, for the community of Christian believers is a partial anticipation of the perfect community of the reign of God. The doctrine of salvation also has close links with eschatology, because salvation is both a reality of partial healing in the present and a future reality of complete and perfect wholeness for which we may hope. In chapter 9 our focus was chiefly upon salvation in the present, now we turn our attention more directly toward those future aspects of salvation for which Christians may hope. The meaning of the sacraments of baptism and eucharist is also tied to eschatology, for the experience of grace in these sacraments is a foretaste of the perfect fulfillment of God's reign.

The pervasive influence of eschatology in the Christian outlook has not always been recognized. The reason much contemporary theology sees the whole Christian vision being shot through with eschatology was the unsettling argument that eschatology is central to the Bible and to the teachings of Jesus. The German scholar Johannes Weiss started the recovery of eschatology in 1892 with the publication of *Jesus' Proclamation of the Kingdom of God*. Albert Schweitzer reinforced the message in 1906 with *The Quest of the Historical Jesus*. These scholars argued that there is an extensive presence of eschatological ideas in Jesus' teaching. Ever since, Christian theologians have been compelled in one way or another to take account of biblical eschatology and interpret its meaning for today. We will join this very important discussion first by looking at the main strands in biblical eschatology, second by distinguishing several major interpretations of those biblical views, and third by examining the chief images of Christian eschatology.

Before we begin our study of biblical eschatology we must face a fundamental difficulty in thinking about the future. The fact is that we cannot know the future in the same way that we can know the past and present. Whereas past and present events and conditions are actualized, the future is pure possibility. The future does not exist as a fact to be known. The truth is that our expectations and hopes for the future are extrapolations or extensions of certain elements in past and present experience. People differ as to what "certain elements in past and present experience" are taken as the key to imaging the future. For Christians the biblical story and above all the story of Jesus are the foundations for forming a vision of the ultimate future. With this in mind, we shall now turn to the principal source of Christian thinking about the future—biblical eschatology.

Biblical Eschatology

From among the diverse eschatological perspectives in the many books of the Bible we shall select four very important versions of thinking about the future.

1. *This-worldly eschatology of the preexilic prophets.* When the Israelite monarchy and religious practice declined after King David and King Solomon, prophets repeatedly warned the Israelites of a coming divine judgment upon the nation for its failure to live up to its covenant with Yahweh. The purpose of the warning was to call the people of Israel back to faithfulness to God. If the nation would repent of its ways, the prophets held out hope for a renewal of the nation led by a devout king like David. This person would be the Messiah, someone anointed by God. This ideal king would usher in a golden age in which Israel would enjoy political glory, social justice, peace, and prosperity (Isaiah 9:2-7). Indeed, all nations would share in Israel's peace (Isaiah 2:2-4; Micah 4:1-4). This is the idea of the reign of God, although it is not identified by that specific name in the Old Testament. When Israel did not repent, judgment of the "Day of the Lord" came over the course of more than a century in several major defeats, the eventual destruction of Jerusalem in 587 B.C., and the exile of many remaining people to victorious Babylon.

It is important to note two features of this eschatology. First, it is a *this-worldly hope*. The ultimate hope for these preexilic Israelites has to do with the well-being of Israel within time and space. There is no hope for the nation or the individual that truly transcends this world and its history. Although preexilic Israelites did not believe individuals were simply annihilated at death, they thought the dead enter a shadowy existence in *Sheol*. People did not look forward to this, for it was a half-existence, not a fulfillment. The residents of Sheol, sometimes called shades, do not enjoy the essence of a good life—worship of God: "For in death there is no remembrance of you; in Sheol who can give you praise?" (Psalm 6:5). The second feature of preexilic eschatology is that it is purely a *communal hope*. What counts is that the nation of Israel continue and prosper.

2. *Apocalyptic eschatology* emerged after some of the Israelites returned from Babylon to Palestine around 538 B.C., and it was especially prominent from about 300 B.C. until the time of Jesus. The Greek word *apocalypsis* means revelation; it is an appropriate name for this outlook, since the adherents of apocalyptic believed that the secret truths of world history had been revealed to them. While there is diversity in apocalyptic thought, we can characterize the major form of apocalyptic eschatology in four points.

First, apocalyptic writers are *pessimistic about history*. Within the present order of history, they expect things to get worse, not better. This reflects the sad straits of Jewish political fortunes as foreign political domination persisted during most of the postexilic period. Like the earlier prophets the apocalyptic authors look to God for liberation, but now they look beyond the order of this world to a totally renewed world. This pessimism about history is often expressed in the belief that the entire cosmos under God's judgment will come to a catastrophic end and a new cosmos will be created by God.

Second, apocalyptic thinkers have a *sharply dualistic view of reality*. They see both good and evil forces in conflict with each other. God is opposed by the devil, who now entered for the first time into the mindset of Israel. Another closely related dualism is between the evil, unhappy present age dominated by the devil and the good, blissful future age in which God will reign. In addition, when God's judgment of the world comes, there will be a separation of the righteous people from the unrighteous. Whereas before both the good and bad were thought to end up in Sheol, now there are separate destinies in heaven and hell.

Third, apocalyptic writings often set forth the *stages of history in God's predetermined plan*. The earlier prophets had a sense of history being open to surprises and new twists, although it is fundamentally shaped by Israel's covenant relationship with God. Now in apocalyptic thought, history is seen as more fixed and determined in advance by a divine plan. Part of the appeal of much apocalyptic eschatology is that it claims to let one in on the divine plan.

Fourth, apocalyptic thinkers believe *the present age is coming to an end very soon*. This means for many that the world will soon suffer a cataclysmic end. There is much interest in ascertaining signs that the end is near.

Prominent in the apocalyptic perspective are certain key images: the last judgment, a powerful emissary from God called the Son of Man who will play the leading role in the endtime events, resurrection of the dead, heaven, hell, and the kingdom or reign of God. One of the earliest expressions of some of these images appears in the Old Testament book of Daniel:

> As I watched in the night visions, I saw one like a human being [Aramaic: son of man] coming with the clouds of heaven. And he came to the Ancient One and was presented before him. To him was given dominion and glory and kingship, that all peoples, nations, and languages should serve him. His dominion is an everlasting dominion. . . . (Daniel 7:13-14)

Here we encounter the images of the powerful Son of Man delegated by God to bring in the reign of God. Later in this same chapter Daniel has a vision of four evil beasts among whom the fourth beast is the strongest. Of this fourth beast Daniel says, "Then the court shall sit in judgment, and his dominion shall be taken away, to be consumed and totally destroyed" (Daniel 7:26). Now we meet the image of the last judgment in which God definitively defeats the forces of evil.

3. *The modified apocalyptic eschatology of Jesus.* There has been debate among scholars whether Jesus returns to the earlier this-worldly eschatology of the prophets or draws heavily upon apocalyptic eschatology. It seems to me that Jesus does some of both. That is, like the prophets Jesus certainly emphasizes the ethical responsibilities of people; he does not abandon the present world and simply look to a new world. He even takes the initiative to form a new community that seeks to live according to his message. Nevertheless, apocalyptic themes and images are prominent in Jesus' teaching. It appears that he expected the present order to end soon under the leadership of the Son of Man. Indeed, the close proximity of the reign of God heightens the need for people to repent and adopt new priorities. So the nearness of the reign of God does not diminish ethical responsibility for the well-being of society, but actually strengthens it. Thus the major point about Jesus' eschatology is that *he makes considerable use of apocalyptic ideas, although he modifies them to incorporate some prophetic, ethical concerns.*

Strong evidence exists for several apocalyptic elements in Jesus' message. Jesus' frequent use of the reign of God language has precedence in Daniel and also reflects the two-age pattern of apocalyptic. Another apocalyptic feature is that Jesus expected great cataclysmic suffering and a last judgment as part of the end of this age: "Blessed are you when people revile you and persecute you and utter all kinds of evil against you falsely on my account" (Matthew 5:11); "Jesus said to them, 'Truly I tell you, at the renewal of all things, when the Son of Man is seated on the throne of his glory, you who have followed me will also sit on twelve thrones, judging the twelve tribes of Israel'" (Matthew 19:28). This last passage from Matthew manifests yet another image in Daniel's apocalyptic scenario—the Son of Man. Furthermore, Jesus appears to have thought the end was very near: "'Truly I tell you, there are some standing here who will not taste death until they see that the kingdom of God has come with power'" (Mark 9:1).

While it seems likely that Jesus took over many apocalyptic ideas, he also modified apocalyptic thought in three major respects. First, he claimed the reign of God was not just in the near future but was also already present in his ministry of preaching and healing: "But if it is by the finger of God that I cast out the demons, then the kingdom of God has come to you" (Luke 11:20). Because the reign of God is so near, Jesus calls people to repent, to change their ways. Second, Jesus refused to follow the fairly common apocalyptic practice of drawing up a calendar of endtime events; he said that no one but God knows the time of the end (Mark 13:32).[1] Third, unlike some apocalyp-

---

1. This view of Jesus' eschatology with the first two modifications is presented by the British New Testament scholar James D. G. Dunn, *Unity and Diversity in the New Testament* (London: SCM, 1977), 318–22.

tic thinkers, Jesus does not entirely give up on the present society and leave it to an impending destruction; he carries on an active ministry in part to renew Jewish society.

4. *Paul's further modification of apocalyptic eschatology.* When we consider Paul's view, we are not dealing with just a single individual's thought. As the most influential early Christian missionary, Paul's understanding of eschatology must have been shared by many other early Christians. *Paul follows Jesus' apocalyptic thinking, but further adapts it in view of Jesus' resurrection and anticipated imminent return.* We see familiar apocalyptic images in this letter of Paul, written about the year 51.

> For the Lord himself, with a cry of command, with the archangel's call and with the sound of God's trumpet, will descend from heaven, and the dead in Christ will rise first. Then we who are alive, who are left, will be caught up in the clouds together with them to meet the Lord in the air; and so we will be with the Lord forever. (1 Thessalonians 4:16-17)

Hope for the ultimate future now is fundamentally shaped by Christian beliefs about Jesus, and centers on the anticipation of Christ's return. Notice that Paul expects to meet Jesus, not some previously unknown Son of Man. Apocalyptic belief is altered in another respect by the early Christians. Whereas apocalyptic thought had anticipated a resurrection of all or many of the dead as part of its endtime scenario, early Christians believe that resurrection has happened already for this single person Jesus. This was not something that previous apocalyptic expected. Paul understands Jesus as the "first fruits" of those to be raised from the dead (1 Corinthians 15:20).

Paul thinks the end is very near, for he expects to be alive when Jesus returns; "then we who are alive, who are left, will be caught up in the clouds." This expectation plus the social position of the Christian churches in the Gentile world influence Paul's ethical teachings. That is, while Jesus called Jews to a reformation of Jewish social relations, Paul works with churches that are tiny outposts in a much larger pagan society. To reform that pagan society in the short time Paul thought remained simply was not realistic. These beliefs affect Paul's ethical teachings. On the one hand, the gospel of Jesus Christ leads Paul at times to envision a radically different order of life *within* the church community: "As many of you as were baptized into Christ have clothed yourselves with Christ. There is no longer Jew or Greek, there is no longer slave or free, there is no longer male and female" (Galatians 3:27-28). On the other hand, Paul advises the early Christians not to change their status in the larger society: "I think that, in view of the impending crisis, it is well for you to remain as you are. Are you bound to a wife? Do not seek to be free. Are you free from a wife? Do not seek a wife" (1 Corinthians 7:26-27). Paul even advises slaves to remain in that condition (1 Corinthians 20–21).

Thus Paul carries on the apocalyptic themes of Jesus, but adapts them to his belief that Jesus himself will soon return to remake the world.

We may summarize this first part of the chapter on biblical eschatology by remembering that there are two major forms of thinking about the future in the Bible. One is the early prophetic outlook that focuses its hopes on the nation of Israel within time and space, and summons Israelites to moral and religious renewal of their society. The other form of eschatology is apocalyptic, which envisions a catastrophic end of the present world and hopes for a new order of things through resurrection of the dead. Elements of both forms are present in the eschatology of Jesus.

Recent Interpretations of Eschatology

It is one thing to describe what views of eschatology were held in biblical times; it is another thing to say what biblical eschatology means for today. This latter question about the meaning of the Bible for contemporary people is a question of interpretation, and it is the subject of the second part of this chapter. We recall that the technical term for this process of interpretation is *hermeneutics.* To interpret any historical document such as the Constitution of the United States or the Bible is a hermeneutical process. The interpretive process is like having a conversation with the historical text.[2] In this conversation we come with our questions and interests, which naturally reflect our historical, social, and personal situation. For instance, I come with questions arising out of my status as a late twentieth-century, white, middle-class male American who has some serious health concerns. Someone else may approach the Bible with the questions of a Guatemalan Indian peasant woman concerned about social and economic progress for her people within a repressive regime. So no one approaches the Bible with pure neutrality. We all bring our concerns, needs, biases, and cultural background to the text.

A genuine conversation involves a double movement. Not only do we ask questions of the Bible, but the Bible also speaks to us and challenges our current understanding of things. A biblical book meets us as a voice with its own perspective and very different cultural situation. If we truly listen to that book and let it speak with its own integrity and strangeness, we are invited and challenged to appropriate that biblical perspective as in some way an answer to our questions. We may even be prodded into asking some entirely new questions. Yet we can never simply duplicate the thinking of Isaiah, Matthew, or Paul; they remain persons from the ancient Near East. We must interpret the biblical book for our time and place. This is the hermeneutical task.

---

2. David Tracy, "Theological Method," in *Christian Theology*, rev. ed., Peter Hodgson and Robert King, eds. (Philadelphia: Fortress Press, 1985), 38–46.

Since the whole of Christian theology involves interpretation of Scripture and tradition, all the theological topics we have dealt with in this book have engaged us in this hermeneutical conversation. Nevertheless, nowhere in theology do the interpretive questions confront us so obviously as with eschatology. While the prophetic eschatology fits rather smoothly with various modern Western efforts to refashion human society according to some social ideology, the apocalyptic eschatology of Scripture confronts modern culture as an alien outlook indeed. What is the meaning of these biblical perspectives on eschatology for people today? The first step in answering this question for ourselves is to reflect on the basic approach to interpreting biblical eschatology. This may sound terribly abstract, but as we examine several different approaches the issue will become more concrete and clear. We will see that one's basic stance toward eschatology even determines which topics will be discussed.

Over the last century very different answers have been given to this hermeneutical question. We shall consider four major interpretations as a way of helping us formulate our own thinking on eschatology.

1. *Fundamentalist apocalyptic eschatology.* By no means do all fundamentalists think in apocalyptic terms, but many do. Those who do take biblical apocalyptic very seriously, but in a literal way. We have seen that apocalyptic employs many images. While the suggestive power of symbols is discernible in all religious thought, apocalyptic is especially rich in symbols. For instance, heightened symbolism is evident in this passage from the only entirely apocalyptic book in the Bible, the book of Revelation.

> Then I saw an angel coming down from heaven, holding in his hand the key to the bottomless pit and a great chain. He seized the dragon, that ancient serpent, who is the Devil and Satan, and bound him for a thousand years, and threw him into the pit, and locked and sealed it over him, so that he would deceive the nations no more, until the thousand years were ended. After that he must be let out for a little while.
>
> Then I saw thrones, and those seated on them were given authority to judge. I also saw the souls of those who had been beheaded for their testimony to Jesus and for the word of God. They had not worshiped the beast or its image and had not received its mark on their foreheads or their hands. They came to life and reigned with Christ a thousand years. (Revelation 20:1-4)

Although the highly symbolic nature of these passages is suggested by the fact that they are presented as visions ("Then I saw"), those who follow fundamentalist apocalyptic understand these visions as literal predictions of events to come. If you recall the distinction between a sign that conveys straightforward information and a symbol that suggests an indefinite number of meanings, then it is clear that fundamentalist apocalyptic interprets these images of biblical apocalyptic as signs. So rather than read this passage as an evocative symbol of God's power to overcome evil and death, the fundamentalist sees it as direct information about future events. One of the central events that fundamentalist apocalyptic expects from the above passage in Revelation is that Christ will return to reign over a thousand-year period of peace and justice on earth. This period is called the millennium, from the Latin word *mille*, meaning thousand. Hence, another common name for fundamentalist apocalyptic is *millennialism*. During this thousand-year period Satan will be bound by God, but will be released to work evil for a time after the millennium.

In keeping with much apocalyptic thought in the intertestamental period mostly prior to Jesus, fundamentalist apocalyptic exhibits an intense interest in ascertaining the *sequence* of endtime events. This is seen in the attention given to the release of Satan after the millennium and his eventual complete defeat. But the most heated debates in fundamentalist apocalyptic circles take place over what is called the rapture and its relation to what is commonly referred to as the tribulation.

The idea of the *tribulation* is derived from Matthew 24: "When he was sitting on the Mount of Olives, the disciples came to him privately, saying, 'Tell us, when will this be, and what will be the sign of your coming and of the end of the age?'" (v. 3). Later in the chapter Jesus says, "Then they will deliver you up to tribulation, and put you to death; and you will be hated by all nations for my name's sake" (v. 9). Still later, "For then there will be great tribulation, such as has not been from the beginning of the world until now, no, and never will be" (v. 21; these quotes are from the Revised Standard Version). The Christian life at all times necessarily involves trials and suffering arising from the conflict with evil, but millennialists believe that the great tribulation will be a time of far greater affliction. Millennialists also commonly interpret a reference to one week in Daniel 9:27 to mean the great tribulation will last for seven years.

Fundamentalist apocalyptic thought also speaks of the *rapture*. In 1 Thessalonians 4:17, when speaking about the return of Christ at the endtime Paul says, "Then we who are alive, who are left, will be caught up in the clouds together with them to meet the Lord in the air; and so we will be with the Lord forever." Millennialists interpret this being "caught up in the clouds" to mean that the true believers will be lifted up out of the intense suffering of the tribulation to be with Jesus. This is the rapture. The question hotly debated among millennialists is when the rapture will take place. Pretribulationists say that the rapture will occur just before the great tribulation. Posttribulationists argue that the rapture will come after the affliction. There are also some midtribulationists who say believers will be raptured after enduring three-and-a-half years of the great tribulation. Of these three groups, the pretribulationists most emphasize that Christ might return at any moment now. Since according to their view Christ's return will not be preceded by the tribulation, there will be no advance warnings of the return.

A significant subgroup within the pretribulationist camp are the dispensationalists. *Dispensationalism* is a theology developed in England by John Darby (d. 1882) who said that the history of God's dealings with humankind is divided into seven dispensations or systems of divine ordering of things. The millennium belongs to the seventh dispensation. Dispensationalist theology has spread widely in conservative and Evangelical circles through the Scofield Bible, a translation of the Bible with explanatory notes by C. I. Scofield (d. 1921) that give a dispensationalist interpretation to the text.[3]

The chief question about all these various schools of fundamentalist apocalyptic is whether the basic approach to the apocalyptic portions of Scripture is sound. Should the apocalyptic images in Daniel, Matthew, Revelation, and other books in the Bible be read as literal predictions of future events or as symbolic expressions of the strenuous struggle between good and evil and God's eventual victory?

2. Existentialist eschatology. The classic statement of existentialist eschatology is given by Rudolf Bultmann (d. 1976), the most renowned and influential New Testament scholar of the twentieth century. Whereas fundamentalist apocalyptic tries to make biblical apocalyptic thought literally binding on Christians today, Bultmann thinks this approach is doomed to make Christian faith outmoded like ancient Greek mythology. Bultmann believes that apocalyptic eschatology must be radically reinterpreted.

The essentials of this interpretation were initially stated during World War II in Bultmann's landmark essay "New Testament and Mythology." Bultmann recognizes that the New Testament frequently presents its message about Jesus Christ with the images and ideas of Jewish apocalyptic as well as eschatological images drawn from another religious outlook of the Ancient Near East—Gnosticism. Bultmann calls these apocalyptic and Gnostic images myth. Thus he understands the New Testament message to be pervaded with ancient mythology. The difficulty, according to Bultmann, is that this ancient mythology is unbelievable to modern people: "To this extent *the kerygma [Christian message] is incredible to modern man, for he is convinced that the mythical view of the world is obsolete.*"[4] The apocalyptic outlook is simply the cosmology of a prescientific age, and it is incredible to people shaped by modern science. A further count against the apocalyptic view is that the return of Christ never took place as most New Testament authors expected;

---

3. For clear statements of millennialist views by supporters see Millard J. Erickson, *Contemporary Options in Eschatology: A Study of the Millennium* (Grand Rapids, Mich.: Baker, 1977), 109–68; and George Eldon Ladd, *The Last Things: An Eschatology for Laymen* (Grand Rapids, Mich.: Wm. B. Eerdmans, 1978), 63–86.

4. Rudolf Bultmann, "New Testament and Mythology," in *Kerygma and Myth*, Hans Werner Bartsch, ed., Reginald H. Fuller, trans. (New York: Harper, 1961), 3.

although Paul and others in the early church anticipated that Jesus would return soon, Jesus still has not returned after nearly two thousand years. In order for the Christian message to gain a hearing in the modern world, Bultmann says the essential Christian message must be disengaged from its mythological trappings of apocalyptic; it must be demythologized.

Bultmann thinks it is possible to demythologize the Christian message, because the heart of this message and of the apocalyptic language itself is an understanding of human existence. The essential Christian message is a summons to turn from a life of trusting in human resources to a life of trusting in God. Human beings are unable to free themselves from their fallen state of trusting in self. What sets people free is the love of God revealed in Jesus Christ. This love of God in Christ meets people in the word of Christian preaching.

> Now, this is eschatological existence; it means being a "new creature" (2 Cor. 5.17). The eschatology of Jewish apocalyptic and of Gnosticism has been emancipated from its accompanying mythology, in so far as the age of salvation has already dawned for the believer and the life of the future has become a present reality. The fourth gospel carries this process to a logical conclusion by completely eliminating every trace of apocalyptic eschatology. The last judgment is no longer an imminent cosmic event, for it is already taking place in the coming of Jesus and in his summons to believe (John 3.19; 9.39; 12.31). The believer has life here and now, and has passed already from death into life (5.24, etc.). Outwardly everything remains as before, but inwardly his relation to the world has been radically changed.[5]

Several features of Bultmann's interpretation of New Testament eschatology are notable. First, Bultmann's eschatology centers on the present rather than the future. He does not expect the whole apocalyptic scenario of end-time events to occur in the near or distant future. Rather, the spotlight is on the present moment in which a person is called to trust in God. Second, accordingly the meaning of "eschatology" has been fundamentally changed. Whereas all the several forms of biblical eschatology that we examined have some significant reference to a temporal future, Bultmann understands eschatology to be what is *qualitatively* better. So he begins the previous quotation with this statement, "Now, this is eschatological existence; it means being a 'new creature.'" And when Bultmann speaks of an "eschatological event," he means an event that may precipitate this movement into a new quality of life by an individual. Third, Bultmann's eschatology focuses upon the individual human being, not on the sacred community as does prophetic eschatology, and not on the cosmos as does apocalyptic thought. Like the existentialist philosophy of Martin Heidegger which he uses, Bultmann con-

5. Ibid., 20.

centrates on the individual in the present moment of responsibility for his or her existence.

Fourth, while Jesus uses some of the symbols employed in apocalyptic, he radically reinterprets those symbols. Many in the early church later interpreted Jesus' message in apocalyptic terms; for instance, Paul expects God will very soon finally defeat evil and bring the present world order to an end. But Bultmann holds that Jesus himself did not proclaim such apocalyptic beliefs. Nonetheless, one remnant from apocalyptic remains in Bultmann's thought, for he believes in the resurrection of Jesus Christ who is now living.

There is no doubt that Bultmann's strong emphasis on trust in God as the essence of the Christian life is right, yet one wonders whether he has made some serious omissions. This mixed reaction reflects scholarly response to Bultmann's view, for he has been supported by some major New Testament scholars such as Ernst Käsemann and Norman Perrin, yet criticized by other biblical scholars and theologians for being unbalanced in all four of these points. On the first point, while Bultmann claims biblical precedent in the Gospel of John for emphasizing the present moment, New Testament scholar Oscar Cullmann says John's eschatological thinking is more accurately expressed in his phrase "the hour is coming, and is now here" (John 4:23). This shows that John thinks in terms of both future and present. In respect to the closely related second point about Bultmann's limitation of eschatology to a qualitatively different way of existence, it must be admitted that this too is a partial truth. The forms of apocalyptic eschatology we have examined look forward to some events which will be last in the temporal sequence of the history of this world order. On the third point, dealing with Bultmann's concentration on the individual, it is clear that the preexilic prophets pay extensive attention to the community and the various forms of apocalyptic envision major changes for human society as well as for the whole universe. In regard to the fourth point, in which Bultmann draws a sharp break between the nonapocalyptic message of Jesus and the apocalyptic thought of the early church, many New Testament scholars do not agree that the division is nearly so sharp. In other words, many other scholars see apocalyptic elements in Jesus' teaching.

3. *Historical, this-worldly liberationist eschatology.* Some, but by no means all, liberation theologians largely ignore or reject the transhistorical, apocalyptic elements in biblical eschatology and concentrate on the prophetic tradition of historical, this-worldly eschatology. Hope is directed toward a better future within time and space. Today it is common for liberation theologians to look forward to a time of peace and justice in human society and care for the earth and other creatures. This vision of a harmonious world inspires efforts in the present to change human attitudes and transform society's ways.

The theology of prominent feminist Rosemary Radford Ruether is an example of a this-worldly type of eschatology. Although eschatology has not been discussed much by feminist theologians, Ruether gives an explicit treatment of the topic in *Sexism and God-talk*, originally published in 1983 and issued in 1993 with a new introduction in which Ruether says the book "continues to be a good statement of what I have to say about the key Christian symbols, my critique of their patriarchal context and content, and my reconstruction of their liberating potential. I would not fundamentally revise it, although I have and will continue to develop particular themes."[6]

Ruether is critical of both Jewish apocalyptic and Greek belief in immortality of the soul, since both look for human fulfillment beyond time and history. The basic shortcoming of these forms of human hope, she says, is that they are unwilling to accept the limits of human life. Ruether asserts that death should be accepted as natural, and we should concentrate on making existence on this planet more equitable for all people and all life forms. So she agrees more with the preexilic prophetic focus on a better life in this world.

She also faults, however, the prophetic expectation of a final, conclusive setting right of things within history. Similarly, she criticizes the apocalyptic hope for a millennium in which a perfect life will be established on earth for a thousand years. The weakness she perceives in these viewpoints is the expectation that all human imperfections will eventually be overcome in one grand conclusion to human history. Instead Ruether proposes a spiral view of history in which each generation has the task of making life relatively better for the next generation. There will be no final resolution.

> This revolutionary transformation cannot be done once and for all. A humane acceptance of our historicity demands that we liberate ourselves from "once-and-for-all" thinking. To be human is to be in a state of process, to change and to die. Both change and death are good. They belong to the natural limits of life. We need to seek the life intended by God/ess for us within these limits. This return to harmony within the covenant of creation is not a cyclical return to what existed in the past, however. Each new achievement of livable, humane balances will be different, based on new technologies and cultures, belonging to a new moment in time and place. It is a historical project that has to be undertaken again and again in changing circumstances.[7]

What about the individual person? What will become of us after death? At first Ruether says the appropriate response to such questions is agnosticism; that is, to admit that we do not know. However, Ruether is far from completely agnostic about what becomes of individual humans after death. She believes that our individual existence ceases at death and is dissolved back into

---

6. Rosemary Radford Ruether, *Sexism and God-talk* (Boston: Beacon, 1993), xv. See also Ruether, "Eschatology and Feminism," in *Lift Every Voice: Constructing Christian Theology from the Underside*, ed. Susan B. Thistlethwaite and Mary Potter Engel (San Francisco: Harper & Row, 1990), 111–24.

7. Ruether, *Sexism and God-talk*, 255.

God/ess from which new persons and individual creatures emerge. God/ess is the everlasting matrix or nurturant reality from which individual beings and even planetary worlds appear and pass away. Ruether actually envisions a sort of immortality in the sense that the good and evil in a person's life is taken up into God/ess and is incorporated into the ongoing world process. So individual persons do not survive, but their achievements and failures do. "That great matrix that supports the energy-matter of our individuated beings is itself the ground of all personhood as well. That great collective personhood is the Holy Being in which our achievements and failures are gathered up, assimilated into the fabric of being, and carried forward into new possibilities."[8] It is at this point that her agnosticism enters, for she says we cannot understand what this means. Since it is beyond our powers to even imagine what this means for us as individuals, we should concentrate our efforts on using our limited life span to create a good community for the next generation within history.

Ruether's eschatology raises many questions, but one of the most important is whether a Christian vision of the future should include a transhistorical hope for a communal and individual life beyond death. The crucial factor in answering this question is to clearly identify the central source for one's thinking about the future and human fulfillment. In other words, what is the basis in the past and present for imagining the future? In Ruether's case, the fundamental source is ecological thought in feminism, science, and nature religions. So when she states her own views on eschatology in *Sexism and God-talk*, she does it by expanding on some ideas of the American Indian Vine Deloria. Jesus is mentioned only once in the chapter and then only in a one-sentence suggestion that Jesus' vision of the reign of God may have shared her spiral view of history in which there are periodic renewals of society. Jesus simply does not figure significantly in her thinking about the future. One should ask whether this is a sound way of formulating a Christian vision of the future. If one affirms the resurrection of Jesus from the dead, then one's thinking about the future will include a transhistorical hope for life and fulfillment beyond death.

4. *A symbolic interpretation of biblical apocalyptic that affirms both individual and communal hopes as well as both historical and transhistorical hopes.* This characterizes the thinking of the majority of theologians today, even though they differ from one another in many respects. Among them we can point to Catholic theologians Karl Rahner, Monika Hellwig, and Anglican John Macquarrie. Even some prominent theologians who put the primary emphasis on the historical dimension of eschatology also have a place for fulfillment in a

8. Ibid., 258.

dimension that is transhistorical or beyond time and history; among them are the Catholic liberation theologian Gustavo Gutiérrez as well as the leading Protestant theologians of hope, Jürgen Moltmann from the Reformed tradition and Wolfhart Pannenberg from the Lutheran tradition.[9]

This is also the basic stance I will take in discussing Christian eschatology. Corresponding to the three elements identified in the approach—a symbolic rendering of biblical apocalyptic, both individual and communal hopes, and both historical and transhistorical hopes—I have three reasons for adopting this stance.

a. While it is possible to interpret biblical apocalyptic language as signs communicating direct information about the future, I think *it is appropriate for us today to understand apocalyptic language as symbolic.* Let's consider again Revelation 20:1-5, which speaks of a thousand-year reign of Christ on earth.

> Then I saw an angel coming down from heaven, holding in his hand the key to the bottomless pit and a great chain. He seized the dragon, that ancient serpent, who is the Devil and Satan, and bound him for a thousand years, and threw him into the pit, and locked and sealed it over him, so that he would deceive the nations no more, until the thousand years were ended. After that he must be let out for a little while.
>
> Then I saw thrones, and those seated on them were given authority to judge. I also saw the souls of those who had been beheaded for their testimony to Jesus and for the word of God. They had not worshiped the beast or its image and had not received its mark on their foreheads or their hands. They came to life and reigned with Christ a thousand years. (The rest of the dead did not come to life until the thousand years were ended.) This is the first resurrection. Blessed and holy are those who share in the first resurrection.

Remember the distinction between the historical meaning of a text and the contemporary meaning of that text; it is one thing to say what a text meant in its own historical setting and quite another thing to interpret that text for people today. For instance, the author of the Genesis 1 creation story used an ancient scientific view of the universe to affirm faith in God as creator. This ancient science saw the universe emerging out of chaotic waters. The universe is shaped like a bowl turned upside down. The round part of the bowl is the sky, which is like a screen on which God has hung the stars. It may have been that the author of Genesis 1 took this picture of the universe

9. Karl Rahner, "The Hermeneutics of Eschatological Assertions,"in *Theological Investigations*, Vol.4 (Baltimore: Helicon, 1966), 323–46; Monika Hellwig, "Eschatology," in *Systematic Theology: Roman Catholic Perspectives*, Vol. 2, Francis Schüssler Fiorenza and John P. Galvin, eds. (Minneapolis: Fortress Press, 1991), 347–71; John Macquarrie, *Principles of Christian Theology*, 2nd ed. (New York: Scribner's, 1977), 351–70; Gustavo Gutiérrez, *A Theology of Liberation*, rev. ed. (Maryknoll, N.Y.: Orbis, 1988), 95–105; Jürgen Moltmann, *History and the Triune God* (New York: Crossroad, 1992), 108–9; Wolfhart Pannenberg, *The Idea of God and Human Freedom* (Philadelphia: Westminster, 1973), 196–202.

as both sign and symbol. In other words, while the author saw rich symbolic meanings about God and creatures in this outlook, he may also have believed it represented accurate information about the structure of the universe. But the basic purpose of Genesis 1 is to express certain religious convictions, not to teach science. So modern people are not bound to believe this ancient view of the world. Jews and Christians today may take this creation story as symbol but not sign; that is, they may agree with the fundamental religious affirmations of Genesis 1 without having to subscribe to its picture of the universe.

It seems to me that something similar needs to be said about Revelation 20. Let's assume for the moment that the author of Revelation thought there would be a literal thousand-year reign of Christ on earth and that Satan would be locked up by God in a deep pit during this period before being released again for a little while. Are we today obligated to adopt this projection of the future? Or does the author make important religious affirmations that may be held without being literally bound to his specific scenario and worldview? At least two things should make us pause before buying into a literal reading of Revelation 20. One is that Revelation is the only book in the Bible that speaks of a millennium. If the teaching were as central as millennialists say it is, then one would expect it to be taught also by other New Testament writers. Another reason to hesitate adopting a literal interpretation is that Revelation 20:4 clearly says that those who will reign with Christ in the millennium are "those who had been beheaded for their testimony to Jesus and for the word of God." This restriction to those beheaded is generally ignored by millennialists. In other words, they are selectively literal in their interpretation.

What significant religious affirmations are being made through the rich symbolism of Revelation 20:1-5? Two suggestions may be made. First, the angel's binding of Satan is a dramatic expression that the power of evil far exceeds human capability to conquer unless God intervenes. Second, the hope for a thousand-year reign of Christ on earth affirms that Christians should not give up on this world and simply wait for a redemption beyond time. The history of Christianity demonstrates this influence, for the millennium has often generated utopian efforts to dramatically refashion human society. Jürgen Moltmann is just one example of a prominent theologian who nurtures this spirit of millennialism or chiliasm (from the Greek word for thousand) without literally expecting Christ to rule on earth for a thousand years. Thus this basic approach identifies the important religious affirmations of biblical apocalyptic without being bound to their literal fulfillment.

b. There is no fulfillment for individuals apart from relations with other creatures. Bultmann is certainly correct in stressing that the Christian message has profound implications for the individual person. Through this message the individual is challenged to examine his or her priorities and called to trust in

God above all else. Nonetheless, there is no fulfillment of the individual apart from relations with other creatures. Who we are as individual persons and how we relate to God are intimately connected with our relationships to other persons and creatures. For instance, if I trust in God above all else, it will deeply affect how I relate to my wife, children, and colleagues as well as to friends, neighbors, and strangers in need. A common theme in the New Testament is that one cannot love God without also loving other people. Over the past century-and-a-half we have become aware that we cannot meet the needs of individuals who are hurting without paying attention to the society in which they live. For example, in today's world not everyone in a society experiences hunger or homelessness; it is almost always the poor who know this suffering firsthand. Similarly, the incidence of rape and sexual abuse is linked with social factors such as frequent media portrayals of violence and of women as sexual objects. It is also becoming increasingly clear that we cannot seek the best for our children and fellow human beings without also caring for the whole community of creatures on earth. So hope for the individual's fulfillment must include hope for the whole human community and the community of earth's creatures.

c. A contemporary eschatology should reflect the very structure of human hope as well as the shape of biblical eschatology. An essential aspect of our makeup as human beings is that we seek to shape our life in accordance with some hope for the future. At the beginning of this chapter we distinguished between the secondary future and the absolute future. Our secondary future is made up of all the dreams and plans we have about such things as progress in school, romance and family life, career, and monetary status. Our absolute future is the ultimate goal toward which our life as a whole is leading. Obviously what we acknowledge as our absolute future will have a great effect on our secondary futures, for our fundamental goal in life will influence our priorities and thus how we envision progress in school, success in a career, and so forth. The impact of the absolute future on how people live today, tomorrow, and next year is assumed in Jesus' call to repent, since the reign of God is near (Mark 1:15). Thus eschatology has implications for how individuals and communities shape their life within time and history; there is an important historical dimension to Christian eschatology.

Christian eschatology also has transhistorical hopes for the future. Admittedly, human longings for fulfillment in life after death are widespread although not universal. But the human wish for fulfillment beyond death is not in itself a solid basis for asserting that there actually will be such fulfillment; merely wishing does not make it so. However, Christian eschatology takes its cues from Jesus Christ. Christian hope for the future is grounded in Christian experience of Christ in the present. Central to this Christian experience in the tradition is that Christ is living, Christ has been raised from the dead and lives. This means that God has given Jesus a transhistorical fulfillment, a perfected existence beyond time and history. When Christ's resurrection is taken seriously, Christian eschatology will have a transhistorical as well as historical dimension.

When we take this approach of a symbolic interpretation of biblical apocalyptic with attention to both individual and communal as well as historical and transhistorical hopes, then we can identify the major themes that should be discussed in Christian eschatology. The themes are (1) the reign of God and the parousia, (2) death and resurrection, (3) last judgment, (4) heaven and hell, and (5) the intermediate state and purgatory. These subjects will occupy our attention in the third part of this chapter. Some authors divide the topics between what they call general eschatology and individual eschatology; other authors divide them among individual, social, and cosmic eschatology. I will not use any such division, for all these themes have individual, social, and cosmic dimensions.

Reign of God and the Parousia

The kingdom or *reign of God* is the central theme of Jesus' preaching and teaching. The Gospel of Mark summarizes Jesus' message this way: "The time is fulfilled, and the kingdom of God has come near; repent, and believe in the good news" (Mark 1:15). This one-sentence summary highlights three aspects of Jesus' message. First, the reign of God refers to a situation in which God rules without opposition and conflict; God's good and wise will is not contested. So in saying that "the kingdom of God has come near," Jesus affirms that this victorious rule of God is close at hand; it is imminent, in the very near future. Second, when Jesus says "the time is fulfilled," he means that this reign of God is also manifest in the present through Jesus' own words and actions. Thus the reign of God is both in the near future and in the present. How can it be both? The most likely answer is that God's present reign is an anticipation and promise of its full, complete manifestation in the near future. Third, Jesus offers people a share in the reign of God, "repent and believe in the good news." As we have noted before, "repent" means to change the direction of one's life. To believe in the good news is to establish a new direction by making God's will one's highest priority.[10]

If this is an accurate statement of the historical meaning of Jesus' preaching, we are still left with the hermeneutical or interpretive question of what this message means for people today. I think Jesus' message of the reign of God has implications for the individual, society, and the cosmos. I also think the reign

---

10. This summary of Jesus' preaching is from Dunn, *Unity and Diversity in the New Testament*, 13–16.

of God, like all the Christian eschatological symbols we will discuss, refers both to a future possibility and to what may be experienced as a present reality.

For the individual, Christian proclamation of God's reign is an invitation and challenge to trust in God above all things and to commit one's life to God as the highest priority. This is not accomplished in a single conversion experience, but is done again and again as one goes through life. Trusting in God and making God first have a profound impact on one's daily relationships and duties. For instance, to trust above all else in God means that a person will not rely for one's worth upon his or her achievements in academics, social relations, sports, or work; one's worth is a gift from God in each moment. Since a person is repeatedly tempted to trust for worth in oneself or some other creature, one is called to repent and believe again and again. According to Bultmann and those strongly influenced by his existentialist interpretation, this meaning of the reign of God for the individual is almost the whole of Christian eschatology.

I would not deny the centrality of this invitation to trust in God, but I think the message of the reign of God also has implications for the whole human race. Reign of God is the central Christian image for envisioning the ultimate goal of human history. Belief in the reign of God as the goal of history is consistent with belief in God as creator and guide of history. To hold that the universe and human beings have been created by God implies that history has a purpose or goal intended by God. Similarly, belief in the providence of God (divine guidance of history) implies that God has some goal in mind. Of course, there can be great latitude and flexibility in how God's goal is reached; chance and creaturely freedom can play a significant role along the way. Nevertheless, fundamental to biblical and Christian notions of God is the conviction that God has a purpose for the world and for humans. So it is that, in most of the Bible, history is understood as linear, that is, not like a racetrack that goes around and around, but like a highway that goes to some destination. The dominant biblical symbol for this goal of world history is the reign of God. In this context, the reign of God refers to a situation in which human beings live with complete trust in God, love for one another, and respect for all creatures. In short, the reign of God is a symbol for harmony, harmony of people with God, harmony of people with one another, and harmony of all creatures. Such harmonious community is the ongoing creation of the divine dance that continuously moves out into what is other, in order to produce an ever-richer unity. The reign of God is not boring uniformity, but ever-interesting variations on the theme of loving community. To use a different metaphor, even in the reign of God the jazz band continues to play and improvise.

Obviously, the symbol of the reign of God portrays the goal of history in very broad strokes. It would be a mistake to take any specific picture of the goal literally. For instance, one vision of the goal of history is given in the Old Testament in Isaiah 65:17ff.:

> For I am about to create new heavens and a new earth. . . . I will rejoice in Jerusalem and delight in my people; no more shall the sound of weeping be heard in it, or the cry of distress. . . . They shall not labor in vain, or bear children for calamity; for they shall be offspring blessed by the LORD—and their descendants as well. . . . The wolf and the lamb shall feed together, the lion shall eat straw like the ox. . . . They shall not hurt or destroy on all my holy mountain, says the LORD.

It is not surprising that in this vision of an ancient Hebrew prophet the nation of Israel and Jerusalem are prominent. Details should not be pressed as an exact blueprint for the future. Yet Isaiah's formulation clearly suggests harmony and an end to suffering.

An underlying assumption of this biblical vision is that God is ultimately responsible for the outcome of history. So unlike secular views which think that humans govern things or that nothing directs a heartless world that will finally make humans extinct, biblical faith holds that God is finally responsible. The reign of God in its fullness symbolizes the situation in which all things in the world eventually conform to God's good will. Then all things will be in harmony.

It may seem that this vision of the goal of history encourages people to withdraw from the problems of the world today and simply look forward to some future paradise. No doubt, some Christians have thought this way. In fact, fundamentalist apocalyptic tends in this direction, for it often sees the present world as doomed to divine destruction in the very near future. So why try to repair a sinking ship? The main responsibility of Christians, according to this view, is to help people escape the ill-fated ship by converting to the Christian faith and being saved from condemnation.

Hope for the reign of God as the goal of human history does not necessarily foster escape from the present world, however. The key question here is the relation between the future "new heavens and a new earth" of God's reign and the present order of things in the world. Apocalyptic generally sees a very sharp contrast between these two ages and situations; the present order is so corrupt that it has very little continuity with the future perfect order of things that God will bring. Prophetic eschatology also sees a contrast between the present and the future fulfillment, but the difference is not so sharp as in apocalyptic. Prophetic eschatology affirms more continuity between present and future, for the renewed relationships established through repentance and faith contribute to the future fulfillment. Not that the reign of God develops or evolves by purely human and natural impulses. Fulfillment still is understood as a gift from God, a fruit of God's promise as it awakens fresh dreams and hopes in the present. For instance, someone who truly believes in God's promise of a future harmony of life will not give in to despair in apparently hopeless situations, such as have existed in the chaos and suffering of some African nations or in the cruelties of civil war in the former Yugoslavia. One who trusts God's promise of the coming reign of God will continue to work for reconciliation even amidst such apparently hopeless circumstances. Thus a prophetic eschatology does not expect God's reign simply to be dropped into our laps and the partial good in human life wiped out; rather, the limited efforts and achievements of people to live now in harmony with one another and with nature will be taken up and perfected in that future fulfillment.

The prophetic outlook on this issue seems more consistent with Jesus' way of operating. To be sure, Jesus employed apocalyptic images and thought patterns, yet Jesus' call to repentance and faith included a summons to participate in the community life of his followers. The general pattern was to serve one another and especially those at the margins of life, rather than to seek personal advancement even at the expense of others. So Jesus did not call his followers to throw up their hands and wait for God to bring in paradise; he urged them to fashion a new community that would reflect the justice and compassion of God's reign. In this way the hoped-for future of God's perfect reign is partially present already in the common life of Jesus' disciples.

So far I have argued that the biblical symbol reign of God has significance for the individual and for all of human history, but now we must ask about its meaning for the cosmos. Does the reign of God have implications for the nonhuman universe? Some apocalyptic thought in the Bible uses imagery that suggests destruction of the existing universe and the creation of a new one. Mark 13:24-25 envisions major celestial changes: "But in those days, after that suffering, the sun will be darkened, and the moon will not give its light, and the stars will be falling from heaven, and the powers in the heavens will be shaken" (compare Matthew 24:29). Some parts of Revelation also might be read as implying the end of the existing world and the creation of another: "Then I saw a new heaven and a new earth; for the first heaven and the first earth had passed away, and the sea was no more" (Revelation 21:1). And in its vision of the new Jerusalem the book says, "And the city has no need of sun or moon to shine on it, for the glory of God is its light, and its lamp is the Lamb" (Revelation 21:23). Generally fundamentalist apocalyptic interprets such biblical passages to mean that the reign of God will exist in a newly made universe after the destruction of the present universe.

It may be, however, that such passages should not be understood so literally. The vision of Isaiah 65, composed after the Babylonian exile, points us in this direction, for it uses language that the New Testament book of Revelation echoes. The prophet speaks for God: "For I am about to create new heavens and a new earth; the former things shall not be remembered or come to mind" (Isaiah 65:17). The prophet goes on to describe a newly created Jerusalem in which there will no longer be distress. Yet in the prophet's new

Jerusalem death will not be eliminated, only early death will not occur. Furthermore, human life would go on much like it had for centuries in Palestine, for people would build houses and plant vineyards. A major change in nature is projected, though, for "the wolf and the lamb shall feed together"; thus while familiar animals would continue to exist, they would no longer feed on each other. This suggests that while the harmony of the reign of God would certainly require fundamental and widesweeping change in the world as we know it now, it might not be necessary that this space-time universe come to a cataclysmic end. Of course, there is sufficient looseness to the symbol of a new heaven and new earth that in fact this universe may come to a catastrophic end. Yet it may also be the case that a radically new order of human and natural life will emerge which, like Christ's body, has both continuity and discontinuity with the present world.

In the New Testament the arrival of the reign of God in fullness is closely linked with the appearance of a figure called the Son of Man. The Christian church identified Jesus as the Son of Man, so Paul and other early Christians expected the reign of God to be fully established at the return of Jesus Christ or at what is often called the *parousia*, a Greek word meaning appearance. Although Paul and other early Christians anticipated that they would experience severe persecution and suffering before God's reign would be fully established, they looked to the future with longing since at the center of the ultimate future would be the person whom they trusted and loved most completely, Jesus. The future was not to be feared, for Jesus would appear again and be revealed in his glory to all.

As we noted before, while Jesus himself did not set forth a timetable of endtime events, he seems to have thought God's reign would come in its fullness very soon (compare Mark 9:1). Paul and many other early Christians expected God's reign to begin when Christ returned within a very short time. This raises an uncomfortable question for Christians: Why the protracted delay in the return of Christ and the full establishment of God's reign? Indeed, does the extended postponement call into question the entire hope for Christ's return and for the reign of God? No doubt, ever since Johannes Weiss and Albert Schweitzer rediscovered the prominence of eschatology in Jesus' message, the delay has been an embarrassment to many Christian scholars. In fact, one of the great attractions of the existentialist and this-worldly approaches to eschatology is that they effectively set aside any hope for Christ's return and a dramatic reordering of the world. They remove the difficulty of the delay by eliminating the expectation. What can be said about the delay, though, if one still holds to the hope for Christ's return and the complete installment of God's reign?

The difficulty is greatest for those who maintain a rather literal reading of biblical apocalyptic, for then one wonders why God has not already dropped the reign of God into our lap, especially when Jesus thought it would come long before now. But if one gives some weight to the prophetic tradition as well as to apocalyptic, then God's reign will not arrive like a tornado—totally unwanted by any people. As we said earlier, Jesus' announcement of God's reign is coupled with a call to change and to reflect the justice and love of God's reign in one's own behavior and community. In other words, God will not simply dump the reign upon humans, regardless of anyone's response. Hence, a possible reason for the delay is that God has not yet received the appropriate response from human beings, so God mercifully extends the time of opportunity.

To briefly recall the main points of this discussion, the message of God's reign calls the individual to trust in God as the lord of one's life, holds out a vision of harmony and justice that inspires efforts to improve social relationships in the present, and envisions a radical reordering of the entire cosmos without necessarily destroying it. Christians may have a confident hope for God's reign, since at its center is the parousia or reappearance of Jesus. Perhaps the parousia and fulfillment of God's reign have been put off as God seeks a more positive acknowledgment from humans.

Death and Resurrection

Death is not only a human experience, for death is a biological phenomenon that affects all living things on earth. Dandelions, hickory trees, earthworms, toads, and humans all have mortality in common. As I commented in connection with Jesus' resurrection in chapter 7, death is an integral feature of the system of life on earth. Without death the evolution of life forms would not take place, and without death the earth would long ago have become terribly overcrowded with living things. Another implication of the presence of death throughout the biosphere is that biological death could not have first entered the world when human beings sinned, for plants and animals were mortal millions of years before humans ever existed. Thus there is good reason to question the idea that biological death first came into the world when human beings sinned. What is needed is a careful examination of precisely what the Bible says about death.

As is the case with many topics, there is not just one view of death in the Bible; the various books of Scripture, composed over more than a thousand years, express some diversity of outlook on death. One common approach to death in Scripture is to focus on how the relationship of humans with God affects the human experience of death. In other words, death simply as a biological phenomenon affecting all life forms does not occupy center stage; what is emphasized is how trust or distrust in God influences the human *expe-*

rience of mortality. For instance, in the story about the first man and woman in the garden of Eden (Genesis 2:4b—3:24), God tells the man, "You may freely eat of every tree of the garden; but of the tree of the knowledge of good and evil you shall not eat, for in the day that you eat of it you shall die" (Genesis 2:16-17). If death here is taken in the biological sense as the end of life on earth, then the warning is not fulfilled; the first man and woman do not in fact end their life "in the day" or at the moment of their sin. But what does surely happen in the moment they disobey God is that they are now alienated from God; this is a metaphorical and theological meaning of death as loss of unity with God. So a note that is sounded several times in the Old Testament is that the dead in Sheol, even though they have a sort of continued existence, do not enjoy fellowship with God: "For in death there is no remembrance of you; in Sheol who can give you praise?" (Psalm 6:5; compare Psalm 30:9; 88:5).

Since the very essence of life is to have fellowship with God, it is a small step to speak of someone alienated from God as dead even though one is physically up and walking around. So Jesus says to a would-be follower, "Let the dead bury their own dead" (Matthew 8:22). And in the Gospel of John Jesus says, "Very truly, I tell you, anyone who hears my word and believes him who sent me has eternal life, and does not come under judgment, but has passed from death to life" (John 5:24). The spiritual death of separation from God has a powerful impact on the human experience of death as the end of earthly life. Ideally people would face the end of earthly life calmly and without fear, for they would place all their confidence and hope in God. So followers of Jesus still must physically die, but what he has done is to "free those who all their lives were held in slavery by the *fear* of death" (Hebrews 2:15; italics added).

The apostle Paul is the chief source of the idea that death originates with human sin. Paul seems to lump death as end of earthly existence and spiritual death together. In his letter to the Romans Paul reflects on how Adam and Jesus have such different influence on their fellow human beings, "For if the many died through the one's trespass [Adam's], much more surely have the grace of God and the free gift in the grace of the one man, Jesus Christ, abounded for the many" (Romans 5:15). Paul seems to believe that the first man's sin brought both biological and spiritual death into the world. "For the wages of sin is death" (Romans 6:23). Paul does not regard death in the natural world as simply a neutral, biological phenomenon, for he says the creation which is in "bondage to decay" groans as a woman giving birth in hope of being set free (Romans 8:19-23). So the distinction between death as end of earthly life and spiritual death, which some biblical authors make, is not made by Paul.[11]

---

11. A clear discussion of biblical teachings on death is given in "Death," *The New International-al Dictionary of New Testament Theology*, Vol. 1, Colin Brown, ed. (Grand Rapids, Mich.: Zonder-van, 1975–1978), 429–47.

Here again we must face the interpretive question of what we today should make of the biblical teachings on death. It seems to me that it does not make sense to adopt Paul's idea that death first entered human and natural life when the first humans sinned. That was a reasonable belief for Paul, since people in his culture thought humans were created at about the same time as other creatures. But now we have good reason to think life on earth existed many millions of years before human beings appeared, and that evolution was a key mechanism in the development of life. It makes more sense today to observe a distinction between death as the end of earthly existence and spiritual death. Then the Christian can say that Christ frees believers from the spiritual death of centering one's life on a creature, from the fear of death as end of earthly life, and from death as termination of any meaningful existence for the individual.

Death as the end of earthly life not only keeps the planet from being vastly overpopulated, it also has great spiritual significance for human beings. The fact that we humans must die and that we are aware of this fact gives human life on earth tremendous importance. Death gives urgency to the issue of what we will do with our life, what sort of persons we will become. If our existence were to stretch on endlessly, we could delay indefinitely the question of our basic direction in life. But death presses the question upon us. Furthermore, death as the end of earthly existence presents us with the ultimate opportunity for faith or unfaith, for trusting in God or trusting in some creature. Death compels us to give up control. Death also forces us to give up all the people and things that we have valued in life. It is the opportunity for the ultimate act of surrender to a loving and wise God. Death has this impact upon us not only at the final moments of life, but also whenever death casts its shadow over us. To live with genuine acceptance of death means to accept the contingency and tentativeness of all our plans and achievements. Awareness and acceptance of our mortality foster humility and dependence upon God.[12]

Christian hope for life beyond death is for resurrection from the dead. This belief in resurrection has its historical roots in Jewish apocalyptic and in the belief of the earliest Christians that Jesus had been raised from the dead as the first fruits of all those humans to be one day raised from the dead. We recall that in Israelite-Jewish history prior to the second century before Christ, the belief was that those who died lived an unsatisfactory half existence in Sheol. Hope was focused upon the future of the nation or community; there was no real hope for life beyond death for the individual. But when hope for restoration of the nation's standing had been battered by the Babylonian exile and later by foreign domination from Persian and Hellenistic rulers, the question of the individual's destiny after death became more

---

12. Monika Hellwig has a concise, insightful discussion of death in *Systematic Theology: Roman Catholic Perspectives*, Vol. 2, 363–65.

prominent. Many but not all Jews accepted the belief that God would in effect recreate individuals after death, that is, raise them from the dead. The only clear, undisputed expression of resurrection in the Hebrew Bible comes in Daniel, "Many of those who sleep in the dust of the earth shall awake, some to everlasting life, and some to shame and everlasting contempt" (Daniel 12:2). In Jesus' day the Jewish group called Sadducees did not believe in resurrection (Mark 12:18). Nevertheless, the apocalyptic belief in resurrection was shared by Jesus and his followers (Mark 12:24-27).

What cemented belief in resurrection for the first Christians was their conviction that God had raised Jesus from the dead. Whereas Jewish apocalyptic held to a general resurrection of many people, the early Christians believed that something totally unexpected had happened, namely, that the one person Jesus had been raised. Christian belief in the resurrection of Jesus has also been the cornerstone of hope for a general resurrection of the dead by later generations of Christians. The primary ground of later Christian belief in Jesus' resurrection is not an historical judgment that the original disciples made a sound assessment of the situation long ago, but rather is the contemporary experience of the presence of Jesus Christ as a living personal reality for Christians. In any case, belief in Jesus' resurrection is the main reason why Christians have commonly shared the ancient apocalyptic belief in a general resurrection of the dead.

We must examine more carefully what resurrection means. While many of our questions cannot be answered, four features of the resurrection belief are discernible. First, the simplest feature is that resurrection means a new life after death for the individual human being. This meaning is expressed with a metaphor, for being made alive after death is likened to rising from sleep. Since resurrection is a metaphor, we should not take the metaphor literally.

Second, it is God who raises people from the dead, so life after death is a fresh gift from the God who created all things. This distinguishes resurrection from the belief that the human soul is naturally indestructible, a belief commonly called *immortality of the soul*. While it is possible to conceive of God creating the human soul as immortal so that immortality would be a divine gift at creation, belief in resurrection goes further in holding that life beyond death is a new gift of God over and above creation. Sometimes the contrast between resurrection and any notion of immortality is seen as absolute, and then all language of immortality is considered out of bounds for Christians. But the contrast is not so sharp. Paul himself in speaking of the resurrection says, "For this perishable body must put on imperishability, and this mortal body must put on immortality" (1 Corinthians 15:53). Catholic theologian Joseph Ratzinger has also convincingly argued that generally church councils and traditional Christian theologians such as Thomas

Aquinas modified Greek philosophical ideas to form a Christianized understanding of immortality as a new divine gift.[13]

Third, resurrection existence is some sort of physical existence. Resurrected persons are a psycho-physical unity, or, in more traditional terms, a unity of body and spirit or body and soul. This also distinguishes resurrection from immortality of the soul, which affirms a nonphysical form of eternal life. The resurrected person is a body-spirit or body-soul unity.

Fourth, resurrection involves both continuity and discontinuity with the current order of human existence. On the one hand, there is continuity, for the risen Jesus is recognizable to his followers as the same person they had known. On the other hand, there is also discontinuity, for Jesus does not simply return to resume his previous earthly life. As we noted in our discussion of Jesus' resurrection in chapter 6, his resurrection involved radical transformation. The risen Jesus is visibly accessible to his followers only through the extraordinary resurrection appearances that the Book of Acts represents as visions and several Gospels represent as events in which Jesus mysteriously appears and disappears. Continuity and discontinuity are both present also in Paul's earlier testimony regarding the general resurrection. In 1 Corinthians 15:35-57 Paul uses the analogy of a seed to talk about the general resurrection. As a seed is sown and emerges as a plant that looks very different than the seed, so in the general resurrection our perishable physical body is sown and an imperishable "spiritual body" emerges. Paul envisions substantial discontinuity between the earthly person and the resurrected person, yet there is also continuity in his thought that it is "this body" that must put on imperishability. A cucumber plant emerges only from a cucumber seed.

These are the main features of the New Testament belief in resurrection of the dead. But is resurrection a reasonable belief for contemporary people or is it a fantastic leftover from the ancient worldview? A definitive answer cannot be given, but a thoughtful interpretation and defense of resurrection has been offered by the British philosopher of religion John Hick. He proposes that we think of the resurrected person as a psycho-physical "replica" of an earthly person who as resurrected exists in a different world with its own kind of space. Hick advances a variety of interesting ideas about life after death, but we will focus on three main points in his argument. First, *Hick distinguishes a "replica" (with quotes) from a replica (without quotes)*. The reasons are that an ordinary replica (without quotes) may exist simultaneously with the original thing and that there may be multiple replicas of the same original. Think, for example, of the statue of Abraham Lincoln in the Lincoln Memorial in Washington, D.C. Many replicas of this statue could be made, and they could

13. Joseph Ratzinger, *Eschatology: Death and Eternal Life*, trans. M. Waldstein (Washington, D.C.: Catholic University Press, 1988), 146–61.

exist at the same time as the original. But by a "replica" (with quotes) John Hick has in mind that there is only one "replica" of the original, and the "replica" does not exist simultaneously with the original. Applied to the belief in resurrection this means that the resurrection person is the only "replica" of the original person and exists only *after* the original person has died.

Second, *Hick says a resurrected person is a "replica" of the original person, for both have the same memories and pattern in body and character*. It is reasonable to think of a "replica" of a human person, for this does not involve the popular idea that a person's body is itself transformed into a new mode of existence. That popular idea *requires* that Jesus' tomb be empty, for it means that Jesus' very body be changed. The difficulty with this notion when applied to the general resurrection is that most people to be raised will have long been dead and the molecules of their bodies at the time of death will have been redistributed in the world. In fact, the actual molecules in our bodies today are not the same as were present there three years ago. The physical constituents of our bodies are constantly changing. So Hick's suggestion is that a "replica" of a person has the same pattern of that person's body as well as the same character and memories, although the physical substances that make up the body are not the same. The pattern of body and personal character as well as the person's memories may be considered information that can be encoded in a message and then decoded back into its original form. For instance, when we listen to a CD of a song, we are not hearing the very same sound waves that the musicians made when they recorded the song. The pattern of sounds made in the recording studio have been translated into certain imprints on the CD and then retranslated by our CD player into sounds that we can hear. So we say we are listening to the same song as the musicians recorded, because the original and its replicas have the same sound patterns. John Hick is saying that the resurrected person is a singular "replica" of the original person, for both have the same memories and patterns in body and character. A person with different bodily form, different character, and without any memories of his or her original life would not be the same person.

Third, *Hick says that a resurrected body exists in the different space of another world*. A body by definition occupies space. So a resurrected body would also fill space. However, it is conceivable that there be another world or even many worlds alongside the world in which we reside. Another world could have its own kind of space with properties and laws different from those of our world. A resident in our world would have no awareness of another world and vice versa. It would also be impossible to go to this other world in the same way that we travel from Chicago to London or from Memphis to New Orleans, for each space is of a different sort. God, of course, would be aware of all worlds. Now Hick suggests that being resurrected is like a person suddenly leaving our present world and appearing in another world.

One would have continuity with the person who lived in the present world, for one would be physically recognizable as the same person and would have the same character and memories. Since the information of one's identity had been translated into a different world, one would be the same person. Yet there would also be discontinuity, for now one would exist in a different world with a transformed body whose constituents operate according to different laws.[14]

Hick's "replica" theory surely does not prove resurrection, but it does offer a reasonable explanation of how we might interpret the belief in a modern worldview. At bottom, though, belief in resurrection of the dead depends on belief and trust in a God who is able to create and recreate. Without God who spans all spaces and all worlds, we would remain defeated by death. In short, whether one accepts Hick's "replica" theory or not, the essential element of Christian belief in resurrection is that the God who raised Jesus to new life promises also to radically transform others.

Finally, we should see how death and resurrection are present as well as future realities of salvation, for all the major images of Christian eschatology refer to both dimensions. The apostle Paul shows the way when he says, "For if we have been united with him in a death like his, we will certainly be united with him in a resurrection like his" (Romans 6:5). Dying and rising with Christ do not occur merely at the end of life, but are central realities of the Christian's present existence. Just as the final act of dying calls for giving up control and surrendering oneself to God, so now the Christian is called in daily life to turn away from sinful inclinations and to give oneself wholly to God. Each day and in countless situations the Christian is summoned to "die with Christ." So death is not an independent factor that one must face alone either in the present or the future; the Christian experiences death in the presence of Christ. Likewise, the Christian participates now in the resurrection of Christ by sharing in Christ's God-centered existence. Although one's physical existence is not yet radically transformed by God's act of general resurrection, one's attitude and behavior can be transformed by God's grace to reflect a new creation. "Therefore we have been buried with him by baptism into death, so that, just as Christ was raised from the dead by the glory of the Father, so we too might walk in newness of life" (Romans 6:4). Baptism is a powerful sacramental symbol of this present and future reality of death and resurrection for Christians. To recall one's baptism day by day is to be mindful of dying and rising with Christ. Thus salvation in both its present and ultimate future forms bears the pattern of Christ's death and resurrection.

14. John Hick, *Death and Eternal Life* (New York: Harper & Row, 1976), 279–90. A brief thoughtful evaluation of Hick's theory is given by Stephen H. Travis, *Christian Hope and the Future* (Downers Grove, Ill.: InterVarsity, 1980), 103–5.

Judgment

We can organize our thought on judgment into four points before looking at several objections to the whole idea of divine judgment.

1. *Judgment means to evaluate or make a discrimination.* It is important to get off on the right foot with the subject of *judgment* by clarifying our understanding of the word. Quite often people equate judgment with condemnation. While this is certainly one meaning of the word, it is by no means the only meaning. It is better to understand that judging means to evaluate, to make a discrimination. For instance, we might say, "In my judgment, this film is very good." One especially significant form of judgment is the verdict handed down by a law court; here a judge or jury makes an evaluation regarding the innocence or guilt of a person. The point is that a judgment can be either positive or negative. When we equate judgment with condemnation, we are assuming that all judgments are negative; then to think of God's judgment means to think only of condemnation. That is to start off on the wrong foot with this important eschatological image, for God's judgment can be either positive or negative. Thus it is possible not to fear God's judgment, but to actually look forward to it as bringing deliverance and freedom.

With this in mind it should not surprise us that Scripture sometimes portrays God's judgment as something to fear and other times as something to welcome. In the preexilic prophets of the Old Testament, the predominant note is judgment as discipline and condemnation of the errant nation; the purpose was to recall the straying Israelites to covenant faithfulness with God. Yet a frequent Old Testament encouragement is that God is a judge who brings justice and salvation to those who suffer injustice (Deuteronomy 10:18). The king of Israel should be like God in being a good judge who has special regard for the needy. So the psalmist prays, "Give the king your justice, O God, . . . May he judge your people with righteousness and your poor with justice" (Psalm 72:1-2). In the New Testament Christians looked forward to the last judgment when Christ would return. They even prayed that it would happen soon. So Paul prays, "Our Lord, come" (1 Corinthians 16:22). This anticipation of the last judgment is also a possible stance for contemporary Christians. Christians need not fear the judgment of God, for Jesus Christ is at the center of that judgment.[15]

2. *Judgment is both present and future.* In most of the Old Testament, God's judgment is expected within time and history, but in the two or three cen-

---

15. Helpful discussions of this topic are given in "Judgment," in *The New International Dictionary of New Testament Theology*, Vol. 2: 361–71.; and Hans Schwarz, "Eschatology," in *Christian Dogmatics*, Vol. 2, ed. Carl E. Braaten and Robert W. Jenson (Philadelphia: Fortress Press, 1984), 571–75.

turies prior to Jesus, Jewish apocalyptic thought looked for a decisive and final divine judgment by the Son of Man beyond this present order of time and history. This apocalyptic outlook is also expressed in the New Testament, and there the Son of Man is identified with Jesus Christ. "When the Son of Man comes in his glory, and all the angels with him, then he will sit on the throne of his glory. All the nations will be gathered before him, and he will separate people one from another as a shepherd separates the sheep from the goats" (Matthew 25:31-32).

God's judgment is expressed both in the present within history and in the ultimate future beyond history. God's judgment as both deliverance and condemnation may be experienced now within the lives of individuals and communities, yet historical judgment is often quite ambiguous. To be sure, selfish and corrupt ways often bring downfall and unhappiness to persons and groups, so a moral structure to life seems to apply. Similarly, virtue in many respects has its own rewards. Nevertheless, there are far too many exceptions to this law of retribution that as we sow, so shall we reap. Thus it is reasonable that Jewish and Christian apocalyptic thinkers have looked beyond history to an unambiguous, definitive manifestation of divine justice.

3. *We should distinguish two aspects of God's judgment.* The aspect that receives most attention is judgment as a sifting *between* people, that is, a separating of the faithful person from the unfaithful, a division between those persons who receive salvation and those who receive condemnation. The other aspect of judgment is a sifting of qualities *within* a person. While none of us is perfectly good, there may be elements of trust and love that bear some resemblance to perfect trust and love. Such partial elements of goodness would be sifted out and carried on into that person's existence in eternity, while the elements of mistrust and selfishness would be refined out. In this way we may think of earthly relationships of love and loyalty continuing into eternity and being healed of any flaws. This gives content to John's thought that those with faith already experience eternal life. In short, judgment is like a refining process that takes place within the human community by separating out the faithful from the unfaithful as well as within an individual by sifting out the sound from the unsound elements in one's character. Both aspects of judgment occur within time and in eternity, but the refining that goes on within time leaves opportunity for further change, while the last judgment is not open to later revision.

4. *Faith and actions are both criteria of judgment.* One may be confused about the criterion or standard of divine judgment. On the one hand, Scripture emphasizes faith in God's mercy as the basis for the last judgment. All have sinned. So a positive judgment is the result of God's forgiveness. "For there is no distinction, since all have sinned and fall short of the glory of God; they

are now justified by his grace as a gift, through the redemption that is in Christ Jesus" (Romans 3:22-24). Because the gift must be accepted, quite often the New Testament insists upon faith in Jesus Christ: "For God so loved the world that he gave his only Son, so that everyone who believes in him may not perish but may have eternal life" (John 3:16). Thus faith in God's forgiveness in Jesus is the criterion for judgment. On the other hand, there are scriptural passages that look to what a person has done as the criterion: "For all of us must appear before the judgment seat of Christ, so that each may receive recompense for what has been done in the body, whether good or evil" (2 Corinthians 5:10; cf. Romans 2:6-10). It is difficult to reconcile fully these two perspectives. Yet there is some overlap in the two notions, for what a person does is an expression of his or her faith. So ultimately what counts is the nature of a person's relationships with God and other people, for these reflect one's fundamental commitment or faith.

There are several objections to the belief in divine judgment. One is that people should not be held responsible for their way of life. Modern culture has made us aware that we are conditioned by historical, social, and psychological forces that limit the scope and power of our freedom. A violent criminal may have been reared by an abusive, chaotic family in a violent society. A kind person may have been reared by a gentle, caring, God-fearing family in a stable society. How is it possible to accurately weigh the degree of personal responsibility amidst such complex influences? One reply is that judgment is rendered neither by limited human beings nor by abstract principles of right and wrong, but is given by the personal God revealed in Jesus Christ. God knows all the factors affecting people's lives, and is able to assess responsibility fairly.

A second objection comes from a powerful strain in modern culture that says God is a libertarian who lets people do whatever they want with their freedom and always forgives them for any mistakes they make. The Christian tradition is more paradoxical in its thinking. Surely, Christians teach that God is superabundantly forgiving, yet they also say that how we respond to the light given us matters a great deal. God not only forgives, but calls for repentance and changing one's ways. Those who do not live with trust in God and commitment to God's ways will be held accountable. Belief in divine judgment implies that humans are responsible to God for the limited freedom that the creator has given them.

A third objection to divine judgment comes in the form of an alternative, namely, reincarnation. A recent study found that 15 percent of Presbyterians active in their church supported reincarnation, so it is important to ask whether such a belief is compatible with Christian faith.[16] Although there are

---

16. James W. Lewis, "Baby Boomers: The Lapsed and the Loyal," *The Christian Century* (May 18–25, 1994), 534.

different conceptions of *reincarnation*, fundamental to all is the conviction that human beings are wholly responsible for both their conscious deeds and their situation in life. One's situation in life—as poor or rich, male or female, talented or untalented, healthy or unhealthy—is determined by one's own actions in previous lives. Everything is governed by strict justice: we reap as we have sown. In this way belief in reincarnation claims to solve the problem of evil, for one does not even ask whether the good and almighty God is responsible for evil; humans are entirely responsible.

From the perspective of Christian faith, the primary question about reincarnation is that it undercuts any sound notion of divine grace. Strict justice is an extremely hard taskmaster. It keeps one in a very long, perhaps even infinite cycle of rebirth, while holding out the hope of finally getting off the cycle through enlightenment. Such a view is fundamentally different than an understanding of God shaped by the story of Jesus. In the Christian story our one life is of immense significance, and hope for fulfillment is grounded in the mercy and transforming love of God rather than strict justice. Trying to combine Christian faith and reincarnation is like trying to mix oil and water.

Heaven and Hell

The notions of heaven and hell employ spatial imagery to talk about God and the relationship of people with God. In the Bible *heaven* has both spatial and theological meanings, much as it does for most people today in the Western world. That is, in the Old and New Testaments at times heaven refers to the distant parts of the universe that hold the stars. Today also when we observe the stars, planets, and moons, we may say that we are looking "toward the heavens." Since people of all eras become aware of the stars and other "heavenly bodies" by looking up, it has been natural to think of heaven as being above.

In the Bible as well as today, this spatial language is sometimes used to affirm certain things about God and our relationship with God. Jesus spoke of God as "heavenly Father" and instructed his followers to begin their prayer, "Our Father in heaven" (Matthew 5:48; 6:9). Such language clearly distinguishes God from earthly fathers. It was common in both the Old Testament and New Testament to think of God dwelling "in heaven" and having the divine throne in heaven (1 Kings 22:19). This spatial imagery makes sense, because the immensity and grandeur of outer space with all its stars is powerfully suggestive of the majesty and greatness of God. So for most of the biblical writers, heaven is the proper place of God. Yet as creator of heaven and earth (that is, the whole universe), God transcends both. So heaven cannot contain God (1 Kings 8:27), and even though God is said to dwell on earth in the Jerusalem temple, Yahweh is not confined to it (1 Kings 8:12-13). With these qualifications understood, heaven is regarded as the dwelling place of God. Thus the Gospel of John understands Jesus as sent by God down from the heavenly realm (John 6:38). The link between God and heaven becomes so close that when Jewish piety showed reverence by avoiding the use of God's name, one substitute was to speak of heaven. This usage is reflected in the Gospel of Matthew, which speaks of the kingdom of heaven rather than the kingdom of God.

When contemporary Christians understand the metaphorical nature of heaven language, they realize that heaven is more a condition or mode of being than a place in our universe. Even though they may continue to speak of someone "going to" heaven or being "in" heaven, the language is not taken literally. Heaven is a symbol for being with God. Since heaven is the metaphorical home of God, to be in heaven is to be at home with God. Furthermore, unity with God brings everlasting life that consists of peaceful, joyful relationships with God and other creatures, so heaven is a fulfillment of the good in relationships on earth as well as a welcome release from the tears, dissension, and death that mar earthly existence.

The various Christian eschatological symbols should not be regarded like countries on a map, each country separated from the others by distinct borders. Rather, there is considerable overlap between some of the eschatological symbols. This is true of heaven and the reign of God, since they both refer to a condition of peace through unity with God. The main difference is that reign of God has a strong horizontal, temporal reference to that ultimate future that fulfills human history, whereas heaven tends to work more as a spatial, vertical symbol of what is above. Another difference is that ever since the early Middle Ages heaven has been interpreted much more individualistically; that is, while reign of God refers to a setting right of the whole community of beings in the cosmos, heaven has been widely understood as the destiny of some individuals at the time of their death. Another symbol with some of the same range of meaning as heaven is the *beatific vision*. The beatific vision is suggested in a few passages of the New Testament. Jesus says the pure in heart "will see God" (Matthew 5:8), and Paul says, "Now we see in a mirror, dimly, but then we will see face to face" (1 Corinthians 13:12). So the symbol of the beatific vision portrays fulfillment of life beyond death as pure joy in truly knowing God.

Nevertheless, heaven may refer to a present as well as future mode of being. To be sure, the New Testament and contemporary Christians generally think of heaven as a condition to be entered in the future beyond death, yet it is possible to regard the present life of faith in God as a foretaste of that perfect unity with God in heaven. This is clearly evident with the symbol of *eternal life*, which has considerable overlap with the symbol of heaven. In both the Old and New Testaments life is viewed as a gift from God, and resurrection comes as a new divine gift. Since the essence of life is fellowship with God, the believer already has eternal life (John 6:40, 47). Thus there may be an eternal or heavenly quality of life on earth that is a limited anticipation of fulfilled existence in heaven.[17]

The Christian symbol of *hell* has its roots in the Bible and includes at least two important New Testament words. One of the words is *Gehenna*, which the New Revised Standard Version of the Bible translates as hell. Gehenna is the Greek form of the Aramaic name for a valley south of Jerusalem. Some centuries earlier Ahaz, king of Judah, had followed the religious practices of neighboring nations, including the sacrifice of his own son on an altar in this valley of Gehenna. Later religious reformers and prophets regarded this sacrilege as the ultimate expression of infidelity to Israel's covenant with God. This tainted valley became the place where executed criminals and other outcasts were buried. As the site of abominable human sacrifice and disgraceful burial, Gehenna was ripe for metaphorical extension into a place of shame and suffering for the unrighteous.

In addition to Gehenna, sometimes the New Testament speaks of *Hades*. In the Greek translation of the Old Testament the Hebrew word *Sheol* was translated with the Greek name for the realm of the dead, Hades; the contemporary New Revised Standard Version carries over Hades into the English. So Hades in the Bible means much the same as *Sheol*, although belief in the resurrection modified the notion of Hades. In the New Testament (as in some earlier Jewish writings) Hades is no longer the everlasting residence of all the dead but becomes the temporary place of suffering for the unrighteous. In Luke 16:23ff. Hades is portrayed as a place of torment from flames. Gehenna is similarly imagined as an "unquenchable fire" (Mark 9:43). Although both Hades and Gehenna are frightening places for the dead, in the New Testament there is a distinction between them. At their death the unrighteous are thought to go to Hades until the general resurrection and last judgment at which point they are cast into Gehenna. This suggests that the unrighteous dead dwell in Hades as souls without a body until they are given a new body at the resurrection.

Hell is linked with spatial imagery, for both Gehenna and Hades are imagined as places. In the New Testament Hades is thought to be a place below, although it is never said that Gehenna is a lower region. In any case, the spatial imagery of hell need not be taken literally, although it is conceivable that Hades and Gehenna are remote places in our universe or places in another world. Most Christian theologians today do not think of hell so much as a

---

17. "Heaven" and "Life," in *The New International Dictionary of New Testament Theology*, Vol. 2:184–96; 474–84.

place, however, but as a mode of being or condition. As the ancient Israelites already saw in their symbol of Sheol, the essence of Sheol, Hades, and Gehenna is separation from God. While the core of life is understood as fellowship with God, the heart of suffering in death is separation from God. Hades is a temporary experience of such suffering and Gehenna is the eternal experience of separation. So heaven and hell are opposites. The joy of heaven is harmonious relationship with God, our loved ones, other people, and other creatures. The suffering of hell, whether in Hades or Gehenna, is separation from God and other beings.[18]

Now we must consider an important question regarding hell: Whether anyone will end up in hell and thereby be eternally unfulfilled and separated from God. This question is raised especially by those who espouse a position called *universalism*, the belief that all people will eventually receive the salvation of reconciliation with God. The case for universalism has been stated very clearly by that eminent British philosopher of religion, John Hick. Like most other Christian universalists, Hick argues that since God is both loving and almighty, God will eventually bring about the salvation of all people. That is, God as loving wants all humans to be saved, and God as almighty will finally accomplish that divine purpose. In support of this position, Hick cites several passages in the writings of Paul. Paul says, "As all die in Adam, so all will be made alive in Christ" (1 Corinthians 15:22) and "God has imprisoned all in disobedience so that he may be merciful to all" (Romans 11:32). In both statements the second "all" can hardly be less inclusive than the first.

There are two major objections commonly raised against universalism. One is that there are numerous biblical passages that speak of eternal damnation. For instance, in Matthew 25:41 Jesus tells a parable that says, "'You that are accursed, depart from me into the eternal fire" and Paul says those who do not know God "will suffer the punishment of eternal destruction, separated from the presence of the Lord" (2 Thessalonians 1:9). Part of Hick's response to this objection is to admit that there are numerous sayings of Jesus that speak of punishment for the unfaithful, but Hick points out that only the Matthew 25 saying of Jesus explicitly speaks of *eternal* punishment. The other objection to universalism is that it does not do justice to the free will of humans. Since humans have free will, some may persistently refuse to be reconciled to God. If so, then the only way God could save all would be to coerce the unwilling and that would violate the God-given power of free will. Because God would not do this, the objection says it is wrong to assert that

18. "Hell," in *The New International Dictionary of New Testament Theology*, Vol. 2: 205–10. Another term used in the New Testament is the *abyss* which is the place to which demons are sent and in which Satan is bound for one thousand years.

God *will* save all. John Hick's reply is that since God has created human beings in such a way that they are "restless until they rest in" God, God does not need to coerce anyone. Like a good psychotherapist who helps a person overcome his or her internal blocks, God assists people in reaching the fulfillment for which their very nature is destined. In fact, says Hick, the frequent biblical warnings about future punishment are part of the divine strategy to help sinners turn their life around, rather than predictions of a condemnation that will certainly happen.

One other element in Hick's argument for universal salvation is that he postulates further opportunities for spiritual reform in another world after death. Since some persons apparently make little or no advancement toward reconciliation with God during their life on earth, Hick believes that there must be more possibilities for repentance and spiritual growth in another existence.

You must make up your own mind about universalism and hell, but perhaps a brief formulation of my own view might aid your reflections. I think Hick is mistaken in his claim that God *will* surely save all people. I have several reservations about his position. It loses any sense of urgency for people to use the limited time they have on earth to act responsibly; in this respect human freedom is evacuated of much of its significance. To be sure, according to Hick, no one would be compelled to trust in God. Yet the need for decision and change could be delayed almost endlessly. Furthermore, Hick too quickly explains away the biblical warnings about possible future condemnation of the unrepentant. Scripture as a whole does better at maintaining the unresolved tension between God's desire to have all be saved and warnings to the hard-hearted. I believe it is better to be more reserved in our thoughts about what happens after death. Christians should certainly proclaim God's intention that all be saved, but we are better off leaving the fate of the unrepentant in God's wise, just, and merciful hands. This means that we should also not claim that God *will* certainly assign some persons to the eternal suffering of hell. Since a person may resolutely refuse to be reconciled, some people *may* end up in hell. Nevertheless, along with this sober realization, we may also *hope* that the God of love will somehow realize the divine desire to save all. This leaves the matter where it belongs—in God's hands.

The Intermediate State and Purgatory

The Christian eschatological symbols together do not form some clear, fully coherent picture of what will happen after death. Many questions are left up in the air. For example, while the Christian tradition clearly affirms the general resurrection when all or at least many of the dead are raised from the dead with a new body, it is not clear what happens to someone at the point of their death. Some have suggested that the dead sleep, as it were, until the general resurrection. More common has been the belief that at the moment of death the souls of the dead experience either heaven or hell and exist in that condition without a body until the general resurrection when a new body is given. This is the question of *the intermediate state*: What happens to the dead between the time of their death and the general resurrection?

One answer has been to say that God exists outside time in an eternal now, and every moment of time is therefore equidistant from God's eternity. So when a person dies and leaves the flow of time, that person experiences no time gap between the point of death and the resurrection. Within time the calendar would show that there was a period between that person's death and the resurrection. Since the dead are outside time in the eternal present, however, they do not wait to be raised. While some are content with this answer, I am dissatisfied with its idea of eternity as timelessness, for it means that there is no movement or development within God and eternity. I prefer to just leave the question of the intermediate state up in the air. As long as Christians trust in God, the mechanics of what happens after death may simply be left to God. Compared to some roughly contemporaneous Jewish writings that spelled out in considerable detail the geography and timetable of the afterlife, the New Testament is very reserved on such matters. Christians today would do well to follow that example.

A significant teaching pertaining to the intermediate state is the doctrine of *purgatory*, which basically says that after death some individuals go through a process of purging that prepares them to enter heaven. Those Christian churches that hold to a doctrine of purgatory envision three possible destinies for individuals after death: some may go directly to hell, the very holy (saints) will go directly to heaven, and most believers will go to purgatory before eventually reaching heaven. So someone in purgatory will finally go to heaven, never to hell.

As Catholic theologian Richard McBrien says, "There is, for all practical purposes, no biblical basis for the doctrine of purgatory."[19] Probably the main historical basis for belief in purgatory was the practice of praying for the dead. For this practice appeal was often made to the deuterocanonical or apocryphal text 2 Maccabees 12:44, "For if he were not expecting the fallen to rise again, it would have been useless and foolish to pray for them in death." The belief in purgatory as a distinct state of the dead emerged gradually after Augustine (d. 430). In the Middle Ages two interpretations of purgatory were advanced. The Orthodox Church envisioned purgatory as a process of spiritual growth and maturation. The Roman Catholic Church thought of purgatory chiefly in

---

19. Richard P. McBrien, *Catholicism*, rev. ed. (San Francisco: HarperSanFrancisco, 1994), 1166.

penal terms, that is, as a period of suffering and punishment for one's sins, although the Council of Florence in 1439 sought to achieve a balance of both notions. The sixteenth-century Protestant Reformation rejected the doctrine of purgatory for two reasons: (1) it contradicts justification by faith, which emphasizes salvation through God's forgiving mercy and (2) it is not taught in Scripture. Purgatory remains today a disputed teaching between Protestants who reject it and Orthodox and Roman Catholics who affirm it.

Richard McBrien represents a common Catholic interpretation of purgatory when he says, "Purgatory is best understood as a process by which we are purged of our residual selfishness so that we can really become one with the God who is totally oriented to others, i.e., the self-giving God."[20] Thus contemporary Catholic theologians have generally adopted the Orthodox version of purgatory as a refining process of spiritual growth; any suffering involved is not some arbitrary punishment inflicted from without but the intrinsic suffering associated with difficult personal change.

Views on purgatory reflect several features of Roman Catholic and Orthodox spirituality as well as Protestant spirituality. Belief in purgatory is consistent with the Catholic and Orthodox emphasis upon grace as primarily a transforming power, while rejection of it follows the Protestant emphasis upon grace as primarily divine forgiveness. Affirmation of purgatory also reflects the Orthodox and Catholic confidence that the Holy Spirit works in and through the practices and institution of the church. Thus they hold that it is sufficient that purgatory is taught in church tradition; it need not be mentioned in Scripture, although it must not be contradicted by Scripture. Protestants are uneasy with a teaching that has no support in the Bible, and commonly think purgatory actually conflicts with the biblical teaching on grace. With their greater stress on the corrupting influence of sin, Protestants are also more likely to say that even some long-standing church practices and teachings can be wrong. Hence, one's assessment of the belief in purgatory takes place not as an isolated item, but as part of a rich complex of attitudes and beliefs.

The difference between Catholic and Orthodox affirmation of purgatory and Protestant rejection has been minimized by some Catholic theologians. Catholic Monika Hellwig says, "There seems to be no reason in the nature of the case or in the tradition for insisting that purgatory means in the literal sense an extension of quasi-time outside worldly time, extended beyond the moment of death."[21] That is, the refining, transforming process of purgatory could take place instantaneously as part of the judgment rendered at an individual's death; there would then be no *period* during which an individual would be in purgatory. I think this interpretation is consistent with a Protes-

20. Ibid., 1168–1169.
21. Hellwig, in *Systematic Theology*, Vol. 2, 369.

tant understanding of grace. If the process of purgation occurs in a moment rather than over some extended duration, however, it seems that prayers for the dead would be pointless except as prayers of thanksgiving and praise to God for their lives. This should mean the abandonment of prayers and masses that are intended somehow to "help" the dead in their purgation process. But Richard McBrien says it is consistent with Catholic principles to feel an obligation of "concern and mutual assistance" toward our dead relatives and friends.[22] Joseph Ratzinger gives a thoughtful rationale for such assistance in the relational nature of personal identity; who we are depends in great part on the nature of our relations with others. Hence, for the living to pray for and forgive the dead assists the dead in being fully formed in love.[23] So differences over purgatory have not been fully resolved. Such differences may not be barriers to further degrees of unity among Christians, however, for purgatory is a relatively secondary doctrine, not a core teaching of any church.

This concludes our discussion of Christian eschatology. We may recall that the discussion had three main divisions. In the first part we saw that the Bible presents two distinct types of eschatology: the this-worldly eschatology of the preexilic prophets and apocalyptic eschatology; Jesus combined elements of both in his teachings. In the second part we tried to sort out our basic approach to eschatology by examining four common approaches in contemporary theology. Then in the third part of the chapter we reflected on the various symbols of Christian eschatology, and interpreted their meaning for today.

Our consideration of eschatology is also a fitting conclusion to our entire study of Christian teachings, for the focus of Christian eschatology on trust and hope in God brings us back to where we began: faith in God. John Calvin begins his great work in Christian theology with the insight that without knowledge of ourselves there is no knowledge of God, and without knowledge of God there is no knowledge of ourselves. I think this is most certainly true. Christian teachings set forth a comprehensive understanding of human beings inextricably related to God, who has created all things and is at work reconciling creatures with God's self and with one another. My hope is that these reflections have not only sparked your interest and imagination, but also helped you think through the fundamental questions of your own life.

22. McBrien, *Catholicism*, 1171.
23. Ratzinger, *Eschatology*, 232–33.

Index